WITHDRAWN

Milton's Kinesthetic Vision in *Paradise Lost*

Milton's Kinesthetic Vision in *Paradise Lost*

Elizabeth Ely Fuller

Lewisburg
Bucknell University Press
London and Toronto: Associated University Presses

PR
3562
.F8
1983

Associated University Presses, Inc.
440 Forsgate Drive
Cranbury, N.J. 08512

Associated University Presses Ltd
25 Sicilian Avenue
London WC1A 2QH, England

Associated University Presses
2133 Royal Windsor Drive
Unit 1
Mississauga, Ontario
Canada L5J 1K5

Library of Congress Cataloging in Publication Data

Fuller, Elizabeth Ely, 1943–
  Milton's kinesthetic vision in Paradise
lost.

  Bibliography: p.
  Includes index.
  1. Milton, John. 1608–1674. Paradise lost.
I. Title.
PR3562.F8   821′.4   81-65862
ISBN 0-8387-5027-3   AACR2

For Cyane
Ovid, *The Metamorphoses,* Book V

Contents

List of Charts

Acknowledgments

To John T. Shawcross, Allen Mandelbaum, John Hollander, D. H. Melhem, and Marjorie Norris—mentors, colleagues, and friends; to all my colleagues and friends at The City University of New York, too numberless to name here; and to Beth Linnerson, who taught me to think as an artist:

My debt of gratitude is an eternal pleasure.

Introduction

Milton's *Paradise Lost* is a work that exists in many dimensions. In its magnitude, richness, and complexity it touches and excites every part of our being and of our world. Yet, as the mind in its perhaps natural desire for order begins to gather the various elements of the poem into a structure of understanding, the poem resists such efforts at every turn, and reading it can then become a painful as well as a rich experience. *Paradise Lost* seems to be constructed in such a way that its different dimensions cannot fit into any single system, or into compatible systems, whether spiritual, rational, emotional, perceptual, or even poetic. It seems impossible to consider it from any single point of view, or in any single frame of reference. The poem is not simply disorganized, random, chaotic, or overly complex. Nor will it resolve itself into any central dualism or conflict. Rather, it seems precisely composed to avoid such relative comforts. It seems to be specifically calculated in its shifting dimensionality to arouse pain and anger in the mind as well as curiosity and delight.

The disjunctiveness, for example, created by two such statements by God about Adam and Eve as "They trespass, authors to themselves in all" (3: 122) and "He sorrows now, repents, and prays contrite, / My motions in him" (11: 90–91)[1] may fissure or wrench the poem's ideological frame, as may the editorial comment that Satan could never have risen from the burning lake of hell where he is chained as the poem opens "but that the will / And high permission of all-ruling Heaven / Left him at large to his own dark designs" (1: 211–13) when juxtaposed with God's comment at the beginning of Book 3 that "no bounds / Prescribed, no bars of hell, nor all the chains / Heaped on him there, nor yet the main abyss / Wide interrupt can hold" the Adversary (3: 81–84). The laws governing the fate of the universe may seem equally contradictory. In Book 7, as he prepares to create the earth and its universe, God tells the Son and the assembled angels that in the last days ". . . earth [shall] be changed to heav'n, and heav'n to earth, / One kingdom, joy and union without end" (7: 160–61). But the poet posits a rather different possibility when in Book 2 he calls the chaos from whose elements God created the universe "the womb of Nature and perhaps her grave" (2: 911).

The representation of character likewise breaks into extremes. God and the Son are now presented as mild, now as wrathful and violent. At one moment, ". . . [from] the seat supreme . . . a voice / From midst a golden

13

cloud thus mild was heard" (6: 27–28); at another, ". . . the Son . . . into terror changed / His countenance, too severe to be beheld / And full of wrath, bent on his enemies" (6: 824–26). Satan is similarly presented in terms of opposites: now he is noble and bold, now he is vicious and shrewd. He is powerful and dangerous, but he is sad and helpless. He is cruel but remorseful. "Confounded though immortal" (1: 53), his "huge affliction and dismay / Mixed with obdúrate pride and steadfast hate" (1: 57–58), he is a creature of doubleness from the beginning of *Paradise Lost*. Adam and Eve, the human heroes of the poem, are likewise portrayed on the one hand as "frail" and pitiable and on the other as magnificent and awesome. Satan refers to the inhabitants of the new creation as "puny" (2: 367), to Adam as his descendants' "frail original" (2: 375), and to the earth as the "frail world" (2: 1030). God beholds them "with pity" (5: 220), Raphael calls Adam to his face "frail man" (6: 346), and Milton refers to the human pair as "innocent frail man" (4: 11).[2] Yet as they first appear to the reader in Book 4,

> Two of far nobler shape erect and tall,
> God-like erect, with native honor clad
> In naked majesty, [they] seemed lords of all.
>
> (4: 288–90)

The plot, like the ideological frame and the characters, is indeterminate in its implications. At the poem's end Michael's teaching arouses in Adam both joy and sorrow. As the archangel speaks of the happier paradise[3] and the new heavens and earth of the future, Adam voices in response the paradox of the fortunate fall as he exclaims:

> O goodness infinite, goodness immense!
> That all this good of evil shall produce,
> And evil turn to good; more wonderful
> Than that which by creation first brought forth
> Light out of darkness!
>
> (12: 469–73)

Yet Adam and Eve's life in the world outside Eden is to be difficult, uncertain, and "wandering." As they descend to the "subjected plain" in the concluding lines of the poem,

> Some natural tears they dropped, but wiped them soon;
> The world was all before them, where to choose
> Their place of rest, and Providence their guide:
> They hand in hand, with wand'ring steps and slow,
> Through Eden took their solitary way.
>
> (12: 645–49)

These lines move the mind so deeply and in so many ways that it is difficult to say exactly how the poem has ended. Such certainties as new heavens and earth or the grave of chaos are here out of focus. The poem seems neither specifically comic nor tragic, neither lyrical nor ironic, neither just nor unjust, neither "sad" nor "happy." It is somehow too profound to be any of these things and profound enough to be all of them. The reader's mind is arrested in a deep understanding that does not know what it understands and is left perplexed and wondering.

Last, *Paradise Lost* is poetically disjunctive. More often than not poetic devices such as similes do not reinforce their referents but instead take the poem into qualitatively different worlds that, once experienced, make it difficult for the reader to return to the dimension of the referent. For example, the bees-and-elves simile at the end of Book 1 moves the mind in such a way that the simile and its relation to the poem become seemingly inexplicable. In this simile the thousands of fallen angels thronging into the hallway of their newly raised infernal palace are likened first to bees in springtime, then briefly to pygmies, and last to fairy elves:

> . . . the spacious hall
> . . . .
> Thick swarmed, both on the ground and in the air,
> Brushed with the hiss of rustling wings. As bees
> In springtime, when the sun with Taurus rides,
> Pour forth their populous youth about the hive
> In clusters; they among fresh dews and flowers
> Fly to and fro, or on the smoothèd plank,
> The suburb of their straw-built citadel,
> New rubbed with balm, expatiate and confer
> Their state affairs: so thick the airy crowd
> Swarmed and were straitened; till the signal giv'n,
> Behold a wonder! they but now who seemed
> In bigness to surpass Earth's giant sons,
> Now less than smallest dwarfs, in narrow room
> Throng numberless, like that Pygmean race
> Beyond the Indian mount, or fairy elves,
> Whose midnight revels by a forest side
> Or fountain some belated peasant sees,
> Or dreams he sees, while overhead the moon
> Sits arbitress, and nearer to the earth
> Wheels her pale course; they on their mirth and dance
> Intent, with jocund music charm his ear;
> At once with joy and fear his heart rebounds.
>
> (1: 762–88)

The image of the bees is appropriate to portray the large number of devils, their thronging movement, and the rustling of their wings; but here the parallels between vehicle and tenor stop. The warmth of the bees' activity in their almost human city and the flowery springtime, the cool and peaceful beauty of the midnight revels, and the feelings these arouse in the reader take the poem far away from the heated and painful conflicts of hell.

The mind is quietly drawn to this new world, to the sunny citadel and the moonlit forest, as it is drawn many times again in other parts of the poem into what is seemingly the same world. Again in Book 1, to describe the enraged and defiant Satan chained in his immensity to the burning lake of hell, Milton uses a simile of a whale slumbering at night on the cool Norway sea:

> Thus Satan. . .
> With head uplift above the wave, and eyes
> That sparkling blazed; his other parts besides
> Prone on the flood, extended long and large
> Lay floating many a rood, in bulk as huge
> As whom the fables name of monstrous size,
> Titanian or Earth-born, that warred on Jove,
> Briareos or Typhon, whom the den
> By ancient Tarsus held, or that sea-beast
> Leviathan, which God of all his works
> Createst hugest that swim th'ocean stream:
> Him haply slumb'ring on the Norway foam,
> The pilot of some small night-foundered skiff,
> Deeming some island, oft, as seamen tell,
> With fixèd anchor in his scaly rind
> Moors by his side under the lee, while night
> Invests the sea, and wishèd morn delays:
> So stretched out huge in length the Arch-fiend lay.
>
> (1: 192–209)

In a similar tone Milton pictures Satan, having escaped his chains, rousing his stricken followers:

> . . . on the beach
> Of that inflamèd sea, he stood and called
> His legions, angel forms, who lay entranced,
> Thick as autumnal leaves that strow the brooks
> In Vallombrosa, where th'Etrurian shades
> High over-arched embow'r.
>
> (1: 299–304)

And in the council in Pandemonium, heartened by their leader's courage and his love for them, the fallen angels' "doubtful consultations dark" about their future break into rejoicing,

> As when from mountain tops the dusky clouds
> Ascending, while north wind sleeps, o'erspread
> Heav'n's cheerful face, the louring element
> Scowls o'er the darkened landscape snow or show'r;
> If chance the radiant sun with farewell sweet
> Extend his ev'ning beam, the fields revive,
> The birds their notes renew, and bleating herds
> Attest their joy, that hill and valley rings.
>
> (2: 488–95)

The reader is touched and relieved by the clarity and peace of the still night world at sea. The whalelike Satan may be dangerous, but the sense of evil is gone. It is a neutral world. The reader is delighted by the brief but heightened joy of the reviving fields and, in some place deeper than thoughts and words, is at once moved into stillness by the poignant tone of the autumn-leaves simile and opened out into a seemingly boundless space. Yet within this space he/she finds small figures that seem both fragile and strong—the city builders; the pilot moored by leviathan's huge side, wondering and waiting; the belated peasant whose heart rebounds with both joy and fear as he watches or dreams the moonlit scene before him. The reader shares some kinship with these small figures, as he/she perhaps likewise shares with the pale arbitress overhead and even with the entranced leaves.

Allured, in Isabel MacCaffrey's words, by the "pathos and undeniable beauty"[4] of this cool world, one might fear that, in the absence of the ability to judge, the mind will yield to its strange qualities and fall into delusion and some kind of death, like the peasant in Book 9 who follows the enchanting light of the will-o'-the-wisp into the bog and drowns:

> . . . Hope elevates, and joy
> Brightens his [Satan's] crest, as when a wand'ring fire,
> Compact of unctuous vapor, which the night
> Condenses, and the cold environs round,
> Kindled through agitation to a flame,
> Which oft, they say, some evil Spirit attends,
> Hovering and blazing with delusive light,
> Misleads th'amazed night-wanderer from his way
> To bogs and mires, and oft through pond or pool,
> There swallowed up and lost, from succor far.
>
> (9: 633–42)

Or will the mind, like Eve in her Satan-inspired dream, be called by some gentle voice to walk forth at night—"the pleasant time, / The cool, the silent . . ."—to be worshiped by nature, to pluck from the fair tree of knowledge, and, no longer "confined to earth," "ascend to heaven" into a spaciousness of spirit in which the earth lies below "outstretched immense, a prospect wide / And various" (from 5: 38–89)?

To escape this uncertainty the reader may, like MacCaffrey, quickly turn to deny such images of temptation as "superstition and false belief,"[5] or like Ann Ferry return from the appreciation of such moments of mortal beauty so evidently loved by the poet as well as the reader to the sad but sane conclusion that, in the final analysis, the mortal world is fallen and measured by the unfallen.[6]

In this way *Paradise Lost* is experienced as divided and disjunctive, a work existing in and drawing its readers into incompatible dimensions, fragmenting the mind, and betraying the natural desire for order and meaning. The poem causes this confusion; but it is the reading experience, the interpretive process, that is most immediately the image of frustration as the mind watches itself turning from painful deliberation to curiosity and delight, as it watches itself moved by the similes yet reactively asserting and retreating to more certain conceptual truths, angry at the disjunction or nonrelation between them, the different dimensions seemingly related only by the corners the mind turns from one into the other. The mind's own answers seem to become the cause of disjunction and perplexity: hence the curious phenomenon that often Milton criticism is the reflection of the very issues it is attempting to resolve. Yet such critical reflectings are, perhaps unconsciously, an act of truth, for the poem itself appears intentionally to participate in and ensure its own disjunctions as it shifts the reader's mind from one mental dimension to another.

Thus, early in Book 1 the poet describes hell in tones that arouse sympathy for the pains suffered there, then quickly turns to share in the condemnation of the sufferers:

> . . . sights of woe,
> Regions of sorrow, doleful shades, where peace
> And rest can never dwell, hope never comes
> That comes to all; but torture without end
> Still urges, and a fiery deluge, fed
> With ever-burning sulphur unconsumed;
> Such place Eternal Justice had prepared
> For those rebellious, here their prison ordained
> In utter darkness.
>
> (1: 64–72)

In a more extreme form of the same strategy, the poet shifts into the relief and peace of the whale simile quoted above, only to shift back into the structure of judgment with more violence than when he left it:

> So stretched out huge in length the Arch-Fiend lay
> Chained on the burning lake; nor ever thence
> Had ris'n or heaved his head, but that the will
> And high permission of all-ruling Heaven
> Left him at large to his own dark designs,
> That with reiterated crimes he might
> Heap on himself damnation, while he sought
> Evil to others, and enraged might see
> How all his malice served but to bring forth
> Infinite goodness, grace and mercy shown
> On man by him seduced, and on himself
> Treble confusion, wrath and vengeance poured.
>
> (1: 209–20)

Following these poetic motions, the reader's sympathetic faculty is abruptly divided from his/her judging faculty; or if the shift is too difficult to follow, his/her sympathetic faculty hits up against what is perceived as the external moral judgment of the editorial authority. In such unexpected shiftings the mind's usual processes of judgment are no longer operable: the familiar frames of ideology, character, action, and art have split and broken apart; the usual relations between them no longer hold; and the poetic structure has split not to break but to open into a new world both dangerous and beautiful, which the mind, stripped of all familiar points of conceptual and emotional reference, must face alone.

Although the splitting of the familiar structures is painful, and the new world uncertain and bewildering, the shiftings into it provide relief by removing the reader from the hell of the poem's intense and seemingly absolute appeals to his/her sympathies and moral judgment to a neutral space where questions of moral judgment seem curiously absent. The reader may safely enter into this space without fearing the "amazed night-wanderer's" fate if he/she imagines that the poem's stern ideological pronouncements are a kind of picture frame instead of a frame of reference, a frame that allows one to consider the qualities and effects of the world within it while assuring its separation from the world in which one makes judgments and identifications, in which, in Adam's words to Eve in his analysis of her dream, one must "affirm" and "deny" (5: 107).

Thus James Whaler in his series of articles on the Miltonic simile, while asserting that the Miltonic simile is homologous and organically related to the fable of the poem, leaves this assertion behind to enter more fully into the simile's separate world and investigate its nature and its effect on the reader's mind and perception without returning to questions of its relation to fable. In this spirit he observes that the simile does not seem to homologate with the referent as far as the motive underlying the act or situation in the simile is concerned, that while "the purpose underlying . . . [the referent] may be sinister, belligerent, evil, vindictive, horrible, destructive; the purpose underlying [the simile] may be, at the same time, peaceful, virtuous, ingenuous, constructive, idyllic, beautiful, charming."[7] He goes on to comment that the simile serves as a "perspective device" that "guides the reader or auditor to a point of survey whence he may observe great events in miniature, serene spectator of processes and perturbations he is relieved from sharing."[8]

Geoffrey Hartman, in his article "Milton's Counterplot," characterizes Milton's similes in a similar way but goes further to define their function as "aesthetic distancing," by which the poet intentionally removes the reader's point of view from the epic action to a nonnarrative lyrical perspective, a "secret arbiter"—sometimes a figure like the peasant in the elves simile, sometimes simply a mood, like the charmed rhythm of Mulciber's fall in 1: 740–46. Occurring repeatedly throughout *Paradise Lost,* these instances of aesthetic distancing form a "counterplot" that establishes behind the "narrative's burning wheel" a "divine imperturbability" and sheds a "calm and often cold radiance" over the poem as a whole. Hartman returns to a theological frame at the end of his study to identify God as the supreme arbiter and to define the ultimate purpose of the counterplot as embodying "Milton's two means of divine justification, man's free will and God's fore-knowledge of the creation's triumph." But this conclusion does not function to lessen the strong sense Hartman has imprinted of the cold mood distanced from theological positions that lies at the center of *Paradise Lost*.[9]

In this coldness the mind is relieved from the painful and blinding motions it has left and becomes slowly inured to them. And as his/her mind clears in this central coldness, the reader begins to see that this world has motions, less violent and dramatic and more sustaining, of its own. In these new motions, the motions of yearning, landscapes and small figures appear. In the nearing of joy to the object of desire the sun breaks on the hills of evening; in the distance of joy from what it yearns for, the angel forms, the autumn leaves, lie thick-strown and still; and in a pause in its struggling journey of desire, the pilot anchors by chance in the lee of the whale-island.

In these same motions the reader will learn to move with the forces of the universe; and, molding them as he/she receives them within his/her own being, be "author to" [him/herself] in an assertive yet consonant reciprocity. In the motions of yearning the desirer is linked to the object of desire, of feeling and perception, by bonds more fluid yet more sure than the rigors of ideological reference structures.

In this way one becomes aware of the simple truth that the truth of what is seen and known is in how it is seen and known. In this truth the painful shiftings of the earlier experience of *Paradise Lost* and of the world may now be experienced as the movements of all the parts of the being participating in the action of knowing. For Milton, truth is in such motion, and it is this truth that he wishes to teach in *Paradise Lost*. Thus, like Coleridge's ideal poet who seeks in poetry to "bring the whole soul of . . . [human being] into activity,"[10] Milton prays in the opening of Book 3 to Holy Light—the "sovran lamp" that, blind, he can only "feel" (3: 22)—for the ecstasy of psychic matter and energy resolving into each other through motion, and for the vision this intermotion yields:

> Shine inward, and the mind through all her powers
> Irradiate, there plant eyes.

> (3: 52–53)

Milton intends his poem to move the reader, not only in the emotional sense of that word but through all the faculties and capabilities of his/her being. The primary mode of both his vision and his poetry is kinesthetic. Knowledge is essentially knowledge of or by means of motion, in both a physical and a psychic sense. Kinesthesia in its physical sense is "the sensation of bodily perception, presence, or movement resulting chiefly from stimulation of sensory nerve endings in muscles, tendons, and joints."[11] Psychic kinesthesia is knowledge, through the motions of yearning and meditation, of the motions of the psyche in relation to the motions of the universe, or is, as Francis Fergusson expresses it in his *Idea of a Theater,* "our direct sense of the changing life of the psyche," a sense experienced through what he terms the "histrionic sensibility."[12]

To destroy rigid mental structures inimical to such experience of motion and to awaken the mind's kinesthetic faculty, Milton shifts poem and mind, in the process Hartman calls aesthetic distancing, from one dimension to another and from one faculty to another. Repeated instances of aesthetic distancing form a counterplot to the epic plot, which functions to educate the reader's kinesthetic faculty by leading—indeed forcing—the mind through various kinds of motions that are neither arbitrary nor qualitatively similar but fall into a particular sequence. This sequence is a declension of mind, for as it progresses through the sequence, the mind is radically altered, articulated into consciousness of all its capabilities. The declension begins in what may be termed the *sympathic* state, a state in which the mind is disturbed by ideological and emotional disjunctions such as those quoted above, and ends in subtle and complex meditative strategies.[13]

A literary criticism that would comment on such a poem must, in the spirit of Northrop Frye's *Anatomy of Criticism,* separate itself from such external frames as theology, philosophy, sociology, morality, and taste, and allow its structures to arise out of the poetry itself. Because *Paradise Lost* is so highly conscious of its own poetic movements—because indeed such a consciousness is part of its subject—it is possible to articulate from it a more disciplined, subtle, and exact literary criticism than perhaps would be possible from most literary works. Northrop Frye must separate criticism from particular works of poetry as well as from the frames just mentioned, but with *Paradise Lost* such a strategy is not necessary. Moreover, because the poem in the formation of its own poetics has absorbed the external frameworks into its own movements, it is further possible to do what Frye rejects as an improper critical concern—to derive from literary criticism a meaning, a vision of life, that is not an "existential projection" of a literary form but, in Michael's words to Adam, the "sum of wisdom" (12: 575–76), attained not only on the "top of speculation" (12: 588–89) but in the "new lands" (1: 290) of the space of meditation.[14]

NOTES

1. All quotations from *Paradise Lost* are from *The Complete Poetical Works of John Milton,* ed. Douglas Bush (Boston: Houghton Mifflin Company, 1965).

2. Ironically, the use of the concept *man* to refer to "human being" is precisely the kind of thinking Milton is working in *Paradise Lost* to disrupt and remold, yet his insight did not cause him to alter his own linguistic habit in this regard. In my quotations from the poem, I have not altered this usage except where it is unusually distracting, and in such cases I have of course indicated the change by enclosing it in brackets. Likewise, in quotations from the work of

literary critics, I have not altered their use of the word *man* to refer to "human," nor have I changed their use of masculine pronouns to refer to terms such as *the reader*.

In my own text, I use *human being, humankind,* or *humanity* instead of *man* unless *man* is referring specifically to a male human. I use *he/she, him/her, his/her,* and *him/herself* as pronouns when they refer to such terms as *the reader, the desirer,* or *the hero.* However, to avoid confusion, I use masculine pronouns in discussions of the figures in Milton's similes—the pilot, the peasant, the mariner, and so on—because Milton conceived of them as male and therefore referred to them with masculine pronouns.

3. Following Milton's practice, I capitalize *Paradise* when it refers to the specific place in Eden, and do not when it refers to a state of mind or spirit.

4. Isabel G. MacCaffrey, *"Paradise Lost" as "Myth"* (Cambridge, Mass.: Harvard University Press, 1967), p. 131.

5. Ibid.

6. Ann Ferry, *Milton's Epic Voice: The Narrator in "Paradise Lost"* (Cambridge, Mass.: Harvard University Press, 1967), chap. 3.

7. James Whaler, "Miltonic Simile," *PMLA* 46 (1931): 1061.

8. James Whaler, "Animal Simile in *Paradise Lost,*" *PMLA* 47 (1932): 552. See also idem, "Compounding and Distribution of Simile in *Paradise Lost,*" *Modern Philology* (February 1931): 313–27; idem, "Grammatical Nexus of Miltonic Simile," *Journal of English and Germanic Philology* 30 (1931): 327–34.

9. Geoffrey Hartman, "Milton's Counterplot," in *Beyond Formalism: Literary Essays* (New Haven and London: Yale University Press, 1970), pp. 113–23.

10. Samuel Taylor Coleridge, *Biographia Literaria* 14, in *The Portable Coleridge,* ed. I. A. Richards (New York: The Viking Press, 1950), p. 524.

11. *American Heritage Dictionary of the English Language, New College Edition,* ed. William Morris (Boston: Houghton Mifflin Company, 1976).

12. Francis Fergusson, *The Idea of a Theater: The Art of Drama in Changing Perspective* (Princeton University Press, 1949; reprint ed., by Garden City, N.Y.: Doubleday Anchor Books, 1953), p. 18.

13. Stanley Eugene Fish, in his *Surprised by Sin: The Reader in "Paradise Lost"* (New York: St. Martin's Press, 1967), bases his study of *Paradise Lost* on the reader's response to the poem. Milton, he says, uses certain literary devices specifically to incorporate this response into the poem as an integral part of it. The reader is made to feel sympathy for Satan and Adam and Eve, and this sympathy is then made to clash with the author's doctrinal intrusions as an educational device: the experience of sin through an identification with the fallen characters immediately and harshly confronted with the truth more effectively brings the mind to Christian virtue than the direct statement of doctrine. Although Fish begins his study with a rhetorical approach, he concludes with an authoritarian theological orthodoxy that is very different from the concept of counterplot here proposed.

14. Northrop Frye, *Anatomy of Criticism* (New York: Atheneum, 1966), "Polemical Introduction," pp. 3–29.

Milton's
Kinesthetic Vision
in *Paradise Lost*

PART I

The Poetics of Milton's Counterplot

---

1   Perceptual Kinesthesia

What ultimately becomes in Milton's declension of mind a complex meditation begins not only in the mind's painful sympathic conflicts but also in the
humbler experience of one of the simplest perceptual truths: that the appearance of an object and the viewer's relation to it are significantly influenced
by their location and movement in space—by the relation of location to
location, location to movement, or movement to movement. A change in
location or movement will change the relation between object and viewer
and will change the appearance of the object.

The perception of these relations is kinesthetic perception, and such
kinesthetic perception is basic to Milton's perceptual process and to his
mode of presentation. This kinesthesia is not only disjunctive but mediative.

As do most works of literature, *Paradise Lost* occurs in space and time
and has characters who move in this space and time. The space or setting of
Paradise Lost is, of course, the whole created and uncreated universe—hell,
chaos, heaven, earth, moon, and the other celestial bodies in the universe,
and the spaces between all of these. As the action of the poem unfolds, there
are shifts in setting from one place to another; and often in these shiftings the
appearance and the nature of the settings change. Because the shiftings
involve such great distances, the changes in appearance are significant. At a
great distance a planet, for example, is an object of perception framed by the
viewer's perception, while at close range the planet, or even a very small
portion of a planet, becomes a large setting in which the viewer is contained.

In his journey from hell through chaos toward the newly created world
and Eden, Satan first sees the earth far off, as he is leaving the gradually
"retiring" chaos, as a tiny "pendent world" hanging "in a golden chain" from
the walls of heaven (2: 1051–52). Then, as he lands on its outer shell, the
universe becomes a larger globe:

> . . . upon the firm opacous globe
> Of this round world, whose first convex divides
> The luminous inferior orbs, enclosed
> From Chaos and th' inroad of Darkness old,
> Satan alighted walks.
>
> (3: 418–22)

Entering inside the universe he flies "amongst innumerable stars" (3: 565), and later lands on Mt. Niphates (3: 742), a vantage point that affords him a view of Eden: ". . . towards Eden which now in his view / Lay pleasant, his grieved look he fixes sad" (4: 27–28). He journeys on to its border:

> So on he fares, and to the border comes
> Of Eden, where delicious Paradise,
> Now nearer, crowns with her enclosure green.
>
> (4: 131–33)

Finally he leaps over the boundary and lands on the tree of life within the garden.

In Satan's movement the earth has changed from a tiny orb to a larger globe, to a patch of green, to a garden with trees, leaves, birds, and so on that then becomes the setting for the next several books. The size and appearance of the earth and Satan the viewer's relation to it have all changed as he journeys.

The same change in the appearance of the earth is represented in Raphael's journey from heaven to Eden in Book 5:

> . . . nor delayed the wingèd saint
> After his charge received; but from among
> Thousand celestial ardors, where he stood
> Veiled with his gorgeous wings, up springing light
> Flew through the midst of heav'n; th' angelic quires
> On each hand parting, to his speed gave way
> Through all th' empyreal road; till at the gate
> Of heav'n arrived, the gate self-opened wide
> On golden hinges turning, as by work
> Divine the sov'ran Architect had framed.
> From hence, no cloud, or, to obstruct his sight,
> Star interposed, however small, he sees,
> Not unconform to other shining globes,
> Earth and the gard'n of God, with cedars crowned
> Above all hills . . .
> . . . .
> . . . Down hither prone in flight
> He speeds, and through the vast ethereal sky
> Sails between worlds and worlds, with steady wing
> Now on the polar winds, then with quick fan
> Winnows the buxom air.
>
> (5: 247–70)

In this passage the change in the earth's appearance occurs less gradually, for Raphael's journey is faster than Satan's.

In these examples a change in the position of the viewer is responsible for the changes in appearance of the object of vision. A similar change of appearance can occur if the point of view shifts from one viewer, or from one position in space, to another. Thus Satan in hell is in early scenes perceived close up—he is as huge as a whale; when he moves "he rears up from off the pool / His mighty stature" (1: 221–22). But later, as he sets out on his "solitary flight" through chaos, he is suddenly seen from a great distance:

> Meanwhile . . . [Satan]
> . . . .
> Explores his solitary flight; sometimes
> He scours the right-hand coast, sometimes the left;
> Now shaves with level wing the deep, then soars
> Up to the fiery concave tow'ring high:
> As when far off at sea a fleet descried
> Hangs in the clouds.
>
> (2: 629–37)

Hell, at first represented as swirling elements metamorphosing around the characters, has taken on a shape and has boundaries, and Satan has become very small. At the beginning of Book 3 this shift is completed as the point of view is shifted to the eye of God and Satan is seen from a point far above hell:

> Now had the Almighty Father from above,
> From the pure empyrean where he sits
> High throned above all highth, bent down his eye,
> His own works and their works at once to view.
> . . . .
> . . . He . . . surveyed
> Hell and the gulf between, and Satan there
> Coasting the wall of heav'n on this side Night
> In the dun air sublime, and ready now
> To stoop with wearied wings and willing feet
> On the bare outside of this world.
>
> (3: 56–74)

These shifts and their effects are not accidental, arbitrary, or merely descriptive, but basic to Milton's perceptual process and to his understanding of perception and its relation to the appearance and nature of the object of perception. He explicitly foregrounds the importance of relative position when he defines the size of the pendent world as "in bigness as a star / Of smallest magnitude" (2: 1052–53). How big is a star? How big is a small star? What this definition is saying is, "the earth is as big as a star that appears small," or "the earth is as big as a star would appear to a viewer far away from it: small."

Milton uses this perceptual strategy as a more explicit device in Book 6, when he describes Satan's armies approaching from the north on the plains of heaven:

> . . . At last
> Far in th'horizon to the north appeared
> From skirt to skirt a fiery region, stretched
> In battalious aspéct, and *nearer view*
> Bristled with upright beams innumerable
> Of rigid spears, and helmets thronged, and shields.
>
> (6: 78–83; emphasis added)

The armies suddenly change aspect, yet there is no designated viewer moving nearer such that the armies look different as in the examples given above. Simply with the words *nearer view* Milton indicates that every object may be represented and perceived from different distances. Similarly, stars, Milton says, "shone / Stars distant, but nigh hand seemed other worlds . . . or happy isles" (3: 565–67); and the earth "a globe far off / . . . seemed, now seems a boundless continent" (3: 422–23).

Likewise Milton foregrounds the importance of movement in determining one's sense of space between objects when he measures Raphael's distance from earth as "within soar / Of tow'ring eagles " (5: 270–71). Space and distance take their measurement from the motion of the beings who move within or through it.

In the examples given above, the shifts in point of view and the accompanying changes in appearance are not experienced as disjunctive, because they occur in a clearly defined space frame. The reader participates in the shift when his/her point of view is anchored in, or represented by, a character, as in Satan's and Raphael's journeys. If the character moves, the reader moves too and shares in the changing perception. In the other instances given above, the reader must shift his/her own point of view, but such shifts are not difficult since the locations or orientation in space are defined in terms like *above, look down, near, far, nigh,* and *distant.* All the changing appearances can be "saved" by the laws of the Galilean-Newtonian space-time frame that govern location and motion and guarantee the integrity of size, shape, and distance. Although an object's appearance may change because of a change in the viewer's spatial relation to it and although it may thus be said that the view of the object is nowhere absolute, nevertheless the nature and integrity of the object may be considered separate from its relation to the viewer because of the Galilean-Newtonian laws. The truth of the appearance and the truth of the relation are in how these are seen and known, but the truth of the object is independent of its appearance, is the object "itself." Indeed, the apparent absoluteness of this second truth allows the experience of change itself a reality of its own and prevents it from becoming disruptive to the viewer.

But there are other shifts in *Paradise Lost* in which this distinction is less easy to make and in which this felt sense of truths and identities is less certain. The changes above were felt as familiar to the reader, even though he/she may never have traveled between planets, because they were represented in terms of objects or persons, spaces, and motions that were governed by the same laws that govern his/her more limited life on earth. However, when one considers, for example, the relation of the time Raphael's journey takes to the distance it covers, the proportionate relation between the variables comprising the frame loses its constancy and these variables and the objects governed by the laws of the frame lose their stability and integrity.

There are different kinds of motion represented in *Paradise Lost*. As Satan enters the "first convex" of the universe (3: 419), his motion is represented in two ways:

> . . . then from pole to pole
> He views in breadth, and without longer pause
> Down right into the world's first region throws
> His flight precipitant, and winds with ease
> Through the pure marble air his oblique way
> Amongst innumerable stars.
>
> (3: 560–65)

"Winding with ease" is motion at an unchanging velocity, or motion that, while it changes the appearance of the stars, is not so disproportionate as to destroy the perceptual relation. "Throwing his flight precipitant," on the other hand, is either accelerated motion or motion at a far greater velocity. Its relation to objects of perception is not described in this passage. In Raphael's flight, however, in the passage quoted earlier, the appearance of the earth is represented as changing much more rapidly, and the precipitous speed of the angel "thither prone in flight" and his apparently more relaxed "sail[ing] between worlds and worlds, with steady wing"—a motion similar to Satan's "wind[ing] with ease"—seem to be the same motion. The Newtonian law that says that constant velocity is inertia even though it is very great would seem to account for a seeming disparity in these two descriptions, but if Raphael's speed is considered in relation to the object of perception, the constancy of the perceptual relation is not so easily resolved. If the speed is great enough, the appearance of the object would change for the viewer into blurred imperceptibility. According to the law of inertia, the flight in itself might be felt as relaxed and stable, or perhaps not felt at all; but in relation to an object of perception, the flight would be felt as dizzying. In this experience, because of the Newtonian sanction, the imperceptibility of the object would not necessarily affect the truth of its integrity and identity, but the perceptual experience becomes wrenching and disproportionate. Carried further, however, as Raphael himself suggests to Adam in their discussion about astronomy in Book 8, velocity may not simply blur but may dissolve an object in motion:

> The swiftness of those circles áttribute,
> Though numberless, to his omnipotence,
> That to corporeal substances could add,
> Speed almost spiritual; me thou think'st not slow,
> Who since the morning hour set out from heav'n
> Where God resides, and ere mid-day arrived
> In Eden, distance inexpressible
> By numbers that have name.

(8: 107–14)

Such a possibility carries kinesthetic perception to an extreme that, while perhaps theoretically or even ontologically disturbing, may not threaten the reader's perception of and certainty about the integrity of the elements and beings composing the everyday world. Yet why then do tangible objects or tangible aspects of the characters in *Paradise Lost* often substantially change appearance or have a double or plastic appearance, almost as if they existed in a frame invaded by the non-Newtonian laws just described? At the end of Book 4, for example, as Satan angrily confronts Gabriel's angelic squadron, he holds "in his grasp / What seemed both spear and shield" (4: 989–90). And throughout the poem Satan himself drastically changes appearance as he metamorphoses into various animals and beings: in Book 3 he changes into a cherub to fool Uriel (3: 635); in Book 4 he becomes the "four-footed kinds"—a lion, a tiger—(4: 395–409) to spy on Adam and Eve; and of course in Book 9, and still more definitively in Book 10, he becomes the serpent. Similarly, at the end of Book 1 in the passage quoted above, the giant devils suddenly at "the signal giv'n" wondrously "to smallest forms / Reduced their shapes immense" (1: 776–90).

In a less substantial but still visibly perceptible sense, Satan repeatedly undergoes changes of physical appearance corresponding to the changes in feeling and character referred to in the introduction. For example as he speaks his tortured and tortuous soliloquy on Mt. Niphates:

> . . . each passion dimmed his face
> Thrice changed with pale, ire, envy, and despair,
> Which marred his borrowed visage.

(4: 114–16)

Such changes produce a disjunction in physical appearance and a disjunction in the integrity of the being's identity when Satan or a significant aspect of Satan is represented as a single object. Thus, as he beholds his followers parading before him in hell, his eye is "cruel . . . but cast[s] / Signs of remorse" (1: 604–5).

The question of the spear-shield is not easily answered. It might be argued to explain Satan's metamorphoses that he is not a real character—he is a fiction, an angel—and it might be argued, from a slightly different angle, that the changes in the appearance of his face are the expressions of feelings and moods not unusual to the human reader, although the image of Satan's eye and what it connotes remain disturbing.

Yet one must ask whether Milton is really describing some changes so "objectively" and others so "fantastically"—in two incompatible modes; one must ask whether Satan is two kinds of being at once—a human character as in a novel and a fabulous creature—when the poet has so specifically fore-grounded this very issue in the giant devils' radical change in size. Although they are essentially incorporeal (1: 789), Milton is nevertheless teasing both the reader who would evade the issue by a literal-minded and limited adher-ence to the Galilean-Newtonian frame and the reader who would evade it by believing in "wonders"—that is, magic.

Such disjunctions distort or deviate from familiar frames of reference; a kinesthetic shift that may be experienced as disturbing in a different way is the entry into the simile world. It is disturbing because, unlike most similes in which the vehicle serves to reinforce the tenor, it seems to move into a different frame altogether. In the simile quoted above in which the fallen angels' love for Satan is compared to the sun at evening briefly returning from behind the clouds to bring the fields back to life, vehicle reinforces tenor—rejoicing breaking through doubt—but there are three other charac-teristics that make it a distancing device. First, the rejoicing followed by Milton's praise of it (2: 486–99) and the pleasantness of the scene do not fit in hell: the tenor itself is already distanced from hell. Second, the length and beauty of the simile takes the reader's attention away from hell for a time that takes on weight in itself and significance as it imprints its contents on the reader's mind. Third, the simile creates, or opens into a space, a world that could be indefinitely extended: tucked into the valley and hills may be farms, villages, churches; flowing through them may be a river; with the sheep may be shepherds; after the day and evening there will be night with lights com-ing on. And so on.

Similarly, the whale and the bees-elves similes are long and they open into a space, a world distant from their tenors and characterized by tones that, as described in the introduction, are curiously pleasant and peaceful. Further-more, in these similes Milton introduces not only the sense of a new point of view, but a new viewer: a figure, perhaps a character, though a character of a different kind from God, Satan, Adam and Eve, and the angels—the pilot, the peasant, and by implication, shepherds.

Where and what is this world? In the frame of the epic, mimetically occurring in the space at least partly defined in terms of a Newtonian cos-mology, it is a space in some other frame; but it is also Vallambrosa and Norway—the world and time of the reader's familiar world, more familiar and predictable, perhaps, than the world of the epic.

In another extended simile in Book 1, Milton again foregrounds this very issue by shifting the poem into a scene similar in every way to the similes just discussed, except that now the new figure and point of view are those of Galileo himself:

> . . . the superior Fiend
> Was moving toward the shore; his ponderous shield,
> Ethereal temper, massy, large, and round,
> Behind him cast; the broad circumference
> Hung on his shoulders like the moon, whose orb
> Through optic glass the Tuscan artist views
> At ev'ning from the top of Fesole,
> Or in Valdarno, to descry new lands,
> Rivers or mountains in her spotty globe.
>
> (1: 283–91)

Such shiftings take the reader far from the simpler perceptual experiences that are one of the beginnings of Milton's declension of mind. Yet, as the poet offered the reader mimetic instances of gradual and participatory motion in which the changes and disjunctions might be mediated, so there are in *Paradise Lost* poetic experiences that act to partly resolve the disjunctions just discussed.

As Satan is described beginning his journey from hell to earth, hell is described in the passage quoted earlier as a "fiery concave tow'ring high" (2: 635), an appropriate characterization since Satan, and the reader, are still inside hell. However, earlier in his farewell speech to his fallen angels, Satan has spoken of hell as "our prison strong, this huge convex of fire" (2: 434), though he is still viewing it from within. In this disjunction in characterization, a mediation is accomplished if the reader supplies a shift in point of view similar to the ones Milton supplies with such words as "now nearer" and "from above." Or mediation can be achieved by saying that Satan describes hell as convex because in his imagination he has already left hell and is viewing it from outside. The distinction between shifts represented mimetically in the epic frame of the poem and shifts that are implied but must be made by the reader, even though the two shifts are otherwise identical, is significant because, in both interpretations of the example just given, the viewer has displaced him/herself in the space of mind rather than in the Galilean-Newtonian space frame of actual movement. Because in this case the distinction may seem little more than technical, the movement from concave to convex serves as a transition to more imaginative shiftings.

In a passage describing Paradise, Milton uses a kinesthetic technique both to represent the motion of the landscape and to awaken the reader's several senses simultaneously such that he/she experiences the scene in all the richness of both the scene and his/her own perceptual complex:

> . . . cool recess, o'er which the mantling vine
> Lays forth her purple grape, and gently creeps
> Luxuriant; meanwhile murmuring waters fall
> Down the slope hills, dispersed, or in a lake,
> That to the fringèd bank with myrtle crowned
> Her crystal mirror holds, unite their streams.
> The birds their quire apply; airs, vernal airs,
> Breathing the smell of field and grove, attune
> The trembling leaves.

(4: 258–66)

In this passage Milton focuses his description as much on the motion of the elements composing the scene and their relation to one another as on the individual elements themselves. Correspondingly, he appeals both severally and simultaneously to the reader's sight, sense of temperature, smell, hearing, and kinesthetic sense of position and motion. This technique has two effects. First, the essence of this landscape is motion and interchange as well as substance and identity. Second, in the richness of the perceptual experience itself the scene seems to be alive. Thus in the last three lines, as Milton puns on the word *airs* and combines the two senses most dependent on the air—hearing and smell—with the part of the kinesthetic sense inseparably related to air—breathing—the landscape itself seems to be breathing and making sound. How deeply this simple descriptive passage, without philosophy, almost unavoidably makes us experience the truth of "the one life within us and abroad" that Coleridge yearned for but could rarely find!

The genius of Milton's simplicity still more simply imprints the same kinesthetic truth on the perceiver's mind in a passage describing Raphael:

> . . . he stood
> And shook his plumes, that heav'nly fragrance filled
> The circuit wide.

(5: 285–87)

Here Milton not only has combined or mixed stimuli and senses, but has combined them in such a way that movement produces a smell, as above sound waves became breathing. But perhaps the most beautiful descriptive passage using such techniques is that of the newly created fish in Book 7:

> Forthwith the sounds and seas, each creek and bay,
> With fry innumerable swarm, and shoals
> Of fish that with their fins and shining scales
> Glide under the green wave, in sculls that oft
> Bank the mid-sea. Part single or with mate
> Graze the seaweed their pasture, and through groves
> Of coral stray, or sporting with quick glance
> Show to the sun their waved coats dropped with gold,

Or in their pearly shells at ease, attend
Moist nutriment, or under rocks their food
In jointed armor watch; on smooth the seal
And bended dolphins play; part huge of bulk;
Wallowing unwieldy, enormous in their gait,
Tempest the ocean.

(7: 399–412)

This is the passage Arnold Stein singles out to show that Milton's descriptive method is kinesthetic, not visual or auditory.[1] Even the shellfish, who do not move, are rendered kinesthetically, so strong is the sense of place and body and relation to surroundings. As Stein says, Milton writes so that the reader knows what it is to *be* a shellfish, not to see it. It is Milton's kinesthetic perceptual style that brings the other senses alive: it is the sporting movement that makes the golden backs visible. Milton even adds the necessary light source, the sun. It is seeing pieces of the fish—fins and scales—against the green of the wave that makes them appear as the reader simultaneously sees and feels their gliding. Movement and sight depend upon and enhance each other.

Such descriptions are not disjunctive; rather, by jarring the perceptual faculties out of their sensuous sloth, Milton makes the motion of their kinesthetic interdependency a mediating force that corresponds to the object of perception. In this mediation fish and mind seem to exist in the same space.

In Satan's perception of convex hell, the Galilean-Newtonian motion was displaced into a new frame, the imagining mind. The Galilean-Newtonian frame was itself framed. Here it might seem that the distinction between these two frames has entirely collapsed, that the two are perfectly coincidental. However, although fish and perceiving mind seem to exist in the same space, this space as a whole is different from the Galilean-Newtonian space, even framed, because it is more psychic than physical: the entire perceiving experience between object and viewer has been transferred not from an "objective" to a "subjective" space, but from a Galilean-Newtonian to a psychic space or frame.

Whereas in the earlier experiences of motion it was the viewer as a whole, as a body, who was in motion (or conceivably the body of the object in motion), here it is the elements of the viewer that are in motion in relation to each other *as* the elements of the object of perception (the landscape) are in motion in relation to one another. The relation between object and viewer is the relation between motions inherent in the natures of each. The motions described in the passages just quoted are subtler and more articulated than the motions of whole bodies because they are not restricted to what can be perceived visually. They are not dominated by the eye. Thus to the eye the viewer in these passages would appear still, though the senses are in motion.

The world represented in these passages is the same world as that framed and governed by Galilean-Newtonian laws, but perceived in a different space. It is the same space in which Satan sees hell as convex, but it is less mechanical because it is filled with intangible and invisible motions as well as tangible and visible ones. This space is a third space, neither the "outer" Galilean-Newtonian space nor the space of a solipsistic or mystical mind, a world of fantasy cut off from the world. It is the same space as the space of the similes.

In the examples given above, the motions and the new space are perhaps not ultimately disturbing, because they have been derived from and sanctioned by everyday experience, "proved upon the senses," as it were, even though they may not be easily measurable by Galilean-Newtonian laws. This everyday experience acts partly as a mediation just as Milton's representation of and appeal to shifting location did in earlier instances.

The reader can participate in this experience, and through this participation Milton teaches new truths and establishes new poetic structures. The new space, though the motions within it are more subtle and complex, has the same felt certainty as the Galilean-Newtonian frame: it is framed, and it is derived from and imprinted through familiar experience.

An emblematic representation of point of view as it exists simultaneously in the mechanical world of Galilean-Newtonian coordinates and in the inner world solipsistically cut off from the motions framed by the third space is Satan as he perches on the tree of life immediately after leaping the bounds into the garden of Eden:

> Thence up he flew, and on the Tree of Life,
> The middle tree and highest there that grew,
> Sat like a cormorant; yet not true life
> Thereby regained, but sat devising death
> To them who lived; nor on the virtue thought
> Of that life-giving plant, but only used
> For prospect, that well used had been the pledge
> Of immortality.
>
> (4: 194–201)

This perception of the tree of life is very different from the perception of Paradise and the fish, just as the point of view of the cormorant is different from the point of view of the poet who represents himself as a bird throughout *Paradise Lost*, a bird retired into the covert of his imaginative third space (3: 37–40), a bird in flight as he moves through his own poem, through his imagination, shifting his attention and focus between and within the dimensions of which *Paradise Lost* consists. Bird is not literally poet, but poet's presence, a point of view somewhere between that of poet, a character, and the reader, an emblem for point of view in itself in the controlled motion. Thus in the prefatory poem to the second edition, Andrew Marvell represents Milton as the bird of paradise:

> Thou sing'st with so much gravity and ease,
> And above human flight dost soar aloft
> With plume so strong, so equal, and so soft.
> The bird named from that Paradise you sing
> So never flags, but always keeps on wing.

(ll. 36–40)

It might seem that these mediations still cannot resolve the shifts and dualities of objects, such as spear-shield, of Satan's eye, and of character discussed above. But if one understands that object or being can be perceived in two different frames, one can consider the possibility that, if the second frame of mind deepened and articulated his/her sense of physical motion—as in the perception of the fishes—and if it allows the perception of motions less tangible than physical motion—such as smell and temperature—it may allow him/her to perceive yet subtler and less tangible motions that would affect his/her sense of the nature of any object of perception.

The most important, perhaps, of these less tangible and more psychic motions are the motions of tone. A shift from a direct mimetic representation into a tonal representation of an object or being, or a shift from one tone to another, signals a change in attitude or point of view of the viewer toward the object that is a less literal point of view than in the passages discussed so far. This shift in point of view may, as do the more literal physical shifts, change the appearance of an object of perception as the viewer's emotional relation toward it changes.

Such tonal shifts occur repeatedly throughout *Paradise Lost*. The poem modulates, for example, from the description of painful hell to the lyrical and sympathetic tone of

> Regions of sorrow, doleful shades, where peace
> And rest can never dwell, hope never comes
> That comes to all.

(1: 65–67)

In a similar shift Milton moves from the description of the burning solid of hell on which Satan must land as he leaves the lake to the sympathy of "such resting found the sole / Of unblest feet" (1: 237–38). Milton's description of the much-admired architect of Pandemonium modulates into a more delightful and less painful lyrical tone even as he describes him falling, as Mulciber, from a Greek heaven:

> . . . thrown by angry Jove
> Sheer o'er the crystal battlements: from morn
> To noon he fell, from noon to dewy eve,
> A summer's day; and with the setting sun
> Dropped from the zenith like a falling star,
> On Lemnos or th'Aégean isle.

(1: 741–46)

Here the shift in tone has rendered Mulciber an object of beauty rather than an object of terror and evil.

Similar shifts are shown in the instances quoted in the introduction where a mimetic description modulates into a lyrical simile—into the scenes of the whale, elves, autumn leaves, and reviving fields. The shift into the editorial condemnation following the whale simile cuts in a different direction: from a lyric sympathy to anger, which radically alters Satan's appearance in the poet's, and perhaps the reader's, judgment.

Complementing the lyrical shifts are many instances of ironic shifting, some of them humorous and lighthearted and some of them sharper and almost as apparently vicious as the outbreaks of anger. The poet's choice of words as he describes the heavenly angels falling on the field of battle before the onslaught of Satan's cannon removes for a moment the seriousness from the contest between good and evil and makes the angels appear comical:

> . . . down they fell
> By thousands, angel on archangel rolled
> The sooner for their arms.
>
> (6: 593–95)

As Adam addresses Eve on the beauties of their garden in his first speech in *Paradise Lost,* he says that their life there is happy and free, for God requires of them only one service:

> . . . not to taste that only Tree
> Of Knowledge, planted by the Tree of Life,
> So near grows death to life, whate'er death is,
> Some dreadful thing no doubt.
>
> (4: 423–26)

As in the preceding example, this comment lifts the reader for a moment from the seriousness of the epic plot and removes from the tree of knowledge its awesome symbolic character such that, because of Adam's innocent point of view, it becomes an ordinary tree. But unlike the description of the rolling angels, this comment also gives the reader a strange pause as his/her knowledge undercuts Adam's innocence. A sharper ironic shift is Michael's editorial comment about the flood he has shown Adam in vision in Book 11: as he describes the "fair atheists" "swimming" in sensuous joy, he quips "[they] now swim in joy / (Erelong to swim at large) . . ." (11: 625–26).

In all of these tonal shifts the appearance of the object of perception changes, and as it changes the viewer's feelings about it change too. A shift in tone signals a shift in faculty, as when, in perceiving a landscape, the perceptual focus might shift from sight to smell. When an object changes appearance because of the viewer's change of physical location, the direction of causality seems to be clear; but in a tonal shift it is more difficult to say whether the change in tone, object, or feeling is primary. For these motions all occur in the same space, the imaginative frame, and it is more difficult to distinguish them than it was to distinguish in the perceptual act the motion of fish from the motion of senses, should one want to do so. Whereas in the perception of the fish the motions between the different parts of the fish resonated with the viewer's inner motions—the motions of the various perceptual faculties, in the tonal perception the motions of the viewer's inner parts are resonant with the inner motions of the object of perception. Of course it might be argued that a tree or spear does not have "inner motions," though a being or an eye does. But in tonal perception the object, even a tangible one, may be said to include the potential functions or attitudes that other objects or beings may have in relation to it. This is a truth that Satan, perched on the tree of life, cannot perceive. Again, it is the same object as is perceived in the Galilean-Newtonian frame, but this object is being perceived in a different frame and therefore different aspects of its nature are revealed. Thus, as with the shifts discussed earlier, a tonal shift signals a shift into the third space—the imaginative second frame—but in a subtler and deeper articulation that renders the space yet more psychic than physical, though it is still not transcendent or separate from the world. The shift into this space is most clearly marked in the similes because the space itself is outlined and imaged.

To understand these more psychic motions in the imaginative frame, one can no longer appeal to known laws or everyday experience. It is the work of the next stage of Milton's declension of mind to make them known; but before this is possible, the exact nature and limits of the third space must be defined. Milton first uses further shiftings to define what it is by destroying identifications with what it is not; for as the mind struggles to understand the new frame it falsely identifies it with various other familiar frames, identifications that must be destroyed. These shiftings are disjunctive and painful; and as identifications are destroyed, the motions within them may become disjunctive too as they begin to assert their own unknown nature. Before, these motions were not felt as disruptive because the viewer still felt that they modulated between truths that were true in themselves. Though the fish may move in new ways, their motion did not destroy their identities. And though the perceptual faculties may mix, they are still discrete and may easily resolve back into their essential natures. Though Satan's attitude may vary, Satan is still Satan and the tree still the tree. Though Mulciber may be perceived as beautiful, Mulciber is still Mulciber the evil angel. And though an object may be viewed ironically or lyrically, this irony and lyricism will pass more quickly than the more substantial object modulated by these tones. In other words, the changing and fluid qualities of perception, thought, and feeling, and of objects, are not felt to take ontological priority over the more substantial identities between or within which these motions occur. But when shiftings destroy the familiar frames by which mind ordinarily measures identities—conceptual, ideological, moral, psychological, even literary and linguistic frames—one is likely to suffer a loss of point of view, of the center sanctioned by these frames, and to suffer a corresponding loss of the sense of the integrity of objects—of a character, of an idea, even of a tree or a spear. Then the qualities of the imaginative space assert themselves in their own right. Tone, more than could physical motion in the examples discussed early in this chapter, becomes a reality as great or greater than the objects it modulates between. These psychic motions at first become more disrupting than the shifts in the Galilean-Newtonian frame because there are no readily apparent laws to govern them. But as Milton forces the issue of how intangible psychic motions can alter appearance and identity, he gradually discovers and articulates their laws. This discovery and articulation through poetic experience is the goal and process of the declension of mind as it unfolds through the counterplot.

NOTE

1. Arnold Stein, *Answerable Style: Essays on "Paradise Lost"* (Seattle and London: University of Washington Press, 1967), p. 151. See T. S. Eliot, "Milton I," in *On Poetry and Poets* (New York: Noonday Press, 1961), pp. 156–64, for his discussion of Milton's style in visual terms; and see C. S. Lewis, *A Preface to "Paradise Lost"* (New York: Oxford University Press, 1961) chaps. 7 and 8, for a discussion of Milton's style in auditory terms.

2 Sympathic Kinesthesia

Milton forces the issue of the relation between the Galilean-Newtonian frame and the imaginative frame in such devices discussed above as the giant devils' "wondrous" change in size and the placing of Galileo in the simile space for several reasons. He wishes to call into question the supremacy of the Galilean-Newtonian frame, but at the same time he wishes to prevent the imaginative space from becoming imaginary or mystical: he will not allow it to be a safe and separate space removed from or transcending the heat and dust of the "real" world, an imagination whose virtue derives from a vague, undisciplined appeal to fantasy and sentiment. By forcing a confrontation of its dimensions with the dimensions of a scientifically rigorous frame he wishes to show that the realm and motions of the imagination have laws equally rigorous, and further, to demonstrate that the laws of this third space when fully understood will subsume these physical laws and in so doing will bring power and wisdom to the mind willing to overcome its fears and enter the third space.

Milton also forces the relation between the imaginative frame and other frames often identified with it—theological, psychological, and even literary frames. The Newtonian frame allows and explains motion as well as position, but often conceptual frames allow only fixed position of mind and restricted motion, the frames taking on the solidity of objects in the mind unlike the physical concepts of space, motion, and time which, because they are more clearly understood, are allowed their motion and insubstantiality. In some of his descriptions Milton shows the reader that, when he/she moves, the appearance of objects changes in relation to that motion. In the less tangible world of concept, Milton similarly shows the reader that he/she habitually gives concepts and frames a substantiality similar to that of objects, and perhaps compensatorily more substantiality precisely because they are in "reality" less tangible. In order to make the reader aware of this habit and to change it, Milton breaks down the substantiality of concept by foregrounding concept and frame and then treating them kinesthetically, just as he did the objects of perception in his kinesthetic physical descriptions. He sets their appearance in motion in relation to the mind's psychic motions.

At the same time, Milton breaks down the mind's habitual reliance on one faculty over another, an attachment that makes the activity of the whole soul, the consciousness of the "mind through all her powers," impossible.

As the reliance on one sense inhibits the full kinesthetic perception through all the senses of the landscape in Paradise, so an elevation of reason or moral judgment or pity to a position of mental domination inhibits understanding and leads the mind to false conclusions.

Milton's aesthetic distancing works to destroy any consistent referential frame the mind might attempt to find or erect within the poem. On the one hand he sets up conflicting references; on the other he erases the boundaries distinguishing one frame from another.

Reference is uncertain and contradictory both within the single simile and within the larger context of the counterplot and of the poem as a whole. For example, in the whale simile, the whale is Satan chained to the burning lake and is also the Satan of the medieval bestiaries, the devil who will draw the unsuspecting Christian to ruinous damnation. In the opposite theological direction, however, the whalelike Satan "prone on the flood, extended long and large / Lay floating many a rood," a clause that not only measures his length but connotes that he is an image of salvation. The whale is also the leviathan created by God in Book 7:

> . . . There leviathan,
> Hugest of living creatures, on the deep
> Stretched like a promontory sleeps or swims,
> And seems a moving land, and at his gills
> Draws in, and at his trunk spouts out a sea.
>
> (7: 412–16)

And last, the whale is the whale of the peaceful scene in the simile affording temporary anchorage to the pilot in his uncertain night journey. The two images of the slumbering leviathan seem neither evil nor good, despite their denotative and connotative references. These various conflicting references render a conceptually framed identification or judgment of the whale impossible.

In a similar referential conflict, Satan appears "involved in" or "wrapped in" mist in Book 9 as he returns to Eden and "like a black mist low creeping" searches for the serpent, fit vessel of his intended deception (9: 75, 158, 180). Yet in Adam and Eve's morning hymn in Book 5 "mists and exhalations," rising and falling as rain, are represented as part of the "ceaseless change" that advances God's praise (5: 183–91).

Even the frame of the counterplot itself is inconsistent. For example, similes of pilots beset by obstacles reappear frequently throughout *Paradise Lost;* yet, whereas in the whale simile in Book 1 Satan is the whale, in several other similes it is Satan who is the ship or pilot. In Book 2, as he beholds the earth in the distance, he is likened to "a weather-beaten vessel [that] holds / Gladly the port, though shrouds and tackle torn" (2: 1043–44). In Book 4, nearer to Paradise, he is likened to sailors nearing the spicy Arabian shores:

> . . . As when to them who sail
> Beyond the Cape of Hope, and now are past
> Mozambic, off at sea north-east winds blow
> Sabaean odors from the spicy shore
> Of Araby the blest, with such delay
> Well pleased they slack their course.
>
> (4: 159–64)

And in Book 9, as he "obliquely" approaches Eve, he is likened to a steersman tacking in inconstant winds into the mouth of a river:

> As when a ship by skilful steersman wrought
> Nigh river's mouth or foreland, where the wind
> Veers oft, as oft so steers, and shifts her sail.
>
> (9: 513–15)

The frame of the counterplot is similarly inconsistent in Milton's use of meteor images. In Book 2: 708–11, Satan the evil angel is represented as a "horrid" comet who causes "pestilence and war," and in 5: 708–11, as a delusively beautiful star—perhaps like Mulciber. Yet in 4: 555–60, it is the good angel Uriel who is the shooting star beheld by the mariner in the autumn night, "when vapors fired / Impress the air." In 9: 634–42, in the simile discussed earlier, it is Satan who is "kindled vapors" that lead the peasant, a figure like the pilot, to ruin. On the other hand, in 12: 629–32, the vaporous mists "gather[ing] . . . fast at the laborer's heel" are the bright cherubim of God.

In 1: 304–13, as they rise up from the burning lake at their leader's call, Satan's followers are likened to Pharaoh's armies, as "with perfidious hatred" they pursue the chosen of God following Moses out of Egypt. But soon after, as Satan directs the flight of his roused angels by waving his spear, the evil Satan-Pharaoh becomes the "good" Moses, who with his "potent rod" calls up the hordes of locusts (1: 338–43). In Book 11, as Michael descends to Paradise to instruct Adam on future days before expelling the human pair from Paradise, he is described in a simile that contains a conflicting reference:

> A glorious apparition, had not doubt
> And carnal fear that day dimmed Adam's eye.
> Not that more glorious, when the angels met
> Jacob in Mahanaim, where he saw
> The field pavilioned with his guardians bright;
> Nor that which on the flaming mount appeared
> In Dothan, covered with a camp of fire,
> Against the Syrian king, who to surprise
> One man, assassin-like had levied war,
> War unproclaimed.
>
> (11: 211–20)

The first army is "good," the second "bad." Milton foregrounds the issue by putting the two references side by side.

Milton forces the issue of reference still more explicitly by using the same image of the sun shining through the clouds to describe both God and Satan. Satan in hell appears as a

> . . . form [that] had yet not lost
> All her original brightness, nor appeared
> Less than Archangel ruined, and th' excess
> Of glory obscured: as when the sun new ris'n
> Looks through the horizontal misty air
> Shorn of his beams.
>
> (1: 591–96)

Similarly, in Book 3 Milton addresses God:

> . . . thou shad'st
> The full blaze of thy beams, and through a cloud
> Drawn about thee like a radiant shrine,
> Dark with excessive bright thy skirts appear.
>
> (3: 377–80)

Thus the references in *Paradise Lost* cannot be fitted into a consistent frame; they are multidirectional. With this technique Milton establishes a world independent of all other frames with its own landscape, characters, and qualities. The process of detaching it from these frames is the counterplot; the world itself is the third space framed and imaged.

At the same time as Milton's aesthetic distancing works to detach this imaginative space from conceptual referential frames, it also works to prevent this space from identifying itself with any literary frames that would separate it from the world. The giant devils' dramatic change in size forces the relation between Newtonian and non-Newtonian measurement not only because it is a wonder in itself, but also because they change size in the middle of the bees-pygmies-elves simile chain, which raises the question whether it is the bees' small size that in some process similar to a distanced physical point of view is responsible for the devils' change in size. This destruction of the boundary between "reality" and the "imagination" does not lessen the power of the imaginative space but rather serves to increase it, because it is implied that the way an object is seen in this space affects the object's reality.

A similar passage in Book 5, whose structure is not made so explicit, describes Raphael as he reaches Paradise:

> . . . Down thither prone in flight
> He speeds . . .
> . . . .

> . . . till within soar
> Of tow'ring eagles, to all the fowls he seems
> A phoenix, gazed by all, as that sole bird,
> When to enshrine his relics in the sun's
> Bright temple, to Egyptian Thebes he flies.
> At once to th'eastern cliff of Paradise
> He lights, and to his proper shape returns,
> A Seraph winged.
>
> (5: 266–77)

Raphael, who as he leaves heaven is an angel "veiled with gorgeous wings" (5: 250), is in this passage likened to a phoenix, or resembles a phoenix or *seems* to be a phoenix; but the phrase "to his proper shape returned" implies that he has *become* a phoenix. In the space of the simile a real act has occurred.

In a slightly different device, the space within the similes in Books 1 and 2 becomes in Books 11 and 12 the "real" world of history. For example, the Moses in the simile discussed above appears as a historical character in 12: 169–226. Milton even includes the same "potent rod" (1: 338, and 12: 211) and "crazed" and "broken" chariot wheels (1: 311 and 12: 210) in the scene.

When in Books 11 and 12 Adam is taken to the mountaintop by Michael and shown in vision all of human history, Milton forces the relation between imaginative space and the Galilean-Newtonian frame in a slightly different way. Instead of confusing the boundaries between them, here Milton telescopes such great space and time into such a limited time and place— Adam's sojourn on the mountain—that the disproportion threatens to burst the poetic boundaries if they are conceptually framed; yet at the same time, because it is the world that is mimetically represented within them, the space cannot detach itself from this world.

Lest the imaginative space become not overly substantial but on the contrary overly fluid, "romantic," or mystical, Milton sets irony and lyric against each other in several similes. For example, in the simile in Book 9 discussed above, the fate of the peasant who follows the enchanting will-o'-the-wisp distances this enchantment by means of irony of action. All these shiftings detach Milton's imaginative space from frames established by literary criticism, and from the critical tendency to define literature through a univocal relation to "reality," whether the relation be imitative of or deviating from some constant reality, and whether this reality be conceived of as transcendent or empirical.

Once the overly substantial reference frames have been destroyed, the objects and images in Milton's universe become not simply multireferential but interreferential. Thus, to describe hell and heaven Milton uses images drawn from the earth. In Book 1, images of blasted trees and uprooted hills are used to describe the landscape and its inhabitants:

> . . . on dry land
> He lights, if it were land that ever burned
> With solid, as the lake with liquid fire,
> And such appeared in hue; as when the force
> Of subterranean wind transports a hill
> Torn from Pelorus, or the shattered side
> Of thund'ring Etna.
>
> (1: 227–33)

The fallen angels are described in the following simile:

> Their glory withered: as when heaven's fire
> Hath scathed the forest oaks or mountain pines
> With singèd top their stately growth though bare
> Stands on the blasted heath.
>
> (1: 612–15)

Similarly, in heaven, Satan as he is struck in battle by Abdiel is likened to an uprooted tree-covered mountain:

> . . . as if on earth
> Winds under ground or waters forcing way
> Sidelong had pushed a mountain from his seat
> Half sunk with all his pines.
>
> (6: 195–98)

In Book 10 after the fall, Paradise begins to change. As the sun alters its course, the temperate weather changes to "pinching cold and scorching heat" that begin to resemble the weather of hell with its "fierce extremes" (2: 599). And as the winds "rend the woods and seas upturn" (10: 700), Paradise begins to resemble the landscape of hell.

Raphael uses such interreferential imagery in his narrations to Adam of war and creation in Books 5 through 7. He describes God's armies and their movement, which are outside Adam's experience, by comparing them to flocks of birds flying, with which Adam is familiar:

> . . . high above the ground
> Their march was, and the passive air upbore
> Their nimble tread; as when the total kind
> Of birds in orderly array on wing
> Came summoned over Eden to receive
> Their names of thee.
>
> (6: 71–76)

Satan's armies are also likened to images drawn from Paradise:

> . . . Satan with his powers
> Far was advanced on wingèd speed, an host

> Innumerable as the stars of night,
> Or stars of morning, dew-drops, which the sun
> Impearls on every leaf and every flower.
>
> (5: 743–47)

Then when he later describes God's gathering of the waters on the third day of creation, Raphael compares the waves rolling into order to armies:

> . . . As armies at the call
> Of trumpet (for of armies thou hast heard)
> Troop to their standard, so the wat'ry throng
> Wave rolling after wave.[1]
>
> (7: 295–98)

Since Adam knows about armies only through the comparison to birds and dewdrops, which are of the same order of generality as waves, one might ask how helpful this simile is to Adam. However, the length and strength of the narration has perhaps created a reality that may then itself serve as a point of reference. But the real point is that Raphael is describing a universe that is interreferential. Milton even calls attention to this truth by the parenthetical comment.

In another set of images Milton sets up not a two-way but a three-way interreferential pattern:

> About him [God] all the sanctities of heaven
> Stood thick as stars.
>
> (3: 60–61)

> . . . th'angelic squadron bright
> . . . .
> . . . began to hem him [Satan] round
> With ported spears, as thick as when a field
> Of Ceres ripe for harvest waving bends
> Her bearded grove of ears, which way the wind
> Sways them.
>
> (4: 977–83)

> [God] sowed with stars the heav'n thick as a field.
>
> (7: 358)

Stars, grain, and angels are all used to describe each other, and the word *bearded* adds a specifically human dimension.

In these descriptions there is no final or primary reference point. To stress this truth still further, Milton breaks not only poetic frames, but also the linguistic frames of diction and syntax. Just as an object like the tree of life is both a physical point of "prospect" and a source of life, so many individual words as Milton uses them can be attached to no one meaning or degree of substantiality, nor can these words be divided into "literal" and "figurative" meanings.[2] For example, the fruits of the trees in the garden are repeatedly pictured or referred to as objects, as in Milton's description of Paradise in Book 4:

> . . . goodliest trees loaden with fairest fruit,
> Blossoms and fruits at once of golden hue.
>
> (4: 147–48)

Similarly, Eve offers real fruits when she "prepared / For dinner savory fruits" for their guest, Raphael (5: 303–4). Raphael uses fruit as an image in his representation of the chain of being in Book 5:

> O Adam, one Almighty is, from whom
> All things proceed, and up to him return
> . . . .
> . . . So from the root
> Springs lighter the green stalk, from thence the leaves
> More airy, last the bright consummate flow'r
> Spirits odórous breathes: flow'rs and their fruit,
> Man's nourishment.
>
> (5: 469–83)

Yet, because the eating of fruit has such significant consequences in *Paradise Lost,* the word is also used in its other sense—consequence of attitude and action. Thus Adam and Eve are first described as "reaping immortal fruits of joy and love" in their "happy garden" (3: 66–67), and the woe to follow their literal eating of the fruit of the tree of knowledge is similarly referred to as "fruit" in the opening lines of the poem:

> Of man's first disobedience, and the fruit
> Of that forbidden tree.
>
> (1: 1–2)

As they begin to experience the effects of their fall, Adam uses the word in both senses:

> . . . we know
> Both good and evil, good lost and evil got
> Bad fruit of knowledge, if this be to know.
>
> (9: 1071–73)

As she arrives with Satan at the forbidden tree, Eve exclaims:

> Serpent, we might have spared our coming hither,
> Fruitless to me, though fruit be here to excess.
>
> (9: 647–48)

And as he formally greets Eve in Book 5, Raphael stresses the meaning or substantiality of fruit as potential attitude and action:

> Hail mother of mankind, whose fruitful womb
> Shall fill the world more numerous with thy sons
> Than with these various fruits the trees of God
> Have heaped this table.
>
> (5: 388–91)

By contrast, Satan, in the same frame of mind as when he perched on the tree of life to get a better view, selects a word to refer to the forbidden fruit that is limited to the literal-minded: *apple*. As he describes the fruit to Eve in Book 9 in an attempt to awaken her appetite, he tells her of "the sharp desire [he] . . . had / Of tasting those fair apples" (9: 584–85); and as he reports success to his hosts in hell, he says:

> . . . him by fraud I have seduced
> From his Creator, and the more to increase
> Your wonder, with an apple.
>
> (10: 485–87)

There are many other words used in a multiple sense by Milton in *Paradise Lost*—such as *root, seed, error*—but a most significant cluster of words is *arms, unarmed,* and *disarmed.* Angel on archangel rolls in heaven because they are encumbered by their arms: "unarmed they might / Have easily as spirits evaded swift" (6: 595–96). Later in Book 10, Adam is described as *disarmed* by Eve's avowal of love in response to his outburst of accusing anger after their fall and judgment (10: 945), a word that, in an epic poem that includes both physically violent battles and the angry words that often prompt angel and human to arm and battle physically, carries great resonance. As Milton's kinesthetic poetry unframes the imaginative space to free and reveal its psychic motions, so Eve's love disarms Adam and meets him in the psychic space in which the urge to arm—less tangible than spears and shields—rises and is quieted by psychic motions that are the true determinants of the more tangible frames and objects.

In a technique related to his handling of diction, Milton often structures his syntax such that the distinction between noun, verb, and adjective is dissolved. Frames like "reality" and "mind" break into common motions and the substantiality of objects is drawn into their motion and quality in relation to other objects.

In his description of hell, for example, Milton uses adjectives referring to emotional states to modify nouns referring to the landscape, as in:

> The dismal situation waste and wild
> A dungeon horrible, on all sides round
> As one great furnace flamed, yet from those flames
> No light, but rather darkness visible
> Served only to discover sights of woe,
> Regions of sorrow, doleful shades.
>
> (1: 60–65)

> . . . yon dreary plain, forlorn and wild,
> The seat of desolation, void of light.
>
> (1: 180–81)

The region is sorrowful, the shades doleful, and the plain forlorn both because they cause these feelings and also because they are themselves sorrowful, doleful, and forlorn. Such usages render the landscape both a
geographical and a psychic "place," a reality that Satan fruitlessly tries to
conceptualize in such contradictory lines as "the mind is its own place" (1:
254) and "which way I fly is hell; myself am hell" (4: 75). The use of "darkness visible" as both direct object and subject further serves to dissolve the
substantiality of both word and place. A similar shifting in syntactic function
occurs in lines like the following:

> Regions of sorrow, doleful shades, where peace
> And rest can never dwell, hope never comes
> That comes to all; but torture without end
> Still urges, and a fiery deluge, fed
> With ever-burning sulphur unconsumed.
>
> (1: 65–69)

"Hope" can be read as the subject of "urges" with "torture" as a first direct
object and "fiery deluge" as a second direct object; or "torture" can be read
as the subject of "urges" with "fiery deluge" as a second subject; or "hope"
and "fiery deluge" can be read as second subjects of the verb "urges" with
"torture" as direct object. All of these readings, and the fact that three are
possible, syntactically image the kinesthetic relations between substance
and psychic energy, and the metamorphoses of one into the other. In the first
reading, the thought "hope urges a fiery deluge" images a psychic energy
turning into matter. In the second reading, "urges" has no direct object
though it is a transitive verb, a syntactic shifting that images pure energy
before it turns into matter. In the third reading, psychic energy severed from
substance urges torture.
    Milton's description of the thunder creates a similar effect through a com-
bination of syntactic structure and imagery:

> But see the angry Victor hath recalled
> His ministers of vengeance and pursuit
> Back to the gates of heav'n; the sulphurous hail
> Shot after us in storm, o'erblown hath laid
> The fiery surge, that from the precipice
> Of heav'n received us falling, and the thunder,
> Winged with red lightning and impetuous rage,
> Perhaps hath spent his shafts, and ceases now
> To bellow through the vast and boundless deep.
>
> (1: 169–77)

Because the thunder like the hail that is "shot" is a "minister" of "pursuit" that bellows through the deep, the word *winged* images the thunder as an arrow that would be the direct object of a subject "archer" who "shoots" it. But, of course, syntactically it is the thunder that is the subject of "spent."

As Milton dissolves the distinctions between substance and feeling and between substance and motion in the passages just discussed, so he dissolves the distinction between substance and quality by using adjectives as nouns in such phrases as "palpable obscure" and "vast abrupt" (2: 406, 409). The "obscure" becomes "palpable" partly because it is a noun, and likewise the abruptness of using the word *abrupt* as a noun enhances the meaning.

In Raphael's account of the creation of living creatures in Book 7, Milton makes intransitive verbs expressing movement transitive, rendering subject and object reversible, stressing the motions between them, and thereby increasing the sense of tremendous energy. To say, as he does, that roosters and peacocks "on ground / Walked firm" (7: 442–43) is usual, or even that "the sounds and seas, each creek and bay, / With fry innumerable swarm" (7: 399–400), though the effect is different; but to go farther and describe birds as "soaring th'air sublime" (7: 421) or say that an insect or worm "creeps the ground" (7: 475) is a syntactic shifting that has quite a different effect. Milton pushes this device still farther in:

> . . . air, water, earth
> By fowl, fish, beast, was flown, was swum, was walked
> Frequent.
>
> (7: 502–4)

These lines startle with the life they convey. It is as if the nouns were struggling to free themselves from nouns into verbs, a process that is then imaged and realized in the magnificent lines rendering the birth of life from inorganic matter commanded by God in Genesis: "let the earth bring forth . . .":

> The grassy clods now calved, now half appeared
> The tawny lion, pawing to get free
> His hinder parts, then springs as broke from bonds,
> And rampant shakes his brinded mane; the ounce,
> The libbard, and the tiger, as the mole
> Rising, the crumbled earth above them threw
> In hillocks; the swift stag from under ground
> Bore up his branching head.
>
> (7: 463–70)

The word *branching* heightens the effect by destroying metaphoric boundaries in a reversal of vehicle and tenor similar to that in the bees-elves and phoenix similes discussed above. In the Galilean-Newtonian scheme, it is the stag's antlers that look like branches and are acting like branches—

growing out of the earth—but here the force of this passage reads: "antlers grow out of the earth and branches look like antlers," an effect made possible by the syntactic technique just described. This passage combines imagistic and syntactic technique to make poetry "fact" in the third imaginative space.

In this deframing process the reader is likely, as mentioned above, to suffer a loss of point of view, of the felt center sanctioned by these frames, and a corresponding sense of the loss of the identity and integrity of objects and beings. A sense of character differs both from the substantiality of tangible objects—because while character is in some respects sensibly perceivable and tangible it is also intangible like an idea—and from the substantiality of concept and ideology—because while equally intangible it is closer to the psychological motions of the observer, and being more mobile is less easily substantialized.

Ordinarily, when one beholds a being or object, one has a sense of its identity and substance without consciously thinking of the frames that help guarantee this identity, for, while conceptual certainty is an important sanction, the sense of character or psychological identity has a priority in a domain of its own, a priority that is less another frame than a center or focus of unity. But when the support of the conceptual frames is destroyed kinesthetically in the foreground of the reader's mind in the manner just described, the duality of Satan's cruel and remorseful eye becomes more disturbing, as does the non-Newtonian disjunction of the spear that is a shield. Or, to consider the process in reverse, the identities of objects and beings normally perceived without recourse to frames are suddenly split apart, such that the mind is forced to consider the question of frames, a question for which it receives no easy answer. In most novels changes or disjunctions of mood may not disturb in this way, but in *Paradise Lost* they do because the question of character is drawn into the question of frames.

As mentioned in the introduction, Satan is represented in terms of conflicting qualities. He is "confounded though immortal"; he is anguished though proud and obdurate; his eye is cruel and remorseful. And though he is filled with hate and revenge, though he is calculating and sarcastic, he is simultaneously gentle and kind, as when he "gently raise[s] . . . [the] fainted courage, and dispel[s] . . . [the] fears" of his stricken angel legions (1: 529–30). The lyrical and poignant tone of Satan's words to Beelzebub as he urges him to seek rest from the burning lake hardly seems obdurate:

> Seest thou yon dreary plain, forlorn and wild,
> The seat of desolation, void of light,
> Save what the glimmering of these livid flames
> Casts pale and dreadful? Thither let us tend
> From off the tossing of these fiery waves,
> There rest, if any rest can harbor there.

(1: 180–85)

Correspondingly, Satan's physical being has no integrity: he repeatedly changes shape and substance; and with the frames gone, the reader cannot hope to answer the question "Who is Satan?" by placing him either in a "real and objective" or in a "fabulous" frame. For his metamorphoses occur both in reality and as similes: he "becomes" the "stripling Cherub" in 3: 636, the beasts of prey in 4: 395–408; but he is "like" the wolf in 4: 183, the cormorant in 4: 196, and the mist in Book 9. However, at one point he is merely "wrapped" in mist, an association less that a simile. Sometimes his form exists in some indeterminate zone between likeness and being: Gabriel's guard finds him "Squat *like* a toad close at the ear of Eve" (4: 800; emphasis added) as he brings her the disturbing dream; but a few lines later Ithuriel touches him with his spear, which causes Satan to "start up in his own shape" (4: 819). Here Satan's physical self is difficult to distinguish from either his likeness in simile (toad) and position (squat) or, more significant, his psychological self, the self who speaks "falsehood" which "returns / Of force to its own likeness" (4: 812–13). The confusion characterizes his most famous metamorphosis into the serpent, who is both a vessel, separate from Satan, that he "enters," *in which* he "constrains," "mixes," "incarnates," "encloses," and "imbrutes" himself (9: 163–88), and his incarnation, an incarnation that is, in 10: 505–15, no longer indeterminate:

> . . . he stood, expecting
> Their universal shout and high applause
> To fill his ear, when contrary he hears
> On all sides from innumerable tongues
> A dismal universal hiss, the sound
> Of public scorn; he wondered, but not long
> Had leisure, wond'ring at himself now more;
> His visage drawn he felt to sharp and spare,
> His arms clung to his ribs, his legs entwining
> Each other, till supplanted down he fell
> A monstrous serpent on his belly prone,
> Reluctant, but in vain.
>
> (10: 505–15)

Satan is disjunctive in inner and outer substance: the line of division does not run between a "real" and a "fabulous" character. There is a continuum of correspondence between Satan's physical metamorphoses and his psychic divisions. To answer the question posed above, Milton is not describing Satan in two incompatible modes—the tangible Satan fantastically and the character of Satan realistically. He is representing both in the same mode. One feels a disjunction in mode because a change in physical aspect is more noticeable and thus apparently fantastic than a shift in psychic aspect.

Such dualities of identity as cruelty-remorse and angel-toad appear throughout *Paradise Lost,* forcing the issue of substantiality, the issue of frame, and the issue of cause. Thus Satan's spear changes, both within and between similes, from a spear to a tall pine, which is then made into the mast of a ship, which changes to a cane (1: 293–95) and later to a magic wand (1: 338).

The disjunctiveness of appearance and possibly character is not limited to Satan. God images himself forth both in the mildness of a golden cloud and in the anger of "sulphurous hail" and "bellowing" thunder "winged with red lightning and impetuous rage." And in Book 6, as the Son's chariot of wrathful Power Divine appears "with fresh flow'rets hill and valley smiled" (6: 784), perhaps a surprising causality.

Disjunctions in identity and frame seemingly run throughout the universal fabric from the least object to the cosmology of the heavens. Sometimes these disjunctions are made to seem casual, almost insignificant, as when Raphael says to Adam "whether heav'n move or earth, / Imports not, if thou reckon right" (8: 70–71), or when Milton says in his description of Satan's journey out of hell, "Thither his course he bends / Through the calm firmament (but up or down, / By center, or eccentric, hard to tell, / Or longitude)" (3: 573–76). But the destruction of frames that such statements effect makes "reckoning" difficult. For in the perception of the disjunctions just discussed, the reader's mind is drawn into the same space as the disjunctions, especially of character; but here the various faculties do not participate in what is felt to be the perception of an integrated object as in the perception of the fish. Rather, different faculties seem to perceive different aspects of the object in a mutually exclusive manner. As one can see an eye as either cruel or remorseful but not both simultaneously, one can similarly feel sympathy for Satan's pain and desire for rest and can see Satan lyrically as a whale in a beautiful and peaceful scene; but when the poem abruptly shifts into the angry editorial commentary following this simile, the reader feels outrage—either against Satan or against Milton and Divine Justice—and loses both the first perception and his/her perceptual center. The poetic movement is an alternating figure and ground: figure becomes ground and ground figure, but it seems impossible to focus on both simultaneously, to have both figure and ground be figure. Sympathy and moral condemnation are felt as mutually exclusive, just as it is difficult to see a spear as both a mast and a cane, and as it is difficult to see flowers springing up in the path of power.

Yet, however disjunctive and painful it may seem at first, Milton's progressive deframing process is not arbitrary or chaotic but follows a declension of mind in relation to universe. The purpose of the declension so far has been to redefine ideological and conceptual structures in terms of psychic motions and forces, forces such as anger and pain, power, or Eve's disarming love. Milton will show in succeeding stages of the declension that the motions of destruction—destruction in terms of the frames—have laws, as do the motions in the physical universe, but the first step has been to define the ideological issues as psychic motions. For most often conceptions and judgments of the nature of things are really sympathic, as opposed to empathic, frames disguised as "objective" and substantial ideological frames. The sympathic frame of mind derives from such psychic forces as anger and pain and the issues arising from them, and the frame is maintained by virtue of an unconscious identification with these forces. The redefinition of such ideology into psychic forces is not a destructive and negative process but the first step toward an empathic relation both to universe and self—an imaginative projection into and participation in the being of another and one's own being—that yields understanding without the identifications and substantializations of ideologies. Since the sympathic forces into which the ideological structures resolve are psychic, the space they occupy may be the same as the space of the mind that is in relation to them, the perceiving and conceiving mind that frames and responds to them with attitudes such as pity and judgment. These responses and attitudes too have laws, as do anger, pain, and love.

This process of redefinition is clearly represented in the plot of *Paradise Lost* as well as in the counterplot, though this representation is perhaps easier to discern from the perspective of the counterplot. In the first stage of the declension, the epic is represented ideologically as the theological contest between good and evil, between God and the concept of "blessed union" of heaven and Satan, who breaks this union in his rebellion. The purpose of heaven as God has created it with the Son as vicegerent is, as Abdiel tells Satan

>   . . . to exalt
> [Their] . . . happy state under one head more near
> United . . .
> . . . .
> . . . all angelic nature joined in one.
>
>   (5: 829–34)

And as God states to the assembled hosts:

>   . . . Him who disobeys
> Me disobeys, breaks union, and that day
> Cast out from God and blessèd vision, falls
> Into utter darkness, deep engulfed, his place
> Ordained without redemption, without end.
>
>   (5: 611–15)

As the plot moves from ideological statement to the representation of Satan's rebellion and its consequences, the declension moves into a dramatic dimension focused more on character, motivation, and psychology. In this dimension Satan is not simply "evil." He is frequently represented as suffering great pain under terrible burdens. The reader is likely to feel pity

for Satan and his faithful angels pictured as withered trees standing bare on
the "blasted heath," their former glory "scathed" by "heaven's fire" (1: 612–
15), or for Satan when his face "intrenched" with "scars of thunder" is
streaming with "tears such as angels weep" (1: 601, 620). It is repeatedly
stressed that Satan has no hope, no rest (1: 66, 237–38), is a ship without a
port (1: 185), and a sea without a shore (2: 1011). Even as he considers his
rebellion in heaven, he is represented as lonely: it is midnight, and Satan
alone is awake. He turns to Beelzebub, "his next subordinate," and says in
pitiable tones:

> Sleep'st thou, companion dear, what sleep can close
> Thy eyelids? And rememberst what decree
> Of yesterday, so late hath passed the lips
> Of heav'n's Almighty? Thou to me thy thoughts
> Wast wont, I mine to thee was wont to impart;
> Both waking we were one; how then can now
> Thy sleep dissent?
>
> (5: 673–79)

It appears that Satan feels "impaired" by the elevation of the Son partly
because he feels unpreferred by his Creator, even feels that the Creator has
broken the union. Satan turns in his feeling of loss to the angel next to him in
eminence for companionship and solace. The root of his sin seems to be
longing for God's love, but his sin serves only to bring him more pain.

As in this dramatic dimension Satan is not simply "evil," so God is not
represented as simply "good." Some critics characterize God, especially in
Book 3 where he makes his longest speeches, by describing his voice as
"toneless," "flat," "calm," and "impersonal," qualities that befit the abstract
truths spoken by a transcendent being.[3] Such adjectives are simply inaccu-
rate. God's voice, especially in Book 3, often sounds testy, frustrated, hurt,
vindictive, rigid—in short, personal. For example, as he observes Satan on
his journey of revenge to earth, God says:

> . . . And now
> Through all restraint broke loose he wings his way
> Not far off heav'n, in the precincts of light,
> Directly towards the new-created world,
> And man there placed, with purpose to assay
> If him by force he can destroy, or worse,
> By some false guile pervert; and shall pervert;
> For man will hearken to his glozing lies,
> And easily transgress the sole command,
> Sole pledge of his obedience; so will fall
> He and his faithless progeny. Whose fault?
> Whose but his own? Ingrate, he had of me
> All he could have; I made him just and right.
>
> (3: 86–98)

The tone of "whose fault? Whose but his own? Ingrate . . ." is hardly flat, but rather is angry and defensive. To "appease" this anger, the self-styled "incensèd Deity" (3: 186–87) wants "proof" of "obedience" (3: 103), "rigid satisfaction" (3: 212), and "payment" of "debts" (3: 246). God is all powerful; he is also volatile. The possibility of his explosion into wrath, even into a wrath that would destroy his creation, is referred to throughout *Paradise Lost*—by the poet, by Gabriel, Abdiel, Adam, the Son, Raphael, and, of course, Satan and his subordinates. For Satan, this possibility is a prime reason for going to Eden:

> . . . here perhaps
> Some advantageous act may be achieved
> By sudden onset, either with hell fire
> To waste his whole creation, or possess
> All as our own, and drive as we were driv'n,
> The puny habitants; or if not drive,
> Seduce them to our party, that their God
> May prove their foe, and with repenting hand
> Abolish his own works. This would surpass
> Common revenge.
>
> (2: 362–71)

Satan has seen the anger of God, which at times is so great that it makes no distinctions. As Abdiel has said on the eve of the war in heaven, he will fly the tents of Satan "lest the wrath / Impendent, raging into sudden flame / Distinguish not" (5: 890–92). The Son mentions the same possibility in response to God's wrath in Book 3:

> Or shall the Adversary thus obtain
> His end, and frustrate thine, shall he fulfill
> His malice, and thy goodness bring to naught,
> Or proud return though to his heavier doom,
> Yet with revenge accomplished, and to hell
> Draw after him the whole race of mankind,
> By him corrupted? Or wilt thou thyself
> Abolish thy creation, and unmake,
> For him, what for thy glory thou hast made?
>
> (3: 156–64)

Adam, as he weighs his decision whether to fall with Eve in Book 9, more optimistically rejects such a possibility, assuming that God would not do anything so irrational:

> Nor can I think that God, Creator wise,
> Though threat'ning, will in earnest so destroy
> Us his prime creatures, dignified so high,
> Set over all his works, which in our fall,
> For us created, needs with us must fail,

Dependent made; so God shall uncreate,
Be frustrate, do, undo, and labor lose,
Not well conceived of God, who though his power
Creation could repeat, yet would be loth
Us to abolish, lest the Adversary
Triumph and say: "Fickle their state whom God
Most favors, who can please him long? Me first,
He ruined, now mankind; whom will be next?"
Matter of scorn not to be given the Foe.

(9: 938–51)

Yet Raphael has told Adam that he would be especially pleased to hear the
story of Adam's creation because he, Raphael,

. . . that day was absent, as befell,
Bound on a voyage uncouth and obscure,
Far on excursion toward the gates of hell,
Squared in full legion (such command we had),
To see that none thence issued forth a spy
Or enemy while God was in his work,
Lest he incensed at such eruption bold,
Destruction with Creation might have mixed.

(8: 229–36)

And Milton, in his description of Satan journeying through chaos, characterizes chaos as "This wild abyss,/ The womb of Nature and perhaps her
grave" (2: 910–11).

Thus the ideological contest between good and evil is in the dramatic
dimension of the poem redefined as a contest between anger and pain. In
terms of the action arising from anger and pain, the contest might appear to
be a contest of power between unequal forces. Indeed, God's wrath and
power are so great that he is capable of destroying the creation out of wrath
even as he created it in love. It is seemingly impossible for a pained Satan to
directly oppose such anger or to find refuge from it. As the poet says in his
comment following the whale simile, God allows Satan to rise off the lake so
that he will bring on his head "treble confusion, wrath, and vengeance," and
as Belial says:

. . . what can force or guile
With him, or who deceive his mind, whose eye
Views all things at one view? He from heav'n's highth
All these our motions vain, sees and derides;
Not more almighty to resist our might
Than wise to frustrate all our plots and wiles.

(2: 188–93)

Ironically, Belial represents God in exactly the same physical posture in
which the reader first sees him in the beginning of Book 3.

The reader's response to this second definition of the contest is likely to be pity for Satan and judgment against God, a response that is disturbingly the inverse of his/her response in the first definition of the contest in terms of good and evil. It is a disjunction impossible to avoid, for the redefinition of the structure of good and evil into the structure of pain and anger is explicitly reinforced in the dimension of plot as Gabriel voices its precise formulation to Satan in Book 4 in answer to Satan's attempt to justify his escape from hell as flight from pain:

> . . . the wrath
> Which thou incurr'st by flying, [will] meet thy flight,
> Sevenfold, and scourge that wisdom back to hell,
> Which taught thee yet no better, that no pain
> Can equal anger infinite provoked.
>
> (4: 912–16)

The reader is forced out of a univocal reliance on the ideological dimension and into participation in the conflict of raw psychic forces both by his/her response to the dramatic representation of God and Satan and by its discursive definition. This second contest, the disjunction between anger and pain, may seem structureless and irresoluble, as in the passages discussed above, and may cause discomfort and alarm; but in the poem's redefinition of its determining structures and in the mind's discomfort, the poem and the declension of mind move into another redefinition of the poem's central conflict: ideological versus emotional valuation, or pity versus judgment. In itself this new disjunction may seem scarcely more mediative than the motions of wrath and pain, but pity and judgment more than anger and pain are feelings of attitude, achieving more distance from the objects of consideration and framing them in the space of mind.

This last redefinition again is represented explicitly in the dimension of the poem's epic plot at the close of Book 4 as Satan confronts Gabriel and his angel squadron at the gates of Eden and where the decision is made to send Satan to play out his drama with Adam and Eve in the "woody theater" (4: 141) of Eden, the space of human mind represented by the newly created human pair.

For the contest between God and Satan—whether conceived of in moral terms or in terms of power—is deadlocked and incapable of resolution despite the almightiness of God. Satan's and God's forces are evenly matched, and a renewal of the war in heaven would only lead to destruction. On the one side:

> . . . th'angelic squadron bright
> Turned, fiery red, sharp'ning in moonèd horns
> Their phalanx, and began to hem him round
> With ported spears . . .
> . . . .
> . . . On th'other side Satan alarmed

Collecting all his might dilated stood,
Like Teneriffe or Atlas unremoved:
His stature reached the sky, and on his crest
Sat Horror plumed; nor wanted in his grasp
What seemed both spear and shield. Now dreadful deeds
Might have ensued, nor only Paradise
In this commotion, but all the starry cope
Of heav'n perhaps, or all the elements
At least had gone to wrack, disturbed and torn
With violence of this conflict.

                                                        (4: 977–95)

The only alternative is for them to part, and to allow Satan to continue on
into Eden:

Th'Eternal to prevent such horrid fray
Hung forth in heav'n his golden scales, yet seen
Betwixt Astraea and Scorpion sign,
Wherein all things created first he weighed,
The pendulous round earth with balanced air
In counterpoise, now ponders all events,
Battles, and realms. In these he put two weights,
The sequel each of parting and of fight;
The latter quick up flew, and kicked the beam.

                                                        (4: 996–1004)

The immense power arising from pain and anger, regardless of their source
in God or Satan, would destroy the creation. Whether God allows the forces
of good and evil to battle for victory by force, or whether he exercises his
own pure power, his anger provoked by Satan, he would, ironically, give the
victory to Satan, for as Satan has said earlier, the "abolishing of his own
works . . . would surpass common revenge."

    To avoid this conclusion, and to escape the deadlock between them, God
instructs Gabriel through the heavenly sign to allow Satan to enter the garden of Eden. In his weighing of the "sequel of parting" and the "sequel of
fight," God indicates to Gabriel that the better solution—for God—is the
sequel of parting. The better solution for Satan may well be the sequel of
immediate fight; therefore Gabriel must in interpreting the heavenly sign
trick Satan into believing it best for him to continue to Eden:

The latter quick up flew and kicked the beam;
Which Gabriel spying, thus bespake the Fiend:
"Satan, I know thy strength, and thou know'st mine,
Neither our own but giv'n; what folly then
To boast what arms can do, since thine no more
Than Heav'n permits, nor mine, though doubled now
To trample thee as mire. For proof look up,
And read thy lot in yon celestial sign
Where thou art weighed, and shown how light, how weak,
If thou resist." The Fiend looked up and knew

His mounted scale aloft: *nor more;* but fled
Murmuring.

(4: 1004–15; emphasis added)

Whereas in the real weighing it is the two sequels that are weighed, Gabriel, although he does say at first that they are evenly matched in arms, tells Satan that it is Satan's lot if he resists that is being weighed against the angels' and is the lighter. In this way he conceals the possibility that Satan might win immediate victory, though he himself would be lost too, by fighting until the elements go to wrack. Satan, fooled by this stratagem—"knew his mounted scale aloft: *nor more*"—flees from force into guile—from confrontation and from entering Eden directly to entering Eden in secret—from the contest of power to the contest of mind.

The war of good and evil, the battle of raw psychic forces of which the universe consists, has been transferred onto "frail" humanity. While on the one hand, in the epic dimension, this transference may seem either ironic or cruel, on the other hand Milton, in the most forceful possible way, stresses the strength and determining power of the human mind by making it the locus, the theater, of the universal drama. At the end of Book 4 Eden becomes the new center of creation, a modulation imaged in the two bridges or pathways built from hell to earth and from heaven to earth. In Book 2 Satan's "track" through chaos is soon made into a bridge by Sin and Death:

> . . . Sin and Death amain
> Following his track, such was the will of Heav'n,
> Paved after him a broad and beaten way
> Over the dark abyss, whose boiling gulf
> Tamely endured a bridge of wondrous length
> From hell continued reaching th'utmost orb
> Of this frail world, by which the Spirits perverse
> With easy intercourse pass to and fro
> To tempt or punish mortals.

(2: 1024–32)

From above, a stairway connects earth to heaven:

> Ascending by degrees magnificent
> Up to the wall of heaven a structure high
> . . . .
> The stairs were such as whereon Jacob saw
> Angels ascending and descending . . .
> . . . .
> Direct against [the gate of heaven] . . . opened from beneath,
> Just o'er the blissful seat of Paradise,
> A passage down to th'earth, a passage wide.

(3: 502–28)

The resolution of the divine conflict and the fate of the created universe now depend on the human inhabitants of the pendent world as they struggle with the motions of pity and judgment in their own being. It is a mission whose outcome is uncertain: they may stand, they may fall; a fall may trigger the volatile power of God to destroy the creation and return it to the womb-grave of chaos. It is a difficult mission: they are forbidden to eat of the tree of knowledge in a universe where it is difficult both to discern the hypocrisy of evil and to perceive the goodness of God. As Milton says, when Uriel is fooled by Satan's disguise as the stripling cherub and by his guileful request for directions to Eden in Book 3,

> So spake the false dissembler unperceived;
> For neither man nor angel can discern
> Hypocrisy, the only evil that walks
> Invisible, except to God alone,
> By his permissive will, through heav'n and earth;
> And oft though wisdom wake, suspicion sleeps
> At wisdom's gate, and to simplicity
> Resigns her charge, while goodness thinks no ill
> Where no ill seems: which now for once beguiled
> Uriel, though regent of the sun, and held
> The sharpest-sighted Spirit of all in heav'n.
>
> (3: 681–91)

Yet Adam and Eve must still be responsible for discerning and choosing wisely. As God says, "they trespass, authors to themselves in all, / Both what they judge and what they choose."

God himself is "unapproachèd" and "invisible," veiled in radiant cloud (3: 3, 375–80), and as Moloch says "inaccessible" (2: 104), or as Satan says, "concealed" (1: 641).

But it is precisely this reliance on such conceptual knowledge that has been deframed: Adam and Eve are not to know truth through a direct discernment, nor even through pity and judgment, but through more subtle psychic motions in the third space of mind. The resolution of the issues of *Paradise Lost* into the conflict between pity and judgment is a resolution only because it defines and focuses these issues: it defines substance as force and it locates the conflict and resolution in attitude and mind.

Though the sympathic motions of pity and judgment have laws, as do anger and pain, they are in themselves as insufficient as the frames they construct and refer to, and can lead to no resolution and fulfillment. Their clash serves rather, as they begin to define themselves as inadequate, to focus the mind on its attitude in relation to the object of pity and judgment and thus shifts it into a yet deeper psychic space, the space of yearning and desire that lies deeper than anger and pain. As the mind is taken from the structure of what should be (good and evil) or from the structure of what is (anger and pain) into the structure of what is desired in relation to these first two structures, it moves out of the sympathic stage into the next stage of the declension of mind. In this succeeding stage, pity and judgment resolve into subtler psychic motions that allow pity and judgment to be understood, and simultaneously the mind's reliance on one or two faculties over others resolves into the motion of all faculties, into the interrelating movement of the emotional, sensible, intuitive, meditative faculties as well as the cognitive faculties, movement that includes and is the psychic correlate of the kinesthetic sense, interrelating faculties that constitute the faculty that Francis Fergusson calls the histrionic sensibility. This kinesthetic mode can lead to a wisdom of far greater depth, subtlety, and precision of thought and articulation than a purely conceptual mode, to a knowing that corresponds to the perceptual apprehension of the vines, waters, and creatures of Paradise in 4: 257–66, and 7: 387–504.

At the conclusion of this deframing process—part of the first stage of the declension of mind that occurs simultaneously with perceptual kinesthesia— the only "frame" remaining is pure frame, a frameless frame, the frame of the third space of incipiently self-conscious mind. Of course, it is difficult to represent pure frame, yet some instances of Milton's aesthetic distancing give the reader the experience of shifting into a frameless dimension, frameless, that is, in terms of conceptual or mimetic definitions. In this experience, at first one seems to suddenly move into an "empty" space; yet the space is not a void or a vacuum. It might be thought of as an aesthetically framed space if all solipsistic and all ideological connotations are removed from the term *aesthetic*.

As there are kinesthetic shifts in space and setting in *Paradise Lost,* so are there shifts in time. Earlier in the perceptual experience of aesthetic distancing, time shifts are probably more wrenching than space shifts because it is more difficult to imagine displacing one's point of view in time than it is in space, for spatial shifts are a physical possibility while time shifts are not. Now, however, after the deframing process of the sympathic stage of the declension, time shifts may be experienced more easily because the mind has been rendered more flexible, and their experience will yield the experience of pure shifting. In Book 3, in God's opening speech about Satan's temptation of Adam and Eve to the Son and the surrounding sanctities of heaven, there is first a smooth shift from present to projected future:

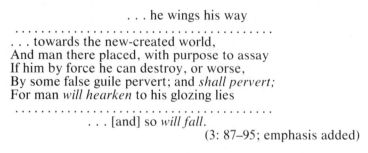

> . . . he wings his way
>
> . . . .
> . . . towards the new-created world,
> And man there placed, with purpose to assay
> If him by force he can destroy, or worse,
> By some false guile pervert; and *shall pervert;*
> For man *will hearken* to his glozing lies
>
> . . . .
> . . . [and] so *will fall.*
>
> (3: 87–95; emphasis added)

But then there is a wrenching shift to the past as his speech continues:

> . . . Ingrate, he *had* of me
>
> All he could have.
>
> (3: 97–98; emphasis added)

God of course speaks from eternity (3: 78), which can be understood conceptually; but dramatically this shift propels the reader, even before Adam and Eve have been introduced in Book 4, to the end of Book 9, after the fall. The past in the shift is past from a different present from the one God is speaking from in Book 3: this present is, from the point of view of Book 3, a future the reader must kinesthetically shift into so that it becomes a present.

The shifts into simile in Books 1 and 2 likewise involve a shift into future time, but because this future time is imaged in terms of place—Valdarno, Fesole—the shift seems less radical.

A shift halfway between the almost abstract time shift in Book 3 and the richly imaged time shift in the similes occurs in Book 10 just after Adam and Eve have fallen and been judged. At this point in the poem, Adam and Eve have last been seen at the end of Book 9 arguing and accusing each other. At the beginning of Book 10, God addresses the angels and the Son; and the Son descends to Paradise to judge first the serpent—Satan has fled—then Eve, and, by implication, Satan, whose head will be bruised by her seed, then Adam. Milton then describes Sin and Death building the bridge across chaos to earth, and Satan returning to hell and his followers. Milton then backtracks to account for Satan's movements between the fall and his return to hell:

> He, after Eve seduced, unminded slunk
> Into the wood fast by, and changing shape
> To observe the sequel, saw his guileful act
> By Eve, though all unweeting, seconded
> Upon her husband, saw their shame that sought
> Vain covertures; but when he saw descend
> The Son of God to judge them, terrified
> He fled, not hoping to escape, but shun
> The present, fearing guilty what his wrath
> Might suddenly inflict; that past, returned
> By night, and list'ning where the hapless pair
> Sat in their sad discourse and various plaint,
> Thence gathered his own doom.
>
> (10: 332–44)

Milton then continues his account of Satan's journey back to hell.

The view of Adam and Eve in their "sad discourse" is perhaps the eeriest and most jarring instance of aesthetic distancing in the poem. This particular discourse does not occur in the time of the unfolding action until much later in Book 10, when the reader first hears Adam and Eve after the judgment talking to themselves and each other about their plight, during which time they mention the serpent's and, by implication, Satan's judgment. The "time" of this action or scene is thus represented twice in the poem in an order the reverse of what might be expected: that the direct mimetic representation come first and the referential representation come second. As it is, however, the antecedent comes after its reference. It is as if the poem has dropped through a hole in time into another time and space, an imaginative pure poetic space that somehow gives the figures and actions within it more resonant life.

In this passage the mind experiences the shock of an emptiness, though the space is not a void, by reason of its sudden distancing from familiar frames and substance. In two other passages the same framelessness exists but the space created by the deframing is experienced as filled rather than empty.

The line describing the coming of God through the Son to judge Adam and Eve after they have broken their pledge deframes the poetic space by means of its syntactic ambiguity:

> . . . he from wrath more cool
> Came, the mild Judge and Intercessor both,
> To sentence man. The voice of God they heard
> Now walking in the garden, by soft winds
> Brought to their ears, while day declined; they heard.
>
> (10: 95–99)

It is as if the voice is walking and the nature of God as voice is less tangible than body, yet voice moves with the assertion and substantiality of body. The nature of God is experienced as the motions of tone, cool and soft; as spirit; as the psychic motions, subtler and purer than anger and pain or pity and judgment, into which the declension of mind next moves. Adam and Eve, still at this point in Book 10 in a sympathic state of mind, "hear" but do not hear, for in the next lines they "from his presence . . . [hide] themselves among / The thickest trees."

In a pair of passages describing the serpent, the same deframing occurs and the same filling with tone. The serpent is judged even though he was unavoidably made the instrument of sin by Satan:

> . . . without delay
> To judgment he proceeded on th'accused
> Serpent, though brute, unable to transfer
> The guilt on him who made him instrument
> Of mischief, and polluted from the end
> Of his creation; justly then accurst,
> As vitiated in nature.
>
> (10: 163–69)

The harshness of this passage perhaps surprisingly gives way to the image of "the snake with youthful coat repaid" in 10: 218, an image used to describe the pitying Son clothing Adam and Eve's nakedness. Taken together, these two passages cancel each other out in absolutist logical terms but create a space in which the image of the snake with its bright new skin may assert itself, create a space—and a time—in which the mind and being may, like the snake in spring, evolve into new life. In their brevity and simplicity, the passage describing Adam and Eve in their sad plaint imprints the experience of the third space in the reader's mind by way of negative reference to familiar frames, and the two serpent passages, like the passage describing the voice of God, imprint in the reader's mind the experience of the psychic motions within the third space, motions that, unlike anger and pain, pity and judgment, are in the final stages of the declension of mind mediatory.

NOTES

1. Anne Ferry in chap. 3 of *Milton's Epic Voice* distinguishes the various kinds of simile Milton uses in the poem, one of which is this simile specifically drawing on edenic imagery familiar to Adam.
2. Isabel MacCaffrey in *"Paradise Lost" as "Myth"* stresses repeatedly that Milton's style is not metaphorical because it makes no such dualistic divisions as literal and figurative.
3. Anne Ferry characterizes God's voice in this way in chap. 3 of *Milton's Epic Voice*, as does Irene Samuel in "The Dialogue in Heaven: A Reconsideration of *Paradise Lost*, 3: 1–417," in *Milton: Modern Essays in Criticism*, ed. Arthur E. Barker (New York: Oxford University Press, 1965), pp. 233–45.

3   The Lyric-Ironic Modal "Structure"

In the sympathic state of the declension of mind, the ideological and emotional faculties dominate the reader's conflicting responses to the poem; but in Milton's focusing and definition of this conflict the mind moves from the violent world of epic and theology into the quieter world of the pilot moored by the whale's side and of the peasant in the moonlit forest. The attention is here shifted from "great things" to "small"—to use Raphael's words (6: 311)—from "shapes immense" to the "smallest forms" of elves, and the dramatic almost substantial exertions of anger and pain yield to the less definite tones of the voice walking in the cool garden and the perplexed bemusement of Adam's wry comment about the tree of knowledge.

The peasant and the pilot are simple people related to the mysteries of sky, earth, and water by intuition and sense more than by rational ideology or universalizing moral judgment. Their encounters with the unknown arouse feelings that are not precisely definable or even distinctly felt and that do not identify what is seen. The peasant's heart rebounds "at once with joy and fear"; he "sees or dreams he sees." The whale is an island, at least until morning, or the island is a whale. In this image of the skiff moored in the shelter of the whale's giant sides the reader senses the presence of some dimly lit, uncertain mystery, or shape, something awesome, huge, and silent. That is all. The elves are small and making music, but as in the whale image the scene is moonlit, dreamlike, with a stillness close to awe. But although these scenes are perceptually, philosophically, or even emotionally vague, they are in some other sense definite and clear: this world, in its "intensity of calm,"[1] communicates a magnetic quality and a certain clarity peculiar to itself. The intensity and clarity are the intensity and clarity of focused yearning, "represented" by the attitude and tone of desirer in relation to desired but existing in its own right distinct from these two poles. For what is stressed by the poet in passages such as these is not so much *what* is seen or is there—its reality or meaning—as *how* it is seen when such considerations are secondary, and the awareness that different angles of vision are possible, that different kinds of knowledges can exist in the considering mind simultaneously and side by side. In such considering, the mind for a time ceases—in Adam's words to Eve after her dream in Book 5—to "affirm" or "deny," or to "approve" or "disapprove," and allows perceptions to "come and go" into the mind, or allows itself to come and go in the terrains of no judgment without, however, "harboring" (5: 95–119).

The primary characteristic of Milton's instances of aesthetic distancing is their suspended quality, their space apart even from the desire for certainty and conceptual definition, and their tone. Adam's comment about the tree of knowledge arrests the mind in a bemused and almost self-conscious irony; the whale and elves similes lift the mind into a lyric space filled with the motions of yearning for a port, yet distracted from the thought of the port into an awareness of the yearning itself and the pause it provides in the journey.

The term *tone* usually refers in literary analysis to the author's attitude toward or relation to the literary material or the reader, an attitude incorporated into the work itself. Tone implies a certain distance from or perspective on the content, a certain self-awareness of the poetry of itself. In *Paradise Lost* it is not so much the author's attitude toward the poem and the reader,[2] or the reader's attitude toward the content and his/her own responses to it,[3] but rather *the attitude implied or called up by the poem in the human psyche in general,* in the psyche as a reality heuristically framed in the third space distinct from the poet, the reader, the poem, and the world. This attitude can be the kinesthetic position or motion of observer in relation to object in the world of mind as well as in the physical world of Galilean-Newtonian space.

In his counterplot Milton extends tone, a momentary perspective on content, into *mode,* into a disciplined experiential consideration of the structures or flows of force informing the mind's attitudes toward the sympathic deadlocks discussed above. Mode is extended tone as allegory is extended metaphor. However, unlike allegory, the essence of mode is its fluid and mobile quality, which is proper specifically neither to the poet as a "self" nor to the reader as a "self" considered as subjective entities expressing and experiencing feelings separate from those feelings and attitudes expressed and aroused in a disciplined way by the poem, nor even proper to the poem "itself" considered as some "objective" artifact. The fluidity of mode allows it to mediate by flowing between and resolving poem and mind into its own structures and energies without losing either poem or mind. The reader's perceptions, feelings, thoughts, and attitudes are brought into the poem in a controlled manner that is a literary device in itself.

While mode does not have a set structure like allegory or ideology, the flows of energy of which it consists move according to certain laws. The energy is yearning; the "structure" of yearning may be thought of as existing in between yearning itself and issues of fulfillment, of attainment of the object of yearning; or it may be thought of as motion existing between and determined by attraction to and repulsion from points in a structure defined by the conceived nature of the object of yearning and by the conceived nature of the attainment desired. This modal structure differs from sympathic structure because here the focus and attention are on the motion more than on the object and the attainment.

The modal stage of the declension of mind shifts the mind's primary concerns from ontology to epistemology, yet it does not thereby set up any duality between poem/mind and "reality," for the interflowing and inter-modulating process occurring in and between poem and mind and the emerging structures and energies come in the end into an alignment in which mind resonates with and reveals the structures and energies of reality that in certain respects poem and mind resemble. This aligning process is the stated epic purpose of *Paradise Lost:* "to justify"—a word that, if one makes an effort to see through the sympathic dimension of its legal, moral, and conceptual definition, "to show to be just, right, or reasonable," means "to adjust or arrange exactly"—"the ways of God to men" (1: 25).

The declension of mind moves through three principal stages. In the first, sympathic structures are deframed and the mind moves into the third space. In the second, the mind comes to know the modal structure in the third space. In the third, the mind moves into meditative modes beyond the more familiar lyric and ironic modes. Thus the modal poem moves and occurs in its own space—a space at times "imaged" as pure space as discussed above, and at times imaged as in the similes—a third space that exists neither in reality nor in the subjective mind, a space that frames the world as does the Galilean-Newtonian frame but in a different way.

As we are related perceptually to objects and settings of the phenomenal world by position and motion in time and space, so are we related emotionally, intellectually, intuitively, and spiritually to the less phenomenal world by the modal positions and motions of yearning. In a fourth "stage," as meditative resonance reveals the nature of the alignment with reality, the mind leaves the third space that has temporarily existed separately for heuristic purposes, and returns to the world, now perceived as a world different from the epic, theological, and empirical world the mind left as it first entered the third space. The declension of mind completed, the counterplot has become plot, and reality is the reality revealed by the proper alignment of mind. Both mind and reality have been transformed. Thus the counterplot is "counterplot" at first, but as the declension of mind proceeds, the counterplot comes to be seen as a reinforcing or even determining structure or movement. The subject or plot of the poem comes to be seen as the subject of the counterplot: the nature and operation of the mind. While in the epic dimension the subject may be falling, the subject of the counterplot and the plot as transformed by the counterplot is the unfalling of the mind as it grows to know itself and the world. In a sense, then, one subject of the poem is finding the subject: first *Paradise Lost* may seem to be a theological epic, then poetic and psychic process, and last, the kinesthetic ontological principles of universe in relation to psyche and their reciprocal evolution.

Whereas the kinesthesia of the sympathic stage is negative and painful, modal kinesthesia is more positive and less painful. Pain is often the result of resistance: in some situations if one yields to what is assumed to be causing the pain, the pain will disappear and the cause will change its nature or appearance. At first the motions of the modal counterplot may be experienced as painful as the mind is distanced from the sympathic ideological and emotional structures whose familiarity may be comforting even though they frustrate and lead to deadlock, and the mind may wish to resist these modal motions with rigidity, as does a critic like MacCaffrey. But if the mind allows itself to enter the third space and yield to modality while watchfully considering the laws of its motion, allows itself to risk knowledge that is not controlled by pity and judgment, the pain will fade, especially as its latent faculty, the histrionic sensibility, begins to stir within—recalled, reinforced, and developed by the counterplot.

This mental process is more fluid than ordinary analytic reasoning, perhaps more like dreaming, especially in the beginning. However, it is important to stress that the modal process has its own structures and energies that are not random or chaotic, but have patterns of flow subject to laws just as the behavior of matter is subject to the laws of physics. The meditative state and vision this process eventually leads to is therefore not a vague or mystical ecstasy. Both the path and the result are disciplined, articulated, and precise, though not perhaps immediately and easily graspable by familiar forms of consciousness.

The Lyric-Ironic Paradigm

The structure of the counterplot may be considered in two ways. As it appears in incarnate instances in the poem, so to speak, it is woven into the plot in a linear sequence. The declension of mind, on the other hand, may be discussed in terms of a paradigmatic structure of its own, even though it may differ from its particular linear representation, from Milton's use of it, and from the reader's particular experience of it. For example, one instance of aesthetic distancing may exist in more than one stage of the declension of mind: it may be sympathic, lyric, and meditative all at once, depending on the mind's perspective and the aspects on which the mind is focusing. The reader may progress in a simple forward movement through the declension, but is more likely to move back and forth between stages. An instance of meditative aesthetic distancing may precede an instance of sympathic conflict in the linear sequence of the poem.

In its paradigmatic sequence, the declension of mind moves from the sympathic deadlock between pity and judgment discussed at the end of the last chapter into the lyric and ironic modes, which together form a paradigmatic structure of their own. This structure of movement in this stage exists as a series of three impulses. In the initial impulse, the mind's shift from the dimension of what ought to be and what is into the dimension of yearning

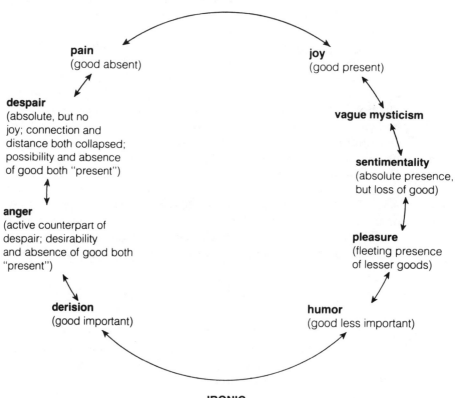

good possible

desirer and desired connected

state: receptive, passive

LYRIC

pain
(good absent)

joy
(good present)

despair
(absolute, but no
joy; connection and
distance both collapsed;
possibility and absence
of good both "present")

vague mysticism

sentimentality
(absolute presence,
but loss of good)

anger
(active counterpart of
despair; desirability
and absence of good both
"present")

pleasure
(fleeting presence
of lesser goods)

derision
(good important)

humor
(good less important)

IRONIC

connection broken

good not possible

state: active, responsible
controlling

and into the third space is experienced as a relief. In the second impulse, the mind moves with and watches the motions of yearning between the various points defined by the relation between the actuality and the conceived nature of the object of desire and by the conceived nature of its attainment. In this growing knowledge the mind in a third impulse begins to consider modality as a structure of fulfillment, at which point modality reveals frustrations and deadlocks of its own. It is these deadlocks that propel the mind into the third meditative stage of the declension of mind.

In yearning, the object of desire is something neither possessed nor absent, yet felt to be in some way present or existent. It is aspects of these two general characteristics of the nature of the object of yearning and the desirer's relation to it that define the poles between which the motions of yearning flow.

In the various examples of ironic and lyric tonal distancing discussed above, it can be seen that both ironic and lyric tones fall into ranges. Irony ranges from the playful humor of angels rolling on archangels to Michael's sharper comment about the flood, and even to the derisive and vicious irony of the editorial attack on Satan following the whale simile. Similarly, lyric aesthetic distancing ranges from the joy of the reviving fields and the beauty of the falling Mulciber to the pain of the hopeless and doleful region of hell in 1: 65–67, and the fiery "resting" of Satan's ublest feet in 1: 237–38. Ironic tone modulates between humor and derision, and lyric between joy and pain. In modal terms, these affective motions may be related in a structure to the relation between desirer and desired (see chart of modal structure).

In the lyric mode, at the pole of pain one is aware of the loss or absence of the desired good; at the pole of joy, one is aware of the good desired or remembered as it is brought to the foreground of the mind in imagination and as the awareness of its absence in actuality is momentarily forgotten. In this mode the attainment of the good is conceived or felt to be in some way possible; and the force of a yearning nearing the actualization or incarnation of love flows between and connects the desired good and the desirer. For the good desired is love, in particular a love that is absolute, present, and permanent as opposed to trivial, absent or distant, and fleeting. The object of desire is indistinctly conceived of at this stage as a substance that embodies love or a being who gives love. Joy is imagined to be the ideal state, and it is imagined that the permanent attainment of the absolute good would make this joyous state a reality, and that its absence will cause pain. In this lyric mode the desirer is in a yielding and receptive state. The two pairs of poles, joy-pain and presence-absence, are causally related by the lyric motions: if the possible good seems absent, the desirer feels pain; if present, joy. But the reverse causality is also operative, if in a lesser degree: if the desirer is in a joyous state, then he/she feels the good to be present; if in a pained state, absent. Thus one cannot label the mode either "subjective" or "objective."

Since the force of yearning flows in two directions, it can be a mediating force that can "invade" the "objective" world and alter its manifestations.

The ironic mode is less affective, and more intellectually attitudinal than the lyric mode. Attainment of what is desired, or a positive connection between desirer and desired, is conceived of as impossible. Whereas in the lyric mode the causal direction absence-causes-pain/presence-causes-joy might have seemed stronger than the reverse because it is a receptive mode, in the ironic mode it is as if the desiring mind, no longer able to bear the uncertainty about the real presence of the good, has actively decided it desires control of the situation, certainty, and relief, and has therefore broken the connecting possibility and also to some extent broken the desire. Even though in the lyric mode the good is conceived of as possible, a certain disconnection always lingers in the background, a potential pain even when most forgotten. In the ironic decision, the faculties of intellect, wit, and practical judgment take over from feeling, and the passive mind becomes active as it takes control and conceives of the absolute good as unattainable.

Whereas in the lyric mode the movement toward one pole or the other is determined by the imagined absence or presence of the good, here the movement between derision and humor is determined by the evaluation of the desired good now considered as unattainable: if it is considered unimportant, irony is at the pole of humor and light-hearted laughter; if it is considered serious and important, irony is at the pole of derision and anger.

As lyric is related to feeling, so ironic is related to judgment and ideology. However, in lyric and ironic modality, the attitude is more important than conceptual conclusions, and the flows of force and the ambiguous gap between desirer and desired become more foregrounded as "realities" in themselves.

Irony can be directed toward the gap itself, toward the object of desire, toward the self or others as responsible for the gap, or can be imagined as directed toward the self from the outside. The issue of responsibility enters in because the desirer desires control and certainty. In the lyric mode this directionality is not so apparent, because when love or joy is imagined to be flowing between desirer and desired and the desirer is a receptive vessel, the question of both directionality and responsibility is less important.

The continuum between desirer and desired is also sometimes considered by the desirer as a continuum between material and spiritual. Even though he/she conceives of the desired as ambiguously substantial, it still seems more absolute and less tangible than the tangible material world immediately visible. In the lyric mode the differentiation is less salient and less keenly felt because the relation between spiritual and material is conceived of as an unbroken continuum, through whose degrees flows the connecting force of yearning almost become love. This conception is expressed in Raphael's picture of the chain of being, followed by the tree image already quoted:

O Adam, one Almighty is, from whom
All things proceed, and up to him return,
If not depraved from good, created all
Such to perfection, one first matter all,
Endued with various forms, various degrees,
Of substance, and in things that live, of life;
But more refined, more spiritous, and pure,
As nearer to him placed or nearer tending,
Each in their several active spheres assigned,
Till body up to spirit work, in bounds
Proportioned to each kind. So from the root
Springs lighter the green stalk, and from thence the leaves
More airy, lest the bright consummate flow'r
Spirits odórous breathes: flow'rs and their fruit,
Man's nourishment, by gradual scale sublimed.

(5: 469–83)

Even pain is a force whose flow may predominate in the consciousness over absence or disconnectedness. In the ironic mode, however, the differentiation between material and spiritual is more apparent, though less painful because they have been actively disconnected. The ironic verbal style reflects this stage: its insistent grossness, inflation, repetition, and use of clichés makes the language materialistic on the one hand; yet on the other, it is entirely unpredictable, wildly energetic and frenetic, taking unexpected turns, and has a strongly felt lack of necessity. These two apparently incompatible characteristics derive from the snapping of the connection between absolute love and the material, which snapping causes the material to fall into grossness and at the same time sets energy free of both incarnation and direction.

Within this lyric-ironic structure, modality is fluid because the two-way causality mentioned earlier causes the modal center of gravity to move from pole to pole within each mode, and also from one mode into the other, defining other poles as it moves.

For example, in response to the pain of the lyric pole of absence, the desirer gains ironic distance from the object and from his/her desire for it and moves perhaps to the ironic pole of light-hearted humor, where it is possible to imagine that, after all, the good desired and its unattainability are perhaps not so important. With the perspective of absolute joy and the gap separating him/her from it in the background, his/her feelings and attitude become less intense, and the desirer moves into not an all-fulfilling joy, but pleasure, by focusing on more attainable goods. Correspondingly, since the good is considered unimportant, the desirer feels no urge to consider questions of responsibility and blame and therefore feels an easygoing, sympathetic attitude toward other beings and toward him/herself. This pleasure, and the presence of the lesser goods, move from the humorous pole of irony toward the lyric pole of joy. However, these joys are fleeting and the goods are not absolute, and these qualities prevent them from yielding an all-fulfilling joy.

If in response to this impermanence, or to the lyric pain of absence, the desirer considers the loss important and serious, he/she will move to the other pole of irony, the pole of derision. In the midst of lesser joys the joy itself may cause the true object of longing to reobtrude itself into consciousness, and then the desirer's distancing irony may break into derision and outright anger as it considers the issue of cause and responsibility in order to gain control. Intellect and wit become tinged with desire and emotion and the modal flow swings toward the lyric pole of pain. Anger is still an active and controlling force, but it can move easily into despair, which, because the desirer still considers the absolute good to be unattainable, is more devastating even than lyric pain. As this despair destroys his/her control, however, yearning may be aroused again, and despair yield to pain and the pain predominate in consciousness over the issue of real presence. Conversely, from the other direction, great pain and consciousness of absence in the lyric mode may push the desirer into despair and thence into anger and irony.

At the other pole of lyric, when the focus on yearning has brought the good desired into the foreground of consciousness, the experience may be absolute, but it is never permanent. To render the state permanent, the desirer may fix on the attainment itself and on the self experiencing it, but then the object is lost, which moves the desirer out of joy into a vague mysticism or sentimentality and into pleasure—thus into the light-hearted pole of irony where lesser goods will move into empty attainment. Or if the desirer attempts through the experience of joy to fix on the absolute itself, its goodness and presence necessarily disappear, and the desirer moves suddenly into the fevered frenzy of Keats's "Ode on a Grecian Urn," a strangely parching "wild ecstasy" beyond the "sensual ear," or drops into a cold and desolate landscape, the "cold hill side" and despair of the starving knight in "La Belle Dame sans Merci."

Modality is by its very nature fluid, but as the mind watching its motions gains increasing consciousness of the points that define the structure within which it moves, it may begin to focus on the issue of fulfillment and imagine that the force of its flows directed by the conceived aspects of the good and the desired joy promises greater and more possible fulfillment than the sympathic structures. Such imagining, however, serves only to make the motions more frenetic and the stopping points more painful. Considered as a structure of fulfillment, the modal structure is a puzzle: though it may provide temporary relief from sympathic conflicts, it provides no constant resting-places, still points, or satisfying conclusions. It is fluid, but its fluidity occurs within a seemingly closed system. When one element or relation necessary to the desired stage of imagined joy is fixed, some other element necessary to its stability shifts and the structure of fulfillment resolves into some other structure. For example, in the motions just described, when the absolute begins to be fixed, the joy and permanence vanish, and the desirer shifts into trivial and fleeting pleasures or a seemingly absolute and eternal despair. Or should the desirer constrict his/her mind and turn away from overwhelming questions to settle for the permanence of the habitual, the joy of the sentimental, or the solid presence of the material, then sooner or later a pall will come over this settled life and turn into frustration and finally anger.

One may not attempt to fix oneself at one point in the structure, nor, to consider the problem in slightly different terms, may one attempt to follow one motion to a conclusion. The lyric impulse draws the desirer like Keats's knight into exhilaratingly magical and mystical lands and simultaneously to the cold hillside with seemingly inexplicable necessity, as in *Paradise Lost* the "romantic" peasant in Book 9 allows himself to be led into the swamp. Similarly, the ironic impulse, whose critical control at first yields exuberance and delight, falls into an obsessive and at times uncontrollable momentum as it struggles to avoid the sanctionless vacuum formerly filled by the flows of yearning. It is this galloping irresolution that afflicts the angels, both righteous and unrighteous, in the war in heaven.

The situation is like two equations with two unknowns, or a number of equations with one too many unknowns to solve. The modal structure is inconclusive and unsatisfying. Its fluidity is not unidirectional like Platonic energies. When one falls from joy into despair, one might think that he/she has exited from the now painful modal structure, yet despair—ironically— does not last long, because one is moved by pain or distracted by secondary pleasures. However preferable the alternatives of unmoving despair or moving uncertainty may seem, the desirer cannot escape the lyric-ironic structure in these ways. All such positions and desires and disappointments are drawn into its perspective and into the laws of its motions. Even such seemingly definitive emotional exertions or withdrawals as anger and despair, even such seemingly definitive acts as murder or suicide, will not free the soul from these motions. The modal structure exists as a totality whose only consolation is that the terms of both desire and denial are more clearly articulated than when the desirer, frustrated by the deadlock of the sympathic structure, first entered it.

Yet it is precisely this experience of the yearning for fulfillment hitting rock bottom that is the pivot that will allow one to turn out of pain. The consolation is real. Because the modal structure is a structure of attitude, it exists to provide not fulfillment, but consciousness. The particular and peculiar structure of unfulfillment that modality articulates precisely defines the falsity of both the object as conceived by the desirer and the nature of the attainment as conceived by the desirer, and further defines their true nature and thereby points the way to the only fulfillment possible.

Yet precisely at this point in the declension of mind, much literature and literary criticism regress to sympathic strategies and attempt to formulate structures of fulfillment by fixing on one point or motion in the modal structure. If in the sympathic stage one is likely to erect and substantialize ideological or emotional forms, in the modal stage one is likely to erect and substantialize literary forms. Thus Northrop Frye in *Anatomy of Criticism* escapes sympathic fallacies in order to analyze his near-modal anatomy—which, however, is deceptively structured because he has drained it of the motions that truly inform it—but in the end falls into a lyric fallacy as he chooses romance—desire at the pole of vague joy—as the "mythos" to ultimately determine his theoretical structure. Frye says, "The structural principles of literature . . . are to be derived from archetypal and anagogic criticism, the only kinds that assume a larger context of literature as a whole." For Frye, literature in the anagogic mode gives the reader "not reality, but the conceivable limit of desire, which is infinite, eternal, and hence apocalyptic."[4] Fixing his definition of literature at this "conceivable limit," he effectively betrays the yearning, for as Milton says when Satan first beholds the beauty of Paradise, joy cannot drive away despair (4: 155–56). Something else, something more—or less—is needed.

Another substantializing literary form is the plot of epic in which the progress of the action to a certain kind of conclusion and the character of the hero serve to bear or incarnate ideologies. Another literary fallacy is the allegorical vehicle-tenor structure that fixes a relation between the two ends of the desirer-desired continuum. Still other literary forms attempt to stabilize the modal structure into fulfillment by inserting into it what might be termed *intermediates*. Two such intermediates are the hero and the symbol. In ritual or myth, forms with which tragedy, for example, begins, a system of identification is set up in which the hero is an intermediate between desirer and desired, an institutionalized solution to the painful gap between them. The hero is an upside-down scapegoat on whom his/her subjects project their ideals and their strength, and give up their own relation to the absolute in exchange for the hero's taking the responsibility for it. There is complicity in this arrangement. If not joy, the hero will have power, dignity, and adulation; the subjects will have security. The hero is identified with the absolute, and the members of the chorus identify themselves with the hero, and in this way the gap is welded shut.

A similar system of identification is the symbol. In its broadest sense, there are many kinds of symbols: institutions, social roles, objects, rituals, words, images, and so on. The symbol's usefulness derives from its simultaneous doubleness—it looks two ways, toward both the material and the spiritual—and its solidity and stability. This solution requires a finely adjusted balance between poles, but if successful, it stops up the gap between desirer and desired.

Other attempted solutions to the unfulfilling motions of modality might be called strategies of accommodation. In their initial impulse comedy and irony or satire gain distance on the false resolutions just described. They are anti-structural. However, usually an ironic form is not random or unfocused in its attacks, but points somewhere else, to some positive vision that, while not ordinarily given much literary space or specificity, is present by strong implication. This vision may be another known structure of values, or it may be simply an undefined yearning for something better. Thus, although irony has no resolution of its own insofar as it points to and is partly anchored by another sympathic or modal form or motion, it is subject in the end to fallacies similar to the other fallacies just described.

Other structures of accommodation are the institutionalization of mysticism; manic-depressive cycles; a philosophical version of the Freudian conception of wit, in which with an odd twist interlocking success and defeat one attains fulfillment through a joke; and a valuation and structuring of society in which the desirers institutionalize the whole ironic structure and drain it of tone to keep it from moving. In such times it is often the strategy of the poets to reinject the tone into the irony around them, and the strategy of succeeding poets to move in counterpart into the whole lyric structure, to superimpose the poles of pain and joy on one another, and to intensify the tone to free it of structure.

Such structures and strategies, lacking the necessary self-consciousness, will eventually fall of their own accord, or fall prey to revolution from without or within as the structure, true to its inherent modal nature, resolves into other structures or is destroyed by the frustrated desirer him/herself. The defeat of accommodations, whether sympathic or modal, is represented in Book 2 of *Paradise Lost,* where in the infernal council Moloch, Belial, and Mammon present three seemingly reasonable solutions to their painful situation in hell. The solution Beelzebub presents for Satan, while cruelly seeking to seduce Adam and Eve by guile, yet wisely proposes that the infernally sympathic consciousness move from the sympathic conflicts of hell to the modal reality of Eden. Yet the mind may not rest permanently in Eden either, but must move on into the motions of a higher consciousness. As the sympathic progress of mind in the first stage of the declension of mind concluded inconclusively in the deadlock between pity and judgment, in which the mind may focus on one or the other but not on both simultaneously, so the second modal stage concludes in the less rigid but unresolved figure-ground reversal of the Proserpine simile in Book 4. Here, as he is describing Paradise, Milton first presents fair Eve, through connotation, as Proserpine—through a vehicle in which the tenor itself is absent: the "field and grove" in the kinesthetic passage quoted above in chapter 2 is not, Milton says

> . . . that fair field
> Of Enna, where Prosérpine gathering flow'rs,
> Herself a fairer flow'r, by gloomy Dis
> Was gathered, which cost Ceres all that pain
> To seek her through the world.
>
> (4: 268–72)

On the one hand, this simile is a painful lyric evocation of loss; on the other, its placement here, before Eve has even been presented in her unfallen beauty and majesty in the epic dimension of the poem, rather than, say, in Book 9, is heavily ironic. Here lyric and ironic motions mutually deframe each other in a kind of alternating figure-ground device that does not allow the mind to settle comfortably into one motion or the other.

In Milton's poetics, fallacious literary structures are broken down just as were the fallacious sympathic structures. His particular use of diction and his syntactic technique, both discussed above, allow no word or object to become fixed and stable as symbol. His use of the vehicle-tenor structure not to connect the worlds of desirer and desired but, by focusing on the gap between them, to open into a third space, allows no allegories. His repeated displacement of point of view allows no hero: in *Paradise Lost* the notion of hero becomes instead point of view in itself in a shared landscape of mind. Ironic impulse, poetically isolated in the representation of the war in heaven for the reader's greater consciousness, gallops into increasingly frenetic and fragmented irresolution. And the lyric impulse, similarly isolated from structure yet attempting to attach itself to the delusively symbolic or evocative object of vision, leads the peasant into the swamp in Book 9. All such exits blocked, the reader is forced to confront the modal structure as the structure of consciousness it was meant to be when he/she first turned from anger and pain, and from pity and judgment, to an awareness of attitude in relation to these.

As the desirer redirects his/her attention away from issues of fulfillment, he/she begins to observe certain characteristics of lyric-ironic modality more carefully. The points between which lyric and ironic motions flow, the points that define the modal structure, are themselves defined in terms of a conceived object of desire and a conceived state of joy in its attainment. As discussed above, it is imagined by the desirer that the absolute good permanently present will yield joy. However, attempts to find fulfillment or conclusion in the modal structure prove futile because, as illustrated above, the attainment of one aspect of the desired state causes the other aspects to disappear. The unceasing motions of desire and frustration between the points seem to prove more determining than the points themselves. Absoluteness cancels out presence, or presence cancels out absoluteness. In the perspective of fulfillment, such apparent incompatibility is painful, but in the perspective of consciousness, the incompatibility helps define a new truth. This truth becomes clear if one considers the modal structure using an affective criterion rather than the ontological criterion used above—lyric connection and ironic disconnection. In affective terms, ironic anger and lyric pain are both "caused" by the absence of the good, and ironic humor and lyric joy are both "caused" by the presence (of some good). This second affective grouping stresses an apparent contradiction in the ontological criteria: pain, for example, is determined modally by connection but affectively by absence. The resolution of this contradiction lies in the notion of "presence" and "absence." Examined carefully, the modal paradigm shows that there are three kinds of presence. First, there is the presence of the felt possibility that, were the conditions right, the good could be attained. Second, there is the presence of the possibility of attainment, in the sense that such conditions are being met or are probable. Thus in pain the good is present in the first sense but not the second; it is present as a possibility, but this possibility is not being fulfilled. The good is present only by dint of the strength of desire. In irony, although the possibility of connection has been rejected, this connection lingers and taunts; and as the mind begins to consider the good important though impossible, moving toward the pole of anger, the presence of the object as something desired returns: the presence of what is missing or lost or denied becomes more excruciatingly intensified by its very absence. Last, there is the presence of attainable good in which the two senses of possibility concur. However, this presence, at the pole of humor, is the presence of closeness and attainment more than of the good.

It might seem that if the desirer turns his/her back on the desired absolute good, it will reappear to torment him/her, and if he/she reaches for it, it will disappear. Again, in terms of the imagined fulfillment, this phenomenon may be frustrating; but as a phenomenon in the perspective of consciousness, it reveals several related truths. The conceptions of presence, taken separately, are all misconceived: if the joy is more present when less in the forefront of consciousness, when not considered absolute as at the poles of anger and pain; and if joy is present when least absolute and least possessed and yet modulates into absence as the good becomes lesser goods, the modal structure is showing that the good desired is not substantial either in absoluteness or materiality and that possession is incompatible with its true nature. Presence and absence considered in terms of either possession or exclusion—as in irony—are absolutes of attitude or relationship, not ontological points, elements, or qualities. The aspects that constitute the conceived nature of attainment are all terms of relation or state—permanence, absoluteness, joy—not of substance. The good desired and its attainment cannot be contained or defined in terms of substance and keeps slipping through and away from such terms. Hence the modal motions. Absoluteness in the sense it has been considered is incompatible with relationality. This incompatibility points up another confusion about the conceived nature of the object of desire: the confusion about whether it is a being or love that is desired. It is ambiguously imagined that to attain love, one must attain—or possess—the being. Or it is imagined that the being is a substance or entity who can give love. The modal structure shows that if the aspects of the desired state or attainment are essentially relational, such a clear distinction between love and entity is not possible. Our desire is for love; therefore what we "attain" is not the object but the love of the object; and because what we know of the object is this love, the object "itself" is in terms of love, or perhaps is love "itself." We begin to sense the truth that perhaps the object is not a substance, but a force, a power.

In this new modal consciousness the conceived natures of object and fulfillment are abandoned as unreal. The awareness of relationality destroys the conceptualizations from which sympathic conflicts derive.

The nature and meaning of relationality become clearer in a less abstract and more specific way when one considers more carefully the relation between the passive attitude of the lyric mode and the active attitude of the ironic mode. As one considers the modal motions in this perspective, one realizes that the metamorphic quality of the modal structure is not entirely externally imposed, and not entirely sinister. In the two-way causality mentioned at the beginning of this chapter, the attitudes the desirer chooses in relation to his/her desires and frustrations affect the motions within the structure and can shift the modal center of gravity. This truth is most obvious, perhaps, in the ironic mode, where it is the decision to distance oneself from the absolute and consider it unattainable that defines the mode in the first place. At the pole of lighthearted humor, the decision to consider the absent good less important has an effect: a degree of pleasure is attained. Yet such an "active" stance is not the same as control or possession: the apparently stronger and more active stance at the other pole of anger must be measured against the more painful sense of absence the desirer feels at the moment of the anger. Expression of anger, while a bulwark against despair and thus a control of attitude, cannot be used successfully to directly attain fulfillment: expressions of anger are likely to be repetitive without culminating in anything, and often invite a boomerang effect, as frequently happens to Satan. As God observes:

> . . . so bent he seems
> On desperate revenge, that shall redound
> Upon his own rebellious head.
>
> (3: 84–86)

Actually, the less directly assertive decision at the pole of humor is as yielding as it is active, as the desiring mind relinquishes its grasp on the idea of the absolute. At the pole of anger, after the repetitions have dissipated themselves and the spirit has fallen into despair, yielding to the movement "natural" to the modal structure, the desirer will feel fear and pain, the motions of lyric, as the active stance modulates into a more passive one. An awareness and conscious experience of such motions and of the relation between assertion and yielding and their effects make the truth clearer that the attainment of love is not something that is simply given to or taken by the desirer, but something that is affected by and partly consists of motions within the self, or rather, motions between the self and the desired object. As the desired love is a force, so is the desirer him/herself a force consisting of different motions.

It is the further experience and consideration of such movements in relation to the movements of the desired that is the substance and process of the next stage of Milton's declension of mind, the meditative modes. The particular strength of active yielding just described replaces the desperate sanction of the desired absolute and of the alternating search for rigid control on the one hand and abject passivity before the absolute on the other.

In such active yielding, as the desirer releases the extremes of attitude, possession and exclusion, turning slightly away without losing awareness of the object of desire, the conflicts of absolute-trivial, spiritual-material, permanent-fleeting, presence-absence, and even joy-pain, drift to the periphery of consciousness. At the center of mind will instead be a resonance, an energy flowing intermagnetically. The feeling accompanying the resonance is a deep and peaceful joy, not a wild ecstasy. However, an exclusive focus on the mediating resonance will result in its loss: awareness of the poles must at this stage be maintained, even briefly focused on and experienced separately, though never isolated or incarnated exclusively. The intensity of absence at the poles of pain and anger and its sharpness serve as a check, as a frame, to contain the resonance and ensure the desirer's discipline. Such an adjustment or "justifying" of attitude in relation to the components and motions of the modal structure is one form of the alignment between mind and "reality" mentioned above, is the "attainment" of the desired good.

The gap between desirer and desired becomes a space in which the modal flows of yearning occur. The poles define and ensure this space. The flows become primary rather than secondary; the forces that are flowing take precedence over the notion of the absolute. The primary point of view cannot attach itself to any one point on the modal compass, but must stand alone in the center of the space and allow the flows in order to experience them. The passive flow of lyric possibility fills this space and becomes the pure flows of resonance; the distance and control of irony become a central brace, the edges of the space, and the lines of resonance. The third space and the upright stance—the "upright heart and pure" that Milton prays for in the invocation to Book 1 (1: 18)—the shared space of mind imaged forth in the landscapes of the similes and the tree of knowledge that centers it are the only "symbols," or rather emblems, more certain than ideological system, than plot, than hero, than symbol, than word. In the space of the upright heart desirer is linked to desired by yearning, not fulfillment, yearning that asserts its own reality and will suggest its own forms, to form into the reciprocal and resonant motions of love, not absolute substance but absolute power.

The two most vital and determining characteristics of the lyric-ironic modal structure are therefore the gap between desirer and desired and the fluidity in themselves. The fluidity is constant: it does not terminate itself by turning into a telic form, substance, or idea, as did, for example, Coleridge's organicism, which, at first based on the analogy of the plant's interchanging relationship with its surroundings, much like the passage describing Paradise discussed above, in the end came to be dominated by the apparently more secure telos of the seed's destiny—not that it grows by interchange but that it grows into a certain kind of plant or whole.[5] In Milton's modality, the distance or sense of distance and the central upright stance are the only permanent structural forms.

The way to "escape" the pains and inconclusiveness of the lyric-ironic structure is not an exit like a door one would walk out of. One cannot leave the structure at one of the points labeled on the diagram, through a door marked "joy" or "pleasure" or "despair." Wilhelm Reich uses such a fallacious mental picture in his conception of the "trap" to introduce his *Murder of Christ:*

> The nature of the trap has no interest whatsoever beyond this one crucial point: WHERE IS THE EXIT OUT OF THE TRAP? . . . THE EXIT IS CLEARLY VISIBLE TO ALL TRAPPED IN THE HOLE. YET NOBODY SEEMS TO SEE IT. EVERYBODY KNOWS WHERE THE EXIT IS. YET NOBODY SEEMS TO MAKE A MOVE TOWARD IT. MORE: WHOEVER MOVES TOWARD THE EXIT, OR WHOEVER POINTS TOWARD IT IS DECLARED CRAZY OR A CRIMINAL OR A SINNER TO BURN IN HELL.
>
> It turns out that the trouble is not with the trap or even with finding the exit. The trouble is WITHIN THE TRAPPED ONES.[6]

The fallacy in Reich's picture of the trap is that the concept of exit implies, or itself constructs, the walls that frame and define it. Despite his disclaimer, this picture affects his thinking throughout his book. Milton's comment on such a structure of thought is the Proserpine simile. His way, as the lyric-ironic structure moves into the meditative modes, is to align the mind so as to achieve a perspective in which the trap appears different, in which both exits and walls disappear and it is then no longer a trap.

The lyric-ironic "trap" as discussed above is so constructed as to allow the desirer neither to exit from it nor to stay in it. If one "exits" through the door of despair, for example, even in suicide, one snaps the relationality of the structure, which causes the modal motions to become more violent sympathic motions; or alternatively, distracting pleasures will in apparent incongruity enter onto the scene of despair. If one "exits" through the door of joy, one will find oneself with the same apparent incongruity in the landscape of despair. Attempting to remain still within the structure turns out to be the same strategy as exiting: balancing at one point or another, one is always thrown into movement toward another point. Keats's divine frenzy cannot be a way of life.

The Ends of Lyric-Ironic Modality: Wonder and Meditation

The ultimate alignment and resonance and the particular peace these bring are not so directly and quickly attained as may appear from the description just given of active yielding. Moving into the meditative modes of the next stage in the declension of mind, the reader embarks on an intricate and arduous spiritual exercise that demands patience and dexterity.

It is at this clearly defined juncture between lyric-ironic modality and meditative modality that the flight of Milton's poetry leaves many other literary forms behind. For Milton, the modal structure has served not to sanction such forms but to frame and define them in the necessity of their insufficiency, and to define the structure of this insufficiency so clearly as to point the way to a higher consciousness. It is difficult to describe the final state of mind achieved by Milton's counterplot in any disciplined manner to a reader before he/she has experienced the meditative modes. To call it simply "union with God" would be to fall into the ideological fallacy from which *Paradise Lost* so carefully distances itself. It would be more accurate to call it "wonder," not because the particular affective state this term denotes or the vision it implies are the ends toward which *Paradise Lost* moves but because it denotes a state of mind in relation to the forces of the universe rather than an ideology.

Wonder is the end of tragedy as defined by Aristotle in his *Poetics,* and the tragic form that leads to wonder, like *Paradise Lost,* specifically breaks down and works through intermediate literary forms to a resolution of higher consciousness. The recognition and wonder of tragedy provide an alternative that resolves the pains of the sympathic and modal structures, but this recognition and wonder are partial. It is the particular nature of this partiality that makes tragedy "tragic": the consciousness it achieves is more a psychic confrontation of the naked truth—with no deviation, mediation, accommodation, or even aesthetic distancing—more a psychic act of courage, than a clear and articulated understanding. Milton provides a different alternative, a resolution that yet partly defines itself in relation to the tragedy and wonder specifically absent from *Paradise Lost.*

Tragedy and its counterpart, comedy, can be defined in terms of the lyric-ironic modal structure and in terms of the vicissitudes of certain of the attempted escapes and accommodations discussed above. Comedy occurs at the poles of humor, pleasure, and sentimentality in the lyric-ironic structure. It is preeminently social because the lesser goods that are sought are more in the space of attention than is the absolute. Also, in the end these goods and pleasures are attained: comedy has a "happy" ending. The tone of the relationships between the people of comedy is more easygoing and sympathetic than in tragedy because the demands are less.

Tragedy occurs at the other two modal poles, where the absence of the absolute is the focus and the desirer feels pain, despair, and anger. The plot of tragedy, as Francis Fergusson points out in *Idea of a Theater,* is a quest.[7] The quest in *Oedipus Rex,* Sophocles' paradigmatic tragedy, is for the answer to the question, "Who am I?" This plot ends in the fall, the ironic recognition that the answer to the question brands Oedipus a sinner. But there is a second "plot," which is the true source of the power of tragedy. This plot is a drama of identification between hero and audience, or chorus, a drama of attitude that proceeds through pity and fear to wonder. Before his fall, as discussed above, Oedipus is an intermediate in a structure in which the chorus identifies with the hero who is identified with the absolute. His fall destroys his godlike status, breaking these identifications, and thereby destroys the solution of the intermediate. As father is revealed to be son, the chorus is thrown into chaos. The reaction to this fall is the second plot. In the turmoil that Oedipus causes by his fall—by upsetting the order of their world and making them precipitously aware of the absence of the absolute— the chorus might be tempted to kill him as a scapegoat, making him who was the vehicle for the absolute the vehicle for their anger, fear, and pain. But the second plot prevents such a conclusion to the first plot. In his own reaction to his fall, Oedipus refuses to fall into despair, accepts his fall, and stands upright spiritually. In his spiritual and psychic self-maintenance, Oedipus recognizes and defines himself as a human being, a brother, not an all-powerful god or father and yet not a passive son. He seems to emerge as a three-dimensional entity out of a two-dimensional background, much as the columnar figures of Giotto emerge from the gold background of medieval art, as the curving, coy figures of a Duccio, writhing in their modal structure, straighten up, exert weight on the ground, carve out a space in the air, and assume mass, clarity, and dignity. This new entity is human being; the new space, human space. Yet this space is not subjective space, for corresponding to the breaking of the identification with the absolute is a breaking of the identification with the self and with the despair that in the hero's first fall is an attachment to the self, to the ego. He gains distance in the second plot from his guilty act, from himself, and from his fall. The answer to the question "Who am I?" is therefore not "a sinner," or "Oedipus," but "a human being."

This self-definition allows both Oedipus and the chorus sufficient strength for pity without despair or the fear that might lead to murderous anger. It allows a mutual recognition. This response leads to a wonder that is different from lyric joy and that gives far greater satisfaction than this imagined joy. Wonder partakes of the sublime, which is the affective state accompanying the tragic hero's strength of self-maintenance as he/she confronts, and even yields to without "deifying," a force approaching the power of the absolute such that he/she is not destroyed and yet the absolute is not avoided. In terms of the modal diagram, the sublime is a diagonal relation combining or balancing the poles of anger and joy: the strength and independence of anger and the yielding of joy (see chart).

Wonder also partakes of the beautiful, the affective state accompanying the hero-become-human's response following the confrontation. As, or if, he/she moves into the realm of action after the confrontation, the hero, now frailer, creates, in a chosen limiting, pleasure, beauty, and forms. Beauty consists of a diagonal relation between the poles of pain and pleasure and moves tragedy toward comedy. Yet beauty is not trivial, for as Northrop Frye points out in "The Argument of Comedy,"[8] comedy usually goes through a dark middle, and tragedy as it ends in wonder exists in a comic context. Wonder may be thought of as the intersecting or balancing of the sublime and the beautiful, where the hero, after his/her tragic recognition and self-definition, might move back into life to form the forces flowing around and against the self into the more everyday forms of beauty.

In *Oedipus Rex* this tragic paradigm is not fully and clearly realized. The second plot—the psychic as opposed to the narrative plot—is embryonic and uncertain, just beginning to struggle out of the sympathic mythical mind and its forms. Furthermore, tragedy itself is not fully conscious. Tragedy is tragic because it is in part an act of mourning: though they were false the desirer cherished his/her desires and ideals. In mourning, he/she must slowly absorb their loss. Yet tragedy is also tragic in a more important sense: the desirer does not fully comprehend the forces he/she confronts. The balanced confrontation of the sublime is the only comprehension possible. This confrontation defines the outlines of the absolute as it strikes against the self and shapes them in relation to the self, and as the self is sculpted out of the hard stone of pain in relation to the universal forces. This sculpting allows escape from the painful vicissitudes of the lyric-ironic structure by shaping its forces into forms of action, the desirer's consciousness sufficient only to adjust anger and joy into the sublime. Yet to achieve this partial resolution, this sculpting necessarily hardens him/her and does not allow the motion necessary for the experience of meditative, even modal, motions. Thus the very consciousness that defines one as a human is a mark of the limitation of sublimity and wonder. The end of tragedy is recognition without consciousness, or inarticulate consciousness. Tragedy may be considered a transitional form in the mind's progress out of the sympathic state into the meditative state of full consciousness.

The recognition and wonder of *Oedipus Rex* appear with greater perceptual clarity in other literary works, although this conclusion still prevents full consciousness. In canto 33 of Dante's *Inferno*, for example, Dante's meeting

LYRIC

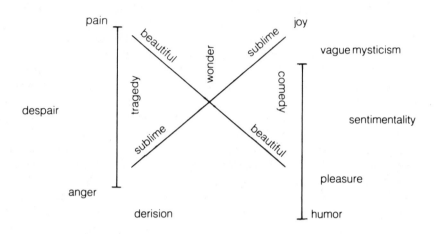

pain · joy

vague mysticism

despair

sentimentality

anger

pleasure

derision · humor

IRONIC

with Count Ugolino more clearly articulates the double-plot structure of tragedy and the poignant human dignity of the tragic hero's spiritual self-maintenance. Ugolino in hell is already dead, has already fallen in the first plot in a space differentiated from the present setting. Here in the frozen pit of hell, the second plot unfolds in its own space. Ugolino suffers and overcomes the pains of the psyche in the measured clarity and beauty of his poetry as he narrates to Dante the story of his imprisonment and death. Here the human space and time are more clearly represented in the straightforward narration, the simple story. It is perhaps difficult after an age of "realism" to appreciate the significance and weight of such a narration emerging from the monstrous and incessantly metamorphic motions of hell and mind. Here also the recognition and wonder is more mutual, occurring between Ugolino, a lesser hero than Oedipus, and Dante, a more knowing chorus, thus establishing a community of human reciprocity rather than that of a lord and a subject whose inequality and lack of consciousness force Oedipus to ask for banishment.[9]

As in *Oedipus Rex* and the narration of Ugolino the hero-intermediate is broken down to allow the mind recognition and wonder, so in a section of Thomas Nashe's *Unfortunate Traveler* the symbol-intermediate is broken down by means of a linguistic satire to allow the mind to enter a third space of wonder. Nashe begins this satire in an epic dimension, which in the first plot describes in allegorical terms the arms of nine knights who are to joust in a tournament to defend a lady's beauty. The knights' ornamental arms ostensibly define the meaning of their being not only in relation to courtly love but also in relation to the absolute love desired in the lyric-ironic structure. But in the course of the description, the vehicles become so visually and materially elaborate, the relation between vehicle and tenor so complicated, and the syntax expressing the allegorical relation so tortuous, that they gradually bury and constrict the knights on whom they are figured, suffocating their humanity. True to the satiric style described above, the vehicle, fearing loss of sanction—fearing absence—asserts its materiality and takes over the literary space, absorbing tenor into itself; and at the same time it explodes into a frenetic energy.

As the sympathic allegorical structure breaks down, this energy begins to express itself in the lyric tones and images of modality. In the end the poetry struggles free as this lyric impulse, chiseled and framed by the pain and absence of meaning, of love, breaks into the third space of wonder. The encumbered and encumbering language of the satire breaks free into a measured, direct, and cold voice similar to the voice of Count Ugolino, and into the stark and simple imagery of "toiling ants and emmets . . . who, in the full of the summer moon . . . hoard . . . up their provision of grain against winter."[10] The motto accompanying this image is "*victrix fortunae sapientia*: providence prevents misfortune." Although this image and motto are officially pictured on the knight's armor, poetically they no longer exist in an allegorical space.

The theme of courtly love has been expanded beyond the romantic desires of the heart to include the singing, blooming, and climbing of the soul, its desires and growth, its nourishment and pain. The image of the emmets at work is poignant because it expresses all endeavor, both the labor itself and the desire for perfection and completion, the disappointment at loss, and the consciousness of these—not the consciousness of the emmets, but the consciousness of the poet and reader, or the consciousness of shared human mind.

The motto that follows this image—"providence prevents misfortune"—is devastating. The pun on the word *providence* defines, exactly if painfully, its sublimity. The linking of "provision" and "providence" balances a bitter vision of hard work against great and unjust obstacles in the absence of any divine providence or grace to care and provide for us, with pity for the frail emmets' painful and innocent perseverance and for the frail humans they represent. This balance consists of a double reference whose modal overtones cut in two directions. There is the verbal irony ("providence") directed against the divine who has abandoned frail humanity coupled with a corresponding pity for those who have been abandoned; but the tone and sense of the image of the work under the moon, the evenness and strength of voice with which it is described, and the cool clarity of the mood and scene indicate that human being has disconnected itself from the passive expectation of divine providence and is gently but insistently working, not in a bitterness wholly apart, but to make its desires into a third reality. The pity the reader feels in this image is not sympathic pity, but wonder at the emmet's solitary perseverance and beauty.

This wonder is hard in tone and closer to the tragic mode than to comic pleasure or joy. It partakes of the sublime in its expression of the self-sufficiency taken from the pole of anger, coupled not with the yielding of joy but with the frailty of despair. But it also partakes of the beautiful, in a certain detachment from the pole of pleasure that carves out the space where these beings can be active and create beauty and form.

In the collapse of the allegorical structure of what should be and what is and in the assertion of the third space, it becomes clear that the essence of poetic verbal structure is the space between vehicle and tenor, or between signifier and signified, a space into which the motions of yearning, the truer meaning, flow.

Milton, with greater consciousness, bypasses the resolution of wonder. Unlike *Oedipus Rex,* Dante's Ugolino episode, and Nashe's description of the nine knights, Milton's resolution has no hard edges, no sculpted figures, no sublime. Tragedy achieves a paratactic resolution in which the columnar self of Giotto's frescoes is defined in opposition to great forces. It is a resolution similar to Yeats's concept of obstacle:

> Nations, races, and individual men are unified by an image, or bundle of related images, symbolical or evocative of the state of mind, which is of all states of mind not impossible, the most difficult to that man, race, or nation; because only the greatest obstacle that can be contemplated without despair rouses the will to full intensity.[11]

Milton focuses instead on the space in which the figures stand, the position of the self, and the motions that pass not only through the space but through the self, which is itself a frame or space. It is as if he expands Giotto's space and puts into it the curving lines of Duccio's figures, and disciplines these. While in the tragic vision the human self is defined, in *Paradise Lost* the self, like all other substances and forms, is distanced. The counterplot is a drama of identification like tragedy, but in it the reader's identification with human being as a substance is broken down, just as are his/her identifications with God, Satan, ideology, anger, and pain. Identifications with an absolute, with persons or things imagined to be vehicles or incarnations of the absolute, with desire itself, with one's pain, with one part of the self, even identification with the self, are the opposite of aesthetic distance. The counterplot labors to detach the reader from such identifications, and in this process sympathy turns into empathy, the imaginative projection of one's own consciousness into another being. True imagination is not identification. Thus the fallen angels in hell fall down in "horrid sympathy" as serpents as they look upon Satan, who has fallen down as a serpent in the passage quoted above, "for what they saw, / They felt themselves now changing" (10: 540–41). The angels in heaven, by contrast, respond to the fall of Adam and Eve with a distanced compassion:

> . . . dim sadness did not spare
> That time celestial visages, yet mixed
> With pity, violated not their bliss.
>
> (10: 23–25)

There is no hero in *Paradise Lost*. The point of view is constantly shifted from character to point of view in itself until it is not even the reader, but the motions of the reader's mind occurring in the space that is framed by the human entity. In *Paradise Lost* the audience-chorus-reader, unlike the Greek chorus, attains the highest consciousness—higher than the consciousness of the characters, except God and the Son—as the counterplot forces him/her free of "subjection" to fallen identifying strategies of mind. *Paradise Lost* is a truly revolutionary poem. For as Milton says, it is bowing down before mediating idols that causes one to sink "before the spear / Of despicable foes":

> . . . the race of Israel oft forsook
> Their living Strength . . .
> . . . bowing lowly down
> To bestial gods; for which their heads as low
> Bowed down in battle.

(1: 432–36)

The plot of *Paradise Lost* is a psychic, not a political, revolution, without which, however, true political revolutions are not possible. The reader no longer lives through a king: such an attitude is what destroys the resonance that is the essence of the relation between angel and God, between human and God, the "union" that Satan breaks when, feeling "impaired"—like the chorus at Oedipus's fall—he "leaves" the throne of God (5: 612, 665–70).

If there is a moment of wonder in *Paradise Lost,* it is when Adam, near the end of Book 12, attains through Michael's teaching not a view of life, but a centered suspension of self and a conscious perspective from which to view life and to act "as in" the presence of God:

> How soon hath thy prediction, seer blest,
> Measured this transient world, the race of time,
> Till time stand fixed: beyond is all abyss,
> Eternity, whose end no eye can reach.
> Greatly instructed I shall hence depart,
> Greatly in peace of thought, and have my fill
> Of knowledge, what this vessel can contain
> . . . .
> Henceforth I learn . . .
> . . . [to] love with fear the only God, to walk
> As in his presence.

(12: 553–63)

This "as in" is the "as if" of all art, the "as" of the third space of the empathic imagination. In this space the naive wonder of tragedy is superseded by an imaginative action that brings the motions of the mind into alignment and resonance with the motions of the universe.

NOTES

1. Hartman, "Milton's Counterplot," p. 121.
2. Anne Ferry in *Milton's Epic Voice* believes that the narrative voice unifies the poem and mediates between its various apparently conflicting elements.
3. Stanley Fish's thesis in *Surprised by Sin* (see intro., n. 13).
4. Frye, *Anatomy of Criticism*, pp. 134, 119.

5. M. H. Abrams, *The Mirror and the Lamp: Romantic Theory and the Critical Tradition* (New York: W. W. Norton and Co., Inc., 1958), pp. 68–69, and 168–75.

6. Wilhelm Reich, *The Murder of Christ* (New York: Noonday Press, 1972), pp. 3–4.

7. Fergusson, *Idea of a Theater*, pp. 28–30.

8. Northrop Frye, "The Argument of Comedy," in *Shakespeare: Modern Essays in Criticism*, ed. Leonard F. Dean (New York: Oxford University Press, 1967), pp. 78–89.

9. Dante, *Dante's Inferno, Italian Text with English Translation and Comment*, John D. Sinclair (New York: Oxford University Press, 1961), Canto 33, ll. 1–90, pp. 405–8.

10. Thomas Nashe, *The Unfortunate Traveler*, in *Elizabethan Prose Fiction*, ed. Merritt Lawlis (New York: Odyssey Press, Inc., 1967), p. 504.

11. William Butler Yeats, "The Trembling of the Veil," in *The Autobiography of William Butler Yeats* (New York: Collier Books, 1965), p. 132.

4 The Meditative Modes

In the final stage of Milton's declension of mind, the meditative modes, the reader's mind is purified of the sympathic tendencies of the lyric-ironic modal structure to identify with or create substances, whether absolute or intermediate. The meditative modes are spiritual exercises in which the gap and the fluidity of mode become heuristically primary realities in order to train the mind to achieve full consciousness of the flows of yearning and its vicissitudes, motions that constitute the reality of both mind and universe. In these exercises, the reader prevents his/her mind from riding the fluidity of tone backward, so to speak, into an unconscious renewal of sympathic identifications and strategies.

Instead, the reader moves onward into the tonally neutral "relativizing" meditative modes, which are still modal, however, because they are attitudes toward the attitudes experienced and brought to the edge of consciousness of the lyric-ironic structure. These two modes are spiritual exercises more than a tangible or conceptual solution like the hero or the symbol. In the first of these modes, simple relativizing, ideas or notions of the mind are set against one another, or into motion with relation to one another, in order to neutralize them, to remove their identifying powers from them. This strategy is different from the second plots of tragedy and linguistic satire because one does not work with just one notion but always with two or more at a time, and always two that are not compatible but move in different directions or against each other. This procedure is less harsh and less disturbing than the breaking of the identifications with hero and symbol because no spiritual attachment is established to either term.

In the second mode, complex relativizing, one experiences by moving with them the various points and forces of the lyric-ironic paradigm, and perhaps even of the sympathic structure, in a histrionic empathy that identifies with none of them. Here there is no longer any need for breaking, wrenching, or harsh distancing, but only for a shifting of attention.

The first of these modes is perhaps more of a special exercise than the second, which is closer to a way of thinking and perceiving, closer to a meditative way of life. The first is entirely toneless and purely intellectual, consciously detached from all judgment and feeling. This intellectual purity prevents this mode from laying any claim to sufficiency in the education of the soul, or to complete truth, because it is too limited. However, this characteristic is momentarily a necessary virtue of the exercise, a necessary step in the progressive aesthetic distancing process. On the one hand, it refines the intellect of the hidden moralistic and sympathic agendas in the ideological strategy of mind discussed in chapter 2. On the other hand, the sharpness and discipline of this mode keeps the mind from straying off into passivity, quietism, vagueness—the mistiness of Frye's romantic fallacy—when it proceeds into the next mode. It helps ensure precision and clarity.

In a way, this mode does not exist in itself. It is completely contentless. It is negative in a pure sense; it is pure shifting. It exists in the spaces between elements, between spaces; whereas in the second mode the reader, though without identification, is filled by all tones as he/she moves into the realm of the energies between mind and object, into the realm of lyric and ironic motions, into anger and pain, and into the realm of the beautiful, the sublime, and wonder, yet never in naked confrontation.

The Simple Relativizing Mode

Simple relativizing, the first meditative mode, is related to the physical and perceptual kinesthesia discussed in chapter 1, to the type of aesthetic distancing that stripped appearances and substances of their absoluteness and determinacy by means of motion. Thus in Satan's and Raphael's journeys the appearance of objects was affected by the observer's motion in relation to them; and in the perception of the fish in Book 7, motion in itself began to take on a reality of its own. Simple relativizing is more intellectual than perceptual: it is a meditation occurring within the space of mind, but its object may be in the Galilean-Newtonian universe. Its purpose is to strip identifications from the "meanings" attached to objects of perception, from the fixed positions of mind one develops in relation to them. The exercise and the experience of its effects are more important than the objects contemplated. The mind's attitude in this meditation is centrally neutral, though not totally and impassively detached. This central attitude is the upright stance whose emblem is the tree of knowledge, a stance prepared for perhaps by the disconnection and independence of the ironic mode as the lyric mode may be the preparation for the experience of modal flows in the complex relativizing mode.

In the exercise one contemplates the countering not of one frame of reference moving in relation to a fixed frame of reference, but of two unfixed frames of reference moving in relation to each other and in relation to the self. One allows oneself to experience these countering motions and their effects but at the same time maintains the neutral stance. The most obvious and clearest example of pure intellectual relativizing in *Paradise Lost* is Adam and Raphael's discussion of astronomy in Book 8. The poet has already in his own earlier references to astronomical structure avoided any commitment to a fixed view. For example, as he describes Uriel returning to heaven after carrying the news of Satan's arrival in the new world to Gabriel, Milton says he proceeds

> . . . downward to the sun now fall'n
> Beneath th'Azores; whether the prime orb,
> Incredible how swift, how thither rolled
> Diurnal, or this less volúble earth
> By shorter flight to th'east, had left him there.
>
> (4: 591–95)[1]

In Adam and Raphael's long discussion, understanding of astronomy in itself is Raphael's secondary purpose: the primary purpose is to detach Adam's sympathic, moral, ideological, and conceptual associations from the astronomical phenomena in order to bring him to an ability and a state of mind in which the truth of astronomy is known in the context of greater truths.

Adam's first comments and questions to Raphael are sympathic:

> When I behold this goodly frame, this world
> Of heav'n and earth consisting, and compute
> Their magnitudes, this earth a spot, a grain,
> An atom, with the firmament compared
> And all her numbered stars, that seem to roll
> Spaces incomprehensible (for such
> Their distance argues and their swift return
> Diurnal) merely to officiate light
> Round this opacous earth, this punctual spot,
> One day and night, in all their vast survey
> Useless besides; reasoning I oft admire
> How Nature wise and frugal could commit
> Such disproportions, with superfluous hand
> So many nobler bodies to create,
> Greater so manifold, to this one use,
> For aught appears, and on their orbs impose
> Such restless revolution day by day
> Repeated, while the sedentary earth,
> That better might with far less compass move,
> Served by more noble than herself attains
> Her end without least motion, and receives
> As tribute, such a sumless journey brought
> Of incorporeal speed, her warmth and light;
> Speed, to describe whose swiftness number fails.
>
> (8: 15–38)

The words Adam chooses, like *admire* and *restless*, which he projects onto cosmological bodies, are sympathic, making the purity of his "reasoning" suspect. Words like *useless, frugal, disproportions, superfluous, sumless,* and *better* are all judgmental, and imply that the stars have intention. In response, Raphael gives Adam exercises, as it were, asking him to set two frames of reference against each other to see both as fixed, both as variable, exercises that teach Adam to "reckon right." The bodies of the universe and their motions may be considered a "book . . . before thee set . . . [to] learn . . . this to attain, whether heav'n move or earth, / Imports not, if thou reckon right" (8: 67–71). Raphael goes on to demonstrate in greater detail this technique of reckoning:

> . . . What if the sun
> Be center to the world, and other stars,
> By his attractive virtue and their own
> Incited, dance about him various rounds?
> Their wand'ring course, now high, now low, then hid,
> Progressive, retrograde, or standing still,
> In six thou seest, and what if the sev'nth to these
> The planet earth, so steadfast though she seem,
> Insensibly three different motions move?
> Which else to several spheres thou must ascribe,
> Moved contrary with thwart obliquities,
> Or save the sun his labor, and that swift
> Nocturnal and diurnal rhomb supposed,
> Invisible else above all stars, the wheel
> Of day and night; which needs not thy belief,
> If earth industrious of herself fetch day
> Traveling east, and with her part averse
> From the sun's beam meet night, her other part
> Still luminous by his ray. What if that light
> Sent from her through the wide transpicuous air,
> To the terrestrial moon be as a star
> Enlightening her by day, as she by night
> This earth, reciprocal.
>
> (8: 122–44)

> Whether the sun predominant in heav'n
> Rise on the earth, or earth rise on the sun,
> He from the east his flaming road begin,
> Or she from west her silent course advance
> With inoffensive pace that spinning sleeps
> On her soft axle, while she paces ev'n,
> And bears thee soft with the smooth air along.
>
> (8: 160–66)

Such considerations are likely to deframe any conceptual structures the mind might construct or refer to in order to understand the motions and to deframe the mind as well. Yet, if the mind retains its neutral stance, it will experience at once a reinforcement of its neutrality and strength and a powerful surge of pure motion or energy.

Raphael uses a slightly different kind of relativizing in the passage commenting upon the speed of his flight from heaven to earth, quoted earlier in chapter 1:

The swiftness of those circles áttribute,
Though numberless, to his omnipotence,
That to corporeal substance could add
Speed almost spiritual; me thou think'st not slow,
Who since the morning hour set out from heav'n
Where God resides, and ere midday arrived
In Eden, distance inexpressible
By numbers that have name.

(8: 107–14)

Here there is a more extreme and more jarring disproportion between rate, time, and distance, a more complex relation of constants and variables. And Raphael goes even further when he increases movement so disproportionately that he wrenches apart the frames of thought that give matter itself its being and certainty. This concept of spiritual speed is perhaps the same as what Adam calls "incorporeal speed," the "warmth and light" of the still sun, a different kind of "motion."

Such kinesthetic contemplation takes Adam and the reader far from the physical shifting that can be felt directly. Raphael uses the word *insensibly* to describe the "three different motions" he is hypothesizing, and it is an insensible kinesthetic motion of the imagination toward which the relativizing of this mode tends, and further, beyond motion felt as disjunctive in the mind too. In the final stage, the mind finds itself in a kind of stillness in motion, or motion in stillness, a state in which point of view and frame of reference have become indeterminate. In this state, one can be aware of the stillness although motion has not ceased because there is no disjunction; and one can be aware of the resonance that the motion has now become, the flow of vibrant energy that in this mode is completely contentless.

The image and feeling of the earth that advances "with inoffensive pace" and that "spinning sleeps / On her soft axle, while she paces ev'n," bearing humanity "soft with the smooth air along," or the image, as Milton puts it at the end of Book 4, of the "pendulous round earth with balanced air / In counterpoise" (4: 1000–1001) bring the mind close to the meditative state. The flow of energy is imaged in the light reflecting "reciprocal" from moon to earth and from earth, the moon's moon, to the moon and in the interinciting "virtue" of sun and stars. In these images of stillness in motion, the kinesthesia and relativizing have not stopped but rather have become adjusted in the right way. The stillness is dependent on the motion, or rather, on the right relation of motions that keeps the stars in their place without Adam's "belief."

There are elsewhere in *Paradise Lost* images of what might be called heavenly kinesthesia, in which the motion is not necessary but is present for the sake of pleasure. The hymns of Adam and Eve in Books 4 and 5 express this kinesthesia both in style and content, and the alternation of night and day in heaven embody the same delight:

> . . . There is a cave
> Within the mount of God, fast by his throne,
> Where light and darkness in perpetual round
> Lodge and dislodge by turns, which makes through heav'n
> Grateful vicissitude, like day and night.
>
> (6: 4–8)

The sexual pleasure enjoyed by the spirits in heaven is perhaps the ultimate expression of this principle: speaking to Adam, in response to his question about love in heaven, Raphael

> . . . with a smile that glowed
> Celestial rosy red, love's proper hue,
> Answered: "Let it suffice thee that thou know'st
> Us happy, and without love no happiness.
> Whatever pure thou in the body enjoy'st
> (And pure thou wert created) we enjoy
> In eminence, and obstacle find none
> Of membrane, joint, or limb, exclusive bars;
> Easier than air with air, if Spirits embrace,
> Total they mix, union of pure with pure
> Desiring; nor restrained conveyance need
> As flesh to mix with flesh, or soul with soul.
>
> (8: 618–29)[2]

After this intellectual relativizing, the first meditative mode may move into a less intellectual stage to experience as an exercise the countering not of abstract concept against abstract concept, but of lyric against ironic, of pity against judgment, of anger against pain, and of justice against injustice. For example, during their discussion of astronomy, Raphael counters Adam's sympathic comments about the planets not only with the pure relativizing "reckoning" just described, but also with the derisive lines about God's "intention" in creating such a complex universe:

> . . . if they list to try
> Conjecture, he his fabric of the heav'ns
> Hath left to their disputes, perhaps to move
> His laughter at their quaint opinions wide
> Hereafter, when they come to model heav'n
> And calculate the stars, how they will wield
> The mighty frames, how build, unbuild, contrive
> To save appearances, how gird the sphere
> With centric and eccentric scribbled o'er,
> Cycle and epicycle, orb in orb.
>
> (8: 75–84)

This is a jolting bit of derision but when the mind has attained to the meditative state imaged by the spinning earth, it can look back and see this derision as an ironic counter to the sympathic trap, as a kind of "counterpoise."

Considered in this way, the comment takes on the neutrality of this mode applied to but detached from feeling. In the same vein, one may contemplate the countering of lyric and ironic in the Proserpine simile, the lyric appearance of flowers in the path of enraged heavenly power, and the seemingly "unjust"—or at least unaccountable—pair of serpent passages in Book 10.

The effects of simple relativizing differ from the solution of tragedy because the exercise specifically includes and makes use of the impasse or deadlock—the counters, neither of which is the viewer him/herself—to spring the mind out of it. The springing out can, further, be the result not only of the disjunction between two answers, but also of the disjunction between question and answer, or of the disjunction between the philosophically inquiring mind and some incisive element in the physical world where the inquiring is taking place—the intrusion of a sound, sight, or movement, like the flowers on the hills of heaven.

The simple relativizing mode brings the reader into an experience of pure motion and energy and to a reinforced neutrality of mind. Furthermore, it more definitively springs the mind from frames into the pure frame of the third space discussed at the end of chapter 2, the space into which the reader suddenly entered in 10: 342–43. This opening of a purely aesthetic space in the mind is necessary to the truly meditative state of mind that one enters in the next mode, complex relativizing, though it does not always occur in such an incisive manner. In this space the reader will experience less perceptual and abstract motions, the motions of yearning purified of sympathic residues in the lyric and ironic modes and purified of lyric and ironic tones themselves. Complex relativizing, while still as neutral as the previous mode, involves all faculties of mind, and instead of being "negative," contentless, empty, or shifting in itself, is wholly positive, combining all tones together in a kind of suspension that is beyond affirming and denying, and beyond the painful and uncertain vicissitudes of the lyric-ironic modal stage.

The Complex Relativizing Mode

While the technique of the preceding mode involved counteracting a motion with another motion and speeding up the sense of motion, and the end result was a release from or cancellation of the anguish of sympathy and judgment and of the lyric and the ironic, the technique of the following mode is rather a slowing up of motion almost to stillness, a calm sojourning in the third space created by distance and maintained by a relaxed discipline, into which are allowed to flow what on another level are painful vicissitudes, and into which flow energy and a quiet joy. The reader thus attains the peace of being filled rather than of release.

Yielding to the magnetism of this third space, as in yielding to the beauty of the elves simile, is not, in this mode, a lyrical or romantic escape, as MacCaffrey and Ferry might imply, a self-indulgent lapse from the world of spirit, for the peasant feels fear as well as joy. The lyric beauty of the whale scene, as discussed above, is countered by erosive ironies, traps for the poetically unwary. The whale is the Satan of the medieval bestiaries, the devil who will draw the unsuspecting Christian to ruinous damnation, as well as an image of salvation. The complex relativizing mode includes such conflict of reference, the beautiful harmony of Mulciber's rhythmic fall from heaven and of the elves' music, and the disciplined clarity of the cold and moonlit world where the "wishèd morn" of daylight understanding "delays." The reader is not indulged: in this world he/she comes to terms with pain, with justice and injustice; in this world more is asked than that he/she follow and obey. Neither the self-identifications of the council in hell nor the fond smugness of the eremites and friars described as the "sport of winds" in the Paradise of Fools (3: 444–97) is tolerated here: the reader is forced into a strength that brings him/her past both piety and the "tough" kind of strength where one says with Eliot's Gerontion, "After such knowledge, what forgiveness?"[3] However, this strength is not so harsh for the reader who has experienced lyric-ironic modality and simple relativizing. He/she is not entering this third space from an ideological perspective like MacCaffrey, being at this point in the declension of mind beyond both conceptual certainties and such expressions of smug despair as Eliot's. Rather the reader experiences and responds to such similes without ideologizing and without pity or despair, but rather with the empathic histrionic sensibility that allows one to yield and move with modal motions without dangerous identifications, a psychic movement that becomes increasingly resonant with these motions, increasingly articulate, and increasingly conscious.

Whereas in simple relativizing the mind maintains a fixed neutral center in its contemplations, in complex relativizing this center is less rigid and less fixed: the neutrality is more a neutrality of mood, almost a central coldness, than of stance. In the first meditative mode, the central stance is necessary because the motions contemplated are often violent. But in the second meditative mode, the movements of meditation and the movements of yearning, occurring more easily in the same space, are less violent and more resonant. The judging and identifying mind is as if suspended in the modal frame, and in this suspension all the motions may pass through it, unobstructed and uncomplicated by affirmation or denial. The less intellectual relativizing of modal and sympathic motions in the final stage of simple relativizing in which the mind is stripped of its mental and emotional positions in relation to them prepares the mind for this neutrality. Yet, unlike simple relativizing, in which the center remains fixed, here the meditative center moves with the modal flows of yearning in order to experience and know them. Though the reader moves with them, he/she does not identify with them: the central neutrality necessary for complete empathy is ensured by the mood of central coldness.

This central coldness is the mood of the moonlit forest where the peasant pauses in his night journey to behold the faery elves, and the mood of the still moonlit night world at sea in the whale simile, its coolness, clarity, silence, and peace. The mind focuses on these images to define its center, and on the simple and restful rhythm of the poetry describing them, on the pause in time and space, and on the absence of any sense of evil or malice. The neutrality and clarity of these similes is distant from their references. It is the neutrality of the uncompelled spirit.

The central coldness is, more emphatically and less lyrically, the mood evoked by Michael's image of paradise after the flood described to Adam in Book 11:

> . . . then shall this mount
> Of Paradise by might of waves be moved
> Out of his place, pushed by the hornèd flood,
> With all his verdure spoiled and trees adrift
> Down the great river to the op'ning gulf,
> And there take root an island salt and bare,
> The haunt of seals and orcs, and sea-mews' clang.
>
> (11: 829–35)

In the complex meditative mode, this cold and spare paradise replaces the warmer and more luxuriant Paradise of Books 4 and 5.

Safeguarded by this central coldness, the mind in meditation moves into the lyric-ironic motions within the third space defined by the similes that, though their references may be inconstant, themselves delineate a separate world. Whereas the relativizing of the first meditative mode was related to the physical kinesthesia of motion and point of view discussed in chapter 1, the relativizing of the complex meditative mode is related to the shifts in tone and simile. In these meditative motions, the reader experiences the clearcut beauty and joy of the reviving fields (2: 488–95), the harmonious ease of the Mulciber simile (1: 740–46), the stricken poignancy of the autumn leaves (1: 300–304), the pleasure of "the spicy shore / Of Araby the Blest" (4: 159–64), the humorously ironic confusion of the pilgrims "blown transverse" by "violent cross-winds from either coast" of the Paradise of Fools (3: 463–97), and the temporary rest of the sea-worn sailors calmed by the sound of the hollow rocks in the shelter of an unexpected harbor:

> . . . as when hollow rocks retain
> The sound of blust'ring winds, which all night long
> Had roused the sea, now with hoarse cadence lull
> Seafaring men o'erwatched, whose bark by chance
> Or pinnace anchors in a craggy bay
> After the tempest.
>
> (2: 285–90)

The small figures in this world characterized by various and varying points and motions of the lyric and ironic modes are many of them pilots and are all of them journeyers or wanderers, like the peasants or like Galileo in his intellectual journeys of discovery through the heavens framed and revealed in his telescope, looking for a port, a harbor, a shore, a home, for peace and rest and fulfillment in their voyages on the seas of yearning. But the pilots never reach a final port: they are always pictured just outside the port, or at a temporary harboring, or in the moment of journeying. The wanderings aptly image the mind as in its meditations it becomes impressed with the different modal motions and becomes articulated into greater consciousness. The journey never ends: the motions unanchor pilot and mind from permanent attachments. Even at the moment of greatest pause, the temporarily anchored ship rides the motion of the waves and the wondering heart moves with joy and fear and must be balanced by such motions. The pilot may not finally anchor, yet by the same token the pilot anchored to the false island does not sink with the whale diving at dawn, for he is seen sailing again in later similes.

As the mind is progressively both detached from modal positions and articulated by modal motions, its cold center is reinforced, giving it greater strength to experience more closely the objects of its meditation in empathic knowledge, and to allow the mind to move into rougher seas, first into the sympathic motions in the world outside the world of the similes in the epic dimension of the poem, then last into the world outside the poem. In this final stage of the declension of mind, the mind gradually develops a self-consciousness and control that allow it to adjust its neutrality in relation to empathic identification with the object of meditation, and to choose its meditations by choosing and adjusting its focus of attention. The meditative activity resulting from such self-consciousness and control yields the mind, not a vague and mystical ecstasy or quietistic transcendence, but rather the finest and most delicate discriminations in perception and then later in action, when it returns to the dimension of affirmation and denial.

This self-conscious mind in meditation centrally focuses not on the pains or violence or inconstancy of the pilots' and peasants' never-ending wanderings, but on another aspect of these images: on their quality of relief, of pause even in the journeying, of suspension. For in this world space is suspended—"by a forest side or fountain." Time is balanced or stopped: the faery elves' revels are at midnight; Michael pauses in his teaching of Adam "As one who in his journey bates at noon, / Though bent on speed" (12: 1–2); "wishèd morn delays" for the seamen moored on the whale; the seamen at the smell of the spicy shore "slack their course." Both fate and free will are suspended: the seafarers find their harbor "by chance," the whale is "haply slumb'ring on the Norway foam." Emotions and judgment are suspended: the peasant "sees or dreams he sees," feels both "joy and fear"; the giant or small devils look like bees, or dwarves, or pygmies, or elves. It is the mind on a "point of balance," to use Geoffrey Hartman's words, that is evoked.[4]

The mind of Aeneas, present by implication in the bees simile as he overlooks the city of Carthage, is balanced between past and future, between pain and promise as he ponders his longing and his destiny. The peasant's mind, mimetically represented, is balanced, suspended, as he wonders whether he sees or dreams the elves, and as he wonders what they might mean. Galileo's mind is suspended between "descry" and "imagine" (1: 290 and 5: 262–63) as he observes the "new lands" on the moon. And the careful ploughman, another peasant at the end of Book 4, balances between hope and doubt, wheat and chaff, as he ponders his crop, bending indefinitely "which way the wind sways" it:

> While thus he spake [Satan to Gabriel], th'angelic squadron bright
> Turned, fiery red, sharp'ning in moonèd horns
> Their phalanx, and began to hem him round
> With ported spears, as thick as when a field
> Of Ceres ripe for harvest waving bends
> Her bearded grove of ears, which way the wind
> Sways them; the careful ploughman doubting stands
> Lest on the threshing-floor his hopeful sheaves
> Prove chaff.
>
> (4: 977–85)

The wind's different directions and the wheat bending to its movement image the vicissitudes of the universe and the meanings and judgments attached to them, but also image the mind as it is yielding to all these motions, calmly relativizing them. The careful ploughman images this suspended mind that "affirms" or "denies" none of them.

It is the same mind that in an unimaged representation is suspended from the battles of hell in the rhythm of Mulciber's fall; it is the reader's mind, the human mind, the human psyche in general. As was discussed in chapter 1, often the point of view in *Paradise Lost* is not simply distanced but is displaced in the similes from the characters of the epic drama, and from the mind involved in this drama, to a new figure. The point of view comes to rest in a small, quiet, undramatic figure in a different space, a different world. But often the same displacement into the third space occurs without there being any designated viewer or place, and the focus falls on the mind as it is balancing, on the motions of the balancing mind rather than on the mind imaged as an entity or person.

This third world is neither within nor without; its images are indeterminate in the official epic and theological schema of *Paradise Lost*. It exists in the motions and flow evoked by the images—hence the image of journeying—attached to or wrenched by neither inner nor outer, neither the identifying self nor the external dictates of ideology, calmly and finely suspended amidst all their motions, the still mind in graceful contemplation.

The meditative mind does not follow or "obey" the objects and images of its meditation, but obeys only its neutral center and its desire to rightly know the motions of yearning, the only "service" required of Adam and Eve by God. Whether Uriel imaged as a shooting star in conjunction with the dangerous "vapors fired," which in another simile image Satan, is "good" or "evil" is less relevant than the observer's attitude in relation to the star and vapors. In this simile Milton has significantly included the observer, another pilot:

> Thither came Uriel, gliding through the even
> On a sunbeam, swift as a shooting star
> In autumn thwarts the night, when vapors fired
> Impress the air, and shows the mariner
> From what point of his compass to beware
> Impetuous winds.
>
> (4: 555–60)

Here the perceiver of the stars, the mariner's mind doubting and weighing, is represented, as well as the stars and vapors. How should it interpret the signs and images? Although the good Uriel appears in a scene with evil vapors and impetuous winds, the mariner makes distinctions and uses the star as a guide in his imperiled journey. It is a point on his compass, an epistemological measuring device rather than an ontological ground to throw his anchor on. The "goodness" of Uriel consists in his perceptual usefulness: the mariner is neither stricken by terror at the fired vapors, like the perplexed monarchs beholding the eclipse in 1: 594–99, nor fascinated, mesmerized, and allured to follow them or the star, like the peasant in Book 9 or like one-third of the heavenly angels in Book 5 beholding the beautiful Satan-Lucifer:

> His count'nance, as the morning star that guides
> The starry flock, allured them, and with lies
> Drew after him the third part of heav'n's host.
>
> (5: 708–10)

It is not so much the identity of the tenor—is it Uriel or is it Satan?—that is the cause of destruction, of "evil," or even its quality—is it beautiful or is it terrifying? It is the viewer's response and relation to it that are determining. Unmeditated ontological identifications belong to the sympathic state of mind; the meditative mind would choose to focus on the beauty, the mood of the morning star, without being drawn after it, a response that would allow the right perception of Satan and that would neutralize and protect the mind from the evil. Satan not followed is not evil.

The rest and peace sought by the journeying figures is not a place, a harbor, or a port, but a state of mind. The pilots and peasants in *Paradise Lost* never reach home; their journeys never end in this sense. The way to

Cathay, to the sweet spicy shores of a paradise sought by many of Milton's mariners, is blocked in Book 10:

> As when two polar winds blowing adverse
> Upon the Cronian Sea, together drive
> Mountains of ice, that stop th'imagined way
> Beyond Pestora eastward, to the rich
> Cathaian coast.
>
> (10: 289–93)

It is the pilot who has achieved the meditative state of mind who finds himself, still in motion, aligned with the forces within and around him, the winds, the mists, and the fires. The Chinese on the "windy sea of land" in Book 3, unlike the fools that are blown to the Paradise of Fools that is the official referent, in the cold and barren space of meditative wisdom build their wagons of cane, erect sails, and use the winds to propel them:

> [Satan] . . . lights on the barren plains
> Of Sericana, where Chineses drive
> With sails and wind their cany wagons light:
> So on this windy sea of land, the Fiend
> Walked up and down alone bent on his prey.
>
> (3: 437–41)

However, it is not the consciously skillful, the shrewd, the expedient mind that attains to an effortless alignment with the motions of the universe: the Satan-mariner in Book 9: 513–16, varying his every move with the river's wind, has no meditative center. For such opportunists the winds become quickly treacherous. True resonance is for those who might be "unskilful," like Adam and Eve sending their prayers to God in 11: 32, but who are detached from the identifications of ontology and self as well as of empirical gain, for those centered in the meditative space—like the "laborer . . . homeward returning" in the closing lines of the poem, for whom the "metéorous" power of God and devil alike might "gather fast" like a fired swamp mist around him, but at his heel, and for whom the fierceness of comets guides and protects, because his chief guide is the providence of his state of mind:

> . . . all in bright array
> The Cherubim descended; on the ground
> Gliding metéorous, as ev'ning mist
> Ris'n from the river o'er the marish glides,
> And gathers ground fast at the laborer's heel
> Homeward returning. High in front advanced,
> The brandished sword of God before them blazed
> Fierce as a comet.
>
> (12: 627–34)

The provident mind has for a time become a world itself, a third space with landscapes, its own time, seasons, and weather, with farms and towns, harbors and ships, and beings peopling it. The absence of a final port, or anchoring of meaning, allows and ensures the existence of such a world. The provident mind is, in Wallace Stevens's words, the "mind of winter," which beholds the winter landscape without identifying with its misery, beholds the nothingness of misery—beholds the bare place relieved of the sympathic— and then hears, in its "inhuman meditation," the protecting and confining watchdogs gone, the sound of the land, the sound of the wind, the sound of the leaves. The mind by moonlight in the third space has come to peace and clarity of vision where the points of the compass are plain, and where the world of both matter and spirit is clearly perceived. It is a "new knowledge of reality."[5]

The Meditative Perspective

After the complex relativizing mode the meditative state of mind becomes more than something temporary that one works oneself into through the techniques of aesthetic distancing that constitute the declension of mind. It becomes the mind's nature or state of being. Beyond disjunction, tension, the instability of metamorphosis, relativizing, or suspension, the union desired with the absolute is restored in the psyche, in the soul; but it is the union of reciprocity, not of possession or identification. The joy of this union is a real joy, though not the joy as desired and imagined in the lyric-ironic state—a possessed and ecstatic joy. It is, rather, almost a by-product of the meditative state.

If the final state of mind in simple relativizing could be imaged by the spinning earth, the earth in counterpoise, the final state of mind in complex relativizing can be imaged by the "self-balanced" earth (7: 242), or the earth "upon her center poised" (5: 579). The flying bird of Marvell's prefatory poem is the meditative song of the bird "in shadiest covert hid," wakefully "tuning her nocturnal note" as she receives the celestial light of meditative vision to "irradiate" her "mind through all her powers," the meditative "thoughts" that, rightly attuned, "voluntary move / Harmonious numbers" (3: 37–55). And this meditating bird-poet evokes the image of the bird who "with mighty wings outspread / Dove-like sat'st brooding on the vast abyss / And mad'st it pregnant" (1: 20–22). In the meditations of both birds appear the worlds of "flocks" and "herds" and "human face divine" invisible to the sight of common day that mourns their loss (3: 44). It is the breaking of the union of reciprocity that allows this vision that is the sin of disobedience in *Paradise Lost*. Union is broken when its nature is misunderstood, when it is confused with possession and absoluteness, which then, because it is not absolute, arouses fear in its apparent indeterminacy.

Of course, once broken, the fear might be greater, for one often identifies most intensely with what is lost or missing. But, as experienced poetically through Milton's counterplot, it is possible to regain in the psyche the reciprocity lost in actuality in the falls. There may be lapses, but these need only be temporary. Sometimes it is necessary to repeat the experiences of the declension of mind again and again to maintain the articulations of vision.

Yet the recovered reciprocity is not wholly limited to the psyche, though this may be the first stage. The psychic vibrations, as it were, of the reciprocity, aligned with those of the universe, pull the being toward a new resonance with and a new participation in its manifestations, its pains and desires, its ideas and its works. In this way the desired reciprocity is also restored in the life-space, in the world that is the subject of epic. The meditative state of mind that it was the task of the counterplot to instill in the reader now becomes a perspective in or from which to perceive and act in the world. This perspective allows one to experience and participate in—not identify with—its vicissitudes without being torn apart by sympathic disjunctions. This new resonance is creative and moving, for it has a certain power to affect and direct the flows and forces it resonates with, provided that one uses one's wisdom to adjudge what is the "necessary thing at the necessary moment."[6]

This perspective is providence, the guide instilled in the reader's mind by the "justifying" of Milton's counterplot. It is this guide that Adam, in the passage quoted above, by loving God with fear and walking as in his presence will "ever . . . observe" (12: 562–64); and it is this guide that Adam and Eve take with them as they descend from Paradise into the plain of the world before them (12: 638–49).

The energy of the purified modal and sympathic motions becomes resonant and creative energy—a kinesis—that, with a sense of necessity that the heavenly stillness-in-motion curiously lacks, forces itself of its own nature down into the faculties, the mind, the body, the senses, "infusing" its "vital virtue" almost like the first creative energy of God (7: 236), into the art, the works, and the life of humankind. This art in *Paradise Lost,* this movement and declension spiritualizing the human psyche, is a true aesthetic, neither detached from the vital concerns of human life in body, feeling, thought, and soul and frozen into any final stasis or form, nor embedded in an unmeditated identification with them.

The human imagination struggling to find, to create, and communicate such an aesthetic is a powerful force, a force different from but perhaps equal in value to the power of the angels. Angelic beings have the power to destroy the creation. Humans do not; they are too frail. But, helpless to resolve the discords of heaven, the heavens anxiously wait and watch humankind in the earthly "theater." The war in heaven had no resolution; the Son's use of measured force stopped it temporarily, but as Gabriel says at the end of Book 4, war could start again at any time. This problem has been transferred to humanity because, though humans might be frail, their frailty gives them, or forces them to develop, another power: the imagination. Not just their reason, for humans are like the angels, unable to discern hypocrisy, but their imagination, the third space in which they can live, and thus come to know, without committing unmeditated and irreversible actions. The best solution, and maybe the only possible one, lies in the strength of this strange power of human imagining, a strength the angels do not seem to have in the same degree, perhaps because they are so powerful that they can and do act at any time, according to their will as much as to their understanding.

Human being may resent this intrusion on his/her innocent bliss but, since it is not simply by reason of punishment or even intention that he/she is given this task, but rather by reason of the potential of human nature, he/she must accept the burden whose evolvement will correspond to his/her own yearnings. So, after some initial pain and struggle, the reader enters into modality and begins the journey in the third space of the imagination, a space presided over not by the sun of the angels nor by the earth of human being, but by that secret "arbitress," the moon, the "ponderous shield" of art, the moon reflecting the sun's light to earth, the human mind, reflecting, pondering, weighing, meditating.

NOTES

1. See also 3: 574–76.
2. See also 1: 423–31 and 6: 350–53.
3. T. S. Eliot, "Gerontion," in *The Complete Poems and Plays, 1909–1950* (New York: Harcourt, Brace and World, Inc., 1952), pp. 21–23.
4. Geoffrey Hartman, "Milton's Counterplot," p. 121.
5. Wallace Stevens, "The Snow Man," pp. 9–10; "The World as Meditation," pp. 520–21; "Not Ideas About the Thing but the Thing Itself," p. 534, in *The Collected Poems of Wallace Stevens* (New York: Alfred A. Knopf, 1967).
6. Gorgias, in Kathleen Freeman, *Ancilla to the Pre-Socratic Philosophers: a Complete Translation of the Fragments in Diels' "Fragmente der Vorsokratiker"* (Cambridge, Mass.: Harvard University Press, 1948), p. 130.

PART II: Flight toward Reality: A Modal Reading of *Paradise Lost*

The progress of the mind's journey through the declension of mind in the third space of the imagination urged by Milton's counterplot begins with the sympathic conflicts in the epic-theological dimension of the poem. In this stage, as discussed above, there is a progression of mind through a first redefinition of the conflict between good and evil into a conflict between anger and pain, a redefinition that leads to a second redefinition of the sympathic agony as a conflict between pity and judgment. This final conflict is a turning point into modality: the mind, in a first impulse toward self-consciousness, relaxes its ideological struggles to pause and consider its own attitudes in relation to them.

As it actually appears in concrete instances in *Paradise Lost,* lyric and ironic modality does not correspond exactly to the lyric-ironic paradigm given above because, although lyric-ironic modality is a separate stage in the declension of mind, in the poem itself the lyric and ironic modes are not completely isolated from the sympathic mode that precedes them and, more especially, from the relativizing modes that follow and supersede them. Perhaps because of the tendency of literary forms to seek resolutions in intermediates that often receive their sanction from isolated lyricism or irony, Milton explicitly foregrounds their insufficiency even as he necessarily uses them to shift the mind out of the falsity of sympathic structures and to imprint on it the first motions of modality. In *Paradise Lost* lyric and ironic are an intermediate stage in a movement that must continue into the meditation of the relativizing modes in order to find the true consciousness and peace that lie beyond. Hence Milton's lyric similes, for example, do not provide the simple pleasure and peace of, say, Homer's similes in the *Iliad,* but are rendered complex by ambiguities, by a cross-countering of referential elements and tones both within the simile and in its relations to other parts of the poem, and often by the predominance of the cold tone proper to the meditative modes over the warmer tone that one might ordinarily associate with the lyric mode. Similarly, Milton's ironic mode is already moving beyond the humor and bitterness usually characteristic of irony into an almost toneless disconnectedness. This disconnectedness represents the nonabsolute relation between desirer and desired itself as well as an attitude of perplexity and wondering that lies between the ironic attitudes of the desirer, which are still partly determined by the conceived nature of the absolute and its attainment, and the neutrality and consciousness of the relativizing modes.

The mind's experience of the final stage in the declension of mind, the meditative modes, does correspond to the description of them given in chapter 4 above, for their nature made it impossible to give a paradigm in the first place. Whereas the lyric and ironic modality in *Paradise Lost* defines itself partly in relation to a lyric-ironic modality existing outside the poem in a cultural and spiritual context, a lyric-ironic modality for which it was valid to give a paradigm, Milton's meditative modality, a less commonly shared experience of mind, defines itself more in its own context and out of its own materials. Therefore it is difficult to frame it in a paradigm. Moreover, such framing is difficult because meditation is an experience whose "answers" are almost a by-product of the experience, an experience that contemplates and moves with images, tones, and flows of force closer to the motions of poetry, and therefore is best "explained" through reference to the instances of this poetry in *Paradise Lost* rather than through reference to a paradigm. Thus, in the reading that follows, the lyric-ironic stage will differ from its discussion above, while the meditative stage will resemble but elaborate upon its discussion in Part I.

The progress of the declension of mind does not correspond exactly to the sequence of instances of aesthetic distancing as they appear in the poem. A device most characteristic of complex relativizing may appear in Book 1 and an instance of sympathic conflict may appear in a later book. This discrepancy results from the complex relations between the various sequences in *Paradise Lost*—story, plot, counterplot, and declension of mind—the totality of whose relations determines the overall "plot." As the mind begins to discover in its reading of the poem, the overall plot cannot be limited to any single one of these sequences. These relations and the plot they reveal will be discussed in their appropriate places as the modal reading unfolds in the following chapters, yet two things must be said here to explain the inclusion of the long sections on the falls—apparently part of the epic plot and not the counterplot—in this reading. First, the causal springs of the epic action itself are revealed to be certain modal concerns; and second, the overall plot that clearly enough begins with God's creating heaven and the angels ends with the reader, in the world into which Book 12 exits, beginning to read *Paradise Lost* in Book 1. His/her reading is a necessity for which the epic and the reality it represents yearn, yet this necessity the reader cannot know until he/she has read and understood the poem.

5　The Lyric Mode

In its first impulse the lyric mode distances the reader from the hellish sympathic conflicts of the epic dimension and acquaints him/her with the two poles of the lyric continuum and all the points between. One of the clearest instances of this lyric shift and the impression it makes on the mind is the simile comparing the fallen angels to autumn leaves:

> Natheless he [Satan] so endured, till on the beach
> Of that inflamèd sea, he stood and called
> His legions, angel forms, who lay entranced,
> Thick as autumnal leaves that strow the brooks
> In Vallombrosa, where th'Etrurian shades
> High over-arched embow'r.
>
> (1: 299–304)

The poignancy of this passage is not the pain that asks for an action or response as the anger of the editorial comment following the whale simile might ask for judgment against Satan, or as the picture of Satan's tear-streaked and thunder-scarred face might ask for pity. Both of these responses are more rhetorical—tending out of words toward action—than poetic—tending toward consciousness. In the simile it is rather the sense of loss and the yearning for the object of loss that are evoked, accepted, and focused upon, separately from the moral status of either the sufferer or the observer. The image, rhythm, tone, and diction reinforce one another to express the fallen angels' state of mind: the pain of hell itself is felt less than the loss of heaven and their yearning for it in its absence. The "thought both of lost happiness and pain," as Milton expresses it in 1: 54–55, torments them more than the nine days' fall, the adamantine chains, or the penal fire (1: 44–53). The autumn-leaves simile is a moment of stillness and pause. Now that the distracting commotion of epic battle is over, the angels are "entranced," "amazed," and "astonished" at their "hideous change" (1: 301–17): it is a moment of dawning insight in which they see clearly, whether they precisely understand it or not, their attitude and feeling about their position, which corresponds to their physical position—"abject and lost." Satan must be aware that this moment of entrancement and stillness might open into the third space, might lead his followers to a more conscious insight, out of the sympathic frame where he operates and into the modal frame. For the first

111

thing he does is to parody their posture and astonishment to make them spring up into the physical stance of "duty," battle and rhetoric, which will then recall the desired mental stance of anger and pain (1: 315–38).

The focus on attitude in this simile signals the shift into modality. In the third space the angels are distanced for a brief moment from their strict punishment and also from what is personal or specific to their situation: the leaves belong to the inhuman, neutral world of nature, like the whale and the craggy bay. We do not pity leaves and judge whales. Moreover, this image is drawn from the world of the poet and reader, making this poetic space a space of shared minds, mind, or the human psyche in general. The "reality" of this space is this psyche's mode of perceiving, thinking, and feeling, the nature of its motions in that fluid modal dimension curiously existing "behind" the punishment and its sting, behind the ideologizing faculty that fixes itself in the sympathic structure.

In the leaves simile the desirer is in the yielding, receptive state proper to lyric (reflected in both posture and tone), and the lyric flow or connection of the felt possibility of fulfillment supersedes any question of action or control. It is as if the yearning evokes the love desired, its source, the "happy realms of light" as much as its loss. Yet the simile is at the pole of pain since its absence in "reality" is stressed.

The simile of the reviving fields in 2: 488–95, on the other hand is one of the most joyful passages in *Paradise Lost,* and it takes the reader out of the sympathic dimension to the other end of the lyric continuum. Though it is not the absolute joy imagined in the lyric structure, this simile embodies a delight in which lesser joys are focused on—on the fallen angels' love for each other—and in which the fleetingness of joy—the sun is the evening sun—is accepted. Yet within these well-defined limits the delight is undiluted. This is not the pleasure of the beautiful, though it is a beautiful simile, because it lacks even the consciousness of tragedy's end. However, as the counterplot does not move in neat stages, this simile can be experienced at different stages with different implications given it by the context of the mind reading it.

The beauty in the Mulciber simile quoted above, the "Dorian mood" of the fallen angels trooping past their leader Satan playing flutes and recorders that can "mitigate and suage / With solemn touches troubled thoughts" (1: 550–60), and the fallen angels' Olympic games, song, and sweet philosophical discourse that "suspend hell" in 2: 521–69, belong close to the same pole of lyric joy.

In between these two similes evoking lyric pain and lyric joy fall instances of aesthetic distancing like the simile of the mariner in 4: 555–60, the simile of the sea-weary sailors anchoring in the craggy bay (2: 284–90), the pilot-whale simile, and the peasant-elves simile. In the first of these similes, it is the mind moving uncertainly on the seas of yearning that is imaged. The simile of the Chinese wagons sailing on the "barren plains / Of Sericana"

likewise images the mind journeying, but it also images the more fully conscious meditative mind moving in resonance with the forces around it. The
scene is so cold and bare that yearning alone seems to occupy it, undisturbed
even by reminders of the good desired or by its distance. It is a "pure" image
and a pure tone because the good is "present" neither in reality nor in
evocation; the detached yearning itself fills the poetic space. This simile may
thus be said to exist in both the lyric and meditative stages of the declension
of mind. In the craggy-bay, whale, and elves similes are imaged a moment of
rest from this journeying and a growing consciousness of the motions of
yearning. The "blustering winds" and the travails they have caused the
seafarers have died down, and the seafarers have found shelter. But the
temporariness of this peace, which they found only "by chance," keeps it in
the realm of fluidity, not of fulfillment.

While the lyric mode serves to distance the reader from the conflicts of the
epic-theological dimension and to acquaint him/her with its own continuum,
it simultaneously serves to introduce him/her to the third space. A single
simile shifts the reader into its own particular space; but because this space
is modal, the inherent fluidity of mode links any one point on the lyric
continuum to every other point, and thus links any one space to every other
simile space. The spaces opened into by the counterplot are one world.
When the reader enters into the space of a simile, he/she enters a world that
is not simply a vague "somewhere" providing relief far away from the heated
epic, but a world positively defined in terms of its own space, time, and point
of view, often represented by a figure or small "character"; its own rhythm,
tone, and mood; and most tangibly in terms of images that further fill out its
dimensions. In the simile of the reviving fields, the herds of sheep might
evoke shepherds, or the evening evoke lights coming on, fires being lit, and
the like. But more than such evocations of particular similes, this new reality
takes on a greater power and permanence because Milton returns to it in
simile after simile throughout *Paradise Lost*. The different views of it may
vary in detail, completeness, and specific mood; but in their varying they
touch all the points on the same lyric continuum, imprinting all its aspects on
the reader's mind and imprinting all aspects of this new world until it becomes comfortable and familiar.

The small figures who appear repeatedly throughout the poem are similar.
Most of them are wanderers, sharing the same concerns, the same yearning
for a port or home, confronting similar obstacles in their journeys such as
darkness or winds, and directing their courses in relation to similar guides,
such as the moon and stars. The night-foundered pilot anchored to the
whale, the sea-worn sailors anchored in the craggy bay, the Chinese sailing
their "cany wagons," the mariner watching the "vapors fired," and the
sailors "slacking their course" to savor the "odors from the spicy shore / Of
Araby the Blest" (4: 159–64), have all been mentioned in the course of earlier
discussions. In all these similes it is their lyric qualities that are fore-

grounded: in the last simile, although it is Satan as he approaches Eden on his mission of revenge who is the tenor, this sinister truth fades before the delight of the simile. In some of his similes Milton further achieves a feeling of great spaciousness, as in the simile comparing Satan to a fleet as he begins his journey out of hell:

> As when far off at sea a fleet descried
> Hangs in the clouds, by equinoctial winds
> Close sailing from Bengala, or the isles
> Of Ternate and Tidore, whence merchants bring
> Their spicy drugs: they on the trading flood
> Through the wide Ethiopian to the Cape
> Ply stemming nightly toward the pole. So seemed
> Far off the flying Fiend.
>
> (2: 636–43)

The geographical names that Milton specifies in this simile and others like it—cold Norway, exotic and warm Bengala, Ternate, and Tidore, the yet further Cape and Pole; the various placing of the anchored ships; and the wide-ranging movement of the sailing ones give this world great scope and a sense of the freedom of space.

Yet despite their apparent promise, the richness of the spicy drugs and the spaciousness of this world remain in the modal dimension: the distance of the desired goal, the time—night—and the dimness of the visual perception—"far off," "hangs in the clouds"—keep the simile fluidly distant from the attainment of the imagined possession or arrival.

Satan is the image of a ship metaphorically as well as in simile as he "sails" in the air on his journey out of hell, through chaos, and toward the newly created earth. He is pictured in Book 2: 918–28, standing on the brink of hell and looking out over the "sea" of chaos, "pondering his voyage" and about to spread his "sail-broad vans / For flight," hoping his "sea . . . [will] find a shore" (2: 1011). The struggles of his journey are likened to Jason's passage between the "justling rocks" and Ulysses' passage between Scylla and Charybdis (2: 1017–20). As he leaves chaos and catches sight of heaven's light he is likened to the "weatherbeaten vessel . . . hold[ing] / Gladly the port, though shrouds and tackle torn" (2: 1043–44). These metaphors and similes picture first the struggle and pain of the voyage, perhaps the storms of the sympathic mode, and then at the last the rest of the harbor not far off. Although Satan is officially evil, the spaciousness of the world in the similes, the evocation of yearning, and the focus on the pleasure dimly perceived in the distance have spilled over into the dimension of the epic, serving to characterize an epic character as well as a small figure. The "glimmering dawn" of the "sacred influence / Of light" (2: 1034–37) and the frail orb of the earth seen far off "as a star / Of smallest magnitude" (2: 1053–54), like the fleet hanging in the clouds, is perceived almost at the periphery of consciousness that merges into the realm of the intuitive or meditative, perhaps shar-ing the same space as the wished morn in the whale simile or the light of the moon in the elves simile.

Raphael like Satan is pictured as sailing in flight—"through the vast ethereal sky [he] / Sails between worlds and worlds" (5: 267–68). Yet in two linked similes he is differentiated in his flight, first from the "less assured" Galileo and then from another pilot dimly perceiving in the distance of the Aegean a "cloudy spot"—the port, the garden of Eden (5: 260–66). Raphael flies and sees swiftly and directly, whereas Galileo is pictured "seeing" in the pause of his imagination and the pilot is pictured beholding the object of vision from a distance.

Some other wanderers who appear with less frequency than the pilots are scouts, explorers, and pioneers. The scout in 3: 543–51, like the pilots, has traveled through a dark and perilous night and then at dawn sees unexpect-edly from the brow of a hill "the goodly prospect of some foreign land" or a "metropolis with glistering spires" gilded by the beams of the rising sun. The quality of the images—they are clear, no longer dimly seen—and the unex-pectedness of the sight make it similar to the delight of the reviving fields. Found by chance like the craggy bay or the whale-island, it is apparently not planned for in the ideological scheme of things; it is, as in other similes, a world the poem turns into as around a corner.

In 1: 675–78, the fallen angels digging for gold are likened to pioneers digging to set up camp. In 2: 570–618, the squadrons of devils roving over the hot and frozen continents of hell to escape or at least distract themselves from their pain are pictured as explorers, in a fruitless journey that places them at the painful pole of lyric, for as they view their "lamentable lot" they find "no rest" (2: 617–18).

A happier wanderer with lesser concerns is the Wordsworthian figure in 9: 445–54, who "long in populous city pent" goes out on "a summer's morn" into the countryside and savors its delights—"the smell of grain, or tedded grass, or kine, / Or dairy, each rural sight, each rural sound."

Another wanderer, both on sea and land, is Aeneas, evoked in the simile likening the devils, who have just built their infernal palace, to the bees. These bees, image of social humanity, themselves recall the passage in Virgil's *Aeneid* (6: 451–54) where Aeneas gazes down at Dido's Carthage, a city in the process of thriving construction, which is an image of life and fulfillment on the one hand, but also of yearning, since Aeneas is still far from Italy and the future city he is destined to build. Aeneas is still a wan-derer who must return to the stormy seas as a pilot before he will reach his own port.

The counterpart of the pilot, wanderer on the sea, is the peasant, who although he may have a home, is always imaged in a homeward journey in his numerous appearances in *Paradise Lost*. He first appears at the end of the simile chain that begins with the bees, as, bound for home, he watches and listens to the elves' dancing and music. He appears again as the "amazed night-wanderer" deluded and frightened by the mists in 9: 634–42, and as the more hopeful "laborer. . . / Homeward returning" in 12: 631–32. In the epic dimension of the poem Adam is represented as a reaper in 9: 838–42: delighted by the prospect of his wandering Eve's return, he has made a wreath of flowers to crown her his "harvest queen." But soon, as he hears of her trespass, "from his slack hand the garland wreathed for Eve / Down dropped, and all the faded roses shed" (9: 892–93).

The counterpart of both pilot and peasant is Galileo, a wanderer in the realm of the distant heavens—or is it in the realm of mind? He appears three times in *Paradise Lost:* in 1: 288–91, gazing at the moon through his telescope; in 3: 588–90, looking at sunspots; and in 5: 261–63, when, "less assured" than Raphael, he perceives "lands and regions in the moon" with that part of the mind between distant vision and imagination.

Some of the representations of Satan as a ship and the representation of Adam as a reaper, occurring in the epic dimension rather than in the third space, operate more like the usual simile, in which vehicle reinforces tenor and in which there is no shifting or uplifting, and they do not have the same effect on the reader's mind as the other, perhaps more properly "Miltonic," similes. They remain in the epic dimension rather than moving into the modal dimension. However, as mentioned above, the Miltonic simile colors these more ordinary similes, drawing the epic toward the third space; and conversely, the doubling of the pilot and peasant images in the dimension of epic plot has the effect of discursively reinforcing and sanctioning what is occurring in the counterplot.

Such metaphorical doubling occurs throughout *Paradise Lost.* Thus Satan, lying in the fiery gulf, says to Beelzebub:

> . . . Thither let us tend
> From off the tossing of these fiery waves,
> There rest, if any rest can harbor there.
>
> (1: 183–85)

Later, as Satan leaves chaos behind, Milton describes him as "glad that now his sea should find a shore" (2: 1011). Adam and Eve after their fall suffer inner "storms" in a passage whose wording quite explicitly defines the mind as the "region" or space in which the storms of the similes occur:

> They sat them down to weep; nor only tears
> Rained at their eyes, but high winds worse within
> Began to rise, high passions, anger, hate,
> Mistrust, suspicion, discord, and shook sore
> Their inward state of mind, calm region once
> And full of peace, now tossed and turbulent.
>
> (9: 1121–26)

In his anguished soliloquy in Book 10, Adam "in a troubled sea of passion tossed" (10: 718), attempts to navigate, like Satan, through what he calls an "abyss of fears / And horrors" (10: 842–43).

The modal wandering that is occurring in the counterplot, and the wandering, sometimes sympathically anguished, that is occurring metaphorically in the epic dimension, both in action and thought, is the wandering of the poet's and reader's minds that is imaged, less literally than in some of the pilot and peasant similes, in Galileo's explorations. This wandering is a theme that is sometimes expressed discursively in the poem. For example, in the invocation to Book 7, Milton fears he will fall from his flight like Bellerophon on "th'Aleian field. . . / Erroneous there to wander and forlorn" (7: 19–20). This wandering is deluded, lost, or uncertain. A wandering with a less definite direction is the "wandering appetite" of Adam and Eve, mentioned in the same invocation (7: 49–50). Eve's fancy wanders in her dream in Book 5, and she does "wander" in 9: 1136. "Wandering thoughts," as Adam says, may seek "anxious cares" (8: 185–87). They may delude and lead one into danger, but not necessarily. As Adam tells Eve after her strangely thrilling but disquieting dream, even evil may wander in and out of the mind if it is not "harbored" (5: 99).

The wandering that does not harbor, but continues its modal journey into the meditative modes, becomes the balancing and balanced meditation of the ploughman-peasant who ponders his wheat at the end of Book 4 and the consonant sailing of the Chinese boats finely attuned to the "windy sea of land"—to air, water, and earth.

Milton's lyric mode itself ensures that the journey will continue: while it initially offers relief from sympathic conflicts and initiates the reader into a new and separate world, in its final impulse it also impresses upon him/her the inherent unceasing fluidity of this world that will allow no final fulfillment or resting-place, and that will become dangerous to those who seek such fulfillment.

As discussed earlier in chapter 2, it is not possible to fix any "meaning" to the simile world—or even to an individual simile—by referring to the tenor, because the relations between the various vehicles and tenors are not consistent. In many of the pilot similes it is Satan who is the pilot, yet in the whale simile Satan is the whale and the pilot is the observer of the whale. Likewise, the carefree wanderer who ventures out into the country on a summer's morn is Satan, but the peasant at the end of Book 1 is some other observer, who beholds faery elves that are Satan and his followers, just as the peasant at the end of Book 12 is fallen human being with the fired mists gathering at his/her heel, mists that are here the cherubim of God but are elsewhere Satan.

The purpose of this pattern of varying relationships between vehicle and tenor is to separate the third space from ideological anchorings, to focus the attention more on what the elements of this space have in common than on their referential meaning.

There is another kind of conflict in Milton's presentation of the modal world that has a different purpose. If one considers a simile in itself and in relation to the simile world of which it is a part, its purely lyric qualities stand out, as, at one stage of the lyric experience, Milton intends them to. But sometimes by the context he places them in, Milton cuts against these lyric qualities at the same time as he is impressing them upon the reader. Sometimes this context is not simply the tenor that conflicts with its vehicle denotatively, but a conflicting distancing device, such as tone. Thus Milton uses the anger of the editorial comment following the whale simile to counter its lyric qualities. In his description of the fallen angels, he uses the autumn-leaves simile to create a lyric mood, but then immediately follows this simile with an alternate one:

> . . . or scattered sedge
> Afloat, when with fierce winds Orion armed
> Hath vexed the Red Sea coast, whose waves o'erthrew
> Busiris and his Memphian chivalry,
> While with perfidious hatred they pursued
> The sojourners of Goshen, who beheld
> From the safe shore their floating carcasses
> And broken chariot wheels.
>
> (1: 304–11)

Now the fallen angels are likened not simply to a neutral image—leaves or sedge—but to the perfidious troops of Pharaoh. The point of view, the still point of observation and dawning consciousness, is shifted from the leaves to a different observer on the shore.

The purpose of these countering devices is to prevent the mind from seeking to harbor permanently, not in a sympathic ideology, but in the lyric mode itself. At this stage of the declension of mind, the countering shifts the mind as a whole out of the lyric attachment; in the later meditative stage, the mind contemplates both poles of the countering, attached to neither. This countering is necessary because there are aspects of many of the similes discussed that are dangerously ambiguous if left to themselves. One must beware of slipping in the fluidity of yearning into a fate as devastating as sympathic destruction. The lyric elements have been temporarily isolated so that the reader might come to know them; but without a care and discipline like those of the mind of the ploughman, which the lyric mode by itself cannot provide, the modal process can turn into, as Adam puts it, "wild work" (5: 112). It is not so much the ambiguity of reference—the relation of the counterplot to its referent in the sympathic dimension—that is danger-ous, as the ambiguity within the world of the lyric simile. The peasant in Book 9 and the mariner in Book 5 cannot be sure of the identity or meaning of what might fascinate and allure them—stars and fired vapors. Yet the difference between their choices makes clear the consequences of following such an allurement. Such an imaginative journey will lead to no truth; in *Paradise Lost* the pilot's lyric journey to the spicy shores is rudely blocked by the icebergs in 10: 289–93.

In terms of discursive judgment, the lyric space is uncertain: it provides no conceptually tangible basis or measurement for "affirming" or "denying." Many of the similes enter a nighttime space. The stillness and coolness of night often provide relief from the heat and fray. As Milton says, it is the "still night . . . / Wholesome and cool and mild" (10: 846–47). Yet it is also the time of uncertain vision, perhaps delusion. In the invocation to Book 3, Milton is surrounded by "ever-during dark" (3: 45). During the beautiful nights in Paradise, the moon

> Rising in clouded majesty, at length
> Apparent queen unveiled her peerless light,
> And o'er the dark her silver mantle threw.
>
> (4: 607–9)

She keeps the sheltering night itself from being too dark. But does the word *apparent* mean that the moon's light is deceptive?

The ambiguous nature of moonlit vision and truth is perhaps nowhere more clearly and fully delineated than in Eve's dream. This space, in which "reigns full-orbed the moon," shares with the similes the cool pale light, the silence, and the freedom of space as Eve beholds "The earth outstretched immense, a prospect wide / And various" (5: 88–89). These qualities are beautiful; as Eve has said to Adam as they prepare to sing their hymn to night:

> . . . sweet the coming on
> Of grateful ev'ning mild, then silent night
> With this her solemn bird and this fair moon,
> And these the gems of heav'n, her starry train.
>
> (4: 646–49)

This time and space are Eve's; she is associated with the moon, and this time and space she would share with Adam.

In her dream she awakens to a gentle voice calling her to share

> . . . the pleasant time,
> The cool, the silent, save where silence yields
> To the night-warbling bird,
>
> (5: 38–40)

and she arises to follow it. But the irony, of course, is that it is Satan's voice calling her, that tells her that the moon "with more pleasing light / Shadowy sets off the face of things; in vain / If none regard" (5: 42–44), a notion ominously similar to the lyric mode of the counterplot itself.

In her dream the counterplot enters more definitely into the dimension of the epic plot. Eve is the pilot, the wanderer, in a realm of her own mind. If she follows the lyric mood in the realm of action, as Adam tells her, she will fall like the peasant in Book 9. Indeed, it is Eve following Satan to the tree of knowledge who is the tenor for this simile. Such linkings between the dimensions of plot and counterplot specify modality as a subject of the epic. Adam and Eve's relation to the inner realm of mind, of dream-vision, and the relation of this realm to the realm of consciousness and action, form one of the major themes of *Paradise Lost*.

At this point in both the plot and the declension of mind, this lyric world is uncertain. The mood of the third space—the mood of stillness, silence, and cold light, presided over by the moon—is its only certainty. But this certainty is not yet conscious or defined because the fluidity of lyric is not yet centered by the upright neutrality of the meditative modes. As Eve says to Adam after she expresses her admiration for the beauties of the night,

> Nor grateful ev'ning mild, nor silent night
> With this her solemn bird, nor walk by moon
> Or glittering starlight, without thee is sweet.
>
> (4: 654–56)

The queen of night, the moon with her starry train, who is mistress of the lyric realm, needs and asks for the centering of a king to walk with her in her fluid psychic realm.

The lyric mode can be only partial; to be a way it must first be countered, clarified, and defined by its counterpart, the ironic mode. As the mind may not stop at any one point on the lyric continuum, but is forced in the separate world defined by the similes to experience all its points and motions, so the mind may not stay in the lyric mode as a whole. In this second stage of the declension of mind, the mind must experience the whole modal structure, ironic as well as lyric.

The function of the ironic mode is to prevent the mind from "harboring" in the lyric mode and from anchoring itself to any intermediate, and to give it a measure of strength and independence necessary for the centering and meditative control in the final stage in the declension of mind by checking and cross-checking it. In this way the whale simile is checked by the editorial anger, the lyric autumn leaves by the perfidious Egyptian troops. Similarly, the scene of the "cany wagons" sailing on the windy plains of Sericana is prevented from falling into lyricism by the image of the pilgrims in the "devious air" of the Paradise of Fools:

> . . . and now at foot
> Of heav'n's ascent they lift their feet, when lo!

A violent cross-wind from either coast
Blows them transverse ten thousand leagues awry
Into the devious air; then might ye see
Cowls, hoods and habits with their wearers tossed
And fluttered into rags; then relics, beads,
Indulgences, dispenses, pardons, bulls,
The sport of winds. All these upwhirled aloft
Fly o'er the backside of the world far off
Into a limbo large and broad, since called
The Paradise of Fools.

                                        (3: 486–97)

In this pair of images the windy sea of land is both imagistically and referentially parallel to the devious winds. But the tones oppose each other, humorous against lyric, an opposition that is ironic. This opposition arrests the mind rather than alluring it. A psychic realm where one disconnects one's yearning from the unattainable absolute and substitutes attainable pleasures—an ironic strategy discussed in chapter 3—and a psychic realm of unrelativized lyric are both limbos, for they lack that necessary, intricate combination of yearning and precision.

The countering of lyric and ironic, in the final impulse of the modal stage of the declension of mind, will bring the mind to a sharp stillness that will allow it the necessary neutrality for the relativizing of the final meditative stage. It is in this stillness that the reader realizes that modality is not primarily a structure of fulfillment, but of a consciousness that alone can lead to fulfillment.

The best example of such countering is the Proserpine simile quoted earlier. This simile is predominantly lyric in tone—poignant, at the pole of pain, though the flowers evoke the delight of the other pole—but it is ironic in situation. The image of Proserpine snatched away from her lyric world by Death is ironic in relation to the many other lyric images where one is snatched from pain to the relief of the lyric world. Further, the placement of this simile here in Book 4 is ironic, for one might expect while the poet is introducing the reader to Paradise that the lyric image might evoke some point of rest beyond irony. Yet, at this moment of arrival and of the poet's supposed highest praise, not of Enna, but of the garden of God, the poem takes an ironic turn into loss and pain. The concisely dovetailed, alternating figure-ground structure of this simile suspends the reader as he/she experiences the two modes simultaneously.

This ironic setting of the two poles of lyric against each other emphasizes the fluidity of the lyric mode that can in itself find no resolution. As Milton, the poet in darkness and solitude compassed round with dangers and evil days, points out in the invocation to Book 7, the lyric Orpheus was torn to pieces by the wild revelers of Bacchus, "nor could the Muse defend her son" (7: 37–38). Milton invokes instead Urania, the muse of astronomy and of precision:

> . . . So fail not thou who thee implores;
> For thou art heav'nly, she an empty dream.
>
> (7: 38–39)

Yet one may not find resolution by refusing to enter the modal dimension in the first place. This refusal is Satan's strategy. His mind in hell almost uncontrollably forces all incipient moments of modal consciousness back into the metamorphic conflicts of the sympathic dimension. He insistently rouses his followers up from their "entranced" state. When his yearning and memory of lost heaven enter into his consciousness, he is possessed by sympathic pain and anger:

> "Is this the region, this the soil, the clime,"
> Said then the lost Archangel, "this the seat
> That we must change for heav'n, this mournful gloom
> For that celestial light? Be it so, since he
> Who now is sovran can dispose and bid
> What shall be right: fardest from him is best,
> Whom reason hath equalled, force hath made supreme
> Above his equals. Farewell, happy fields,
> Where joy for ever dwells! Hail, horrors, hail,
> Infernal world, and thou, profoundest hell,
> Receive thy new possessor: one who brings
> A mind not to be changed by place or time.
> The mind is its own place, and in itself
> Can make a heav'n of hell, a hell of heav'n."
>
> (1: 242–55)

His testiness ("Be it so") and his sarcasm ("farewell, happy fields. . . hail, horrors . . .") destroy the patience necessary to yield to a third space where he might experience the modality of "happy fields." Focusing on "reason" and "force," and on the absolutes of "heav'n" and "hell," his mind will not change, shift, or yield to the "places" or "times" the reader experiences in the simile world. This strategy, however, will not allow him control over his own mind, as he claims. For later, in the beginning of Book 4, he is still in the hell of his own sympathic state. As he says in his anguished soliloquy on Mt. Niphates:

> Which way I fly is hell; myself am hell;
> And in the lowest deep a lower deep
> Still threat'ning to devour me opens wide,
> To which the hell I suffer seems a heav'n.
>
> (4: 75–78)

Once inside Paradise, with the scenes of beauty spread out before him, Satan still refuses to yield. As he admires God's new creation he mourns:

With what delight I could have walked thee round,
If I could joy in aught, sweet interchange
Of hill and valley, rivers, woods, and plains,
Now land, now sea, and shores with forest crowned,
Rocks, dens, and caves; but I in none of these
Find place or refuge; and the more I see
Pleasures about me, so much more I feel
Torment within me, as from the hateful siege
Of contraries.

                                                    (9: 114–22)

Satan's mind is so "fixed" (1: 97) and inflexible that he is unable to shift his attention or focus, as the reader does, in the aesthetic distancing of the counterplot, unable to involve himself in the kinesthetic resonance—the sweet interchange—of the scene, or to enter into the mental third space, the "place or refuge" that would allow him to enjoy the world of the shores and forests that is literally before him, not even in a simile. Refusing delight because it does not fit into his rhetorical and ideological scheme of things, he will find no refuge, but will fall into an "abyss" of mind until, ironically, "in heav'n much worse would be. . . [his] state" (9: 123). It is partly his state of mind that creates his surroundings: are the "rocks, dens, and caves" in this passage meant to recall the "rocks, caves, lakes, fens, bogs, dens" of 2: 621? Would the "hills and valleys, rivers, woods, and plains" of heaven be "shades of death" for Satan? The beautiful resonant motions of the land-scapes of Eden—as perhaps the motions of the seas and fishes discussed above in chapter 1—though ironically presented both in Book 4 and in Book 9 through Satan's eyes, are invisible to him.

   One must allow oneself to wander, and pause in the temporary ports that are themselves part of the journey, in the lyric world; one must allow oneself to be calmed, inspired, and changed by the lulling winds even though they may soon rise into capricious gusts or destructive storms. One must enter the world of modality and experience the odors promised by the spicy shores even though a direct or easy route to these desired shores will eventually be denied, as one is brought to a colder paradise whose mood will yet offer greater promise.

6 The Ironic Mode: The Garden of Eden

It is even more difficult to isolate the ironic mode in *Paradise Lost* than it is to consider the lyric mode in itself. There are passages in the poem that serve to illustrate the different points on the ironic continuum, but these are less frequent than in the lyric mode. A heavily, almost viciously, ironic passage at the pole of pain and anger—anger directed against the desirer—is the editorial comment in the description of the heavenly stairs connecting heaven and earth that Satan beholds in his journey toward earth in Book 3:

> The stairs were then let down, whether to dare
> The Fiend by easy ascent, or aggravate
> His sad exclusion from the doors of bliss.
>
> (3: 523–25)

Yet the word *sad* complicates this moment of irony. Satan's taunts and puns as he rolls up his newly made cannon in the war in heaven are sarcastic, but more humorous, moving away from the pole of pain and anger:

> . . . witness heaven,
> Heav'n witness thou anon, while we discharge
> Freely our part. Ye who appointed stand,
> Do as you have in charge, and briefly touch
> What we propound, and loud that all may hear.
>
> (6: 563–67)

Adam's comment, "whate'er death is," shares this middle ground of the continuum. "Angel on archangel rolled" (6: 594) and the "hills amid the air encountered hills" (6: 664) of the war in heaven are close to the pole of humor. The fluttering cowls and habits—the sport of winds—in the Paradise of Fools, visually and kinesthetically similar to the flying hills, are entirely humorous. The fall of Mulciber might be seen as this humorous motion crossing in the metamorphic fluidity of the modal structure into the pleasure close to the lyric pole of joy.

But such moments are not common in *Paradise Lost*. More often Milton's irony is curiously toneless. When the reader reads the lines "whate'er death is," or Milton's editorial insertion "No fear lest dinner cool" as Adam and Eve are serving Raphael the fruits of Paradise (5: 396), he/she does not really laugh; for laughter is simultaneously stopped short in a kind of bewilderment. As in the Proserpine simile, Milton's irony is often more the irony of situation than of tone, or a combination of both, which leads the mind beyond modal attitudes into something closer to understanding. The point of view is not, as in the paradigm, simply disconnected from the absolute in response to the impossible desire for the absolute in order to allow the desirer some control and a release into humor, just as Milton's irony does not allow an unqualified relief. Rather, the point of view is disconnected from its own attitude and tone, from its ironic control, even while being engaged in it. This irony is situated somewhere between the paradigmatic irony and the simple relativizing mode: it has moved beyond simple irony in that it takes an attitude toward its attitude and knows itself to be a structure of understanding more than of fulfillment. But this knowledge is not a full consciousness that is absorbed and resonates through the mind, for it is detached from the lyric mode and therefore from motion. It is not neutral like the meditative modes, but static.

Whereas lyric distancing takes the point of view, in successive instances like doors or windows, into another world that can be described and considered in its own right, ironic distancing, because of the nature of irony, must be considered in relation to the ground or structure it depends on to distort. For while lyric moves toward something, irony is always primarily looking back. In *Paradise Lost* the instances of irony tend to be clustered in two places: the presentation of Eden and Adam and Eve in Books 4 and 5 and the war in heaven in Books 5 and 6. The structures against which the irony is directed are the paradisaic state and the heavenly state in the context of the evolution of the universe. In the second case there is a corollary irony directed against angelic communication with human being. This formulation is somewhat oversimplified, for the irony in both cases is multidirectional and complex, but the perception toward which this mode moves in conjunction with the other modes is that it is impossible to understand the creation, and impossible for the creation to continue to exist, without the participation of the imagination taking place in the third space, the full consciousness of which heaven and Eden lack.

In the Paradise Milton presents in Books 4 and 5, the lyric mode has reached the desired port—the "spicy shores" of its imagined joy and fulfillment. As Raphael arrives in Paradise and makes his way toward Adam and Eve, Milton describes him as coming "through the spicy forest" (5: 298). It is here that Adam and Eve, "yet the only two / Of mankind . . . [reap] immortal fruits of joy and love, / Uninterrupted joy, undivided love, / In blissful solitude . . ." (3: 65–69). As discussed earlier, this picture is ironically undercut by the journeys of Satan and Raphael, which do "interrupt" their solitude. Yet Milton's presentation of Eden further undercuts the picture of Paradise itself because his irony is directed in an intricate way simultaneously against both human nobility and human frailty.[1] The purpose of this double irony is to reveal, as happened when the sympathic state of mind split into pity and judgment, a basic though often hidden fissure in the nature of Paradise as usually imagined: that those who live in Paradise curiously enjoy great strength combined with the passivity proper to lyric. As Northrop Frye says, describing the hero of romance, in his classification of heroes that is the basis for his theory of fictional modes:

> If superior in *degree* to other men and to his environment, the hero is the typical hero of *romance,* whose actions are marvelous but who is himself identified as a human being. The hero of romance moves in a world in which the ordinary laws of nature are slightly suspended: prodigies of courage and endurance, unnatural to us, are natural to him.[2]

Such a state of things is not allowed to stand in *Paradise Lost* and is revealed by the counterplot to be a distortion of the truth of the modal structure. While undercutting habitual ways of imagining Paradise—a process directed to the reader—Milton's irony also presents Paradise as it is for Adam and Eve. In this second function, the counterplot and the epic plot are drawn into the same dimension.

Milton's garden of Eden is a curious entity. It is tangible and substantial, impressing one as being very "real" in this sense, but at the same time it seems rather precarious. It is not the garden of pastoral or religion—diaphanous, pure, mystical, or transcendent—by virtue of being distanced in wish or memory. It is not lyrical or, to use Frye's term, romantic. Yet it is not "real" in the sense of modern realism; it is not "concrete" or "empirical," as critics like Lewis or Eliot have emphasized, whether in praise or blame.[3] Nor does it have the "reality" of symbol, of an intermediate. Rather its tangibility is closer to the tangibility of the emblem, which has a certain meaning beyond itself yet also a certain materiality, even grossness, instead of the symbol's resonance. There is a quality about the emblem of Eden that lingers somewhere between arbitrariness and self-consciousness, as though the golden calf, its ornateness slightly overblown in its maker's effort to assert its substantiality on whatever level possible, should hint in a secret smile, while cutting a smart figure in space like a Bernini sculpture, that it is only an idol, which implies some further wisdom.

Milton's Eden is anti-lyrical, anti-romantic, anti-realistic, and anti-symbolic, his ironic distancing cutting in different directions to maintain a precarious substantiality. His irony moves against different backgrounds or structures instead of against a single structure or corresponding structures as most irony does. Further, whereas irony usually points to or implies some positive value or vision without giving it much literary space or specificity, Milton's irony moves away from one structure to point to another of the structures it has moved away from in another instance. The purpose of this multidirectional ironic movement is to prevent Eden from becoming fixed at any one level or point. The movement at this point in *Paradise Lost* takes place in a closed system in order that the movements cancel each other out and thereby reveal the unreality of absolute conceptions and of inter-mediates, as well as the futility of irony itself in any final sense. In this way Milton's ironic strategy is baroque: he creates a material entity that, through its exaggeration and even grossness, reveals a certain self-consciousness of its materiality's insufficiency, a twist that both diffuses its reality and offers its materiality as the only vehicle of perception available to an observer apparently created to perceive primarily through the senses.

The particular instances of irony in Book 4 occur along a continuum: at one end the multiple disconnection is achieved by the technique of dovetail-ing the lyric and ironic characteristic of the Proserpine simile; at the other end it is achieved by an exaggeration of materialism into near-grossness. Both have the effect of stopping the reader's mind, placing it between doubt and wondering—in the ordinary sense of the word—but without springing the mind into some other space.

The Proserpine simile, as mentioned above, is poignantly lyric in tone, but ironic in its context. If one focuses on the simile itself, the device is at the lyric pole of fear, loss, and pain; if one focuses on the context, unfallen Paradise and joy, the simile is more humorous, almost irrelevant. The confu-sion or perceptual dizziness resulting from this device, similar to some op art, is resolved by the introductory negative comparison to lost pastoral, "Not that fair field of Enna," which takes the simile close to relativizing. Just as the pain of the lyric tone counters an identification with the joy of Para-dise, the "not" counters an identification with the pain of the fall, cause of "death . . . and all our woe" (1: 3), woe that is characteristic of the reader's state of being.

In the Proserpine simile the point of view grounded in the Eve-figure (and also in Ceres) is passive, as is characteristic of the desirer in lyric, especially in relation to Dis. In the later comparison of Eve to Pandora, the point of view is more active, and Pandora is more responsible than the helpless Proserpine. This simile is predominantly ironic, though it is still a double device of dovetailed lyric and ironic:

> [Eve] More lovely than Pandora, whom the gods
> Endowed with all their gifts, and O too like
> In sad event, when to the unwiser son
> Of Japhet brought by Hermes, she ensnared
> Mankind with her fair looks, to be avenged
> On him who had stole Jove's authentic fire.
>
> (4: 714–19)

Again, introducing the fall into the description of unfallen Paradise is ironic; but further, the tone of the simile is ironic, arising from Pandora's foolish-ness. She is a more comic figure than Proserpine because her fate was unnecessary. However, the situation has a lyric aspect—its "sad event" as Milton calls it—that such a foolish and trivial act could loose such dispropor-tionate pain on the world. The felt disjunction between the trivial cause and the enormous consequences[4] dovetails the lyric mode into the ironic simile. It also pushes both modes toward a fuller consciousness, by showing that the desirer's control characteristic of the ironic mode, disconnected in at-titude from the absolute perspective, puts him/her in a vulnerable position by making things seem trivial because lesser goods have been disconnected from the absolute good, which is now considered unimportant in relation to the pain its absence causes—a strategy that robs him/her of a fuller con-sciousness. This consciousness of what allows and what prevents conscious-ness is one goal of Milton's irony: the mutual countering in this simile, showing up the limits of both the lyric and the ironic modes in a kind of cancellation, arrests the mind in a way that makes one question one's modal attitudes.

A passage with this same effect of turning itself inside out (from ironic to lyric) is the one directly preceding Adam's first speech, the passage describ-ing Satan changing himself into different animals:

> . . . About them round
> A lion now he stalks with fiery glare;
> Then as a tiger, who by chance hath spied
> In some purlieu two gentle fawns at play,
> Straight couches close, then rising, changes oft
> His couchant watch, as one who chose his ground
> Whence rushing he might surest seize them both
> Gripped in each paw; when Adam first of men
> To first of women Eve, thus moving speech
> Turned him, all ear to hear new utterance flow:
> "Sole partner and sole part of all these joys."
>
> (4: 401–11)

The mind must experience a strange jolt watching the tiger-Satan stalking the two gentle fawns, shifting his ground to get the best angle from which to seize them "gripped in each paw," while Adam says to Eve "Sole partner," the two passages strongly linked by the word "when." The juxtaposition is ironic, even humorous (in a macabre way), because Adam and Eve are certainly not alone in their bliss. But the image of the innocent and vulner-able fawns itself is lyric, and the moving human speech that turns Satan from his stalking is noble.

The passage is multidirectional. The picture of Adam and Eve as fawns cuts against their nobility and grandeur, making them frail and lyrically poignant; but the picture of noble beings beset by a tiger of which they are so unaware that even when told about it they are still unaware (Adam's "what-e'er death is") undercuts the delicate lyricism as well as their nobility and makes them seem not innocent, but ignorant, foolish, and somewhat comical, like Pandora. But then the power of their ability to speak cuts against this comical view. The cumulative effect of these motions is to make the device more critical than ironic or lyric: the reader is made to wonder about their attitude and position. He/she does not really laugh at their innocence, or even pity or fear for it, for all these reactions are balanced into what might be called a sympathy for the whole situation, as he/she wonders about the degree of control and responsibility Adam and Eve have in their context. They might be as responsible as Pandora for their error, but they may not be responsible for this situation in which things seem trivial, and for the insufficiency of the ironic mode. The gods in the Greek myth who are more powerful than Pandora still have their foolish moments, which makes her both more responsible than Adam and Eve—the Greek gods and humans at a certain point share the same disjunctive and arbitrary universe and the same inconsistent natures so she has more relative power—and less responsible— the universe is disjunctive. But the sense of this universe is not applicable to Adam and Eve's Eden, which has been created by God's mind and is not the result of some divine flirtation.

However, this countering of innocence by perhaps inescapable limitations of situation is in turn countered by another aspect of Adam and Eve's attitude toward these limitations of being partly disconnected from the absolute: they focus their attention on and yield to the pleasures of lesser goods. At the pole of pleasure, evoked in such lines as "from that sapphire fount the crispèd brooks, / Rolling on orient pearl and sands of gold, / With mazy error under pendent shades" (4: 237–39) and "golden tresses . . . in wanton ringlets waved / As the vine curls her tendrils, which implied / Subjection . . . yielded with coy submission . . . and sweet reluctant amorous delay" (4: 305–11), the partial cutting off from the absolute imposed on them becomes almost a disregard for it, a kind of laxity and indulgence in the trivial, as beautiful and innocent as this luxuriant wandering—or erring—is. God's later comment to Raphael that they may be "too secure" seems apt in light of these lines.

In the defining of the nature of Eden by the intersectings and clashings of modal lines of force moving in different directions, some passages, like the ones just discussed, are dovetailed, some are simply neutral or noncommittal, and others take the dovetailing into a heavier, more wrenching irony.

Occasionally Milton inserts a brief, noncommittal, distancing comment into his description of Eden, as in "Hesperian fables true, / If true, here only" (4: 250–51), and as in the repeated use of the verb *to seem* in this passage introducing Adam and Eve:

> Two of far nobler shape erect and tall,
> God-like erect, with native honor clad
> In naked majesty seemed lords of all
> And worthy seemed, for in their looks divine
> The image of their glorious Maker shone,
> Truth, wisdom, sanctitude severe and pure,

Severe but in true filial freedom placed;
Whence true authority in men; though both
Not equal, as their sex not equal seemed.

(4: 288–96)

The irony becomes heavier, though it still cuts in more than one direction, in lines such as the poet's quip, "No fear lest dinner cool," (5: 396) and Satan's leering and sarcastic comment, "These two / Imparadised in one another's arms, / The happier Eden" (4: 505–7). From the critical perspective on their innocence, the irony is directed against Adam and Eve, but its harshness breaks the connection of the dovetail that stops the reader's mind and instead sets it in motion; what was before lyric in the perception of loss—from the reader's point of view, not Adam and Eve's—now inserted into the description of Eden, becomes ironic at the pole of anger. However, this irony turns against the reader, for at this point in the modal declension of mind between lyric-ironic modality and the neutrality of relativizing, such harshness denotes a slipping back into the sympathic, where dinner must be kept warm, and where sensual pleasure is completely disconnected from the absolute and turned into a lesser pleasure that has lost all resonance.

Satan's materialistic comment lacks consciousness; Milton's does not. There are other uses of materialistic irony that are less heavy and more enjoyable, though still self-conscious and self-critical in a humorous way. Sometimes Milton's description of Paradise becomes almost "too much," as both the objects described and the words used to describe them become rich, opulent, exaggerated, just short of grossness. The lines quoted, "crispèd brooks / Rolling on orient pearl and sands of gold / . . . ran nectar" (4: 237–40), have this opulence, as do to a greater degree the "Groves whose rich trees wept odorous gums and balm" a few lines later (4: 248).

These passages are at the ironic pole of materialistic pleasures, which the desirer enjoys with the confidence of detachment from the absolute and with even a slight self-indulgence. However, that this attitude is self-conscious— the sly smile of the baroque golden idol—is evident in Milton's bravura description of the elephant who "To make them mirth used all his might, and wreathed / His lithe proboscis" (4: 346–47). Such lines are a picture of excess, both in content and in style, yet such mirthful and unashamed extravagance again cuts two ways—against the judgmental restraints of the fallen sympathic state as well as against the complementary indulgent reduction of a multilayered reality to the level of the material.

This modal perception of Eden, in which there is no resonance but rather the precarious insubstantiality of different pieces held together almost by being shoved up against each other, like relativizing with no third space and no point of balance, cuts against traditional conceptions of Paradise as absolute joy or intermediate, an ironic process that results in stasis. This ironic process is directed against the fallen reader, but it is also directed to the consciousness of Adam and Eve at this point in the progress of *Paradise Lost* in order that the reader may better understand their nature as well as his/her own as their descendent. In this way the counterplot and the epic dimension become one.

There are several passages in the poem, some in Book 4 and some later, that specifically raise the question of human being's relation to God and their responsibilities in relation to each other. As discussed in chapter 3, the question of responsibility is a key structural component of the ironic mode. As in the presentation of Paradise itself, these passages at this point in the declension of mind move ironically in a closed pattern of cross-counterings that directs criticism—by assigning responsibility—both toward God and toward human being. These cross-counterings create a stasis that arrests the ironic process and the mind engaged in it and directs irony against the ironic strategy itself: the assignation of absolute responsibility to either God or human—to desired or desirer—is a false strategy that derives from the false conceptions that form the points of the structures in which both sympathic and modal motions move.

In Adam's first address to Eve in Book 4, he says that the power that made them must be infinitely good to have given them happiness "who at his hand / Have nothing merited, nor can perform / Aught whereof he hath need" (4: 417–19). Such a thought makes Adam and Eve seem unnecessary and their existence a token for some other issue. However, Adam's statement is only half true, for they are needed, though why and in what way they are needed is an intricate question. But this apparent inability to do anything God could need is reinforced by Satan's genuinely astonished reaction to hearing of God's "sole command" to them—not to eat of the tree of knowledge:

> . . . Knowledge forbidden?
> Suspicious, reasonless. Why should their Lord
> Envy them that? Can it be sin to know,
> Can it be death? and do they only stand
> By ignorance, is that their happy state,
> The proof of their obedience and their faith?
>
> (4: 515–20)

In a sense they are frail and somewhat useless in the scheme of things, almost decorative. If their mode of being strips them of most power, what is their reason for being? However, Adam's colloquy with God in 8: 357–451—later in the poem but earlier in terms of the story's time—cuts against such a train of thought, showing that God does have serious need, which may be satisfied by less obvious forms of power than angels or even himself, indeed forms that have unique powers of their own. Adam tells God immediately after his own creation that he is not fully happy in his solitude in Eden and wants the fellowship of an equal, and God in his reply asks:

What think'st thou then of me, and this my state?
Seem I to thee sufficiently possessed
Of happiness, or not? Who am alone
From all eternity; for none I know
Second to me or like, equal much less.
How have I then with whom to hold converse
Save with the creatures which I have made, and those
To me inferior, infinite descents
Beneath what other creatures are to thee?

(8: 403–11)

Adam's answer to this question perhaps is true—"Thou in thyself art perfect
. . . [and] Best with thyself accompanied seek'st not / Social communication" (8: 415–29)—yet it also shows a disregard of the question, an unwill-
ingness to confront its implications and a preference to focus on happiness
attainable in his own state. Coupled with the passages quoted above describing their yielding to the pleasures of Paradise in near laxity, such a turning
aside from considering the possibilities for happiness in power and excellence so great that it is eternally alone cuts against any pathos in Adam's
innocence. The sense of near complicity in his state is reinforced when he
sinks into sleep immediately after he is told that his wish will be granted
"exactly to . . . [his] heart's desire" (8: 451), even though it is equally true
that it is the strain of such high "celestial colloquy" that has exhausted him.

   Eve's lyric dream breaks into this stasis and shows that the true nature of
Paradise lies beyond static notions, whether they be the stasis of absolute,
intermediate, or ironic attitude. In her dream Eve enters into the third space
of lyric yearning. She wanders, deluded by Satan but drawn by her desire for
more love and the admiration that would be evidence of love, a desire that
she shares with all created beings and God as well. This yearning she has
already expressed in the hymn to night in Book 4, which Satan shrewdly
plays on. She has asked Adam "But wherefore all night long shine these
[stars], for whom / This glorious sight, when sleep hath shut all eyes?" (4:
657–58). Satan answers: "heav'n wakes with all his eyes / Whom to behold
but thee, Nature's desire?" (5: 44–45). She is also tempted to eat the fruit, as
she does in the dream, by Satan's promise of ascent into flight and new
spaces.

   On the one hand, this dream tempts Eve into the dangers of the undiscriminating fluidity of an isolated lyricism. But on the other hand, it is a
modal motion that points up the insufficiency of the ironic mode and of stasis
in general. It makes clear that the mind and the universe, and the relation of
human to God, are essentially kinesthetic and dynamic, and that knowledge
of him and of their own nature is likewise dynamic. Indeed, Eve's dream
may be seen as an instance of lyric distancing that counters the status quo in
Eden as it is in Book 4, as an instance of counterplot occurring in the
dimension of the epic. Satan's invasion may be seen as not simply an evil

mission of revenge, but as an urging that will force Adam and Eve, like the reader, out of an intermediate security and into a growing knowledge of God.

The tree of knowledge and the command not to eat of it, if understood as blind obedience, or will, is the pin that holds this whole static pattern of mind and being together. On the one hand, it keeps Adam and Eve from falling into sympathic or lyric destruction; on the other, it maintains a stasis that makes true knowledge impossible. Eve's dream represents a threat to this dominance of ignorant will—the fruit of irony and a misconception of the tree of knowledge—yet it simultaneously offers a lyric threat of its own. The dream intrudes into their falsely secure happy state and forces them to respond to it. Though it is troubling, it offers the beginnings of a new kind of knowledge in a new space, an offering that significantly precedes Satan's actual temptation in the realm of action.

In his response Adam shows some understanding of the nature of dream: in it one can "come and go," evil can come and go, and one may watch and experience it if one does not "approve," or "disapprove"—identify. But Adam goes on to define dreaming as essentially "wild work," "misjoining shapes," to be governed by reason (5: 100–113), a judgment derived from reason and will. Adam and Eve's final response is their orisons, in which they praise God and his works as they begin their day's work (5: 153–208). This hymn, like their earlier hymns and like the heavenly song and dance and the images of heavenly pleasure, is a patterned motion-in-stillness—or stillness-in-motion—"let your ceaseless change / Vary to our great Maker still new praise. / Ye mists . . . Rising or falling . . ." (5: 183–91)—that is not related to the motions of the sympathic or modal state, and therefore is amost gratuitous in Adam and Eve's present plight. However, Adam and Eve do add one significant note—fear—to their hymn: instead of praising the night as part of the varying of God's creation as they did in the earlier hymn, they now image the heavenly song and dance about God's throne as "day without night" (5: 162) and close the hymn with the prayer "and if the night / Have gathered aught of evil or concealed, / Disperse it" (5: 206–8).

As Milton says, "so prayed they innocent," a prayer that restores calmness to their troubled thoughts, and they begin gardening, leading "the vine to wed her elm," image of Adam and Eve's marriage. This activity brings a significant response from God: "Them thus employed beheld / With pity heav'n's high King" (5: 219–20), and in this awareness of the insufficiency of their state he calls Raphael, "the sociable spirit," and sends him to converse with Adam and Eve, to warn them not to swerve from their obedience. Their happy state is threatened on the one hand by their vulnerability, on the other by being "too secure" (5: 238), and also now by fear. A lack of modal consciousness makes their state further precarious because it results in the apparent disjunction between trivial cause and momentous consequence.

The continuance of their happy state will depend on how they develop their understanding of the relation between will, reason, and the third space of Eve's dream. Their fear may cause them to cling to the security of will or it may draw them into the motions of yearning.

The nature of Eden—in terms of both perception and structure—at this point in *Paradise Lost* is inconclusive as regards the declension of mind and as it affects the epic plot of the poem. What is missing is tone, the yearning of mode, the third space of the lyric similes in which yearning itself is part of the center of awareness, as in the simile of the "cany wagons" on the windy sea of land. Just as lyric isolated from the rest of the modal structure leads to ambiguity, limbo, delusion, and perhaps "wild work" and destruction, ironic isolated from tone leads to a vaguely unsettling inconclusiveness and gratuitousness, either to stasis or to the "wild work" of the war in heaven (6: 698). What is needed is that intricate combination of yearning and distance that is the human imagination.

NOTES

1. This technique makes it difficult to identify with any character as an entity as one might tend to do in a novel, an approach that is the basis of A. J. A. Waldock's analysis of *Paradise Lost, "Paradise Lost" and Its Critics* (Cambridge: University Press, 1961). See especially pp. 17–19.

2. Frye, *Anatomy of Criticism*, p. 33.

3. See chap. 1, n. 1.

4. E. M. W. Tillyard, in *Milton*, rev. ed. (New York: Barnes & Noble, 1967), analyzes Adam and Eve's fall as a result of levity of mind. See pp. 220–33.

7   The Ironic Mode: The Fall in Heaven

As in the presentation of Eden, Milton's irony in the account of the war in heaven functions to define the reader's perception of heaven as well as the nature of heaven itself. If the irony in his presentation of Eden is anti-lyric, anti-romantic, and anti-symbolic, the irony in his presentation of the war in heaven is anti-epic and anti-theological. This irony cuts against traditional conceptions and images of glory that are often the subject of epic and theology in the fallen world, and it further cuts against the conceptions and images the heavenly beings, including God, have of themselves and their state of being. In this second function, the counterplot makes clear that the principal subject of *Paradise Lost* is the modality of reality and modal consciousness of it, and that the spring of the particular story of the heavenly and earthly falls is the lack of modal consciousness. A passage that concisely conveys the flavor of Milton's irony as well as defines his epic subject by way of negative reference appears in the invocation to Book 9:

> Since first this subject for heroic song
> Pleased me long choosing, and beginning late;
> Not sedulous by nature to indite
> Wars, hitherto the only argument
> Heroic deemed, chief mast'ry to dissect
> With long and tedious havoc fabled knights
> In battles feigned (the better fortitude
> Of patience and heroic martyrdom
> Unsung), or to describe races and games,
> Or tilting furniture, emblazoned shields,
> Impresses quaint, caparisons and steeds,
> Bases and tinsel trappings, gorgeous knightss
> At joust and tournament; then marshalled feast
> Served up in hall with sewers and seneschals;
> The skill of artifice or office mean,
> Not that which justly gives heroic name
> To person or poem.
>
> (9: 25–41)

In a phrase like *tilting furniture* Milton represents the stuff of epic glory in overblown materialistic terms, undercutting its grandeur in one direction and materialialism itself in another. The light-hearted and extravagant quality of this humor is characteristic of the humor of the war in heaven, as the battling angels are cast as epic heroes; and images like the "hills amid the air encountered hills" (6: 664) have the same mechanistic quality as the tilting furniture, the humor partly deriving from the deanimation of living beings.

This ironic strategy is simpler than the ironic structure of Eden, but it is complex in its implications. The irony keeps its essentially light-hearted "gamesome" quality (6: 620), typical of the pole of humor in the modal paradigm, no matter where it is situated on the ironic continuum—from the flying hills, to Satan's heavier sarcasm when he fires his cannon (6: 558–630), to the angrier derision of God directed against Satan's ultimately futile efforts (5: 718–37). Even more curious, unlike most irony, which becomes tighter and more condensed until it breaks into the vision of the alternate structure or into a third space, the humor in the war in heaven becomes freer, looser, and more indulgent as the heavenly battle becomes increasingly violent and destructive.

The irony in the war in heaven is more humorous—has more tone—than in the presentation of Eden, because it is more disconnected and more gratuitous. Satan has disconnected himself from the absolute, and there is a sense in which the irony itself represents this original "falling," the breaking of union (5: 612) and resonance that leads in the dimension of the epic plot to the particular gap between desirer and desired absolute that characterizes the modal structure as discussed in chapter 3. There is a close relation between this fall and the style of typical irony: the perhaps seemingly incompatible materialism coupled with a frenetic free-floating energy, and the repetition coupled with unexpectedness. These characteristics may be seen as the result of the breaking of resonance.

The steps of the angels' fall in the plot reflect this modal breaking and its results. When Satan feels impaired by the Son's elevation, the first thing he does is not to attack God, but to "leave" him (5: 669), to break away in pain and anger. The next step, represented in 2: 752–67, is that he suddenly feels "miserable pain" in his head, and sin is born, as well as knowledge ("can it be sin to know?" [4: 517]). Another result is war: "Meanwhile war arose, / And fields were fought in heav'n" (2: 767–68). Then last, death is born ("can it be death?" [4: 518]) from the distortion caused by fear and pain: "this odious offspring. . . breaking violent way / Tore through my entrails. . . with fear and pain / Distorted. . . " (2: 781–84). It is significant that the war is grammatically represented as a subject with intransitive and passive verbs: "war arose" and "fields were fought" rather than "the angels fought wars." The state of war was a natural consequence of the breaking of the magnetic force between spirit, the source of energy, and matter. Now knowledge and war have replaced wisdom and true power ("strength from truth divided" [6: 381]); and resonance has turned into random energy and a fragmented materialism that is characteristic of war, and also of chaos.

The unfallen angels are helpless to stop this increasing fragmentation; it is only finally stopped by the intervention of the Son. For all their rectitude and power, they join in the rage of battle. In Raphael's words:

> . . . ours [the unfallen troops] joy filled and shout,
> Presage of victory and fierce desire
> Of battle . . .
> . . . .
> . . . Now storming fury rose
> . . . .
> . . . together rushed
> Both battles main, with ruinous assault
> And inextinguishable rage.
>
> (6: 200–217)

This rage leads them also to join in the literal dismantling of heaven. "Rage prompted them" to tear up and throw the hills, as described in 6: 635–70. They too are part of the strangely increasing humor.

The conclusions to be drawn from this puzzling situation are complex and perhaps surprising. It appears that the unfallen angels participate, indeed collaborate, in the disconnectedness started by Satan and his followers. Furthermore, the disjunction between trivial cause and momentous effect discussed above in relation to the Pandora simile is here enormous, and has a curious twist: the creation may go "to wrack, with ruin overspread" (6: 670), but in a way the ruin would be inconsequential, for essentially the spirits, both fallen and unfallen, are immortal. As Beelzebub says to Satan

> . . . the mind and spirit remains
> Invincible, and vigor soon returns,
> Though all our glory extinct.
>
> (1: 139–41)

Or as Raphael describes Satan's wounding by Michael's sword:

> [his sword] . . . deep ent'ring shared
> All his right side. Then Satan first knew pain
> . . . .
> . . . but th'ethereal substance closed
> Not long divisible, and from the gash
> A stream of nectarous humor issuing flowed
> . . . .
> . . . soon he healed; for Spirits, that live throughout
> Vital in every part, not as frail man
> . . . .
> Cannot but by annihilating die;
> Nor in their liquid texture mortal wound
> Receive, no more than can the fluid air.
>
> (6: 326–49)

Thus even the fallen Satan is not so disconnected from the absolute as one might suppose.

There is another disjunction between the angels' power and the inability of the plot to reverse itself, or come, in Aristotelian terms, to any recognition: in other words the war in heaven is a poor work of art. Its action, the soul of art, is defective.

All the aspects of this strange situation derive from the nature of the ironic structure in the war in heaven, which, as mentioned above, is more disconnected than the irony of the paradigm and the irony of Eden. This statement may seem to have obvious application to the fallen Satan but to contradict the reality of heaven for the faithful angels like Abdiel, who are not more but less disconnected from the absolute, being nearer to God than is the human desirer in the modal paradigm. However, although the disconnectedness of the fall may be the most obvious, it is not the most basic or determining disconnectedness in the war in heaven. For modally, all the angels are disconnected.

Whereas human mind in irony—and Satan in action—disconnects itself from the absolute in order to gain distance from the pain of yearning or disconnects itself in the opposite direction in order to gain distance from an insufficient intermediate, and yet in the closed fluidity of mode still yearns, the angels, who are close to God even when disconnected in the fall, are more significantly disconnected from the tension of the ironic distance itself, and from yearning too. They are disconnected from modality altogether and from the consciousness it affords. The structure of resonance from which the fall occurs in the plot and the structure of resonance toward which the declension of mind moves in the counterplot are the same, with one important difference: the final resonance will be in consciousness as well as in being.

The comedy of the war in heaven arises, in the first stage of the reader's reading of it, from the parody of human epic heroes. The seriousness of death removed—because angels cannot die—the fighting may be portrayed humorously and its basic silliness revealed. The angels are satirizing us. But the battles are also comic because the angels themselves, who should know better because they are wiser, are similarly engaging in silly actions. What this double irony shows is that, regardless of death or survival, war is in itself inconsequential. It is more meaningful as a game, and from this point of view the silliness becomes pleasure. But from a serious point of view, it reveals the basic materialism to which power and reason expressed in physical battle ultimately reduce.

The unfallen as well as the fallen angels are caught in a paradox inherent in the heavenly structure of obedience and of mind, which is revealed in both their rhetoric and their actions. Basically, it is a structure of reason, will, and strength without the third space of imagination and without yearning. This structure is set forth in several places in *Paradise Lost*. As he comforts Eve after her bad dream, Adam represents the mind as composed of several faculties; the "lesser" ones such as fancy and the senses "serve / Reason as chief" (5: 101–2). Likewise Raphael represents the faculties in a hierarchical structure, with reason at the top: "reason is her [the soul's] being" (5: 487). The angels, though more highly placed than human being, are represented by Abdiel in his debate with Satan in terms of a similar hierarchy in their relation to God: disobedience is "to serve the unwise" or to serve oneself as does the Satan "enthralled" to himself. Obedience, and freedom, lie in serving the worthier:

> Unjustly thou deprav'st it with the name
> Of servitude to serve whom God ordains
> Or Nature; God and Nature bid the same,
> When he who rules is worthiest, and excels
> Them whom he governs. This is servitude,
> To serve th'unwise, or him who hath rebelled
> Against his worthier, as thine now serve thee,
> Thyself not free, but to thyself enthralled;
> . . . .
> Reign thou in hell thy kingdom, let me serve
> In heav'n God ever blest, and his divine
> Behests obey, worthiest to be obeyed.
>
> (6: 174–85)

Abdiel sees the war in heaven as a contest between reason (the faithful angels) and force (Satan). From the perspective of the counterplot, heavenly obedience consists in adhering to God's commandment not to break union by means of a combination of will and focusing on the object of obedience, the commandment itself, without swerving. The "reason" of heaven is not the reason of consciousness or empathy. If they take their attention off the commandment, it is difficult for the angels to make distinctions and they become almost helpless. Thus Satan is "unperceived" by Uriel in Book 3:

> . . . neither man nor angel can discern
> Hypocrisy, the only evil that walks
> Invisible, except to God alone,
> By his permissive will, through heaven and earth;
> And oft though wisdom wake, suspicion sleeps
> At wisdom's gate, and to simplicity
> Resigns her charge, while goodness thinks no ill
> Where no ill seems: which now for once beguiled
> Uriel, though regent of the sun, and held
> The sharpest-sighted Spirit of all in heav'n.
>
> (3: 682–91)

Beelzebub and the angels lured to Satan's cause in Book 5 are similarly helpless when their attention is focused on him rather than on the commandment:

> So spake the false Archangel, and infused
> Bad influence into th'unwary breast
> Of his associate.
>
> (5: 694–96)

> . . . all obeyed
> The wonted signal, and superior voice
> Of their great Potentate.
>
> (5: 704–6)

When the commandment and the union are broken, reason is set against force, as Abdiel puts it. But far from being a simple and clean duel between good and evil, it is a "brutish . . . contést and foul, / When reason hath to deal with force" (6: 124–25), as the puzzled Abdiel says—brutish and foul for all, unfallen as well as fallen. For the battle of reason against force is necessarily redefined in terms of force—force against force. When Abdiel returns from Satan's assembly to the assembly of the faithful, God says that Abdiel has won the verbal contest with Satan, and that

> . . . The easier conquest now
> Remains thee . . .
> . . . .
> . . . to subdue
> By force, who reason for their law refuse.
>
> (6: 37–41)

But the battle turns out to be less simple than this formulation, for the good do not win so easily. As Raphael tells Adam:

> . . . strange to us it seemed
> At first, that angel should with angel war
> . . . .
> . . . But the shout
> Of battle now began, and rushing sound
> Of onset soon ended each milder thought.
>
> (6: 91–98)

Or as Abdiel ponders:

> . . . wherefore should not strength and might
> There fail where virtue fails . . .?
>
> (6: 116–17)

Reason does not remain reason, or manifest itself as reason, for the mild thoughts of the good angels quickly turn to "fierce desire / Of battle" (6: 201–2), "storming fury" (6: 207), and "inextinguishable rage" (6: 217). And the fallen do not simply fall by the swords of the unfallen. Rather, the contest is a clashing that widens the breach and increases the chaos, not one that achieves a resolution or a restoration of resonance. The unfallen do not act like heroes as they become involved in materialism and fragmentation, and eventually participate in the literal dismantling of heaven.

On the first day of battle, their innocence gives them strength:

> Such high advantages their innocence
> Gave them above their foes; not to have sinned,
> Not to have disobeyed.
>
> (6: 401–3)

The "dreadful combustion" might "disturb, / Though not destroy, their happy native seat" (6: 225–26) at this point. But on the second day, as both armies begin to dig up the soil of heaven (6: 468–523 and 635–69), the destruction reaches a point where "now all heaven / Had gone to wrack" (6: 669–70) without the intervention of the Son. The fallen are blinded by their anger and the unfallen by their rectitude and zeal. In an irony greater than that directed against Adam and Eve's innocence, the angels who fall are represented as sheep as they follow Satan "unawares"—"the starry flock" (5: 709)—and as they are driven out of heaven as "a herd / Of goats or timorous flock" (6: 856–57). Although both of these metaphors refer to those who fell, it is the traditional image of the faithful and innocent that is used to describe them. There seems to be no distinction between sheep and goats.

A pointed instance of irony directed against the unfallen angels as they begin to tear up the hills makes Milton's evaluation of epic martial glory clear:

> . . . But they stood not long;
> Rage prompted them at length, and found them arms
> Against such hellish mischief fit to oppose.
> Forthwith (*behold the excellence, the power,*
> *Which God hath in his mighty angels placed*)
> . . . and to the hills
> . . . .
> . . . they ran, they flew.
>
> (6: 634–42; emphasis added)

But perhaps worse than this physical chaos is what the rupture in the heavenly community has done to the minds of all the angels. As Michael exclaims to Satan:

> Author of evil, unknown till thy revolt,
> Unnamed in heav'n, now plenteous as thou seest
> These acts of hateful strife, hateful to all,
> Though heaviest by just measure on thyself
> And thy adherents: how hast thou disturbed

> Heav'n's blessèd peace, and into Nature brought
> Misery, uncreated till the crime
> Of thy rebellion!
>
> (6: 262–69)

Because as Abdiel says, the heavenly community is "all angelic nature joined in one" (5: 834), the brutish contest is a breach in the mind that affects them all. The further irony is, however, that a breach acts to bind them more closely together in some ways once the resonance is broken, as they are thrown up against each other in identifications, just as in an extreme ironic style the detached frenetic energy piles up repetitions.

The irony of the war in heaven makes clear that the formulation of the war as reason against force does not fit the reality. Angelic "reason" is an innocent though zealous will focused on an external commandment. When it swerves, "war arises," war between force and force, between rhetoric and rhetoric, and between irony and irony. Abdiel's claim that his reason is battling Satan's force is not a great deal more valid than Satan's claim that God's force has subdued his reason: "Whom reason hath equalled, force hath made supreme" (1: 248). Satan's reason is flawed, and we laugh at the pretensions and futility of his sarcastic irony as he rolls up his cannon:

> . . . Eternal might
> To match with their inventions they presumed
> So easy.
>
> (6: 630–32)

But we also laugh at his characterization of the faithful as "Ministr'ing Spirits, trained up in feast and song" (6: 167). For though Satan is wrong, in his breaking away he expresses an intuition, distorted as it is, of a truth not represented in the structure of heavenly wisdom, a structure that, though joining reason, will, and love, is unconscious of the truth that there is a space between God and angel, and between angel and angel, filled with resonance and joy, but sometimes filled with yearning.

As Raphael tells Adam, whereas human being's highest faculty is discursive reason, the angels' is intuitive reason (5: 489). Further, they serve God not only out of obedience maintained by will, but out of love:

> . . . freely we serve
> Because we freely love, as in our will
> To love or not; in this we stand or fall.
>
> (5: 538–40)

And they feel sympathy for the fallen angels; recounting the war to Adam is painful for Raphael. It is

> Sad task and hard, for how shall I relate
> To human sense th'invisible exploits
> Of warring Spirits; *how without remorse*
> The ruin of so many glorious once.
>
> (5: 564–67; emphasis added)

But even with this capacity for remorse, their love, and their intuition that is directly related to the object of knowledge, the structure of mind in heaven lacks the consciousness of empathy and therefore does not allow for an adequate representation of the true structure of resonance that is the special nature of heavenly union. The structure of mind is not aligned with the structure of reality. In Abdiel's representation of it, for example, in 6: 174–85, the regal and martial terminology, similar to the physical destruction he engages in, and the rigid hierarchical structure obscure the structure of resonance. The images of heavenly kinesthesia are also inadequate because there is no representation of distance, no space. Though in one sense it was the fall that made modality necessary, in another sense modality was necessary before the fall, both to decrease the possibility of swerving and to enrich the heavenly experience.

Because the structure of union is one of resonance, not of possession, even in the unfallen state there is a gap, or distance. Satan, like Eve, senses the reality of this gap, but he must *act* to resonate with it because the opportunity to experience it imaginatively in the third space is lacking in the structure of understanding. He feels this gap as loss in his speech to Beelzebub in 5: 673–79, a loss that is the pain of lyric. For Satan, the Son's elevation has seemingly broken the union of the one soul, and the resonance that existed in reality but not in understanding has fallen into the two extremes of lyric and ironic for him: "to begirt th'Almighty throne / *Beseeching* or *besieging*" (5: 868–69; emphasis added). There is no lyric mode in heaven before Satan's speech to Beelzebub expressing his need for companionship. Had there been modal consciousness in heaven, Satan's pain might have opened the way to greater understanding, but the lack of such a modal perspective forces him to act, and thus fall.

Another aspect of the structure or heavenly union that is hidden by the hierarchical structure of mind is its reciprocal nature: it is not only a structure of resonance, but one of reciprocity. God is a desirer as well as desired, as he indicates to Adam in their celestial colloquy in Book 8. Despite their "free love" of God, their direct intuition, prompt hymns, and capacity for remorse, it is not clear that the angels have any real empathy for God. God sends them on missions that stem from an obvious need for help from the angels that he cannot provide for himself, which they zealously perform but are content to accept as "obscure." For example, Raphael tells Adam that he would like to hear about the creation of human being because

> . . . I on that day was absent, as befell,
> Bound on a voyage uncouth and obscure,
> Far on excursion toward the gates of hell,
> Squared in full legion (for such command we had),
> To see that none thence issued forth a spy
> Or enemy, while God was in his work,
> Lest he incensed at such eruption bold,
> Destruction with Creation might have mixed.
> Nor that they durst without his leave attempt,
> But us he sends upon his high behests
> For state, as sovran King, and to inure
> Our prompt obedience.
>
> (8: 229–40)

The mission is of course "obscure" because they are in the dark depths of hell, but it is also obscure because they think their service is ritual and decorative ("for state") rather than necessary. They are aware of God's anger in a practical sense and know how to respond to it, but they are not wholly aware of the sources of this anger. One wonders how they would respond if asked what God asks Adam in Book 8. Abdiel, the model of angelic virtue, is "constant" (5: 902), upright, "single" (5: 903), "dreadless" and "unterrified" (6: 1 and 5: 899); the unfallen angels are "fearless" (6: 804). These qualities keep them from swerving but make them incapable of the empathy necessary to perceive the reciprocity of their union. Abdiel's uprightness and singleness are not so different from Satan's proud fixity (1: 97). Adam and Eve, by contrast, are neither single nor fearless; they are by their creation forced into reciprocity, and by their frailty forced into a fear that ensures modality. God himself, in the war in heaven, is represented—by himself or by the angels?—in a nonmodal perspective: "he sits / Shrined in his sanctuary of heav'n secure" (6: 671–72).

The lack of the lyric perspective in this irony of heaven, like the lack of the ironic perspective in lyric, produces the same "wild work" as the wild work of the lyric "mimic fancy" in Eve's dream. As God says:

> War wearied hath performed what war can do
> And to disordered rage let loose the reins,
> With mountains as with weapons armed, which makes
> *Wild work* in heav'n, and dangerous to the main.
>
> (6: 695–98; emphasis added)

The weapons of the angels were essentially "idle weapons," though they nearly destroyed heaven (6: 839). Only one conclusion is possible to this war: it is ended by the pure though measured power of God and the Son. But this is not a real ending; it is not a resolution. The gap is widened, the expulsion of the fallen makes it a definitive split, and then the breach is closed: "Disburdened heav'n rejoiced, and soon repaired / Her mural breach . . ." (6: 878–79).

As for Satan, though immortal Spirit, the fall causes him pain and fear (6: 393–97), pain that can lead to the death of the spirit in another sense: as Nisroch says after the first day of battle:

> . . . pain is perfect misery, the worst
> Of evils, and, excessive, overturns
> All patience.
>
> (6: 462–64)

Without a still center, without the counterpoise of meditation, without patience, the spirit falls into the painful kinesthesia of hell, which is in the constant motion of metamorphosis and distortion. It is the distortion of pain and fear that causes death (2: 783–87).

The good angels, on the other hand, "disburdened," return to their heavenly kinesthesia, motion-in-stillness with no evolution. Though they have experienced "misery," in the end their "holy rest" is "untroubled" (6: 271–72). Both the kinesthesia of hell and the kinesthesia of heaven are motions without the third space, a kind of absolute kinesthesia that is incapable of the movement of development. Although the breach introduced fear and pain into heaven, there was no mental correlate to confront it; therefore the unfallen angels remained "fearless" and the fallen were distorted by fear.

The implications of the ironic structure of the fall and war in heaven make it clear that some evolution is required for the creation to continue in any meaningful way. This evolution cannot take place in the structure of heaven. Thus God creates earth and human being:

> [I] will create
> Another world, out of one man a race
> Of men innumerable, there to dwell,
> Not here, till by degrees of merit raised
> They open to themselves at length the way
> Up hither, under long obedience tried,
> And earth be changed to heav'n, and heav'n to earth,
> One kingdom, joy and union without end.
>
> (7: 154–61)

This opening of the way is the only service asked of Adam and Eve.

In one sense, the angels are more highly developed beings than Adam and Eve: the bliss of motion-in-stillness and stillness-in-motion that is their state is the end toward which the evolution of mind moves. They are certainly superior in terms of power and knowledge. But they are less developed than Adam and Eve in another sense; for when there is a breach in their state, they are not yet at the modal stage of development that can handle the breach. Hence the inconclusive character, simultaneously unsettling and irrelevant, of the war in heaven, in terms of both mode and plot. The angels are like child prodigies who both know a great deal and know rather little, in the sense of a full consciousness resonating through all the parts of the whole soul.

That the angels' state is tentative is indicated by Milton's choice of words as he introduces Abdiel's debate with Satan: "[Abdiel] thus his own undaunted heart *explores*" (6: 113; emphasis added). Though noble and well-intended, his exploration seems awkward and stiff compared to the explorations of the wanderers in the counterplot, because he has no space in which to explore. He is too single. The third space of resonance is double or multiple, since it exists between poles and is reciprocal between beings. He is too constant to enter the third space of yearning, to look at the reflection of the moon like Galileo, or to gaze into the pool like Eve (4: 453–65). Instead, he would spring upright to gaze at the sun, like Satan (4: 29), or like the phoenix-Raphael (5: 272), the phoenix whose life is seemingly an undeveloping kinesthesia of interchanging life and death like heaven and hell. All these are blinded by the sun, unlike Milton who, blind to the sun, feels it kinesthetically, and retires into the third space of the imagination necessary to the evolution of the mind and the universe. This space is not the breach of war but the way to be opened by human being, a destiny whose unfoldment heaven awaits—a destiny to be evolved by a man who turns his eyes "straight toward heav'n" (8: 257) and who springs upright by "quick instinctive motion" (8: 259) and by a woman who pensively seeks her image in the fluidity of a "clear / Smooth lake, that seem[s] . . . another sky" (4: 458–59) coming to know each other in growing reciprocal consciousness, and coming to know God and the universe in the centered yet fluid movement of the meditative human imagination.

8   The Ironic Mode: The Art of Raphael

While the account of the war in heaven is being presented by Milton to the reader in a special ironic mode, it is also being presented by Raphael to Adam and Eve in a slightly different ironic mode. After their innocent response to Eve's dream—the prompt eloquence of the morning hymn that resembles the pleasurable kinesthesia of the angels' hymns—God pities them and sends Raphael "such discourse [to] bring on / As may advise . . . [them] of . . . [their] happy state" and to warn them of the danger posed by Satan's advent into Eden.

> . . . this let him know,
> Lest wilfully transgressing he pretend
> Surprisal, unadmonished, unforewarned.
>
> (5: 243–45)

Despite the good intentions of the "sociable spirit," a certain irony undercuts the way Raphael communicates this message to Adam and Eve. Commenting on the difficulty of telling a story about spirits to "human sense," Raphael proposes to solve it by "lik'ning spiritual to corporal forms" (5: 573). This allegorical strategy does not bear the same relation to the truth as most allegory, in which the poetic vehicle (usually earthly) points to its detached truth (usually spiritual or abstract). Rather, the allegorical form as a whole reflects the problem itself more than it provides a solution: the gap between poetry and truth reflects and is consequent upon the false structure of mind in heaven that does not correspond to the reality of the modal structure of heaven. Raphael's art, which is supposed to help Adam and Eve, has the same insufficiency as the heavenly consciousness: it is nonmodal. The reader may perceive this irony from the perspective of the counterplot, but Adam, at this point in the perspective of the epic, cannot. Raphael's mission has the effect of instilling into Adam and Eve the insufficiency of angelic mind and making them more rather than less vulnerable to Satan.

Adam is eagerly receptive to this influence, for his and Eve's destiny as stated by God is to "open to themselves a way," and the angel's visit provides the first clear opportunity. Adam is exhilarated by his first exchanges with Raphael, and is impatient to hear more. Indeed, his thirst for knowledge becomes a need greater than the desire for food and drink.

147

> . . . Thy words
> Attentive, and with more delighted ear,
> Divine instructor, I have heard, than when
> Cherubic songs by night from neighboring hills
> Aerial music send.

(5: 544–48)

> . . . while I sit with thee, I seem in heav'n,
> And sweeter thy discourse is to my ear
> Than fruits of palm-tree, pleasantest to thirst
> And hunger both, from labor, at the hour
> Of sweet repast; they satiate, and soon fill,
> Though pleasant, but thy words, with grace divine
> Imbued, bring to their sweetness no satiety.

(8: 210–16)

This is a thirst that can no longer be slaked by heavenly hymns.

Yet Raphael's art does not lead them into the third space of the imagination, where the resonant nature of the universe could be known through modality. In a distorted sense, Adam and Eve have already been there in Eve's dream, which is the first "opening of the way" represented by Milton in Eden. Raphael does not acknowledge this space at all; his communication is too direct and "prompt" for the "pause" and "delay" necessary to experience the dream-space. In fact, his account of the war and his other discussions about astronomy and creation are not primarily addressed to Eve, but are a man-to-man colloquy with Adam. His style, as "prompt" and "unmeditated" as Adam's and Eve's beautiful but insufficient hymns, is reflected in his initial response to God's command to go to Eden:

> So spake th'Eternal Father, and fulfilled
> All justice; nor delayed the wingèd saint
> After his charge received; but from among
> Thousand celestial Ardors, where he stood
> Veiled with his gorgeous wings, up springing light
> Flew through the midst of heav'n; th'angelic quires
> On each hand parting, to his speed gave way.

(5: 246–52)

This directness is related to the "unmixed" character of the heavenly state. The Son in Book 6 expels the fallen angels so that God's "saints" will be "unmixed" and "from th' impure / Far separate" (6: 742–43). Adam is "filled / With admiration and deep muse" by the account of the war and of the "evil [which] soon / Driv'n back redounded as a flood on those / From whom it sprung, impossible to mix / With blessedness" (7: 51–59).

The word *unmixed* describes Raphael's style aptly. He responds to Adam's thirst and to Adam and Eve's plight with a fragmented and unresonant art that is directed to their reason, their will, and their fancy and not to their imagination. This art is alternately composed of philosophy, poetry, and stern admonishment, as disconnected from one another as the faculties to which they separately appeal. Raphael's philosophy is represented by the several ladderlike pictures of both the reality of the universe and the reality of the structure of mind, as in the tree image in 5: 69–82, the "scale of Nature" in 5: 509–12, and Abdiel's hierarchy of service in 6: 174–85. His epic poetry, the "terrible example" as he calls it (6: 910), is a discordant combination of violence, humor, and an occasional sweetly lyrical simile, which reinforces the disjunction discussed earlier in relation to the Pandora simile between the catastrophic and the trivial. On the one hand, he pictures the war in heaven with the image of the comical flying hills and, on the other hand, he concludes the tale with the harsh warning:

> . . . listen not to his temptations; warn
> Thy weaker; let it profit thee to have heard
> By terrible example the reward
> Of disobedience.
>
> (6: 908–11)

This humor and this sternness might be seen as elements detached from the two poles of the ironic mode, and detached from modality. The lyric or "edenic" similes that Raphael uses now and then to relate heavenly truth to the world that Adam is familiar with—rural Eden—are similarly disjunctive. Sometimes they are violent images, sometimes sweet, childlike images adduced without much thought. They are neither appropriate to their referents nor do they lead into the third space.

Thus Raphael compares both Satan's army and the army of the faithful, whch are equally militant, to delicate images of dewdrops and birds:

> . . . Satan with his powers
> Far was advanced on wingèd speed, an host
> Innumerable as the stars of night,
> Or stars of morning, dew-drops, which the sun
> Impearls on every leaf and every flower.
>
> (5: 743–47)

> . . . the powers militant
> That stood for heav'n . . .
> . . . moved on
> . . . .
> . . . high above the ground
> . . . and the passive air upbore
> Their nimble tread; as when the total kind
> Of birds in orderly array on wing
> Came summoned over Eden to receive
> Their names of thee.
>
> (6: 61–76)

In using such similes Raphael patronizingly projects a pseudo-lyrical view of reality onto Adam, selectively reinforcing the weaker aspects of lyric perception and the state of innocence.

Raphael represents these same armies when they begin to battle in terms of violent disruption of Adam's peaceful earth. Thus when Abdiel strikes Satan,

> . . . Ten paces huge
> He back recoiled; the tenth on bended knee
> His massy spear upstayed; as if on earth
> Winds under ground or waters forcing way
> Sidelong had pushed a mountain from his seat,
> Half sunk with all his pines.
>
> (6: 193–98)

And when Satan and Michael confront each other:

> . . . two broad suns their shields
> Blazed opposite, while expectation stood
> In horror; from each hand with speed retired,
> Where erst was thickest fight, th' angelic throng,
> And left large field, unsafe within the wind
> Of such commotion; such as (to set forth
> Great things by small) if, Nature's concord broke,
> Among the constellations war were sprung,
> Two planets rushing from aspéct malign
> Of fiercest opposition in mid sky,
> Should combat, and their jarring spheres confound.
>
> (6: 305–15)

For Raphael, the collision of planets may be a "small" occurrence, and the uprooting of mountains an even smaller one; but for Adam such images are terrifying and "overturn the patience," especially since his earth has not known storms and earthquakes in its unfallen state. Although these images have a certain aptness as a picture of what earth will be like if he disobeys, they reflect an inappropriate strategy because, drawn directly from Adam's world and not from the space of the imagination, they reinforce a terror that might make him more vulnerable to a fall that will make them come true.

The disjunction between trivial and serious is accentuated further when Raphael later describes the "idle weapons" used in the comic broils of heaven as the same uprooted mountains. Adam's mind must here take a leap into a perspective in which what is serious and dangerous to him on earth is made to seem slight. This disjunction has the effect of diminishing the space and reality of earth in Adam's perception.

Raphael even more explicitly constricts the space earth occupies in the mind in his formulaic direct comparisons of earth to heaven, as when he describes the angels resting after their joyous feasts:

> . . . roseate dews disposed
> All but the unsleeping eyes of God to rest,
> Wide over all the plain, and wider far
> Than all this globous earth in plain outspread
> (Such are the courts of God).
>
> (5: 646–50)

or when he describes the march of Satan's army:

> Regions they passed, the mighty regencies
> Of Seraphim and Potentates and Thrones
> In their triple degrees, regions to which
> All thy dominion, Adam, is no more
> Than what this garden is to all the earth
> And all the sea.
>
> (5: 748–53)

Such condescending and literal-minded representation shows a lack of imagination that is not very different from Satan's perception of the fruit.

Raphael's similes do not have the distance of the third space. They are too brief; and they have no pause, no still mood, no yearning, no resonance. They cannot function to expand Adam's imaginative potential into the space that would enable him to see earth in its resonance with the yearning and distancing of mind, and in its resonance with heaven, the true union toward which human being is destined. Raphael's distancing between heaven and earth is a disjunction because he does not represent it in a way in which the viewer can see the change as it takes place, either through a change of position, as in Satan's and Raphael's flights, or through the modulation of tone or mood. Raphael reduces the kinesthesia of both body and mind to static, rationalistic formulas that have the effect of expanding Adam's mind into the literal spaces of heaven instead of into the spaces of the imagination in which the principles "behind" heaven and earth resonate. This effect leads to "affirmation" and "denial," to "obedience" and "disobedience."

Raphael's art has opened a gap in Adam's mind, has opened it to a "doubt" and fear (8: 13) that he expresses in his questions about astronomy in the beginning of Book 8. Insufficient as it was, whatever resonance Adam thought he had before the account of the war in heaven is entirely broken. Eve's dream and the foregrounding of issues such as free will and the possibility of falling necessitated by the purpose of Raphael's mission make an "opening" in the "scale of Nature" and are part of the "open[ing] to . . . [themselves] at length the way"; but Raphael's strategy effectively seals off this way and instead opens up to him the spaces of heaven and the fear of chaos. This is not very different from Satan's purpose in Eve's dream. Their strategies are different, but complementary. Raphael's diminishing of earth must reinforce the appeal of Satan's "be henceforth among the gods / . . . not to earth confined" (5: 77–78).

It is significant that after the account of the war in heaven "hate in heav'n" is still "unimaginable" to Adam, and that the expulsion of evil "impossible to mix with blessedness" calms his mind—"Whence Adam soon repealed / The doubts that in his heart arose . . ." (7: 59–60). This calming is not so different from the calming of the hymn to morn, which led God to pity them and send Raphael in the first place.

Although Adam has repealed the doubts and later in the beginning of Book 8 politely says his thirst for knowledge is allayed, his politeness perhaps stems in part from his deference to the superior being. For new doubts follow: "something yet of doubt remains, / Which only thy solution can resolve" (8: 13–14). This preface leads to the questions on astronomy, which indicate the exact nature of his doubt. The enjoyment of a Nature's bounty that was earlier perceived as "unsparing" (5: 344) and "unmeasured out" (5: 399) has given way to fear of disorder if Nature is not "wise and frugal" (8: 26). This fear follows upon the disjunctions of Raphael's account of the war in heaven and perhaps also upon the powerful vitality of the account of creation in Book 7, which makes Raphael's initial ladderlike representations of reality seem flimsy indeed. Whereas the ladder appeals to reason, the vitality of Book 7 appeals to the kinesthetic faculty; but because it follows the galloping fragmentation of the war in heaven and because Raphael has not given this energy imaginative space, it appears chaotic to Adam. Adam has asked earlier in Book 5, "Can we want obedience?" (5: 514), and the angel's answer was "you are free." But his picture of freedom opens up to Adam the raw forces of the universe more than opening him up to the forces and spaces in his own mind. And this opening does not take place "by degrees" (7: 157) but with an abruptness that "overturns / All patience" (6: 463–64) and that leads to Adam's clinging to the insufficient ladder pictures and to the regression of understanding in the fall.

For Adam's questions in the beginning of Book 8 indicate that he wants a return to order, but Raphael responds with the unsettling mental motions of simple relativizing, which must have a different effect on Adam from that on the reader, whose mind has already proceeded through the lyric and ironic stage of the modal declension gradually and in a controlled manner. For Adam, Raphael's technique causes further disruption, because he does not allow the pause, the central neutrality necessary to the simple relativizing mode. Rather, he alternates the setting of motion against motion with jolting sympathic admonishments to "obey." Because it is fragmented, his colloquy with Adam slips into the sympathic realm of affirmation and denial. Repeatedly focusing on the anchor of the will and the issue of obedience rather than on consciousness, Raphael fragments Adam's mind.

For the calmer mind of the reader, Raphael's relativizing technique— "whether heav'n move or earth, / Imports not, if thou reckon right" (8: 70–

71)—shifts the center of consideration from the heavens to the mind beholding the heavens, and then to a resonant alignment with the invisible energies of the universe behind visible manifestations such as planets and the sun. The technique also shows the reciprocal nature of the relation between greater and lesser forces.

The irony is that this moment of one of the clearest representations of truth in *Paradise Lost* has the worst possible effect on Adam because Raphael is a poor artist and psychologist. For this he is a villain, however unintentional. Since he has closed off Adam's imaginative space, this technique is not a strategy of mind for Adam but a new picture that further destroys the earlier hierarchical picture Raphael first gave of the structure of reality. In terms of that first picture, it *does* "import" whether "greater" or "brighter" moves, and it is more or less "excellent."

There is a further irony when Raphael concludes this upsetting presentation by telling Adam not to concern himself with such matters anyway:

> Think only what concerns thee and thy being;
> Dream not of other worlds.
>
> (8: 174–75)

Adam, who was created by God to open to himself the way to heaven at length has first been violently exposed to the raw forces of heaven and then told not to concern himself with the other world to which the way is supposed to lead. Raphael has radically severed the resonance between earth and heaven, and has similarly severed Adam's shattered reason and his will from his dreaming faculty—his imagination.

Adam's reply is equally ironic as he politely assures Raphael that he has "fully satisfied" him and "freed [his mind] from intricacies" (8: 180–82). But again, he is not satisfied, for he offers to tell the angel his own story,

> . . . subtly to detain thee . . .
> . . . .
>   . . . in hope of thy reply.
> For while I sit with thee, I seem in heav'n.
>
> (8: 207–10)

Adam's story takes the poem into a further ironic turn, for it is in the context of this colloquy with Raphael that Adam tells the story of a creation and a form of being that *does* include a structure of mind more closely corresponding to the principles of the universe. However, the irony is that Adam's mind, even as he tells this story, is focused more on pleasing the angel in order to get more heavenly wisdom from him than on the greater and more evolved wisdom of his own creation. This human creation is difficult for the angel to fully understand because of his own structure of mind, which does not make distinctions between literal and spiritual space.

Raphael, though sociable and kindly intentioned, is the poet of epic war, external and literal war. At one point in his account of the war in heaven, he pauses briefly to say how difficult it is to convey to Adam heavenly events:

> . . . for who, though with the tongue
> Of angels, can relate, or to what things
> Liken on earth conspicuous, that may lift
> Human imagination to such highth
> Of godlike power?
>
> (6: 297–301)

The St. Paul whom Raphael is echoing would continue, "Though I speak with the tongues of men and of angels, and have not love, I am become as sounding brass, or a tinkling cymbal" (1 Cor. 13:1). Raphael's art is the brass of war and tinkling of pseudo-lyricism. He omits the perspective and space of love, of yearning, that could "lift / Human imagination" to its destined height. The effect of his visit to Eden is that when he leaves, Adam and Eve are riper to fall.

9   The Creation of Adam and Eve

Adam's relation of his own and Eve's creation articulates in a clearer and more direct way than in Book 4 the nature of the edenic state of being. The creation of Adam and Eve is a "repair" (7: 152) not only of the breach in heaven caused by Satan, but of the heavenly structure of mind: they are different from the angels in their structure and in their relation to the universe. The two principal differences are that they are two instead of one, and that yearning—modality—is created as part of their being.

Adam is born into a context of dream and yearning. His first memory is finding himself on the grass "as new-waked from soundest sleep" (8: 253). As he first joys in the kinesthetic experience of his own movement and the movement of the things and creatures around him, he yearns to know his origins, who has made him. Pensive, he soon sinks into sleep and has a dream that his question is answered by the coming of God, who takes him "raised . . . over fields and waters"—as was Eve in her dream—up the mount of Paradise and into the garden. He awakens to find the dream "all real" (8: 310). Soon in his solitude Adam yearns for another like being and "presumes" to ask the God who comes at his calling to satisfy this yearning. Again Adam sinks down into sleep and a trance, in which his "internal sight," "fancy," witnesses the creation of Eve. Her first act is to "disappear" from his sight. "Left dark" he "wake[s] / To find her" (8: 478–79).

This structure of yearning, calling, and dreaming sets up a dynamic resonance in which the connection between beings, between desirer and desired, is not "prompt" but delayed across a distance or space. Adam must ask for God to respond: "called by thee I come thy guide" (8: 298) and "whom thou sought'st I am" (8: 316). The identity of God whose name is "I am" is he "whom thou seeks't," is what is yearned for and only revealed through this yearning.

This new distance or space is not the space of real action; neither is it even the third space of the imagination, but rather a kind of dramatic space somewhere between action and poetry. When God first answers Adam's request for Eve he sets up a hierarchical structure more mechanical and dissatisfying than the heavenly hierarchy because God is farther removed above Adam and the animals are farther removed below Adam than the angels are removed from each other by the heavenly orders and degrees. However, in this new space, God's first answer is a straw man; he tempts

155

Adam to do in dialogue what Satan was tempted to do in action—protest in an action that arises from a sense of yearning. This interplay of questioning and responding is a resonant relationship between protagonists that, having the magnetism of both cooperation and combat, leads to an evolution dependent upon reciprocity.

This evolution is not predetermined: by setting up this new third space God is involving himself in the time of his creatures in a new way that will better allow him to understand them from their point of view. Behind the hierarchical structure Adam challenges, there is another structure waiting. God himself is evolutionary, and responsive to change. Although he says to Adam "with these [animals] / Find pastime, and bear rule; thy realm is large," Adam asks again because he notices that God "seemed / So ordering" (8: 374–77). In this "seemed" there is room for movement and change. God's manner is firm but mild, and the firmness does not destroy the mildness or conflict with it, but visibly modulates between the two. Adam says to Raphael,

> . . . Sternly he pronounced
> The rigid interdiction, which resounds
> Yet dreadful in mine ear, though in my choice
> Not to incur; but soon his clear aspéct
> Returned, and gracious purpose thus renewed.
>
> (8: 333–37)

God's firmness does not prevent Adam from pressing his point, does not overturn his patience.

The creation of human being as male and female is a new structure within the overall universal structure. They occupy a space in which, being equals, they can form a less stressful and precarious harmony than if they were unequals; yet in which their being unlike creates a distance across which they must know each other in a more conscious resonance than in the heavenly union. Adam and Eve are one being made into two, but in this reformation, they are different qualitatively from angelic being as well as quantitatively.

Eve is more a new kind of being than Adam, for her nature corresponds to the space in reality that is unrepresented in the heavenly structure of mind. She is in herself a space, a dimly known fluid space that Adam must come to know. Adam is the principle of uprightness or centrality that, as he enters and yields to the space, the fluidity centers around. This pair is not primarily sexual, as the preceding phraseology might imply, nor is it a simple imagination-reason dichotomy. Rather it is a spiritual structure that, while it corresponds to the physical, is better understood in terms of psychic modality.

Eve is the pure lyric principle, in a presympathic and almost premodal form. (For the lyric mode as described in chapter 3, and chapter 5, is postsympathic, or postlapsarian.) She is pure fluidity and pure space, undefined and uncircumscribed by poles and forces as in the lyric paradign. It is as if magnetism were freed from its field. She is not the imagination, because she cannot maintain the center necessary to stay in modality and then move into the relativizing modes. She is too fluid and undiscriminating to avoid dangerous attachments. On the other hand she does not form lasting attachments or identifications: she can let them go almost as easily as she made them.

Adam is more like Abdiel and the righteous angels, and therefore less a new kind of being. He is upright and stands firm in the swirl about him. But like Eve and unlike Abdiel, he is presympathic and almost premodal reason and will: he is the *principle* of uprightness and centrality, he is pure structure rather than adherence to a specific command. Both Adam and Eve are detached from power and knowledge. They are created to incarnate the state of *mind* that moves to correspond to the structure of the universe, a state of mind that the angels lack.

When they are first created, Adam and Eve do not yet know each other; instead they are specifically created with the *impulse* to know each other. In this evolving knowledge, Adam and Eve are a couple, a dovetail structure that does not cancel itself out but allows the two parts to bring each other to more conscious and vital life. In this way, God answers the need reflected by Satan's fall, the need for an appropriate mind structure. The structure of the universe and the structure of heavenly love are insufficient, for beings created in God's image but not equal to him will feel the gap between them just as God himself feels it. As he says to Adam:

> What think'st thou then of me, and this my state?
> Seem I to thee sufficiently possessed
> Of happiness, or not? Who am alone
> From all eternity; for none I know
> Second to me or like, equal much less.
>
> (8: 403–7)

But love alone cannot fill this gap, either for the superior or inferior. Consciousness and empathy are necessary. Adam is created to feel the same solitude as God, created first to yearn, not to love; he is born into a modality that opens the way to true consciousness and love. He feels first the gap of Eve's absence, then after her creation the gap of the difference in their natures, and yearns to know her. As he says to Raphael:

> . . . though divinely brought,
> Yet innocence and virgin modesty,
> Her virtue and the conscience of her worth,
> That would be wooed, and not unsought be won,
> Not obvious, not obtrusive, but retired,
> The more desirable; or to say all,
> Nature herself, though pure of sinful thought,
> Wrought in her so, that seeing me, she turned;

> I followed her; she what was honor knew,
> And with obsequious majesty approved
> My pleaded reason. To the nuptial bow'r
> I led her.
>
> (8: 500–511)

The knowledge described in this passage is of several kinds. In this newly created form of consciousness, reason must seek and woo beauty and love, which is "retired" into a different space, but that, once sought, turns to reason.

Thus in the edenic state the declension of mind and evolution are built into the created structure. Adam's feelings for Eve seem to him both the "sum of earthly bliss which I enjoy" and a weakness, even a failing in nature. But this sense is characteristic of the state of yearning itself. In contrast to the angelic state, one might say that Adam has been created already "fallen" because he is born acting on the sense of gap that in Satan's act leads to an immediate and "real" fall. But in this new configuration, the purpose of the gap is to impel evolution. Thus he complains of his delight in the rest of Paradise: unlike his feelings for Eve, it "works in the mind no change, / Nor vehement desire" (8: 525–26).

The solution to his feeling of "weakness" is the change of coming to know Eve and her coming to know him. It is this knowledge of each other—self-knowledge—in the dynamic third space that leads to knowledge of God. Human being is created to be "self-knowing, and from thence / Magnanimous to correspond with heav'n" (7: 510–11). This evolving knowledge corresponds to the structure of the universe partly because it has drawn God into a dramatic and historical movement in which he must participate with his creations, and because of this historical dimension, the "correspondence" is a process less of agreement than of a reciprocity characterized by tension as well as cooperation.

This process has already begun before Raphael's visit, although some of it is revealed not in Book 4 but in the discourse of Book 8. Adam by instinct springs upright when he is first created (8: 257–61), yet he soon enters the space of dream in the reclining of sleep or trance (8: 286–95), a state to which he returns several times in *Paradise Lost* when he is to "see" with his "internal sight."

Similarly, although when Eve is first created she follows her own fluid nature, she soon turns to the upright principle represented by Adam. In her "inexperienced thought" she "lays her down" to gaze into the "unmoved" lake like a Narcissus, loving her own image, not only "equal" but identical, hence not resonant, because the distance of unlikeness is lacking. But a voice warns her and "invisibly" leads her to Adam, standing upright "tall / Under a platane" (4: 477–78). He gently but firmly seizes her hand, and she yields.

Ironically, the wisdom of Adam's and Eve's creation and of their tentative but significant first movements toward self-knowledge is negated by the context in which it is told. In his story Adam reveals the dimension of the third space and the potential of the imagination developing in the dramatic space of edenic life, but in his innocence and deference to Raphael he gives more sanction to the angel's words than to the memory of his own experience. In describing his uneasiness about the felt gap in his relation to Eve, Adam imitates his auditor's hierarchical terminology and thought-patterns:

> . . . [in Eve's presence] transported I behold,
> Transported touch; here passion first I felt,
> Commotion strange, in all enjoyments else
> Superior and unmoved, here only weak
> Against the charm of beauty's powerful glance.
> Or Nature failed in me, and left some part
> Not proof enough such object to sustain,
> Or from my side subducting, took perhaps
> More than enough; at least on her bestowed
> Too much of ornament, in outward show
> Elaborate, of inward less exact.
> For well I understand in the prime end
> Of Nature her th'inferior, in the mind
> And inward faculties, which most excel
> . . . .
> . . . yet when I approach
> Her loveliness, so absolute she seems
> . . . .
> All higher knowledge in her presence falls
> . . . .
> Authority and reason on her wait,
> As one intended first, not after made
> Occasionally.
>
> (8: 529–56)

Words like *prime, inferior, excel, absolute,* and *higher* pervert the truth of their nature as two parts of the human psyche and force Adam into a choice between two equally false conceptions of their relationship: either Adam is "first" or Eve is "first." In an evolutionary reality, "first" does not mean "superior"; and in the configuration of their creation they are complementary beings in which both Adam and Eve yield. In this passage Adam is describing Eve from an external and rationalistic point of view that misconceives her nature: she is the inner space and not "inferior in the . . . inward faculties," though he is right in saying that they are "less exact." But "less exact" does not mean "inferior": this equation turns a quality into a quantity. Adam's mistake is not that he overvalues her but rather that he undervalues her because he misvalues her. Nature's "failure" in subducting his rib does not make him weak or inferior, but creates a space in him that yearns for the being created out of what was removed, a space that corresponds to Eve's nature just as the rib out of which she was formed corresponds to Adam's nature. This configuration is the reality of love and of the heart, the heart that perhaps is the flesh that "fills up" and "heals" the "wide . . . wound" left by the subduction, or a heart that pulsates in the newly created space.

Raphael's response to Adam's speech about Eve is a "contracted brow" and a stern reply that on the surface appears to direct itself more to Adam's literal-minded hierarchical conceptualization than to the pains of yearning giving rise to it. Raphael's reply is couched in the beginning and the end in the same terminology and seems to advise Adam to have more "self-esteem" and to invert his inappropriate adulation of Eve so that he remains Eve's "head" and she acknowledges this dominance. The end of the speech returns to the ladder-picture of universe and mind used in Book 5.

However, buried in this reading is a second reading, in which Raphael is telling Adam to take Eve more seriously and learn to know and value her better, not through reason but through the kinesthetic faculty. This rhetorical movement makes the whole speech a strange weave of incompatible conceptions. The intricacy and importance of this speech warrant quoting it in its entirety:

> Accuse not Nature, she hath done her part;
> Do thou but thine, and be not diffident
> Of wisdom; she deserts thee not, if thou
> Dismiss not her, when most thou need'st her nigh,
> By attributing overmuch to things
> Less excellent, as thou thyself perceiv'st.
> For what admir'st thou, what transports thee so,
> An outside? Fair no doubt, and worthy well
> Thy cherishing, thy honoring, and thy love,
> Not thy subjection. Weigh with her thyself;
> Then value. Ofttimes nothing profits more
> Than self-esteem, grounded on just and right
> Well managed; of that skill the more thou know'st,
> The more she will acknowledge thee her head,
> And to realities yield all her shows:
> Made so adorn for thy delight the more,
> So awful, that with honor thou may'st love
> Thy mate, who sees when thou art seen least wise.
> But if the sense of touch whereby mankind
> Is propagated seem such dear delight
> Beyond all other, think the same vouchsafed
> To cattle and each beast, which would not be
> To them made common and divulged, if aught
> Therein enjoyed were worthy to subdue
> The soul of man, or passion in him move.
> What higher in her society thou find'st
> Attractive, human, rational, love still;
> In loving thou dost well, in passion not,
> Wherein true love consists not; love refines
> The thoughts, and heart enlarges, hath his seat

In reason, and is judicious, is the scale
By which to heav'nly love thou may'st ascend.

(8: 561–92)

Adam has said in his speech that precedes that he is transported by passion when he "beholds" or "touches" Eve. Raphael tells him not to rely so much on his sense of touch, but to "*weigh* with her" himself. This "weigh" is the kinesthetic faculty of mind, like the "ponder" at the end of Book 4. Similarly, in the curious passage that fits least with the hierarchical schema, Adam's sense of sight is called into question: Raphael says that Eve's outside was created beautiful to delight him but was also created "awful" so that he love with honor his "mate, who sees when . . . [he is] seen least wise." Adam's "beholding" is no more superior than his sense of touch.

In the beginning of Raphael's speech (ll. 561–70) there is a syntactic and logical conflict in pronoun reference. The "she" in "she deserts thee not" would appear to be "wisdom" if the reading sequence runs from the antecedent "wisdom" forward to the "she." But as the speech proceeds, the "her" in "weigh with her thyself" is Eve, whose identity as the "she" in the last lines of this section is established by the content—"valuing an outside"—which carries over from Adam's preceding speech. But if the rhetorical beginning, or center of weight and significance of Raphael's speech is read as "Dismiss not her"—the most direct response to Adam's undervaluing of Eve, just as the apparent advice to be Eve's head is the direct response to his overvaluing her—then, reading radially both backward and forward from this center into the rest of the passage, the three "her's" in lines 564–70 would all refer to Eve; the "she" in "she deserts thee not" would be, first, Eve—who does desert him in Book 9 when he dismisses her—and would be, second, in the historical and psychic sequence, "wisdom," who will desert Adam if Adam dismisses Eve and Eve deserts. For wisdom is the result of Adam and Eve's being together the sum of earthly knowledge as well as of earthly bliss, and the way to heavenly knowledge and bliss. Adam "needs Eve nigh," and he needs her inward faculties and space more than her outside. When Raphael says "Dismiss not her . . . by attributing overmuch to things less excellent . . . an outside," what should follow is advice to "value her inside," but Raphael omits this step, which makes the sequence disjointed as he switches instead to the issue of "subjection." This line also lends itself to two readings: Adam should love, honor, and cherish, not subject himself to, the fair Eve; but neither should he subject her to himself. This second sense is supported by the syntactic parallelism of "subjection" with the verbs "cherishing" and "honoring."

The alternative to subjection is, in Raphael's sequence (as opposed to the implied sequence of outside-inside), to "weigh with her [himself]," an idea the angel does not clearly explain. But if read carefully, the lines indicate a path for Adam to follow different from the apparent hierarchical one of dominating her. Raphael does not say "weigh her with yourself" but "weigh *yourself* with her, then value." And he does not simply recommend to Adam "self-esteem," but "self-esteem grounded on just and right well-managed"— an idea that is allowed to remain vague. The fruits of this "skill" in which Eve is weighed rather than dismissed will be that she will acknowledge him without dominance.

But what appears most strongly as the alternative to "subjection"—the center of the hierarchical schema as represented, for example, by Abdiel's heavenly structure of service—is "love" (8: 569, 577; 587–92). In the perspective of the second reading, the closing section of Raphael's speech does not say that passion overturns love and that the dominance of reason and of the scale of nature will "refine" it and make it heavenly, but rather that it is *love* that "refines the *thoughts,*" love that enlarges the heart, love that has its "*seat* in reason," love that is "judicious," and love that *is* the "scale by which . . . [they may] ascend." The wisdom of this love is a high coition of souls, of the one soul of which Adam and Eve are each a complementary part.

Adam's reply to Raphael comes closer to a consideration of Eve's "inside"—which was missing in the angel's discussion—when he says:

> Neither her outside formed so fair, nor aught
> In procreation common to all kinds
> . . . .
> So much delights me as those graceful acts,
> Those thousand decencies that daily flow
> From all her words and actions.
>
> (8: 596–602)

But when he goes on to say that these "declare . . . / Union of mind, or in us both one soul," (8: 603–4) he is using Raphael's terminology, the "union" of the defective heavenly conception rather than a word like *reciprocity,* which Raphael introduced in his inept presentation of astronomy and which Adam himself has experienced. Also he hurries over his discussion of union, hardly listening to his own words, in order to defend himself against Raphael's apparent admonishment: "Yet these subject not . . . still free, / [I] approve the best, and follow what I approve." With these words Adam collapses the double nature of Raphael's speech into the first hierarchical reading, focusing on only one implication of the word *subject,* and thus casts the edenic state in terms of the heavenly state it was created to help evolve. In his "approving" and "following," Adam sounds like Abdiel retorting to Satan. Adam does not yet know what the "best" is.

At the end of his reply, Adam asks Raphael about the nature of heavenly love, which Raphael describes as the undistanced nonmodal kinesthesia of total mixing, total union. This view is as inapplicable, even as harmful, to

Adam as the hierarchical view. Both lack the third space. But Adam's deference to Raphael fixes these two views firmly in his mind.

Raphael's parting words further reinforce Adam's selective understanding of the angel's speech about Adam's relation to Eve.

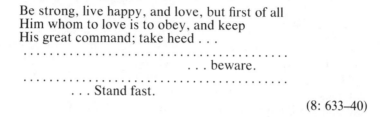

> Be strong, live happy, and love, but first of all
> Him whom to love is to obey, and keep
> His great command; take heed . . .
> . . . .
>   . . . beware.
> . . . .
>   . . . Stand fast.

$$\text{(8: 633–40)}$$

"Whom to love is to obey" can be read in two directions, but the emphasis on strength and on the "command" makes obedience prior to love, and will prior to skill. The third space of dream and dramatic action has been lost.

In this context, Adam's parting words are ironic: "Gentle to me and affable hath been / Thy condescension" (8: 648–49). For in his "condescension," Raphael has dismissed and distorted what is particular to the newly created human nature. While he returns "up to heav'n," Adam is left in "the thick shade" (8: 652–53).

Raphael's failure to sanction the reality of the human configuration and to help increase Adam and Eve's understanding of it—their mutual self-knowledge—undermines the purpose of his mission and makes them more, not less, vulnerable to Satan's guile. But their vulnerability and Raphael's shortcomings are reinforced by another irony, the irony of timing. The human configuration takes *time* to unfold, created as it is with the impulse and potential toward evolution, unlike the angels, who are fully developed at the moment of their creation. Even though in the end this movement will yield greater consciousness and fulfillment, Adam and Eve are both before and after Raphael's visit in an unformed and fluid state. The threat posed by Satan's invasion is a monkey wrench in this gradual development, an occurrence that God hastily tries to remedy after the fact by sending Raphael.

For the angels and God as yet have only an embryonic understanding of the nature of time in the whole evolutionary reality; they do not fully grasp the qualitative distinction between "in a moment" and "at length" (7: 154–58). Perhaps they believed that they could close the breach in heaven caused by the war, turn their backs on Satan, and start afresh with the creation of Adam and Eve, the creatures of time. But the reality is that Adam and Eve were created in the context and dynamic of Satan's fall, whether their creator is entirely conscious of it or not. The evolution from angelic to human being is not a change from static to dynamic reality, but a change from a nonmodal to a modal mind-structure to correspond to a reality that

always was dynamic. Therefore, if Adam and Eve are to be the new structure that will solve the problems caused by the old structure, they must also
confront and resolve the forces represented by Satan. The termination of the
war in heaven by arbitrary force solved the material problem of the continuing existence of the universe, but left the problem of mind unsettled. At their
creation the inevitability and necessity of Satan's invasion of Eden were
perhaps not seen, but at the end of Book 4 it becomes obvious when Gabriel
and his angels act in accordance with forces that have been set in motion by
the war in heaven and Satan's expulsion.

The edenic state is not "freed from intricacies" (8: 182). It is subtle and
complex, unlike a simply conceived ladder of direct ascent. But this lack of
simplicity is compensated by the innocence that is also part of their creation,
that protects them from the dangers attendant upon the intricacy and upon
the length of time it takes for human nature to unfold toward its destined
end. This innocence is like a bubble or shield, a third space that allows and
ensures the indirectness of meditative knowledge rather than the direct
knowledge through action as occurred in the war in heaven. The function of
the tree of knowledge in this state is specifically to break or block the search
for direct understanding and to safeguard the third space. Its offense to
reason is precisely its "meaning": it is a signpost to deflect the mind away
from direct reason into another path, meditation. It has no other "meaning";
its positive function is as a sign and principle of meditative neutrality.
Adam's nature also partly represents this neutrality. Hence in Eve's first
view of him he is standing "Under a platane" (4: 478).

Within this space of innocence, detached from power and direct knowledge, the growth of Adam's and Eve's self-knowledge takes place in a tentative, exploratory manner that is reflected in their often oversimplified
verbalizations about their nature. But what their style of action, thought,
and expression lacks in subtlety and consistency is made up for by their
exuberance and flexibility. This is an "innocence" whose formulations
should not in the beginning be taken at face value, but whose energy and
intuitive gropings should be allowed and guided.

Thus Adam's excessive and inexact praise of Eve in 8: 521–59 is at once
an enthusiastic expression of feeling and an intuition of her value and reason
for being. It is not simply "subjection" but an expression of the yearning to
know this as yet mysterious new entity, and therefore should not be reprimanded outright, but selectively and gently reprimanded, and then guided
toward a more discriminating view of her.

Similarly, even before Raphael's visit, Eve describes and evaluates herself in the simplistic hierarchical terms used by Raphael and Adam when she
recalls to Adam their first meeting. After her Narcissus-like self-
contemplation, she has yielded to Adam's call, and says:

> . . . thy gentle hand
> Seized mine, I yielded, and from that time see
> How beauty is excelled by manly grace
> And wisdom, which alone is truly fair.

(4: 488–91)

Similarly, she has prefaced the reminiscence by saying:

> . . . I chiefly . . . enjoy
> So far the happier lot, enjoying thee
> Pre-eminent by so much odds, while thou
> Like consort to thyself canst nowhere find.

(4: 445–48)

These pictures are only "correct" if understood as a tentative attempt to express the first appreciation of the male principle of uprightness by the female principle of fluidity and space. But it is incorrect if taken as an absolute hierarchical scale of value. For Eve is herself the "like consort," not "like" in the sense of identical but "like" in the sense of "equally valuable." As she asserts Adam's virtue she forgets, for the moment, her own, though perhaps she is not aware of it yet. If this partial and embryonic attempt at expression is taken as it is and frozen into a fixed formulation, it will be false.

The evolution of the edenic state before and during Raphael's visit is already beginning to take place in the trial-and-error process of mutual self-knowledge, sometimes too enthusiastic, sometimes too timid, sometimes needing correction, and sometimes needing encouragement. Moreover, this growing process occurs in relation to forces outside Eden in a kind of *stretching* resonance with the universal structure, which not only opens their own way in relation to it, but also changes the universal structure itself. This evolutionary stretching replaces such "breaking" as "breaking union."[1]

The style of Adam's and Raphael's exchanges often reflects this growing process. As they begin to share their meal of fresh fruit, "sudden mind arose / In Adam . . . to know / Of things above his world" (5: 452–56); yet he asks Raphael his first question about the excellence of things in heaven with "wary speech." Similarly, as Adam, more delighted by Raphael's speech than by food or even the angelic hymns, makes his "request" for Raphael to tell of the war in heaven, he frames it in careful terms that seek to extend his knowledge without abruptness:

> . . . what thou tell'st
> Hath passed in heav'n some doubt within me move,
> But more desire to hear, if thou consent,
> The full relation, which must needs be strange,
> Worthy of sacred silence to be heard.

(5: 553–57)

Raphael's style of response to such overtures is uneven. At times, as already discussed, he takes Adam's and Eve's tentative explorations at face value and destroys their flexibility. At other times, however, especially in the beginning of his visit, the colloquy proceeds according to the stretching principle from his side as well as from Adam's, and his answers reveal the same spirit of risk and tentativeness. For example, when he says that though the "secrets of another world" are "perhaps / Not lawful to reveal," he will tell the story for Adam's good (5: 569–70). Raphael acknowledges this style of Adam's stretching the law when he says, after Adam asks about the creation of earth, "This also thy request with caution asked / Obtain" (7: 111–12). Such statements are faithful to the spirit of the third dramatic space between God and Adam in which Adam "presumes" to press his request for a mate.

This picture of Eden as dynamic process is different from the static picture outlined in the discussion above of irony in Book 4. That first perception of Eden results partly from the reader's preconceptions about the nature of Paradise and from Milton's ironic response to these. However, the static irony also arises from the dangers of Adam and Eve's momentary peace, after Adam has found his Eve, after the pains of yearning, and before the challenge of Satan. For perhaps a continuing infusion of yearning is necessary to prevent them from becoming "too secure"—a security that would destroy the energy and consciousness of modality and arrest the evolution of mind.

But it is not security and complacency that destroy their state; it is the distortion of their structure of mind. First Raphael's moralizing tendencies come to dominate the colloquy so that it loses its stretching resonance, and then this plasticity is further destroyed partly by Satan and partly by Adam and Eve themselves. As Milton expresses it after Adam and Eve fall, "innocence, that as a veil / Had shadowed them from knowing ill, was gone" (9: 1054–55), the innocence that was their separate space of indirect but growing knowledge.

NOTE

1. Barbara Kiefer Lewalski discusses paradise as process in her article, "Innocence and Experience in Milton's Eden," in *New Essays on "Paradise Lost,"* ed. Thomas Kranidas (Berkeley and Los Angeles: University of California Press, 1969), pp. 86–117.

10 The Fall in Eden

The war in heaven was a contest of force; the fall of Adam and Eve is a contest of mind. Frequently throughout *Paradise Lost* it is said that Satan uses guile, not force, in his temptation of the human pair. His seduction of their minds and nature is similar in strategy if not in intent to Raphael's: they both literalize the modal and break the resonance into the dualism of material and transcendent—conceptions that are equally literal-minded.[1] This breaking then releases tremendous energies that because they are now without form work almost randomly for good or evil.

Raphael, addressing himself mostly to Adam, closes off the spiritual third space of the psyche and opens up the specious though "real" (literal) spaces of heaven, thereby obliterating the feminine principle in the psyche represented by Eve. He simultaneously turns the resonant tree-ladder image into a rigid hierarchy, thereby perverting the masculine principle in the psyche, the principle of meditative neutrality that is also represented by the tree of knowledge.

If Raphael's art is allegorical, Satan's might be considered a perverted romanticism. Addressing himself to Eve, Satan focuses on the fallacies, whether stated or implied, in Raphael's "reason" and gives them a further twist. He enters and sanctions the third space of the imagination, of Eve's dream, that Raphael has stripped of reality, but perverts it by identifying it with the specious heavenly space. He turns it inside-out and it collapses, with the result that their "eyes [are] . . . opened" but their "minds . . . darkened" (9: 1053–54). This is the reverse of the mental process in the invocation to Book 3 in which the eyes are blind but the mind illumined.

Satan likewise takes Raphael's picture of the tree—which in association with the ladder image the sociable spirit has unwisely used both as an image of human being's destined ascent (5: 469–512; 7: 505–16; 8: 586–94) and indirectly as an image of sin (8: 167–78)—and uses its inconsistency to destroy Raphael's order of obedience. The fall of Raphael's order allows Satan then to substitute his own version of the tree image as a literal means of ascent.

As Satan's fall was not directly prompted by aspiration to Godhead but rather in the first instance by feeling cut off from God, the "blessed union" seemingly broken by the Son's elevation, neither is Adam and Eve's fall directly motivated by the aspiration to Godhead or the desire to escape the bondage and limitation of a suffocating Paradise, but rather by fear of the apparent chaos of the universe revealed by Raphael and a consequent desire for certainty and control. This second fall is more complex than Satan's, though its workings are more articulated and perhaps therefore easier to understand.

In the first fall there were two primary participants, God and Satan—a higher and a lower being—each with his faithful followers. The distinctions between all of these participants were defined more by the difference in power, in "order and degree," and by their behavior in relation to the hierarchical structure of consciousness in heaven than by their "real" differences in nature, character, or form or by articulations of thought or action in relation to the modal reality of being. As the structure of consciousness failed to reflect this modal reality, so did their "character" or form fail to reflect or embody it. The second fall is more complicated, for there are now five beings or kinds of being instead of two—God, Satan, Adam, Eve, and Raphael—and these beings are more differentiated than were God and Satan. Having acted on his intuition of the unacknowledged modal gap, Satan has fallen into a sympathic state radically different from heavenly being. Adam and Eve have been created as two different but complementary principles of being into a more modal form than the angels. Raphael in his exchanges with the human pair has in his art more than his character introduced a fifth form, attempting and failing to mediate between the older and newer kinds of being. These five "characters" are more *different* than unequal. The fall of Adam and Eve—in fact the possibility of their fall—brings a sixth "character" or form—the Son—into more articulated being. After the war in heaven the Son becomes less an agent and follower of God and more a principle of being differentiated from him, in stretching resonance with him. Indeed, the Son becomes a principle of modal forming in the face of pure power.

The second fall is a moving set of interactions between these five beings that takes place in several interlocking steps. In brief, Adam, the masculine principle perverted by Raphael, fails to be the true masculine force for Eve, who, already undervaluing her own virtue and undervalued in Book 8 by both Adam and Raphael, asks Adam for strength. Failing to get it she seeks to supply this strength for herself by imitating Adam's imitation of Raphael. Satan in his seduction provides the specious means for this self-strengthening; and Eve, feeling "equal" to Adam, enjoins him to share the fruit. Adam, forgetting the dramatic and resonant nature of his relation with God and Eve in the face of sudden loss, focuses on his misconceived "union" with Eve—a concept learned from Raphael—and submits to "what seems remédiless" (9: 919) in a falsely imagined structure.

This sequence is ironic because Eve's colloquy with Adam in the beginning of Book 9 is an instance of potential evolution similar to her recounting of the dream in Book 5 and to Adam's dialogue with God in Book 8. What could even be termed "breaking" on Eve's part could be turned into "stretching," if sanctioned but guided by Adam. Had Adam responded to her here in Book 9 as he had earlier in Book 5 or as God had responded to him in Book 8, Book 9 might have marked a major step forward in their understanding of each other and contributed toward a stronger and more resonant "union." Had Adam once again yielded to and entered the space of dream, of trance, of poetry, however reluctantly, he might better have understood the implications of Eve's suggestion that they part. Instead, their exchange is a reaction to and a reflection of Raphael's visit more than a consideration of Eve's doubts. Adam's response is dominated by a focus on a mechanical, pseudo-masculine reason and will external to the third space.

The groundwork for the fall—Adam's and Raphael's colloquy—has been laid by the end of Book 8. Eve has left them in the beginning of Book 8 just as Adam has asked Raphael his question about astronomical motion, though Eve says later that she has overheard some of their conversation (9: 275–78). As Adam's queries to Raphael reflect a new fear of the bounty, immensity, and energy of the universe in relation to their place in it and a desire for order and reassurance, so the "thoughts" Eve presents to Adam in 9: 213–25, reflect the same uncertainty. Adam's question to Raphael is essentially the same one that Eve had asked Adam earlier in Book 4 just prior to her dream:

> . . . wherefore all night long shine these, for whom
> This glorious sight, when sleep hath shut all eyes?
>
> (4: 657–58)

But Adam's rephrasing of it in terms such as *spaces incomprehensible, useless, frugal, disproportions, superfluous, restless revolution, sumless journey,* and *incorporeal speed* (8: 20–38) must be unsettling for Eve, especially as it sharply contrasts with the previous orderly and reassuring explanation Adam gave her in answer to her question (4: 660–88). Before, the bounties of the creation were a source of delight, not of fear. Thus Paradise is described in Book 5 as "wild" and "wanton":

> A wilderness of sweets; for Nature here
> Wantoned as in her prime, and played at will
> Her virgin fancies, pouring forth more sweet,
> Wild above rule or art, enormous bliss.
> . . . .
>   . . . the mounted sun
> Shot down direct his fervid rays to warm
> Earth's inmost womb, more warmth than Adam needs.
>
> (5: 294–302)

Similarly, when Raphael first arrives as their guest in Eden, Adam instructs Eve to:

> . . . go with speed,
> And what thy stores contain, bring forth and pour
> Abundance, fit to honor and receive
> Our heav'nly stranger; well may we afford
> Our givers their own gifts, and large bestow
> From large bestowed, where Nature multiplies
> Her fertile growth, and by disburd'ning grows
> More fruitful; which instructs us not to spare.
>
> (5: 313–20)

And Adam says to Raphael as he invites him to eat:

> . . . Heav'nly stranger, please to taste
> These bounties which our Nourisher, from whom
> All perfect good unmeasured out descends.
>
> (5: 397–99)

But at the end of the angel's visit, this spontaneous perception of bounty has changed markedly. Now Nature is "frugal," and the possibility that her hand might be "superfluous" is cause for alarm.

This uneasiness is the context in which Eve begins her colloquy with Adam in Book 9:

> Adam, well may we labor still to dress
> This garden, still to tend plant, herb, and flow'r,
> Our pleasant task enjoined, but till more hands
> Aid us, the work under our labor grows,
> Luxurious by restraint; what we by day
> Lop overgrown, or prune, or prop, or bind
> One night or two with wanton growth derides,
> Tending to wild.
>
> (9: 205–12)

On the surface of it, perhaps the picture of "unmeasured" bounty is difficult to reconcile with Raphael's picture of the scale of Nature with its measured steps, but the disturbance in Adam's and Eve's minds goes far deeper than a theoretical consideration of how bounty is related to measurement. Confronted by the breach in the order of things introduced by Satan in the dream and intensified by Raphael's account of the war, the motion of heavenly bodies, and his description of her, Eve expresses her fear to Adam and then seeks aid from him in the form of a reassertion of their natures. Such a response would lead to further understanding of each other, another step in their destined evolution.

Her error is that she speaks less directly here than she did after her dream in Book 5. Then she said:

> . . . I this night—
> Such night till this I never passed—have dreamed

> If dreamed . . .
> . . . .
> . . . of offense and trouble, which my mind
> Knew never till this irksome night.
>
> (5: 30–35)

Now she speaks in an ambiguous and tortuous style that is the cautious and polite style Adam has used with Raphael carried to a nearly absurd conclusion:

> . . . Thou therefore now advise
> Or hear what to my mind first thoughts present:
> Let us divide our labors, thou where choice
> Leads thee, or where most needs, whether to wind
> The woodbine round this arbor, or direct
> The clasping ivy where to climb, while I
> In yonder spring of roses intermixed
> With myrtle, find what to redress till noon.
> For while so near each other thus all day
> Our task we choose, what wonder if so near
> Looks intervene and smiles, or object new
> Casual discourse draw on, which intermits
> Our day's work, brought to little, though begun
> Early, and th'hour of supper comes unearned.
>
> (9: 213–25)

What Eve is saying is not primarily that she thinks they should "divide their labors," but that they should perhaps divide their labors *because* she fears the inroads of the chaos reflected in the "wantonness" of Paradise. This thought is the core or energy center of her speech. Her emphasis on work and "earning" reflects the same fear and the same desire to make order and exert control. It is also a reaction to Adam's and Raphael's misevaluation of her in Book 8: she is responding to Raphael's apparent admonishment to Adam to love in her what is higher, not what is lower or carnal:

> What higher in her society thou find'st
> Attractive, human, rational, love still
> . . . .
> [love] . . . hath his seat
> In reason . . . and is the scale
> By which to heav'nly love thou may'st ascend,
> Not sunk in carnal pleasure.
>
> (8: 586–93)

It is the "higher" and the "reason" that are foregrounded and the "attractive" and "love" that are buried as Eve in her address to Adam tries to remedy ("redress") her felt deficiency—her "graceful acts," her "loveliness" and smiles—by shifting their behavior away from apparent carnality and toward the values Raphael expresses—higher reason and strength.

Last and most important, Eve is asking Adam in poetic language for support and love, for she feels weakened by Raphael's and Adam's devaluation of her and now has no identity. This felt need for support is communicated by the imagery Eve uses to describe their divided labors—"to wind the woodbine round this arbor" and to "direct the clasping ivy where to climb." Both images describe the traditional vine-tree relationship that is used in the early books of *Paradise Lost* as an emblem for Adam and Eve's marriage. In 4: 306–8 Eve's hair has been described as "wanton ringlets waved / As the vine curls her tendrils, which implied / Subjection, but required with gentle sway." Adam is pictured as standing "fair indeed and tall" under the platane in 4: 477–78; and Eve is later described as "leaning" on him in 4: 494–95. In Book 5 their marriage is a direct analogy for their gardening:

> . . . they led the vine
> To wed her elm; she spoused about him twines
> Her marriageable arms.
>
> (5: 215–17)

That their relationship must be more than the dependency and subjection this image suggests is indicated by the placement of the analogy—immediately after Eve's dream when Adam's support of her arouses God's pity—and by the description of some "embraces" as "fruitless" (5: 215).

However, what Eve senses is that she and Adam have been divided—by Raphael—and that they must become close again by valuing themselves and each other. Eve is "seeing" when Adam is seen "least wise." Unfortunately, she expresses this closeness in an image that is easily mistaken for dependency and subjection, which at this point in their evolution are outmoded. What Eve needs is what the tree image, if taken rightly, does express: the inner "tree" incarnate in Adam, the inner male principle of steadfastness and meditative neutrality.

In addition to this support from Adam—the assertion of himself in relation to her—Eve needs him to assert the value of her nature. For Eve's fluid self, her own virtue, has lost what frail sanction it ever had. When she says to him in her veiled poetic style to go where "choice leads thee, or where most needs . . . to wind the woodbine . . .," she is saying "choose me, I am in need." She is giving him only one "choice," since both tasks are the same. This felt lack of value is stated more directly after her fall as she considers whether to share the forbidden fruit with Adam:

> . . . Shall I to him make known
> As yet my change, and give him to partake
> Full happiness with me, or rather not,
> But keep the odds of knowledge in my power
> Without copartner? So to add what wants

> In female sex, the more to draw his love,
> And render me more equal, and perhaps,
> A thing not undesirable, sometime
> Superior; for inferior who is free?
>
> (9: 817–25)

And when she offers the fruit to him, she says:

> Thou therefore also taste, that equal lot
> May join us, equal joy, as equal love.
>
> (9: 881–82)

Her earlier hierarchical formulation and appreciation of their marriage is no longer valid, but the need for mutual understanding and joining integral to their natures has not changed.

In his reply to her plea for help, Adam is insensitive to her poetic meanings and selectively focuses on the least important—if most obvious—of her "thoughts": "let us divide our labors." He does not hear what she is really saying, partly because her thoughts and feelings are confused and her speech indirect, and partly because he is listening more to Raphael than to Eve. In so doing, he "disobeys" the hidden but more important "command": "dismiss not her when most thou needst her nigh" and love with honor "thy mate, who sees when thou art seen least wise." Adam is "least wise" in his reply to Eve. Ironically, as he denies her true support, he focuses, whether consciously or not, on the vine-tree image that Eve has used in her plea for a reassertion of their human natures. In Eve's speech the regressive image indicates how deeply aware she is that the breach between them is serious and the need to repair it desperate. But in Adam's reply the image serves as a symbol for Raphael's hierarchical thought-structure. On the surface, Adam does what Eve asks, as reflected in the words "leave not the faithful side / That gave thee being, still shades thee and protects" (9: 265–66). His image of himself as the protecting tree would seem to answer exactly the expressed need of the vine. But the word *shades* is perhaps a clue to the falsity and irony of Adam's strategy, for he answers in terms of hierarchy, will, and obedience that diminish Eve rather than respect her.

He does tell her of her value to him, but it is her "looks and smiles," "refreshment," "delight," and "tender love" that he selects to praise, to "choose," and not her true feminine nature—her imaginative inward faculties. These more superficial delights are not without value, but Adam has chosen the wrong time to stress them. He is right to "doubt" the wisdom of their being separated, but as he expresses this doubt he stresses her weakness without him, not the particular strength of her nature which, when joined to his, is the strength that can withstand Satan. When she protests, he goes even farther in his false characterization of her feminine nature by telling her that he wants to "avoid the attempt itself" that Satan might make on her.

His response to her comments about their work shows a similar inappropriateness. While Eve in her plight needs order and strength and a means of assertion, Adam not only stresses her weakness, but stresses the delight of their work as opposed to its labor (9: 235–43). He is not wrong, but he is in his attitude toward both Eve and their work "valuing an outside"; for while it is true that the work of their literal gardening in the external Paradise is not meant to be hard labor, their internal *psychic* work is "strict" and difficult. Adam is ignoring their inner natures and inner work—the space to which he was introduced in his creation, Eve's creation, and Eve's dream. He is responding with his severed and externalized reason rather than with the empathic faculty with which he was created. Further, he is literalizing Eve's poetic speech. When he says "The wife, where danger or dishonor lurks, / Safest and seemliest by her husband stays, / Who guards her, or with her the worst endures" (9: 267–69), he is debasing their natures and their evolutionary mission into the domestic, for which Milton aptly calls him "domestic Adam" (9: 318).

Adam similarly perverts his own masculine nature by externalizing it, by emphasizing will, obedience, and reason's "keeping strictest watch" (9: 350–63). Ironically, he does say that their state is "secure from outward force," that it is "within himself / The danger lies, yet lies within his power" (9: 348–49), but he passes quickly over the truth of this "within" to represent the "power" in external terms and thereby rhetorically bury the idea of the power of inward faculties. The following discourse on will and the exhortation to Eve to "obey" is a strategy similar to Raphael's parting speech in Book 8. Adam perverts meditative neutrality into will and collapses the third space, effectively "dismissing" Eve even before he tells her to "Go . . . rely / On what thou hast of virtue, summon all, / For God towards thee hath done his part, do thine" (9: 373–75). Such words are heavily ironical, for Adam has dismissed Eve's virtue, assigning pseudo-masculine values to her as well as to himself: he has not "done his part."

The progress and effect of Adam's speech are not intentional, for balancing such comments as "the husband guards the wife" are appeals to the true reciprocal nature of their marriage, as in "[Satan] watches . . . with greedy hope to find / . . . us asunder, / Hopeless to circumvent us joined" (9: 257–59). But because he values her outside, not her inside, this statement can carry little force.

The consequence is that Eve, uncertain of both herself and Adam, feels compelled to seek her own strength and tries to become another Adam, using Raphael's and Adam's picture as a model. When Adam tells her to stay by "her husband . . . who guards her," her answer is to stress her "firmness":

> . . . that thou shouldst my firmness therefore doubt
> To God or thee, because we have a foe

May tempt it, I expected not to hear.
. . . .
His fraud is then thy fear, which plain infers
Thy equal fear that my firm faith and love
Can by his fraud be shaken or seduced.

(9: 279–87)

She protests against their condition in Eden, which she now sees as a "narrow circuit" (9: 323) and questions whether they can be happy if not "endued / Single with like defense" (9: 324–25). The "narrow circuit" is not Eden, but the realm of the mind that Adam has, like Raphael in 5: 748–53, diminished into nothingness. The essence and strength of their relationship collapsed, Eve feels exposed to the threatening universe unless she can rely on her own strength:

And what is faith, love, virtue, unassayed
Alone, without exterior help sustained?
Let us not then suspect our happy state
Left so imperfect by the Maker wise
As not secure to single or combined.
Frail is our happiness, if this be so,
And Eden were no Eden thus exposed.

(9: 335–41)

The word *exterior* is evidence of the collapse of the third space for Eve and also of the essential worthlessness of Adam's new conception of what sustains. In her brave talk, Eve sounds like an epic hero seeking "temptation" and "trial," to use Adam's words (9: 364–66), seeking proof of self-worth by conquests in the external world—the world of knights, explorers, and pilots seeking control over adversaries, winds, seas, and heavens.

Adam has turned their world inside-out, slackly removing the strictness from the evolution of the mind and placing it on an externalized will. Eve with her assumed braveness goes off to garden alone. When Satan spies her, she is among the rosebushes, her work reflecting her weakened state of mind:

. . . oft stooping to support
Each flow'r of slender stalk, whose head though gay
Carnation, purple, azure, or specked with gold,
Hung drooping unsustained; them she upstays
Gently with myrtle band, mindless the while
Herself, though fairest unsupported flow'r,
From her best prop so far, and storm so nigh.

(9: 427–33)

The strategy of Satan's temptation of Eve is addressed to her doubts and need as Adam's colloquy with her was not. Satan acknowledges and praises her particular feminine nature; he gives her an order and a principle of strength to replace the masculine principle Adam has withdrawn; and he gives her love—the three things Eve has asked for but fails to receive from Adam. The fulfillment, even the relief, this approach seems to promise is indicated by Eve's choice of words as she answers Satan's offer of the fruit: "the cure of all, this fruit divine" (9: 776). Her exchange with Adam has left her wounded and ill.

Satan's temptation succeeds with Eve as much for the genuine sympathy it contains as for its calculated cleverness and desire for revenge. Even the calculations are in their way sympathetic, for they are inextricably involved in his own pain and confusion, regrets and hopes.

His sympathy for Adam and Eve is inspired both by his unexpected delight in the beauties of Eden and by his perception of their frail condition as similar to his own plight. When, like the scout catching sight of the metropolis glistering in the rising sun, he first sees the new world from the stairs between heaven and earth,

> Such wonder seized, though after heaven seen,
> The Spirit malign.
>
> (3: 552–53)

When he first sees Adam and Eve, "earth-born . . . / Not Spirits, yet to heav'nly Spirits bright / Little inferior," his "thoughts pursue [them] / With wonder" and he feels he "could love" them, "such grace / The hand that formed them on their shape hath poured" (4: 360–65). In Book 9 he expresses, perhaps more clearly than Raphael, the reciprocity of heaven and earth:

> O earth, how like to heav'n, if not preferred
> More justly, seat worthier of gods, as built
> With second thoughts, reforming what was old!
> . . . .
> Productive in herb, plant, and nobler birth
> Of creatures animate with gradual life
> Of growth, sense, reason, all summed up in man.
> With what delight could I have walked thee round,
> If I could joy in aught, sweet interchange
> Of hill and valley, rivers, woods, and plains,
> Now land, now sea, and shores with forest crowned,
> Rocks, dens, and caves.
>
> (9: 99–118)

Even as, imbruted in the serpent, he comes upon the Eve he is seeking to seduce, his first reaction is a spontaneous pleasure that makes him for a moment forget his intended revenge. As the city-dweller "conceives delight" from the beauties of the rural morning (9: 445–54), so Satan takes

Such pleasure . . . to behold
This flow'ry plat, the sweet recess of Eve
Thus early, thus alone; her heav'nly form
Angelic, but more soft and feminine,
Her graceful innocence, her every air
Of gesture or least action overawed
His malice, and with rapine sweet bereaved
His fierceness of the fierce intent it brought.
That space the Evil One abstracted stood
From his own evil, and for the time remained
Stupidly good, of enmity disarmed,
Of guile, of hate, of envy, of revenge.

(9: 455–66)

As their beauty arouses his admiration, their vulnerability arouses his pity:

. . . [I am] no purposed foe
To you whom I could pity thus forlorn,
Though I unpitied.

(4: 373–75)

The word *forlorn,* placed as it is, refers equally to Satan and the human pair. When he hears that they are forbidden to eat of the fruit of the tree of knowledge, he exclaims in genuine indignation:

. . . Knowledge forbidden?
Suspicionless, reasonless. Why should their Lord
Envy them that? Can it be sin to know,
Can it be death? And do they only stand
By ignorance, is that their happy state,
The proof of their obedience and their faith?

(4: 515–20)

Their beauty and frailty touch the emptiness within him and evoke confused feelings in him. Although the form these feelings eventually take is the temptation, this temptation may be seen as a kind of love-song to Eve. Couched in the style of a courtly amorist, his extravagant praise and his gifts are a "show of love" (9: 492), not only because they are "feigned" but because they are the perceptible form Satan's "love" takes. Moreover, Satan and Eve's colloquy is a form of coition: the setting of the temptation scene is the third space represented by Eve, which Satan enters as once Adam had entered the space of dream. Of course, this coition is not the high coition of complementary spiritual principles that was the purpose of Adam and Eve's creation. If Adam's behavior in dismissing Eve and externalizing the realm of mind is a prelude to a kind of psychic onanism, Satan and Eve's behavior is a kind of mutual psychic rape. Adam's spiritual "withdrawal" from Eve and from the edenic state has left them "exposed." The essence of the edenic state as an interknowing of two complementary psychic principles is represented with the image of human coition in Milton's first description of the garden in Book 4:

> . . . delicious Paradise,
> Now nearer, crowns with her enclosure green
> As with a rural mound the champaign head
> Of a steep wilderness, whose hairy sides
> With thicket overgrown, grotesque and wild,
> Access denied.
>
> (4: 133–38)

In this psychic and physical joining, Adam and Eve are not "divided," and access is denied to such as Satan, who must "disdain due entrance" (4: 180) to get into the garden.

The sexual undertones in Satan's temptation of Eve are made quite explicit by the conception of the fall as a "seduction," and by such devices as the representation of Satan as an "erect" snake when he first approaches Eve:

> . . . the Enemy of mankind, enclosed
> In serpent, inmate bad . . . toward Eve
> Addressed his way, not with indented wave,
> Prone on the ground, as since, but on his rear,
> Circular base of rising folds, that tow'red
> Fold above fold a surging maze; his head
> Crested aloft, and carbuncle his eyes;
> With burnished neck of verdant gold, erect
> Amidst his circling spires, that on the grass
> Floated redundant. Pleasing was his shape,
> And lovely, never since of serpent kind
> Lovelier; not those that in Illyria changed
> Hermione and Cadmus, or the god
> In Epidaurus, nor to which transformed
> Ammonian Jove, or Capitoline was seen,
> He with Olympias, this with her who bore
> Scipio, the highth of Rome. With tract oblique
> At first, as one who sought accéss, but feared
> To interrupt, sidelong he works his way.
>
> (9: 494–512)

Some of the serpents in this chain of similes are the forms that mythical gods took to father military conquerors.

Milton's language reinforces the sexual implications of such an image. The phrase "sought access" invokes the image of Paradise in Book 4. Later in the seduction scene Milton describes Satan's "words replete with guile" and "impregned with reason" winning "easy entrance" into Eve's heart (9: 733–38). As he begins his courtly flattery, Satan says to Eve:

> . . . all things . . .
>   . . . thy celestial beauty adore,
> With ravishment beheld.
>
> (9: 539–41)

Satan's "love-song" is a "ravishing" of Eve, but at the same time his behold-ing of her "ravishes the beholder." In his use of this reversible phrase "with ravishment" Satan reveals that he is as much a victim of rape as Eve. Their dismissals have left them both "exposed"; the seduction is mutual and col-laborative. The "rapine sweet" that "bereaves" his "fierceness" is a more explicit reference to this inverse victimization.

That this love-song is not a high coition but a seduction that leads to a fall is not something that Satan and Eve "intend," plan, and carry out. Rather it is an almost secondary consequence of their psychic structures, whose "cause" is a more primary, conscious, and controllable self-formation. Of course, this self-formation has taken place and continues to take place partly in response to other beings and events that share their resonant reality. Eve's state of mind is partly "determined"—as outlined above—in reaction to Raphael and Adam and their representations of reality. Similarly, Satan's thoughts and acts occur in response to the flawed structure of heavenly mind as well as to the pain of his own yearning. In the formation of self one's attitude toward place, event, or creature is intimately related to one's at-titude toward the universe as a whole.

The beginning of Satan's self-formation may be most clearly seen in his soliloquy on Mt. Niphates. Satan in his revolt in heaven has acted partly on his intuition of the modal nature of reality. But because the rhetoric of heaven implies that its structure is one of possession and identification, the elevation of the Son makes the modal space a painful breach, a breaking of union. The space turns into a void; power and love become confused and turn into a raw and violent energy; and God, ruling in an "excess of joy" (1: 123), is absolute. Satan's expulsion from heaven widens this gap, and in response he struggles to build a psychic structure corresponding to the uni-versal structure as he perceives it. During the war in heaven, Satan's thought processes are not articulated, but on Mt. Niphates he pauses, like Abdiel in 6: 113–26, to explore his own heart.

The searching train of thought in this soliloquy shows that he does not understand excatly what prompted him to do what he did. He says God "deserved no such return / From me" (4: 42–43), yet the "debt immense of endless gratitude" (4: 52) for his creation and his good was such a burden on him that he felt that more power would "quit / The debt" (4: 51–52). This debt made him "Forgetful what from him [he] . . . still received" (4: 54). What Satan does not or cannot articulate is that he felt God's love to be a burden because, though Satan was powerful, he could give nothing to God in return since God is so much more powerful. The opportunity for real reciprocity is not provided for in heaven in any obvious way. True love is reciprocal, and reciprocity is not passive but requires a certain strength that is not the same as raw power to create from nothing or to destroy utterly. This strength of love is flexible and measured by empathic judgment in relation to the movement of its object. It is proper to angel and human as well as to God.

It is this reciprocal love and empathy that God wants. As he says in Book 3, he created angels and humans free so that they could choose to love not necessity, but him (3: 100–111). But in the unevolved structure of heavenly mind, this desire for love becomes confusedly expressed in such terms as *obedience, allegiance, proof,* and *gratitude* (3: 90–111)—which are not what God wants.

This rhetorical and perceptual confusion makes real reciprocity difficult and serves to turn the structure of raw power into an actuality and to aggravate the pain of yearning. For if Satan feels unable to give love in return, the reciprocity falters, the apparent gap widens, and he feels a greater need for love, which in turn widens the gap still further because this need can only be answered by reciprocal love, not by received love. To resolve this dilemma he withdraws his love entirely (leaves the throne of God—5: 669–70), since it is felt to be so inadequate, and tries to rise in power ("one step higher"—4 50) in order to control the gap and thereby need less. He misconceives the nature of power that goes with love; therefore this strategy does not work but leads to more pain.

Aware that something is wrong with his perception of the gap, Satan alternatively tries in his soliloquy to explain his feeling of burden in terms favorable to God:

> Forgetful what from him I still received,
> . . . [I] understood not that a grateful mind
> By owing owes not, but still pays, at once
> Indebted and discharged; what burden then?
>
> (4: 54–57)

But without the idea of resonance, this self-accusation is not successful, for "paying" is not the same as "giving." The burden is real, which he feels but cannot understand. He goes on to ask himself, "Whom hast thou or what to accuse, / But Heav'n's free love dealt equally to all?" (4: 67–68). The answer for Satan to this self-accusing rhetorical question is "No one and nothing," but the true answer is that the "dealing out" is to blame: such love is not enough; consciousness, empathy, and reciprocity are also necessary.

He yearns to relent (4: 79), but since he is stuck in the perception of a hierarchy in which love is determined by raw power, he sees relenting only as a way to return to the same painful state. Assuming that the structure is absolute, he says:

> But say I could repent and could obtain
> By act of grace my former state; how soon
> Would highth recall high thoughts, how soon unsay
> What reigned submission swore: ease would recant
> Vows made in pain, as violent and void.
> For never can true reconcilement grow
> Where wounds of deadly hate have pierced so deep;
> Which would but lead me to a worse relapse
> And heavier fall; so should I purchase dear
> Short intermission bought with double smart.
> This knows my Punisher; therefore as far
> From granting he, as I from begging peace.
> All hope excluded thus, behold instead
> Of us outcast, exiled, his new delight,
> Mankind created.
>
> (4: 93–107)

Satan forms his unclear and confused perception of heaven into his own psychic structure, a process reinforced by the official rhetorical structure of heaven and by many actions on the part of God and the Son. This psychic structure then prevents him from either seeing or allowing the many instances of "unofficial" evidence that the nature of the universe is not absolute but stretching. For just as the rhetorical structure does not fit the reality, so the reality does not fit the rhetorical structure. But Satan does not see this other half of the truth. He proudly proclaims, as if it were a virtue or something to be desired, the fixity of his mind:

> . . . Yet not for those [God's dire arms],
> Nor what the potent Victor in his rage
> Can else inflict, do I repent or change,
> Though changed in outward luster, that fixed mind.
>
> (1: 94–97)

He is:

> . . . one who brings
> A mind not to be changed by place or time.
> The mind is its own place, and in itself
> Can make a heav'n of hell, a hell of heav'n.
>
> (1: 252–55)

That this attitude and mind-structure are the greatest "hell" is made clear by Milton from the beginning:

> . . . he with his horrid crew
> Lay vanquished, rolling in the fiery gulf

> Confounded though immortal. But his doom
> Reserved him to more wrath; for now the thought
> Both of lost happiness and lasting pain
> Torments him; round he throws his baleful eyes,
> That witnessed huge affliction and dismay
> Mixed with obdúrate pride and steadfast hate.
>
> (1: 51–58)

His own escape from hell belies his characterization of the structure of the universe. At the end of the council in Pandemonium he says:

> Well have ye judged, well ended long debate,
> Synod of gods, and like to what ye are,
> Great things resolved; which from the lowest deep
> Will once more lift us up, in spite of fate.
>
> (2: 390–93)

If one can say "in spite of fate," no fate exists for one to contest. Satan, though not without struggle, is able to leave behind the conditions that cause him pain and are the basis for his thought and actions. When Gabriel asks Satan why he has broken the bounds of his punishment, Satan retorts, "Let him surer bar / His iron gates, if he intends our stay / In that dark durance" (4: 897–99). But the absence of absoluteness in the iron gates implies that there is a corresponding lack of absoluteness in "intention." God's observation to the Son in the beginning of Book 3 confirms this flexibility of "fate":

> . . . seest thou what rage
> Transports our Adversary? Whom no bounds
> Prescribed, no bars of hell, nor all the chains
> Heaped on him there, not yet the main abyss
> Wide interrupt can hold.
>
> (3: 80–84)

Although Satan bases his action on a rigid conception of fate, his intellectual characterizations of reality are changeable and contradictory. He boasts in a statement that is both assertive and vague that he and his followers have "put to proof his [God's] high supremacy, / Whether upheld by strength, or chance, or fate," "by old repute, / Consent, or custom" (1: 132–33; 639–40). His understanding of the creation of the new world swings between two opposite conceptions. On the one hand, God created human being to "supply / Perhaps [their] . . . vacant room," but on the other hand this new creation is "more removed [from heaven] / Lest heav'n surcharged with potent multitude / Might hap to move new broils" (2: 834–37). Heaven seems to be filled with a dangerous "excess of joy" at the same time as it is a gaping vacuum.

Such contradictions might make him wonder, but his mind remains "fixed" and all his faculties hardened against modality, even delight. For example, during the painful war in heaven, at the sight of the "fresh flow'rets" springing up before the chariot of power and wrath, he and his followers "this saw . . . but stood obdured, / And to rebellious fight rallied their powers / Insensate, hope conceiving from despair" (6: 785–87). They are perverse because they conceive hope from despair instead of from the beauty directly in front of them. As the narrative voice comments:

> In heav'nly Spirits could such perverseness dwell?
> But to convince the proud what signs avail,
> Or wonders move th' obdúrate to relent?
> They hardened more by what might most reclaim,
> Grieving to see his glory.
>
> (6: 788–92)

Satan's reactions to his perceptions of Eden are somewhat different from this obdurate resistance in heaven and hell. After his long journey out of hell he has come to a new world that, more modal by its very nature, elicits a more complicated response than the structure of reality in heaven. The beauties of Paradise are initially an answer to his pain and arouse in him the spontaneous expressions of delight quoted above. However, in the end this pleasure has the same effect on him as the joy of heaven, for each experience of delight falls into pain and desperation. As he gazes at the new creation from the stairs between heaven and earth, his wonder quickly sours into envy:

> Such wonder seized, though after heaven seen,
> The Spirit malign, but much more envy seized
> At sight of all this world beheld so fair.
>
> (3: 552–54)

As he first sees the Adam and Eve whom he "could love," he exclaims:

> O hell! what do mine eyes with grief behold!
> Into our room of bliss thus high advanced
> Creatures of other mold, earth-born perhaps,
> Not Spirits, yet.
>
> (4: 358–61)

> . . . sight tormenting! thus these two
> Imparadised in one another's arms,
> The happier Eden, shall enjoy their fill
> Of bliss on bliss, while I to hell am thrust,
> Where neither joy nor love, but fierce desire,
> Among our other torments not the least,
> Still unfulfilled with pain of longing pines.
>
> (4: 505–11)

Similarly, the reciprocal "sweet interchange / Of hill and valley" (9: 115–16) and the sweetness of Eve in the "flow'ry plat," which at first bring him joy and even a degree of conceptual clarity, soon turn from delight into torment.

> . . . the more I see
> Pleasures about me, so much more I feel
> Torment within me, as from the hateful siege
> Of contraries; all good to me becomes
> Bane, and in heav'n much worse would be my state.
>
> (9: 119–23)

> But the hot hell that always in him burns,
> Though in mid-heav'n, soon ended his delight,
> And tortures him now more, the more he sees
> Of pleasure not for him ordained; then soon
> Fierce hate he recollects.
>
> (9: 467–71)

This "self-formation" in which Satan is hardened against modality might in heaven and hell appear to be an unavoidable cycle, but here in Eden the manner in which Satan turns from delight to pain makes its directed nature quite clear. For once Satan reaches Paradise, these moments of beauty are given to him as freely as the "doleful shades" of hell. Even the joy he feels in beholding them demands no payment, sacrifice, or labor. But at this moment of choice Satan turns away from beauty and love. The choice is not even between joy and pain, or good and bad, or love and hatred, since the good has already been given to him. Rather, the choice is whether to keep this good or actively spurn it and turn toward evil, which he does. Thus, though "abstracted from his own evil," Satan *"recollects"* "fierce hate" and "excites" "all his thoughts / Of mischief" (9: 471–72).

> Thoughts, whither have ye led me, with what sweet
> Compulsion thus transported to forget
> What hither brought us? Hate, not love, nor hope
> Of Paradise for hell, hope here to taste
> Of pleasure, but all pleasure to destroy,
> Save what is in destroying.
>
> (9: 473–78)

His mind is fixed, and all his efforts are directed toward maintaining the fixity, not to changing or yielding to a new focus of attention.

This rigidity, more extreme than but similar to Raphael and Adam's pseudo-masculinity, stems from Satan's fear of losing control. This fear is understandable in hell, for as a result of his fall the landscape of his mind and domain is not the sweet interchange of hill and vale but the raging "siege of contraries," the metamorphic inconstancy of hell. The pain of the war in heaven "overturned all patience"; this pain "is perfect misery, the worst / Of evils," is the pain that "all subdues" (6: 457–64). Fear and pain have "distorted" the shape of his psyche and given birth to death (2: 783–89).

The fear is even understandable in heaven, where because of its nonmodal structure the Son's elevation creates an apparent breach. But in seeking to exert control in Eden, Satan is turning away from a beauty and love whose interchanging nature is more easily intelligible, not from a heavenly void or from the fires of "hot hell" (9: 467) toward which he does turn. For him, pain is relief from pain and beauty is cause of pain, a pain perceived to be greater than the pains of hell. It is not so much love "ordained" for someone else that causes him pain, as love itself—whether it is love felt by him for someone else ("whom my thoughts pursue with wonder, and could love"), love offered to him, or love between others. Because Satan understands love in terms of possession and not of modal resonance, and because the love he is exposed to is not possessed (because it cannot be), the very distance that is integral to its nature is felt as an absence and causes pain and emptiness instead of joy and fulfillment.

Here in Eden the particular nature of his misperception of love becomes clear: it is the modal space more than a hierarchical difference in power that terrifies him, for he can love Adam and Eve as he could not love God because they cannot be perceived as powerful or absolute. They distinctly manifest the simultaneous strength and frailty inherent in all beings— including God—living in a reality whose essential nature is reciprocity.

If the space of love is perceived as a void, or alternatively as a violent excess, then it is logical that relinquishing one's control and yielding will result in loss, even rape, of one's being. Behind this fear of loss of control is the more basic and primal fear of dissolution, which is inseparably related to the loss of love because the universe is a structure of love, of yearning. Satan does not seek to expose himself to such pain in either earth or heaven: "neither here seek I, no nor in heav'n / To dwell" (9: 124–25).

It is their being that the fallen angels, except Moloch, value most and strive to maintain even in hell. As Belial says in response to Moloch's proposal that they storm heaven, to incur further wrath from God would lead to further despair and dissolution,

> . . . Sad cure! for who would lose,
> Though full of pain, this intellectual being,
> Those thoughts that wander through eternity,
> To perish rather, swallowed up and lost
> In the wide womb of uncreated Night,
> Devoid of sense and motion?
>
> (2: 146–51)

But Belial's proposal is to sit still and suffer quietly, a fixity that will supposedly preserve the "sense and motion" that is integral to their being. Satan by contrast moves to leave hell and go to Eden, but once there he does not seek to expose himself to the motions of love.

On earth as in heaven, rather than yield to a dangerous goodness, he will exert control. This power tactic will now take the form of revenge, a psychic destruction of Adam and Eve rather than outright war. All of Satan's speeches in which he has initially burst forth into spontaneous delight follow this progression from joy to pain to hatred and revenge. His indignation at the commandment not to eat the fruit quickly becomes the "fair foundation laid whereon to build / Their ruin!" (4: 521–22). The address to Adam and Eve that begins with wonder, praise, and love concludes with:

> Ah, gentle pair, ye little think how nigh
> Your change approaches, when all these delights
> Will vanish and deliver ye to woe,
> More woe, the more your taste is now of joy;
> Happy, but for so happy ill secured
> Long to continue, and this high seat your heav'n
> Ill fenced for Heav'n to keep out such a foe
> As now is entered; yet no purposed foe
> To you whom I could pity thus forlorn,
> Though I unpitied. League with you I seek,
> And mutual amity so strait, so close,
> That I with you must dwell, or you with me
> Henceforth.
>
> (4: 366–78)

But he does not seek to dwell in Paradise "unless by mast'ring heav'n's Supreme" (9: 125). Achieving total power himself is envisioned as the only control that would end his pain. He turns from the pleasure of beholding the sweet Eve, who abstracts him from evil, to "recollect" his hatred and find "pleasure" in destroying her, and through her, human being and the rest of the new creation (9: 470–94).

This sequence of thought and feeling is the manifestation of a process in which modality is reduced to a dynamic of sympathic identification that has laws of its own, a process in which the resonant structure becomes a determinant one. It is a process that Michael Lieb refers to as the dialectics of uncreation.[2]

In his inability to perceive modality in heaven and in his refusal to see it in Eden, Satan in his mind has, more definitively than the rhetorical structure of heaven, cast the qualitative differences of being such as God-angel, masculine-feminine, and love-power into quantitative notions of "equality" and hierarchy, in which the only distinction between beings, faculties, and forms of energy becomes one of degree—"superior" or "inferior." In this structure a resonant relation with either world or another being is impossible. To conceive of universe and mind in hierarchical terms is the first stage of uncreation. In the second stage one resorts to the possessive and identifying strategies of "horrid sympathy" (10: 540), whose motivation is to attain relief from the painful gap but whose dynamic actually serves to intensify the pain by further destroying the only medium in which relief and fulfillment can take place.

If the space of yearning is perceived as resonant and reciprocal, then yearning becomes a love that is dramatic and empathic. But if the space of yearning is perceived as a gap only, it will be a fearful void that turns yearning into desperate need and turns power into a desperate desire for control. A cyclical dynamic is set in motion in which this division between love and power intensifies the sense of the void and in which need and control are driven into the perverted extremes of lust and violence. These are the passions of the fallen angels when they become the mythical gods, described in 1: 365–521, who "fill / With lust and violence the house of God"—the resonant space (1: 495–96). The combination of these two passions is rape, which may be considered the consummate form of identification. The less extreme forms of "horrid sympathy"—such as pity, worship, and subjection—are modifications of the same basic pattern.

In subjection, one seeks to control the painful gap and absolutely assure oneself of receiving love by dominating the "inferior" giver of love. In a subtler form of subjection, one seeks to make another like oneself. Or one subjects oneself to the giver of love in worship, a yet subtler form of coercion in which superior power is allowed the giver, who therefore must give love because he/she is the only one who is in a position to do so. In pity, the most obvious form of identification, one sees the other in his/her pain as oneself, or sees oneself in another and becomes the other.

These strategies are contradictory and futile. In subjection and worship, the enforced power difference cuts the beings off from one another more relentlessly than ever. In pity, a reaction against the cruel consequences of subjection and worship, the now-painful gap of degree is closed as is the gap of quality, a strategy that causes new pain as the identities of the beings are erased.

At the end of all these strategies, one finds oneself alone. Identification destroys identity and love. Because the original motivation of the sympathic process is to escape the lonely void, the mind cannot stop at such a conclusion, and so must move on. These strategies cannot even provide the security and relief of fixity that Satan seeks; subjection, worship, and pity are unable to maintain their identity because to stop is to fall into the hole of loneliness. Like some sinister perpetual motion machine they endlessly metamorphose into one another more resolutely than the fluid positions of the lyric-ironic structure.

Identifying with another's pain provides no ease, because if one is identified with the other the suffering becomes one's own. This pain then arouses hatred, not love, for the other who has caused the pain and erased his/her being, and arouses a corresponding desire for control over this source of pain for relief from it. But subjecting another causes the other pain too, and the imminent loss of the subject as the giver of love causes the master to pity the subject—hence the irony in which the victimizer pities the victim—or perhaps to worship him/her. But if worship is to attain insidious power sufficient for its coercive ends, the object of worship will resent the subjection and abandon or attack the worshiper, which it is free to do by dint of its official "superiority." Sometimes, however, the strategies of subjection and worship are dovetailed in a collaboration between tyrant and subject: the tyrant dominates the subject to receive love, but because this love is not satisfying the subject has power over the tyrant, who submits to it in order to assure him/herself of love and shoulders the subject's burdens because he/she does not understand the reason for the lack of satisfaction. The relation between King Oedipus and his subjects follows this pattern.

The sympathic state of mind is caught in a cycle that ever more tightly constricts the psychic space for the sake of a control that serves to fuel it. There is no direct explanation for the abrupt alternation or combination of these various "shows of love." They are only understandable—"logical"—in terms of the original dynamic. Although the internal logic may be consistent, however, the structure as a whole is nonsensical because the principles on which it is based have no validity, even no reality. Only the resonant structure is real. If one does not allow the modal space, there can be no filling of it. As William Butler Yeats says to the rose of his yearning:

> Come near, come near, come near—Ah, leave me still
> A little space for the rose-breath to fill!
> ("To the Rose Upon the Rood of Time")[3]

Satan's desperate and absurd machinations manifest a psychic fall corresponding to the material and modal fall in the war in heaven, in which heaven goes "to wrack" and irony is fragmented beyond tonality. Just as the created universe almost falls back into the chaos of elements that are mixed and embattled (see 2: 890–914) instead of "conglobed / Like . . . to like" or "Disparted" (7: 239–41), so in the psychic fall the faculties lose their articulation and become confused; the energies of being lose their resonant form and become indistinct and violent; and the distinction between one being and another is lost.

This identifying dynamic is demonstrated in Satan's relation to his followers and in his responses to Eden. In Book 5, when he leaves the painful throne of God, he immediately turns in his loneliness to Beelzebub, his "next subordinate," for love, and in poignant tones asks him how he can sleep while Satan wakes, for this difference creates a breach between them:

> Sleep'st thou, companion dear, what sleep can close
> Thy eyelids? And remember'st what decree

Of yesterday, so late hath passed the lips
Of heav'n's Almighty? thou to me thy thoughts
Wast wont, I mine to thee was wont to impart;
Both waking we were one; how then can now
Thy sleep dissent?

                                                    (5: 673–79)

Though different in degree, Satan and his followers are "as one" in quality
and have little or no separate identity. When he sees their pain, his "cruel
eye" casts "signs of remorse" (1: 604–5). In this sympathic relation, they are
mirrors to each other in which to read and seek their own thoughts and
feelings. After Beelzebub presents Satan's plan during the council in hell and
asks who will undertake it:

                      . . . all sat mute,
          Pondering the danger with deep thoughts; and each
          In other's count'nance read his own dismay
          Astonished.

                                                    (2: 420–23)

Such sympathy is a form of narcissism. As Sin puts it to Satan: "Thyself in
me thy perfect image viewing / Becam'st enamored" (2: 764–65). This process leads in the end to the "horrid sympathy" in Book 10 in which "what
they saw, / They felt themselves now changing" (10: 540–41); or in other
words, a sympathic relation is a sin that gives birth to death, to the erasure of
being.

The fallen angels in hell seek to cement the specious security they find in
their sympathy into "united force and fixèd thought" (1: 560), into "union,
and firm faith, and firm accord, / More than can be in heav'n" (2: 36–37). As
Milton says, "Devil with devil damned / Firm concord holds" (2: 496–97).
But in the end their concord is held together by obedience and subjection to
Satan, and Satan is alone. For when the distance established by qualitative
difference is collapsed into sympathy, one turns to power to maintain one's
identity, a power that may seem to ensure firmer union but that actually
isolates one from the object. At the end of the council in Pandemonium,
Satan must take the journey to Eden alone: "This enterprise / None shall
partake with me" (2: 465–66). In the strategy of subjection, one must hide the
pain within to avoid arousing pity in the other that might in turn arouse
hatred in the other toward oneself. This hiding is best accomplished if one is
somewhat separate from the subject. As Satan says in his soliloquy on Mt.
Niphates:

                    . . . Ay me, they little know
          How dearly I abide that boast so vain,
          Under what torments inwardly I groan;
          While they adore me on the throne of hell,

> With diadem and scepter high advanced,
> The lower still I fall, only supreme
> In misery.
>
> (4: 86–92)

Satan is simultaneously caught in the other end of the strategy of worship: his subjects are coercing him to give and find love for them, and to maintain his subjection Satan agrees to be worshiped:

> . . . is there no place
> Left for repentance, none for pardon left?
> None left but by submission; and that word
> Disdain forbids me, and my dread of shame
> Among the Spirits beneath, whom I seduced
> With other promises and other vaunts
> Than to submit.
>
> (4: 79–85)

For the same reason, he cannot "melt" at the sight of Adam and Eve in Eden:

> . . . should I at your harmless innocence
> Melt as I do, yet public reason just,
> . . . .
> . . . compels me now
> To do what else though damned I should abhor.
>
> (4: 388–92)

Satan feels tormented because in this power structure he receives not love, but respect and adoration. He confuses adoration with love. His monarchy is similar to the one he thinks caused him pain in heaven, only he is in a different position. As Gabriel points out in Book 4 to the Satan who in hell protests that he will not "bow and sue for grace / With suppliant knee, and deify his power" (1: 111–12):

> . . . who more than thou
> Once fawned, and cringed, and servilely adored
> Heav'n's awful Monarch?
>
> (4: 958–60)

In worship, a form of narcissism like sympathy, the worshiper "deifies"—what Satan in 1: 112 protests he will never do—the object of worship in order to assure him/herself absolutely of receiving love. To secure this impossible assurance, the worshiper relinquishes all power to the worshiped-giver and simultaneously makes the love-object similar to him/herself—makes him/her over in his/her own image. Though the object is unequal, he/she is "like." In a reversal of sympathy, the worshiper sees the perfect image of the

worshiped mirrored in him/herself. It might seem that worship is less narcissistic than sympathy because though subject and object in worship are like,
they are unequal, while in sympathy they are both like and equal. But this is
not the case. For pity opens one up to the pain and terror of the true power
of love that cannot be understood or formed by quantitative structures, and
indeed destroys them. Therefore the erasure of being in pity can be the
erasure of falsely conceived being. Releasing him/herself into the flow of
this love, the subject realizes that he/she and other objects—or subjects—
are not entirely "like" nor entirely "unlike": they are like enough to allow
reciprocity and they are unlike enough to allow and ensure the qualitative
form necessary to keep the plastic medium modal, to keep it from collapsing
into quantitative vacuum and the violence of identification. Worship, on the
other hand, is a strategy that uses sympathy to obtain greater control for the
self and thus is more narcissistic. By giving the deified all power, the worshiper forces the deified to take all responsibility and thereby has control
over him/her and simultaneously safeguards against the erasure of being
that occurs in the identification of pity. Making the deified similar adds to the
worshiper's control, for then what the giver gives will exactly correspond to
the worshiper's own nature and needs. The subject feels that this strategy is
necessary because he/she cannot conceive of love between differents. This
misconception emanates from fear of an uncontrolled love. Satan in heaven
has tried to control God by means of abject adoration, as Ahaz "the sottish
conqueror" Milton describes in 1: 475–76 "adore[s] the gods / Whom he [has]
. . . vanquished." When this strategy fails, Satan seeks security in hell:

> Here we may reign secure . . .
> . . . .
> Better to reign in hell than serve in heav'n.
>
> (1: 261–63)

The control and security come to predominate over the desire for love
because love was understood in terms of control in the first place.

However, the violent instability of "secure" hell forces Satan to voyage to
Eden to seek some other form of control. His various responses to Adam
and Eve follow the same basic identifying dymanic, but their articulation is
more differentiated as he swings, in speeches such as the ones quoted in part
earlier in this chapter,[4] from joy into loss, pain, and pity, to intensified pain,
to hatred, back to pity, and to redoubled hatred.

In 4: 366–78, phrases like *mutual amity so strait, so close* aptly characterize the identification Satan seeks, while words like *gentle pair* and *forlorn*
show the pity still mixed with the viciousness. Destroying "this man of clay,
son of despite" (9: 176) in this "mutual amity" will provide no relief and no
control, but true to its cyclical dynamic such action will "back on itself
recoil" (9: 172) and lead to the very "worse relapse / And heavier fall"

(4: 100–101) he seeks to avoid. However, in Satan's identifying strategy, it is logical to look for ease in destruction, for destruction is the extreme form of control:

> . . . neither here seek I, no nor in heav'n
> To dwell, unless by mast'ring heav'n's Supreme;
> Nor hope to be myself less miserable
> By what I seek, but others to make such
> As I, though thereby worse to me redound.
> For only in destroying I find ease
> To my relentless thoughts.
>
> (9: 124–30)

Although Satan's behavior shows a certain internal logic, now that he has reached Eden his frantic exertions to avoid being overwhelmed are unnecessary and absurd. In hell perhaps such strategies of mind were difficult to avoid, the pain too great to relinquish control and yield. As he said on Mt. Niphates, "never can true reconcilement grow / Where wounds of deadly hate have pierced so deep" (4: 98–99). But now, by dint of his arduous epic-lyric journey, he has successfully left hell behind and reached a new space and time where joy and peace of both mind and world almost forcefully arrest the painful motions of evil.

Modal consciousness is more possible here than in heaven or hell, for Eden was specifically created modal and not absolute. In such a reality one has the opportunity to switch one's focus of attention and so receive new influences. In this distancing, one can choose to allow—to "approve" in experience—perceptions that place one in the third space, choose to yield to gentle forces instead of violent ones and so attain respite from the siege of contraries. This perception then deepens into awareness, experience, and consciousness of the true resonant structure, and then it becomes "real."

Because this reality is resonant and not unidirectional, and because it is also a structure of mind, one can choose the joy directly through images of joy without possessing—either in the mind or in reality—the source or cause of joy and proceed from attention to perception to consciousness and experience, a process that joins one to the source of joy. There is a sense in which joy, like pain, can be primary, not secondary: as Nisroch says during the war in heaven, "pain is . . . the worst of evils" (6: 462–63). Pain itself is an evil, not simply the consequence of evil; and joy is a good, not simply the consequence of good. Even in the heavenly state, the source of joy or joy conceived of as something given externally cannot of itself provide joy. Consciousness and resonance of mind are necessary to make it an actual reality. It always was an act of choice and reception not very different from approving the graceful interchange that Satan praises in Book 9, though here this truth is made clearer.

Satan has been prepared for modal perceptions by his journey—the "way

[long] . . . / And hard, that out of hell leads up to light" (2: 432–33)—perhaps similar to Adam and Eve's destined "way" or to the journeys of the pilots and the reader. Satan is the first wanderer to take the modal journey out of the afflictions of the sympathic state that Adam and Eve do not know.

If the perception of edenic beauty startles and causes pain by virtue of its contrast to Satan's pain, the "pain of *longing*" (4: 511; emphasis added) he feels in beholding Adam and Eve embracing could itself serve as a transitional form closer to his experience of the gap in heaven and of pain in hell. However, he is "obdúrate" and "relentless" in the face of all such influences. When he actually reaches the light at the end of the modal journey, all he can say is:

> O thou that with surpassing glory crowned
> Looks't from thy sole dominion like the god
> Of this new world; at whose sight all the stars
> Hide their diminished heads; to thee I call,
> But with no friendly voice, and add thy name,
> O sun, to tell thee how I hate thy beams
> That bring to my remembrance from what state
> I fell, how glorious once above thy sphere.
>
> (4: 32–39)

He places it in the context of his past, and does not see it as something new. In addition to destroying the image of joy in his own perception, he destroys the modal bridge modulating between pain and joy. In hell he has impatiently roused up his followers from their moment of patience, of meditative pause, as they lay "entranced" like autumn leaves in the lyric perception of their loss. Now in Eden he similarly breaks the mood of "wonder" that suspends hell (4: 362–65); snaps the longing into "bliss" and "torment," into dualities and degrees—"happi*er* Eden"; and snaps the interchange into the "siege of contraries," and thus "to hell . . . [is] thrust" (4: 505–11; 9: 114–23).

Satan reacts in this way because he fears that yielding to beauty will thrust him into a void worse than hell. His void is similar to the void Paul de Man sees as the ultimate reality, a reality revealed through what he perceives as the utterly unbridgeable gap between vehicle and tenor in romantic as well as allegorical poetry.[5] But Satan's experience of the sweet interchange and his expression of it give the lie to this rigid idea. It shows him that the third space with the kinesthetic movement that takes place within it is not a void, not an empty psychic space nor a rigid one, but a liquid and plastic medium, sustaining as water sustains a boat, or as the "pure marble air" sustains Satan as he "winds with ease" among the stars in 3: 563–65.

This "void" is alive; and though Satan's pain is great, the exertion required to continue his false strategy in the face of it is greater and more exhausting. The resonant structure does not simply disappear when God, human, or angel are unable to perceive it, or choose not to perceive it.

Therefore much of Satan's energy must be used to oppose its insistent maintenance of its own being. Although it modulates into its own opposing forms in response to the movements of the created beings within it—the resonance becoming more violent and apparently random and chaotic—it simultaneously makes available forces that sustain. A reversal of the fall is always possible until the universe falls so far as to return entirely to the original chaos, the "womb" and "grave," although this reversal returns not to any exact point in the past but to the principles with which it will move forward. The exertion against the reversal of the fall requires as much effort as the exertion against the misperception of reality that precipitated the fall.

In the reversal the meditative space is attained both through perceptions that are themselves meditative or already in the third space and through the shifting nature of the poetic and perceptual process itself that opens into the space. The sweet interchange is itself meditative; the simile of the reviving fields in 2: 488–95 is meditative in a separate space; and the movement from hell to the simile is a shifting that in itself moves the mind out of the sympathic state into the modal state. For Milton the "void" is the emptying of sympathic motions only, and is the space called to attention and into existence by the poetic activity, the distancing between vehicle and tenor that "lifts" the mind.

The shiftings of this process are sometimes gentle, sometimes painful. The sweet interchange is gentle; the view of Adam and Eve in each other's arms is somewhat more painful, serving to foreground and break Satan's false notions of love as well as to show him new delight. The torments of hell are the most painful shiftings and might be considered a "punishment that fits the crime": the crime itself—Satan's misperception of the identifying dynamic as the way to love—represented in a form so extreme that its absurdity becomes painfully obvious and it is broken down. At the same time, this form of punishment serves to emphasize the reciprocal nature of the universe that Satan has difficulty seeing. For although he has broken the resonance of love in heaven, he does not escape reciprocity entirely; he only changes its manifestation. For to live "single" or "alone" is not possible in this universe. Even God cannot expel and sever Satan once and for all. Satan's actions, as in the laws of physics, produce reactions. His perception of things, his state of mind, and his actions performed on the basis of these partly "determine" his fate because they affect the behavior of the universe in which he must live. As Abdiel says after vainly trying to dissuade Satan from rebelling:

> O alienate from God, O Spirit accurst,
> Forsaken of all good! I see thy fall
> Determined, and thy hapless crew involved
> In this perfidious fraud, contagion spread
> Both of thy crime and punishment. Henceforth
> No more be troubled how to quit the yoke

Of God's Messiah; those indulgent laws
Will not be now vouchsafed; other decrees
Against thee are gone forth without recall;
That golden scepter which thou didst reject
Is now an iron rod to bruise and break
Thy disobedience. Well thou didst advise.
Yet not for thy advice or threats I fly
These wicked tents devoted, lest the wrath
Impendent, raging into sudden flame
Distinguish not; for soon expect to feel
His thunder on thy head, devouring fire.

(5: 877–93)

Once chosen, Satan's attitude "determines" the arousal of God's wrath. But this wrath, the iron scepter to "break . . . disobedience," strives in conjunction with the gentler modal perceptions to bring the misperceiving mind back into resonance with the true universal structure. Even the exhausting exertion of energy required to maintain false structures serves a purpose: to make the mind so weary of them that it pushes them away and sinks into a stillness—like the fallen angels in 1: 300–313—receptive to modal influence.

This universe in which the fires of wrath may "distinguish not" is not entirely rational, just, or totally predictable; but it is vital, organic, and structured by principles rather than "fences," by principles whose flexibility makes return possible and makes it open to evolution.

Satan is like the "injured lover" (5: 450) focusing more on what he has not received than on what he can give—give freely and uncertainly, not in a prepared structure. He wants justice, certainty, and rational control more than he wants to live with God, the forces of the universe, and the forces within himself. His love must be safeguarded by this certainty and rigid structure—to love he must first "vanquish." Hence his genuinely guileless surprise when he hears that Adam and Eve are forbidden to eat of the tree of knowledge: "Can it be sin to know, / Can it be death?" But he has already seen the distorted forms of Sin and Death at the gates of hell and the overturning of patience and the perversions of fear and pain consequent upon breaking the union of heaven for the sake of the control of knowledge. For in a universe that is in motion, the security of such knowledge produces only violence and chaos. Satan refuses to allow the "short intermission" of meditative pause, seeing it as a "submission" whose "ease would recant / Vows made in pain"—in yearning—"as violent and void" (4: 96–97). But his form of knowledge leads to the violent and void state, while the meditative pause restores patience and, in the end, allows one to live in a graceful and knowing consonance with the universe.

Although this identifying dynamic leads Satan to seek destruction and revenge focused on frail Eve, both the selection of Eve and the form his revenge takes contain the same admixture of genuine sympathy and "love" as his initial perceptions of edenic beauty. For him as for Eve, the temptation and fall are a curious interweaving of their failure to perceive modal reality and their striving to make it more real.

The precise structure of Satan's motivation is made clear in the last words of his prelude to his "address" to Eve:

> . . . Then let me not let pass
> Occasion which now smiles: behold alone
> The woman, opportune to all attempts,
> Her husband, for I view far round, not nigh,
> Whose higher intellectual more I shun,
> And strength, of courage haughty, and of limb
> Heroic built, though of terrestrial mold,
> Foe not informidable, exempt from wound,
> I not; so much hath hell debased, and pain
> Enfeebled me, to what I was in heav'n.
> She fair, divinely fair, fit love for gods,
> Not terrible, though terror be in love
> And beauty, not approached by stronger hate,
> Hate stronger, under show of love well feigned,
> The way to which her ruin now I tend.
>
> (9: 479–93)

The strategy Satan chooses shows the fear of love characteristic of the identifying dynamic described above, but behind this fear is a love "not terrible"—as long as it is controlled by the "strength" of hate, the extreme form of the desire for control. Eve in particular appeals to Satan, not only because she is weaker than Adam and therefore an easier victim, but also because her love and beauty touch him in a way that Adam's "heroic" qualities cannot. For it is Eve's feminine nature that has been created to correct the flaw in the heavenly structure of mind, to correspond to the resonant modal gap between God and angel to which Satan in his pain intuitively responded by rebelling. Eve is not only the object of his yearning, but the incarnation of it. Eve is the "love fit for gods" missing in heaven, and he is rightly drawn to her. Eve is likewise drawn to Satan, for his concerns and experience with the pain of the modal gap is a form of acknowledgement that Adam refused to give her. Though this mutual attraction is in this sense positive, it is also characterized by certain misperceptions, for it is not Eve but the configuration of Adam and Eve together that most truly corresponds to the structure of reality. But Adam seems too much like Abdiel for Satan, as by now he is for Eve, for him to perceive Adam's true nature. Moreover, Eve and Satan at this point experience the modal gap of yearning as a "wound" more severe than the "commotion strange" (8: 531) Adam and Eve felt when first created, because for both Eve and Satan the third space has been collapsed into the gaping void and the narrow circuit.

Drawn to Eve, Satan in his temptation acknowledges and praises her and the space she represents; but unable to understand the true nature of this space, he makes her over in an image corresponding more to his own perceptions and needs, at the same time offering this image to her in her plight, which he perceives as similar to his own. This strategy is founded on hope as well as hatred, hope for a revesal of the fall, but a reversal of a particular kind, which he substitutes for the modal reversal too terrifying for him to allow.

Satan's temptation takes the form of a seduction, which on the one hand serves not to reverse the fall but to bring further pain on himself and to involve Eve and then Adam in the psychic fall described above. At the same time, however, Satan's strategy serves to involve him in edenic being and in its initial stages attempts to form a new structure of attitude and communication that begins to move out of the sympathic cycle. For the form Satan's stronger "hate" takes to control love and the fear of love is a "show of love well feigned." This feigning hides the hate and therefore may be seen as a deception, but it is also the form the hate takes, its incarnation. In a universe that is not unidirectional, this effort turns the cycle into a progression in which rape becomes, if not high coition, seduction.

Unlike the identifying strategies, seduction has a controlled form; but unlike the apparently absolute structure of heaven, it is not rigid but flexible. The courtly "love-song" is a new kind of art in *Paradise Lost,* succeeding Adam's philosophy and Raphael's epic. These three forms of art may be seen as a progression: Raphael's epic was disjunctively composed of the central tale of physical war and fragments of lyric, irony, and philosophy. Raphael and Adam's later philosophy in Book 8 and the beginning of Book 9 sought unity through an intellectual control that was more rigid and less active. Now Satan's amorist style reenters the realm of action, but it is action of a new kind that involves mind and spirit as well as body, and that, unlike war or rape, seeks an acceptance from the object instead of capitulation. Because the desired end in seduction is mutual, its form is not in a primary relation either to the speaker or to the object but is in relation to both at once, or is in relation to the relation between them. Unlike pity, courtly poetry seeks an end in action; and unlike philosophy, the end sought is personal and historical. This form is neither coercive nor aesthetically detached, but rhetorical and evolutionary.

The love-song marks an evolution in its speaker's relation to the universe, and in his/her representation of it. It sets up a resonance, a magnetism, between speaker and object, between desirer and desired. It exists in a third space separate from both, the space of yearning that is not yet actual but yearns to be so. The form is stretching rather than "obedient," yet it is careful not to break the resonance lest it lose the beloved object. The speaker as poet and desirer strives both in art and in action to maintain the resonance and fit the poetry to the listener, unlike Raphael when he explained astronomical motion to an unprepared Adam in Book 8. Satan's love-song is the first attempt in *Paradise Lost* at a resonant poetic.

The sequence of epic-philosophy-courtly poetry reflects the historical development of Western poetry and also reflects a progression in structures of behavior that is perhaps more paradigmatic than historical. The identifying strategies outlined above may be seen not only as cyclical but as linear, starting with violent subjection (vanquishing the subject in action), moving into worship (passivity in the realm of action and thus entering the realm of mind), then moving into pity (a relation entirely in the realm of mind that begins to exist in a motion between the beings), and then moving into seduction (a relation that begins to move between mind and action).

Although Satan's temptation is in part a real attempt to move beyond the pains of the identifying cycle and closer to an approximation of resonance and fulfillment, it is intuitive and groping rather than wholly self-conscious. Its style is awkward and artificial; and lacking self-consciousness it remains an approximation that eventually leads both Satan and Eve astray. Whereas Adam externalized the internal into scholastic formula, Satan internalizes the external into courtly poetry, the space of fancy. Because Satan's address to Eve is the first attempt at a resonant poetic, it is exaggerated and artificial for perceptual reasons—so that it can be clearly seen and not dissolve back into the cycle. Satan must fabricate in his art a distance that has never existed in the official structure of representation; in the absence of a model he uses exaggeration and extravagant flattery to fortify his construction. The simultaneous approach and avoidance characteristic of courtly poetry is a form intermediate between identification and true resonance.

Because of this emphasis on the construction of this intermediate, fancy eventually takes on a life of its own separate from the space of resonance that it was fabricated to approximate. Its evolutionary drive turns into glittering and flaccid wish-fullfillment; and because it is cut off from the source of its energy, it either evaporates—leaving one on Keats's cold hillside—or becomes a beautiful but elusive and illusory form whose beguiling leads the desirer, as the will-o'-the-wisp leads the peasant in 9: 634–42, into the bog.

Seduction as a form appeals to Eve because it comes closer to corresponding to the edenic state than any other poetic form thus far available. Now that Raphael and Adam have closed off the third space and collapsed it in the structure of official representation, the edenic state cries out for a new, corresponding structure of representation, of perception and understanding. For on the one hand, even though Raphael and Adam ignore it, the reality of the third space still exists, just as the modal reality of heaven still exists even though God and the angels may not perceive it, and just as Satan still exists even though he is expelled from heaven. On the other hand, this reality calls for more than existence: as the reality of heaven called for a corresponding structure of mind, so the edenic structure of reality and mind calls for a corresponding consciousness and form of consciousness. Adam's retort after the fall that Eve longed "to be seen / Though by the Devil himself" (10: 877–78) is as much an explanation as a judgment. Satan's love-song in part appeals to Eve because it is a relational form existing between mind and reality rather than a strictly imitative form, and thereby answers Eden's present need. But this relationality also makes it an optimal tool for revenge. On the one hand, because Eden is a state in which relationality is already a reality—a state in which mind and reality do not exist as separately as they do in heaven, for the structure of corresponding mind *is* Adam and Eve's reality, their reason for being—there is less danger here than there was in heaven of being cut off from resonant reality, whether of "reality" or mind, and more opportunity of finding corresponding representational forms. However, for the same reason there is a greater danger of Eve's slipping from the realm of mind into the realm of action, in which the "real" can be turned into the literal and then fall.

The first stage of Satan's temptation is successful in a positive sense, for in it he acknowledges, praises, and represents Eve as a separate space in relation to heaven. In phrases like *heaven of mildness, thy awful brow, more awful thus* retired, *celestial beauty, thy beauty's heav'nly ray,* and *resplendent Eve* (9: 532–68, 607; emphasis indicated), Satan answers her earlier question about the stars to Adam in Book 4, "Wherefore all night long shine these, for whom / This glorious sight, when sleep hath shut all eyes?" (4: 657–58)—a question whose searching and yearning tone is prelude to resonance more than scholastic or even scientific formulation. This style defines, almost like the setting of a psychic scene, the third space, because Satan is referring to the heavenly phenomena not attached to their externalized reality as in Raphael and Adam's structures, but in themselves and in relation to Eve.

However, because of certain misperceptions, the rest of Satan's temptation goes wrong in relation to any hope for a reversal of his fall and leads instead to Eve's fall and a second fall for himself. The seduction that begins as an approximation of love ends as an approximation of rape: while Raphael and Adam closed off the third space in consciousness, Satan opens it up to consciousness, but in such a way that it collapses more completely in the realm of mind for himself and in the realm of action for Adam and Eve. The effect is similar to letting the air out of a balloon. It is this collapsing of someone else's space and the psychic space in general that is the essence of rape. Onanism and rape are attitudes or acts closely akin to each other: Raphael and Adam's withdrawal from the inner realm of mind and their simultaneous externalized elevation of the masculine principle are not very different from Satan's perverted invasion of the inner psychic space.

His love-song goes awry for two related reasons. First, although he recognizes and acknowledges the third space, his appreciation of it is excessive and his understanding of it too literal; therefore he confuses and undervalues the masculine force in relation to it. Second, his recognition degenerates from the initial approximation of reciprocity into the identifying strategy of coercive worship as he tries to possess and control the third space with a rigidity inappropriate to it, a rigidity that regresses to the rigid hierarchical stances of Abdiel, Raphael, and Adam.

The first mistake in Satan's address to Eve is that he identifiies her with her third space and simultaneously places her at its center. Instead of being a space of meditation between mind and universe, the third space is identified literally with Eve's person and described in terms of her physical rather than her psychic beauty—her "fair outside." Thus Satan says:

> Wonder not, sovran mistress, if perhaps
> Thou canst, who art sole wonder, much less arm
> Thy looks, the heav'n of mildness, with disdain.
>
> (9: 532–34)

With these words the meditative wondering is collapsed into the "wonder" of Eve's "looks." As he goes on to tell her that all things and creatures "gaze" on her and "adore" her, he reinforces the materialistic inversion of Eve's inside into her outside and makes her the "goddess" and "empress"— the center—of this space. As such, Eve herself replaces the masculine principle of central neutrality in her own feminine space, becoming "superior" in a quantitative hierarchy in which masculine beings become her "inferior" servants. While this conception may "redress" the imbalance caused by Raphael and Adam—in its elevation of the feminine principle to superiority and even an apparent self-sufficiency—it is a misperception that, no less than Raphael and Adam's elevation of the masculine principle, destroys the qualitative distinction between masculine and feminine that is necessary to high coition.

This confusion in Satan's perception and representation of Eve reflects and reinforces a confusion of masculine and feminine within his own nature, which then comes to permeate his behavior in relation to her in the rest of the temptation scene and destroy his new art. For Satan, being an angel, includes in himself the aspects of being that the creation of male and female in Eden answered in a more differentiated and perceptible form. These aspects were originally meant to be articulately joined in one complete psyche, the form to which human being will evolve after a fuller consciousness of the two principles of being than was possible in heaven is attained on earth through the joining in high coition of separate masculine and feminine beings.

Because Satan's fall consisted of leaving and then being expelled from the upright masculine hierarchy represented by Abdiel and by the structure of mind in heaven, he has lost much of his masculine strength and has taken on some of the feminine virtue of the gap he intuited. For without the right centering of the masculine principle, this fluid space has become the metamorphosis of hell: there was no second structure waiting to "catch" Satan when he rebelled, as there was for Adam in Book 8. In a way, Satan has been partly "uncreated" as an angel. However, although his new formlessness causes pain and near loss of being in hell, once he reaches Eden perhaps he has the opportunity of recreating himself and attaining through modal declension greater consciousness than a Raphael.

His love-song represents the beginnings of such an attempt, but his inarticulate sympathic state of mind and being makes his relation to Eve difficult. It is unclear to him whether as the incarnation of the modal gap she is a qualitatively different being existing in a complementary relation to him or a being similar to him. The answer is of course that she is both—that separate beings as well as principles within the psyche are related to each other in resonance rather than identification or opposition alone. While it is this truth that makes love and evolution possible, it also makes perception and understanding more difficult.

Satan senses that she is different from the more masculine spirits of heaven and approaches her "retired" and "awful" space as a "single" being (9: 536–37). But it is this difference that incarnates and fills part of his own nature, that is the "fit love for gods" and even the "fairest resemblance of [her] . . . Maker fair" (9: 538). Because of the relief it brings him, this incarnation evokes praise, and worship. But because it so nearly incarnates part of himself, he wants to make it his own, to control it, and therefore his worship runs the risk of becoming coercive and sympathic. This desire is increased by the unprecedented perceptibility of the modal reality, which apparently makes control of it, and fulfillment, more possible than before. Complementing this push toward control is the danger that because of Eve's similarity to part of his own being, Satan will identify with her in the mirror-like relation described above once this new correspondence has become familiar and natural rather than opposite or "awful." Rightly understood, the intricacy of this reality of similarity and complementarity and of parts and wholes makes for a finely attunable medium for growth and fulfillment; if not understood, it can turn into a labyrinth.

Satan's answer to these difficulties in the next stage of the seduction scene is to image himself and Eve each as similar beings with masculine and feminine natures welded together, the qualitative distance between them gone. As described above, he makes Eve the masculine center of her own feminine space. Satan is masculine as the serpent "erect amidst his circling spires" (9: 502); but as he moves with "tract oblique" (9: 510)—rather than straight—and "curl[s] many a wanton wreath in sight of Eve" (9: 517), he becomes more feminine, or effeminate. And when he describes himself to her as "wound" "about the mossy trunk" (9: 589) of the tree of knowledge in order to reach the fruit, he becomes a vine like Eve, the feminine principle that cannot stand alone and needs the support of the masculine tree.

In this last image, Satan has lost the approximation of resonance of his first images of Eve. Without complementarity the feminine alone cannot suffice, any more than the masculine alone can suffice in heaven. In this insufficiency he once again resorts to identifying strategies and his love-song falls through confusion and stubbornness into a calculated revenge that gives form to his hatred of Eve more than to the delight she aroused in him. Whereas in heaven he became the tyrant, he now becomes the fawning worshiper. Because he is yielding to the fluid feminine space without maintaining the central neutrality, he must seek the control gained through the coercive helplessnes of worship, the strategy of the simultaneously powerful and passive hero in the romantic paradise of Northrop Frye. In the destruction of the true principle of disciplined neutrality, the neutrality is destroyed; high coition becomes impossible; and the relation falls into the confines of the merely "personal" and the vastness of the vague.

This worship does not solve Satan's difficulties because Eve is as insufficient as he is; she cannot support him even as empress. In the image of the serpent-vine wound around the tree, Satan indicates that neither one is a tree; they are both vines that need support. To fill this need, to accomplish the active fulfillment of the passive and coercive hero and heroine's romantic destiny, Satan in the next stage of his love-song invokes the magic apple and the tree of knowledge. Satan offers Eve the fruit in order to give her the power of ascending to heaven, which will enlarge and give her greater power over her noble domain. This power is something that she is entitled to by dint of her position of empress of the superior feminine space and that will accrue to Satan as her controlling servant. This conception of the virtue and function of the tree of knowledge is not consistent with Satan's initial conception of the feminine space but is added to it as a kind of overlay because the first conception has failed. For if the feminine space is superior and self-sufficient, as Satan implies in his praise of it, then eating the fruit is unnecessary. This inconsistency and the real motivation for seeking such power—that Eve and Satan are weak and desperate—are hidden by the official rhetoric. This conceptual doubleness is not a fully conscious deception on Satan's part, but emanates in part from his genuine confusion and struggle to form a structure of understanding and behavior in the face of the newly incarnated feminine principle.

Ironically, the means Satan offers Eve to ascend to heaven is a literal-minded version of Raphael's trees and ladders, the masculine imagery no longer of a master but of a servant. By eating the fruit, Satan suggests that Eve may ascend "proportionately" from human to angelic being since he the serpent has by eating it ascended from animal to human being. Again, this ploy may be seen not only as a clever deception but as an attempt to conceptualize the hierarchical masculine rhetorical structure in a new way and thereby rectify his initial errors. Instead of seeing it only as a power structure, Satan now sees it also as an evolutionary structure. "Proportionate" is his version of "by degrees." However, not understanding the exact nature of the joining of masculine and feminine and the consequent resonance between mind and universe, he images this ascent as direct, literal, and primary rather than as the secondary and indirect consequence of resonance that it is. Therefore, in Satan's use of it, the ladder principle does not join earth with heaven but rather serves to puncture the space from inside.

Satan's version of ascent derives from the confusions of Raphael's pictures of the tree, which in conjunction with the ladder image the sociable spirit has variously used as an organic image for human spiritual growth (5: 479–82), as a mechanical image with well-defined degrees and steps of humanity's destined ascent (5: 470–79, 483–90, 508–12; see also 7: 157), and indirectly as an image of sin (8: 167–78). This inconsistent use of imagery causes several problems. First and most obvious, there is a conflict between the concepts of ascent as good and of ascent as evil. Second, there is a conflict between the tree as a picture of organic growth and the ladder as a picture of hierarchy with discrete steps and relative values. Third, all these images work against the real nature of the tree of knowledge as a neutral principle. Finally, Raphael has nowhere offered a picture of the third space, of the joining of high coition, or of the resonant relation of human psyche with the universe.

The aspect of Raphael's tree-and-ladder imagery that comes closest to representing this resonance is the process of transformation that takes place along the chain *between* the various elements that compose it, as in the descriptions of eating and making love. Eating occurs along a vertical continuum that goes from the material to the spiritual and is an activity in which the kinesthetic transformative process is as important as the results of the transformation. When Adam asks Raphael whether spirits eat as humans do, the angel answers:

> . . . what he gives
> (Whose praise be ever sung) to man in part
> Spiritual, may of purest Spirits be found
> No ingrateful food: and food alike those pure
> Intellegential substances require
> As doth your rational; and both contain
> Within them every lower faculty
> Of sense, whereby they hear, see, smell, touch, taste,
> Tasting concoct, digest, assimilate,
> And corporeal to incorporeal turn.
> For know, whatever was created needs
> To be sustained and fed; of elements
> The grosser feeds the purer: earth the sea,
> Earth and the sea feed air, the air those fires
> Ethereal, and as lowest first the moon;
> Whence in her visage round those spots, unpurged
> Vapors not yet into her substance turned.
> Nor doth the moon no nourishment exhale

> From her moist continent to higher orbs.
> The sun, that light imparts to all, receives
> From all his alimental recompense
> In humid exhalations, and at even
> Sups with the ocean.
>
> (5: 404–26)

The passage lends itself to various "meanings," depending on the direction of emphasis. On the one hand, this picture of eating may be used, as Raphael soon does use it, as an analogy for the spiritual ascent of human being:

> Wonder not then, what God for you saw good
> If I refuse not, but convert as you,
> To proper substance. Time may come when men
> With angels may participate, and find
> No inconvenient diet, nor too light fare;
> And from these corporal nutriments perhaps
> Your bodies may at last turn all to spirit,
> Improved by tract of time, and winged ascend
> Ethereal, as we, or may at choice
> Here or in heav'nly paradises dwell;
> If ye be found obedient.
>
> (5: 491–501)

Here the emphasis is on the spiritual, and the angel's moralistic diction and tone reinforce this emphasis. In the earlier passage, however, the "descent" is stressed equally with the "ascent" as the complementary part of a process composed of two motions and existing out of both necessity—the need for sustenance—and pleasure. This kinesthetic process is shared by human, angel, and even the heavenly bodies—the moon feeds and the sun "sups with the ocean." This whole two-directional process is "contained within" both the angelic and the human "substances" or entities. This "contain" is the closest Raphael comes to defining the third space in which the resonant process takes place.

In Raphael's discussion of love with Adam in Book 8, human coition similarly is described as occurring along a vertical continuum from physical to spiritual. Here the emphasis is on "high" love as opposed to "low" carnal passion, an emphasis that obscures the nature of the "true love" the angel purports to describe. For this love is as two-directional as eating and is less vertical. Since Adam and Eve are two equal rather than hierarchical principles, they join in a manner resembling the spiritual "horizontal" union of angelic love more than the vertical conversion of material food into spiritual energy. In human high coition, two complementary bodies and two complementary spirits join simultaneously. The motions of love gather body and spirit into one motion; only in this sense does love occur along a vertical continuum. Body is not transformed in the same way as food. Love is two-directional in two ways: in the "horizontal" reciprocity between masculine and feminine and in the "vertical" reciprocity between bodies and spirits. Love is more multidirectional than eating, for in eating one must start with the material food before one can experience the transformation of it into energy. Also food is "inferior" to the beings that eat it, who are both material and spiritual, and therefore a true reciprocity cannot take place between them. Coition, however, can start as an inrush of nontangible psychic energy that yearns to touch, as well as the reverse in which physical desire is spiritualized.

Both eating and coition are partly intangible, for the same neutrality necessary to meditation is necessary to the pleasures of eating and coition. The center of the pleasure experienced in both does not derive solely from literal "tasting" and "touching" but rather from the processes and motion they set off. The transformation of food into energy in the body is as real a pleasure as the literal engorging of the object, and even as "tangible," though it is experienced and perceived kinesthetically rather than with the senses of taste and touch. The experience of such kinesthetic pleasure and "knowledge" is more obvious in making love, where being filled and transported by "higher" spiritual or psychic energy can be as perceptible and as powerful as physical touching, the blending of spirits as real as the blending of bodies. Such total coition is as real if not as seemingly simple for humans as for angels:

> . . . if Spirits embrace,
> Total they mix, union of pure with pure
> Desiring; nor restrained conveyance need
> As flesh to mix with flesh, or soul with soul.
>
> (8: 626–29)

Thus Raphael describes to Adam the love of angels, but humans also may attain to such purity in their resonant coition, more articulate if less unconstrained. One purpose of the commandment "not [to] taste or touch" (9: 651) is to encourage and ensure the attainment of this total pleasure.

A third source of this kinesthetic pleasure in addition to eating and coition is meditation or contemplation. The "horizontal" motion of the joining of complementary psychic principles is nowhere represented by Raphael, but the motion of energy through the various faculties of mind is indicated in his account of the higher part of the process in which material food is transformed into spirit:

> Man's nourishment, by gradual scale sublimed,
> To vital spirits aspire, to animal,
> To intellectual; give both life and sense,
> Fancy and understanding, whence the soul
> Reason receives, and reason is her being,
> Discursive, or intuitive: discourse

> Is oftest yours, the latter most is ours,
> Differing but in degree, of kind the same.
>
> (5: 483–90)

In his response to Raphael, Adam more explicity casts contemplation into the same ascending pattern as food and love:

> O favorable spirit, propitious guest,
> Well hast thou taught the way that might direct
> Our knowledge, and the scale of Nature set
> From center to circumference, whereon
> In contemplation of created things
> By steps we may ascend to God.
>
> (5: 507–12)

This contemplation takes place or is "contained within" the third space—the space more proper to "intuitive" than to "discursive" reason—but this is nowhere made clear. Because of this inadequacy and because of the inconsistencies in Raphael's use of the ladder-tree imagery and in the conceptions they represent, the verticality and a rigid primacy of hierarchy and ascent in the end subsume the other more organic and kinesthetic aspects of the complex of ideas just discussed. Raphael condescendingly reserves the intuitive faculty for angels, and the discursive structures then serve to obscure the processes by which human being will find and make the way to the one heaven and earth. "Open[ing] to themselves at length the way" (7: 158) becomes indistinguishable from "soliciting their thoughts with matters hid" (8: 168). This conflict allows Satan to ask Eve, with an incredulity that is perhaps partly geniune:

> Indeed? Hath God then said that of the fruit
> Of all these garden trees ye shall not eat,
> Yet lords declared of all in earth or air?
>
> (9: 656–58)

As a result of the irony of such a query that so briefly and simply points up its central fallacy, Raphael's schema easily collapses, and so does any remaining shred of confidence Eve may have in it. Satan's strategy of speaking from the serpent has the same effect: it destroys the apparent hierarchical order of the universe and in so doing increases the sense of chaos and confusion that Eve already feels as a result of Raphael and Adam's colloquies. Her first response to Satan's address is:

> What may this mean? Language of man pronounced
> By tongue of brute, and human sense expressed?
>
> (9: 553–54)

The specious masculine order entirely collapsed, Satan seeks to reinforce the remaining feminine space by reinterpreting the principle of ascent and fabricating a new order. He counters Raphael's confusing and inconsistent literal-mindedness with a literal-mindedness that is simpler and apparently more reasonable. Raphael's transformation of the kinesthetic process into a static and rigidly graded continuum has severed the material from the spiritual and earth from heaven because it has destroyed the motion and energy in which they share. Satan repairs this destruction by reconnecting earth and heaven by means of the magic apple, for by eating this fruit human being will ascend and "be as gods" (9: 708), a prospect that echoes Raphael's "time may come when men / With angels may participate" (5: 493–94). However, Satan's way, unlike the sociable spirit's, is not complex, indirect, or confusing but is quick, direct, easy, and tangible. No "tract of time" is necessary, no "gradual scale," no "way at length, under long obedience tried." Satan's way is "ready, and not long" (9: 626). It is direct: linking earth and heaven directly he makes "intricate seem straight" (9: 632) and flattens out the difficult resonant structure. Although the frustration of "degrees" has been removed, however, the ascent is not chaotic but is still orderly: it is "proportion meet" (9: 711) that humans should be as gods since Satan as serpent has by eating the fruit become "as human." Finally, Satan's way is tangible, certain, and apparently more organic than Raphael's way: it is to touch and taste the fruit literally and directly rather than using it as a meditative symbol of neutrality or as an image of gradual and natural growth in which the seed and tree, by virtue of a reciprocal relation with earth, water, and air, yields its telos—its full growth and its flowers and fruit—as an almost secondary consequence of its primary reciprocal nature.

Satan's strategy is a perversion and a disaster, because such literal-mindedness destroys the organic nature of both the tree image and human being's relation to it more emphatically than Raphael's strategy did. For in reaching directly for the fruit at the top of the tree, Satan is reaching not for something high in himself that has grown or could grow from a seed in himself but for something external to himself that heaven has and he lacks. He does not understand that the ascent is to take place within human being first, an ascent that then will correspond with heaven to yield the "one kingdom" in which " earth [is] . . . changed to heav'n, and heav'n to earth" (7: 160). Satan's act breaks this resonant process by recasting the image so that earth is at the "bottom" and heaven at the "top" and further, by touching and tasting the fruit. Because taste and touch have a more direct materiality than seeing, hearing, smelling, or moving, there is greater danger that they will be misunderstood and wrongly acted upon, their spiritual aspect lost. Appropriately enough, Satan's temptation focuses on these two senses in eating and sex. He tells Eve that before he ate the fruit, he discerned nothing but food or sex and "apprehended nothing high" (9: 573–74). Actually, he does not even discern or enjoy food or sex because he has no understanding or feeling for the resonant and kinesthetic nature of pleasure. He is like compulsive eaters and nymphomaniacs, who indulge themselves physically but always want more, whose hunger and pleasure are alike a death that ceaselessly devours them. Thus Sin is ever devoured by the monster children engendered with her by her son Death:

> [Death] Me overtook, his mother, all dismayed,
> And in embraces forcible and foul
> Engend'ring with me, of that rape begot
> These yelling monsters that with ceaseless cry
> Surround me, as thou saw'st, hourly conceived
> And hourly born, with sorrow infinite
> To me; but when they list, into the womb
> That bred them they return, and howl and gnaw
> My bowels, with their repast; then bursting forth
> Afresh, with conscious terrors vex me round,
> That rest or intermission none I find.
> Before mine eyes in opposition sits
> Grim Death my son and foe, who sets them on,
> And me his parent would full soon devour
> For want of other prey.
>
> (2: 792–806)

Satan's sin is to mistakenly divide food and sex from what is "high" and yet to perceive what is high in terms of a literal touching and tasting that confine them to a narrow circuit contrary to their true multidimensional nature. This rendering of the complex resonant structure into something simple and tangible is an extreme form of identification that destroys the medium necessary for "ascent" and destroys physical pleasure as well, since like spiritual pleasure it depends on reciprocity.

The strategy appeals to Eve for two reasons. First, it not only praises her feminine space, but expands it further, freeing her from the "narrow circuit" into the spaces of heaven, as in her dream in Book 5: "not to earth confined, / But sometimes in the air, as we; sometimes / Ascend to heav'n," as Satan puts it (5: 78–80), or as Eve herself phrases it, speaking of the fruit in Book 9, "Thou open'st wisdom's way" (9: 809).

Second, the clear and articulated order Satan gives Eve allays the fear introduced by Raphael in Book 8 of the overwhelming immensity of the universe and of its seemingly chaotic bounty. Satan's ladder of ascent controls the expansion into the spaces of heaven, and in a way that serves Eve's nature instead of diminishing it. Satan's use of Raphael's rationalistic pictures especially appeals to Eve because after the colloquy with Adam she is herself trying to find a firm and rational principle to take Adam's place in her psyche and to "redress" her own inferior status by becoming more masculine. Satan has already placed her in the center of her space and the universe; now he further gives her the ladder of ascent, the tree, to cling to.

This tree is an approximation of the Adam whom she has lost, more tangible than the metaphorical platane and more tangible even than Adam himself.

The temptation of Eve perhaps has a special appeal to Satan: he hopes somewhere in the back of his mind that by debasing himself and serving Eve he will be able to rise proportionately if she rises. In this coattails strategy he decides, in a new attempt to understand the universal structure, to start at the bottom of the chain of being by "imbruting" himself in the serpent and so perhaps automatically rise "by degrees" back up to the top whence he fell. If human beings, made of clay, "creature[s] formed of earth / . . . exalted from so base original" (9: 149–50) can live in beautiful Paradise and have "angel wings, / And flaming ministers" "subjected to . . . their service," perhaps Satan in his "foul descent" into "bestial slime" can hope to enjoy a similar fate (9: 149–71).

In this mutual appeal Eve eats the fruit, an act that exactly mirrors Satan's false rhetorical picture. Because this word and act are neither in themselves resonant nor in a resonant or dramatic relation to one another—are not in a relation in which word, act, and universe correspond to one another in a neutral space, or in which word, act, or universe slightly offset one another such that they stretch into evolution—Eve's mirroring action precipitates the collapse of the third space, which turns the relation of elements within it into the identifying dynamic. The modality is literalized, the world is broken into the material and the heavenly, and the psyche is broken into fancy and externalized reason. The world of the literal and external is the "real" world, but not the real world, for reality is not literal or external but resonant. Although Eve's eating the fruit is an act in the realm of action, the fall it precipitates is not primarily a physical fall but a psychic fall that has physical repercussions.

The nature of the "knowledge" gained from the fruit is not resonant consciousness, but the power—or the necessity—to "subdue" externals in the literal spaces of earth and heaven as knights, explorers, pilots, and astronomers. "Armed" with knowledge, fallen humanity becomes both the epic hero that Eve told Adam she wished to be and the scientist "dieted by" the tree that Satan calls "mother of science" (9: 680).

The "retired" space has been turned inside-out, becoming the "capacious" mind. As Satan says when he describes his eating of the fruit, he "spared not" (9: 596), promising Eve a new bounty that allows them to turn their thoughts to "speculations high or deep / . . . and with capacious mind / Consider . . . all things visible in heav'n, / Or earth" (9: 602–5). That this capaciousness is specious is indicated by Satan's word *visible:* what is perceived in true consciousness is not primarily something visible or tangible, but rather "insensible" (8: 130), kinesthetic and resonant principles behind these visible manifestations.

In this knowledge the mind loses its flexibility and becomes simultaneously rigid and twisting, monomaniacal and dualistic. Eve becomes "fixed on the fruit" (9: 735) as she considers eating it, and worships it after she has eaten (9: 795–807). This fixity, like Satan's obduracy, makes the mind resistant to modality and leads instead to that symptomatic form in which much philosophy expresses itself, the paradox, the "obliquity" that a false straightness must produce when it refuses the intricacy of modality. As she considers the fruit, Eve "muses" to herself in such forms as:

> For good unknown sure is not had, or had
> And yet unknown, is as not had at all.
>
> (9: 756–57)

Similarly, Satan "reasons":

> Deterred not from achieving what might lead
> To happier life, knowledge of good and evil?
> Of good, how just? Of evil, if what is evil
> Be real, why not known, since easier shunned?
> God therefore cannot hurt ye, and be just;
> Not just, not God; not feared then, nor obeyed:
> Your fear itself of death removes the fear.
>
> (9: 696–702)

Such lines aptly illustrate the "credulity" and "amazement" (9: 644, 614, 640) into which "wonder" has fallen, the latter a pun that reflects both Satan's physical and mental motion.

As Eve "engorges without restraint," the restraint and disciplined neutrality of innocence is gone, and she becomes "mature" in a knowledge that breaks into "truth" and "fancy," into "seeming," a split mediated by "expectation high" instead of by the yearning that mediates in dramatic evolution. As Milton describes her first reaction after eating the fruit:

> . . . such delight till then, as seemed,
> In fruit she never tasted, whether true
> Or fancied so, through expectation high
> Of knowledge.
>
> (9: 787–90)

As Eve says to herself, her experience "open'st wisdom's way" and "giv'st access" out of the narrow circuit (9: 807–10). However, the "truth" is that the third space of meditative "retiring" has become narrower, constricted like Satan's "serpent prison";[6] the external world has become a limitless waste; and heaven has become unreachable. As Eve says:

> . . . thou open'st wisdom's way,
> And giv'st access,though secret she retire.
> And I perhaps am secret: Heav'n is high,
> High and remote to see from thence distinct
> Each thing on earth.
>
> (9: 809–13)

This turn of events in which it is difficult to tell what is closed and secret and what is transcendent and open is as much to be hoped for as feared. The third space has become the "secret" and effeminate space of fancy severed from transcendent "truth," which is equally secret.

As it develops, the initial approximation of resonance in Satan's love-song has snapped. Desiring in his frustration and misperception a total "union"— falling prey to the possessive pull of the telos that lurks within romanticism and destroys its organic nature—Satan's poetic falls into a rigid allegory in which the absoluteness of the link between vehicle and tenor becomes more important than the distance between them, more important than the process in which two poles are established in order to open a space in which resonant perception, the only true "meaning," can take place. This allegory destroys the space that is the very locus of poetry and of "truth," and then easily falls into "realism"—the realism of Keats's "cold hillside" and of Coleridge's "Ne Plus Ultra" and "Limbo," the realism of the capacious wasteland.

The simile of the "amazed night-wanderer" following the will-o'-the wisp into the bog (9: 634–42) defines Eve's state of mind in the modal perspective. Its modal intricacy straightened (9: 632) by Satan the "wandering fire," the simile becomes an ordinary allegorical simile, an illustration in which the "poetic" vehicle corresponds directly to the "content," the "meaningful" tenor: the peasant falls, Eve falls. Part of the strategy of Milton's counter-plot will be to save the explorers, pilots, and astronomers from the bog by taking them out of the literal world and putting them back into the third space of the imagination, to unfix Eve from the center of her space and make her "wander" in a world that is fluid and neutral.

Eve in her fall believes that she has now been made equal to the rational Adam, "redressing" the deficiency she felt as a result of Raphael's and Adam's attitude toward her and for which she separated herself from Adam. In her new acquisition of power, she debates with herself whether to share the fruit with Adam:

> . . . Shall I to him make known
> As yet my change, and give him to partake
> Full happiness with me,or rather not,
> But keep the odds of knowledge in my power
> Without copartner? So to add what wants
> In female sex, the more to draw his love,
> And render me more equal, and perhaps,
> A thing not undesirable, sometime
> Superior; for inferior who is free?
>
> (9: 817–25)

But she decides to share her "happiness" with him in case God is right and the serpent wrong and "death ensue" for her alone, an occurrence that might possibly leave Adam to enjoy a second Eve, a thought worse than death

itself—"a death to think" (9: 830). For the love and yearning she feels for
Adam as an integral part of their creation has now, by virtue of the further
division in their state consequent upon the fall, become "an agony of love till
now / Not felt" (9: 858–59), a division greater than the equality she has
gained.

To reinforce the equality and close this gap, Eve therefore offers Adam
the fruit:

> Thou therefore also taste, that equal lot
> May join us, equal joy, as equal love;
> Lest thou not tasting, different degree
> Disjoin us, and I then too late renounce
> Deity for thee, when fate will not permit.
>
> (9: 881–85)

This offer should appeal to Adam, cast as it is in the same quantitative
rhetoric he used in the beginning of Book 9. Adam is "amazed" at Eve's
story and offer, as Eve was amazed by Satan. He is aware that her virtue as
feminine principle is lost, and feels this loss deeply: the garland he has made
to greet her upon her return "down drop[s], and all the faded roses shed" (9:
893), and he exclaims sadly:

> How art thou lost, how on a sudden lost,
> Defaced, deflow'red, and now to death devote!
>
> (9: 900–901)

At the same time, he feels the same bonds of yearning as Eve, and resolves
to die with her:

> . . . with thee
> Certain my resolution is to die;
> How can I live without thee, how forgo
> Thy sweet converse and love so dearly joined,
> To live again in these wild woods forlorn?
> . . . .
> . . . I feel
> The link of nature draw me: flesh of flesh
> Bone of my bone thou art, and from thy state
> Mine shall never be parted, bliss or woe.
>
> (9: 906–16)

In his desperation, Adam falsely perceives his bond with Eve as a direct
link and their relation as identifying:

> So forcible within my heart I feel
> The bond of nature draw me to my own,
> My own in thee, for what thou art is mine;

> Our state cannot be severed; we are one,
> One flesh; to lose thee were to lose myself.
>
> (9: 955–59)

Similarly, he perceives the universal structure as absolute, and "submit[s] to what seem[s] remédiless" (9: 919), exclaiming in Satan's words, "past who can recall, or done undo? / Not God omnipotent, nor fate" (9: 926–27). Faced with the prospect of losing Eve, he thinks of the "wild woods forlorn" in which he lived prior to her creation, forgetting his dramatic and evolutionary exchange with God that brought her to him in the first place. Both he and Eve remember instead Raphael's facile representation of their state. Eve answers Adam's decision with the same formulation:

> [I] . . . gladly of our union hear thee speak,
> One heart, one soul in both.
>
> (9: 966–67)

Adam partakes of the fruit, another mirroring act that matches his, Raphael's, and Satan's rhetorical structures and Eve's act, a mirroring that further collapses their resonant relation. Adam, like Samson, is "shorn of his strength"—his masculine principle of upright neutrality. Without this resonance their high coition falls into burning lust, the first effect of their fall (9: 1011–45). Now that they are "mature in knowledge" the veil of innocence is destroyed, the innocence that preserved the meditative indirectness necessary to resonant consciousness:

> [They] soon found their eyes how opened, and their minds
> How darkened; innocence, that as a veil
> Had shadowed them from knowing ill, was gone.
>
> (9: 1053–55)

This innocence shielded them not simply from knowing ill, but from perceiving the raw energies of the universe unmediated by creative and meditative forms. Adam now fears beholding the face of God and angel:

> . . . How shall I behold the face
> Henceforth of God or angel, erst with joy
> And rapture so oft beheld? Those heavenly shapes
> Will dazzle now this earthly, with their blaze
> Insufferably bright. O might I here
> In solitude live savage, in some glade
> Obscured, where highest woods impenetrable
> To star or sunlight, spread their umbrage broad
> And brown as evening! Cover me, ye pines,
> Ye cedars, with innumerable boughs
> Hide me, where I may never see them more.
> But let us now, as in bad plight, devise

> What best may for the present serve to hide
> The parts of each from other.
>
> (9: 1080–93)

Desiring now to hide from angel, God, the energy of the universe, and each other, Adam and Eve go "into the thickest wood"—as later they hide "among the thickest trees" when they hear the Son coming to judge them—to find the fig leaves to cover their loins:

> . . . they chose
> The fig-tree, not that kind for fruit renowned,
> But such as at this day to Indians known
> In Malabar or Deccan spreads her arms
> Branching so broad and long, that in the ground
> The bended twigs take root, and daughters grow
> About the mother tree, a pillared shade
> High overarched, and echoing walks between;
> There oft the Indian herdsman shunning heat
> Shelters in cool, and tends his pasturing herds
> At loop-holes cut through thickest shade. Those leaves
> They gathered, broad as Amazonian targe,
> And with what skill they had, together sewed,
> To gird their waist, vain covering if to hide
> Their guilt and naked shame, O how unlike
> To that first naked glory! Such of late
> Columbus found th'American so girt
> With feathered cincture, naked else and wild
> Among the trees on isles and woody shores.
>
> (9: 1100–18)

In their fall they have lost their nobility and become mere "savages," and have also lost their peace of mind:

> They sat them down to weep; nor only tears
> Rained at their eyes, but high winds worse within
> Began to rise, high passions, anger, hate,
> Mistrust, suspicion, discord, and shook sore
> Their inward state of mind, calm region once
> And full of peace, now tossed and turbulent.
>
> (9: 1121–26)

These seas of pain and mistrust are the landscape of hell, of the sympathic state of mind. Yet at the same time they are the setting in which the pilots will begin their modal journey in the counterplot. The savage in the fig-tree simile is also the Indian herdsman, for whom the cool pillared arches provide psychic shelter and peace of mind as well as material for physical covering, initiating the restoration of the veil and the space of innocence.

After Eve's fall, Satan similarly "back to the thicket . . . [slinks]" (9: 784) and later returns to hell in a specious triumph that soon turns to torment.

The fall of human being has a somewhat different meaning for Satan than for Adam and Eve: for him the form of the temptation was a form of mind and art more than an action, and therefore his failure constitutes a fall in his own mind that seconds and corresponds to the fall in action of the war in heaven. As Milton phrases it in 10: 332–33, Satan "after Eve seduced, *unminded* slunk / Into the wood fast by" (emphasis added). This second fall is more devastating than his first fall, because the complement of mind that could by resonant and dramatic process reverse the fall in the realm of action is now destroyed, and now his fall is complete. This dramatic stretching between art and mind and action, the "as if" of the third space thereby collapsed, Satan becomes the serpent whose form he took. The medium of control gone, he falls down uncontrollably from the throne of hell into the monstrous serpent. Similarly, all distance between them as individual beings collapsed, his followers must share his "fate," and they all fall down in "horrid sympathy" for him who made them like him (see 10: 504–84).

For Adam and Eve the fall is less devastating, because in Eden mind and reality are not separate as in heaven and the resonance maintains itself more easily. Thus this kind of mirroring is less possible. Perhaps more important, however, unlike Satan, Adam and Eve would be more likely to notice that the savage wood sometimes has cool and pillared walks.

Although Adam and Eve's initial response to their fall is "mutual accusation" (9: 1187), the Son's judgment of them and their ultimate response to this judgment show a flexibility and a movement that is the renewal and continuation of the evolution brought to an impasse in the beginning of Book 9. First, since the expulsion of Satan and his hosts from heaven in Book 6, an evolution has taken place in the configuration of God and the Son's relation to each other, to the universe, and to the beings within it subject to their judgment. After the fall of Adam and Eve, the Father says:

> . . . fall'n he is; and now
> What rests but that the mortal sentence pass
> On his transgression.
>
> (10: 47–49)

This statement is quite rigid; but the Son's reply to it, different from his replies in Book 6, bends its structure and alters its nature. Then he said:

> O Father, O Supreme of heav'nly Thrones,
> First, highest, holiest, best, thou always seek'st
> To glorify thy Son, I always thee,
> As is most just. This I my glory account,
> My exaltation, and my whole delight,
> That thou in me well pleased, declar'st thy will
> Fulfilled, which to fulfill is all my bliss.
> Scepter and power, thy giving, I assume,

And gladlier shall resign, when in the end
Thou shalt be all in all, and I in thee
For ever, and in me all whom thou lov'st.
But whom thou hat'st, I hate, and can put on
Thy terrors, as I put thy mildness on,
Image of thee in all things; and shall soon,
Armed with thy might, rid heav'n of these rebelled,
To their prepared ill mansion driven down
To chains of darkness, and th'undying worm,
That from thy just obedience could revolt,
Whom to obey is happiness entire.
Then shall thy saints unmixed, and from th'impure
Far separate, circling thy holy mount
Unfeignèd halleluiahs to thee sing,
Hymns of high praise, and I among them chief.

(6: 723–45)

But now he is no longer simply a replica of God, but in a resonant relation to him. He answers:

Father eternal, thine is to decree
. . . .
. . . *but* thou know'st
. . . .
. . . that I may mitigate their doom
On my derived; *yet* I shall temper so
Justice with mercy.

(10: 68–78; emphasis added)

This rhetorical strategy is similar to that in Book 3 as the Son firmly responds to the Father's long speech concerning the fall of human being and its consequences (3: 80–134):

For should man finally be lost . . .
. . . .
. . . That be from thee far,
That far be from thee, Father.

(3: 150–54)

As the Son comes down to seek Adam and Eve in the garden, he expresses dissatisfaction with the effects of their act on their resonant relation with him:

. . . I miss thee here,
Not pleased, thus entertained with solitude.

(10: 104–5)

But in his judgment he is both judge and servant, and he pities Adam and Eve as well as passing sentence upon them (10: 209–14). And in his return to

God he diplomatically "appeases" him by recounting "what had passed with man . . . mixing intercession sweet" (10: 227–28). This "mixed" style is a change from the "unmixed" ideal expressed during the war in heaven.

Although Adam and Eve's first reaction to their judgment is anguish and despair, it soon modulates into a flexibility corresponding to the Son's. Whereas Satan's fixity and misperception exacerbate and perpetuate his fall—he continues to fall and to be punished over and over again, fall and punishment being by now indistinguishable—Adam and Eve fall once and move on.

> . . . so oft they [Satan and his followers] fell
> Into the same illusion, not as man
> Whom they triumphed, once lapsed.
>
> (10: 570–72)

At first, in his soliloquy (10: 720–844) Adam, in a "troubled sea of passion tossed" (10: 718), falls into a hell of sympathic reasoning and feeling that recapitulates the state of mind of Books 1 and 2. His concluding words succinctly characterize the downward spiral into which such strategies of thought lead:

> . . . Thus what thou desir'st
> And what thou fear'st, alike destroys all hope
> Of refuge, and concludes thee miserable
> Beyond all past example and future,
> To Satan only like, both crime and doom.
> O Conscience, into what abyss of fears
> And horrors hast thou driv'n me; out of which
> I find no way, from deep to deeper plunged!
>
> (10: 837–44)

However, this train of thought is stopped by Eve. As Adam calls out for Death to end his torment (10: 854–62), Eve, desolate to see him so afflicted, "soft words to his fierce passion . . . assayed" (10: 865). At first he angrily retorts, "Out of my sight, thou serpent!" (10: 867); and he goes on to describe her fall in literal-minded and rationalistic terms that nevertheless accurately characterize the severed state of mind that brought it about. He accuses her of "longing to be seen / Though by the Devil himself" (10: 877–78), says she is "supernumerary / To my just number found," and asks why God "that peopled highest heav'n / With Spirits masculine, create[d] at last / This novelty on earth?" (10: 887–89). But Eve's response, a dramatic instance of distancing that refuses to accept a false or "remédiless" structure, offsets rather than mirrors Adam's state of mind: she asserts, directly and strongly, the fluid and spacious virtue of her own nature and counters his "reason" with her love:

> He . . . from her turned, but Eve,
> Not so repulsed, with tears that ceased not flowing,
> And tresses all disordered, at his feet
> Fell humble, and embracing them, besought
> His peace, and thus proceeded in her plaint:
>   "Forsake me not thus, Adam, witness Heav'n
> What love sincere and reverence in my heart
> I bear thee."
>
> (10: 909–16)

This declaration is one of the major turning points in *Paradise Lost,* for Eve is the first being to give love that exceeds both her power and the pain of her own loss, who loves more than she wants to be loved. Unlike Satan, she gives regardless of the structural justifications. As she said of the gods in Book 9 after she has eaten the fruit: "[they] envy what they cannot give" (9: 805), not what they are not given. Though her perception of the gods may be wrong, her perception of the nature of envy and love is clear. Here in Book 10 she is "immovable" in her assertion of her love for Adam and her demand for peace between them. And it is peace that is the first step in the counter-plot, in reversing the fall, and indeed in the creation itself (7: 216–17; see below, Part III). The strength Eve shows is not a masculine strength but the strength special to her own feminine nature. Adam is "disarmed" by Eve's response. With this one word Milton signals the victory Eve's asserting love has achieved not only over their division and despair, but over the entire epic frame of mind.

Although the configuration of Adam and Eve as a couple each with different natures in some ways increased the risk of division and a fall, it also has a built-in aesthetic distancing and flexibility: when one is "seen least wise," the other sees from a different perspective that allows recovery and resonant evolution.

In her action, her dramatic expression of love in the face of wrath, Eve herself has changed and has forced the relation between her and Adam to evolve beyond the hierarchical structure in terms of which they were introduced in Book 4 and in terms of which they first pictured themselves. And Eve, who under the pressure of this structure in which Adam is "author and disposer" acted like a serpent in Book 9, in Book 10 acts like the Son in her countering of rage with love, in forcing the structure of things to bend and stretch. As God says to the Son in Book 3, the Son is his "sole complacence" because he has found "peace / . . . under wrath" (3: 274–76).

> . . . [thou] hast been found
> By merit more than birthright Son of God,
> Found worthiest to be so by being good,
> Far more than great or high; because in thee
> Love hath abounded more than glory abounds.
>
> (3: 308–12)

Yet Eve needs the assertion of the strength particular to Adam's nature to direct her love and fluidity, for after they have recovered heart, they begin to think of the sorrows that will befall their children—"miserable it is / To be to others cause of misery" (10: 981–82)—and Eve carries her own train of thought too far in suggesting that they "seek Death" to prevent it. Thus she returns to the same despair out of which she wrenched Adam by her expression of love. But Adam, stronger now, counters with an assertion of his unrightness and reasons in a more distinguishing and less sympathic way than in his soliloquy:

> She ended here, or vehement despair
> Broke off the rest; so much of death her thoughts
> Had entertained as dyed her cheeks with pale.
> But Adam with such counsel nothing swayed,
> To better hopes his more attentive mind
> Laboring had raised.
>
> (10: 1007–12)

Instead of responding univocally to the structure of their present state and its relation to heaven and instead of focusing on their loss, he more precisely focuses on the "mixed" and intricate nature of the judgment. He says to Eve that her desire for self-destruction "implies / . . . anguish and regret / For loss of life and pleasure overloved" (10: 1017–19), not a nobility of mind that is detached from life, pleasure, and love. Here Adam is referring to the modal state of mind—of yearning for something lost that fluctuates between the perception of the object desired and its loss—as it is in the process of slipping back into the sympathic state. Warning against such a fall, Adam "calls to mind" the double nature of the sentence: that though they will sometimes live in pain and though they will die, their future life will also provide shelter from pain and the means to alter it. He also calls to mind the Son's attitude and tone: that whereas they had expected wrath, they were judged with "mild / And gracious temper" (10: 1046–47). Responding in kind, Adam interprets the Son's "look serene / When angry most he seemed and most severe" (10: 1094–95) as an opening for change and remedy, and decides to act on this possibility instead of assuming that the structure of judgment and of the course of events is rigid, as he had when he ate the fruit:

> How much more, if we pray him, will his ear
> Be open, and his heart to pity incline.
>
> (10: 1060–61)

While Satan's inflexibility in the face of what he perceives as an inflexible universe constricts him more tightly, Adam and Eve's articulate fluidity arrests the sympathic motions of the infernal mind and begins to reopen the third space. While Satan chooses violent anger, precipitous action, and pain, the Son and the human pair choose instead the flexible firmness of "yes . . .

but" and "that be far from thee," choose peace and pause, and mildness and delight. That such firmness is a greater strength than violence is indicated by Satan's line "To be weak is miserable" (1: 157): he focuses on misery and pain, which makes him weak, which distorts his physical being. Milton describes his first "metamorphosis" as he speaks on Mt. Niphates:

> Thus while he spake, each passion dimmed his face
> Thrice changed with pale, ire, envy, and despair,
> Which marred his borrowed visage . . .
> . . . .
> For heav'nly minds from such distempers foul
> Are ever clear.
>
> (4: 114–19)

These "distempers" are the monsters that populate hell, where

> . . . Nature breeds
> Perverse, all monstrous, all prodigious things,
> Abominable, inutterable, and worse
> Than fables yet have feigned, or fear conceived,
> Gorgons and Hydras, and Chimeras dire.
>
> (2: 624–28)

For Satan's focusing on pain sustains and perpetuates the landscape of woe that partly depends for its continuance on a mind that acknowledges it. In contrast, when the angels in heaven hear the "unwelcome news" that Adam and Eve have fallen,

> . . . dim sadness did not spare
> That time celestial visages, yet mixed
> With pity, violated not their bliss.
>
> (10: 23–25)

To focus on and reserve a space for bliss, while maintaining a clarity of mind, prevents the collapsing of psyche into pity and the sympathic labyrinth. Similarly, this space can provide shelter from the painful landscape and open into a reversal of the fall in which monsters are dispelled.

Adam and Eve's reactions to each other as beings with qualitatively distinct virtues and their reactions as a pair show, just as do God and the Son's reactions, a countering of different perspectives. Though such perspectives are not yet the meditation of the last stage of the modal declension leading to a full consciousness of the principles of their own being and of the being of the universe, nevertheless they return the pair to the third space of dramatic interchange of Adam and God's colloquy in Book 8. In this space they are beginning to know each other in a way that will gradually join them in a truer union than the unarticulated "individual soul" of Raphael's conception, a conception that led Adam to fall.

In the end, the joining of the two principles of being must take place within each psyche as well as between beings. For although Adam and Eve were created as separate beings, they are both principles of the one complete psyche, in this sense "one individual soul." The human configuration is a kind of learning laboratory that allows, indeed enforces, an empathic inter-knowledge: because they are parts of the same psyche, masculine and feminine tend toward each other; but because they are different, they tend toward opposition. The movement resulting from simultaneous or alternat-ing identification and opposition springs one into empathy, and into the relativizing modes. In meditation, the right relation between the principle of upright neutrality and the fluid third space will yield two new faculties or actions of psychic being: right reason and imagination, which, fallen, were reason and fancy.

NOTES

1. William Empson, although from a different point of view from the one taken here, points out in *Milton's God* that Raphael's formulations of the structure of reality echo the formulations Satan uses in his internal debates and in his temptation of Eve, and that Raphael's instruction weakens rather than strengthens the human pair. *Milton's God* (London: Chatto and Windus, 1965), chap. 4, pp. 147–81.

2. Michael Lieb, *The Dialectics of Creation: Patterns of Birth and Regeneration in "Para-dise Lost"* (Amherst: University of Massachusetts Press, 1970), Part II: "The Process of Uncre-ation," pp. 81–201.

3. William Butler Yeats, *The Collected Poems of W. B. Yeats* (New York: the Macmillan Company, 1956), p. 31.

4. The four principal speeches are: 4: 358–92; 4: 505–35; 9: 99–178; 9: 455–93.

5. The essays on literary artists and critics that constitute Paul de Man's *Blindness and Insight* are all variations on the theme that the romantics were deluded in believing that the sign and meaning could be unified or connected and that the final function of literature and criticism is not to yield the fulfillment of any yearning for "presence or plenitude" but to reveal the absolute and primary reality of the void. This void can be filled by neither life nor art; the failure that the void is or necessitates does not lie in the self but in the fundamental nature of things. The most we can attain is a consciousness of these truths, a consciousness that derives not from absence or yearning but from the "presence of nothingness." All art and criticism, even roman-tic "blindness," can reveal this "insight" to the reader who understands or is receptive to this structural truth. Thus de Man says that "Rousseau's theory of representation is not directed toward meaning as presence and plenitude but toward meaning as void" (p. 127). It is easy to see that de Man's structuralism collapses different stages of consciousness into a single non-modal and nondevelopmental perspective. Paul de Man, *Blindness and Insight: Essays in the Rhetoric of Contemporary Criticism* (New York: Oxford University Press, 1971).

6. In his note to 9: 187–91, Douglas Bush refers to Keats's comment: "Whose spirit does not ache at the smothering and confinement—the unwilling stillness—the 'waiting close'? Whose head is not dizzy at the possible speculations of Satan in the serpent prison? No passage of poetry ever can give a greater pain of suffocation" (*Complete Works*, ed. H. B. Forman, 3: 265).

11   The Meditative Modes: The Art of Michael

Although Adam and Eve's response to their fall and judgment is more flexible and their relation to the universal structure is more truly histrionic than Satan's, their way to the space of bliss is still to be long and gradual. In Books 11 and 12 they will more completely reenter the third modal space collapsed in their fall, but the modality is no longer dramatic, lyrical or ironic, or masculine and feminine, but meditative. Here in their exchange with Michael they begin to move into the two relativizing modes, a further stage in the declension of mind and in the evolution of the universe.

In Book 10 the Son delivered the judgment; in Books 11 and 12 the archangel Michael is sent to execute its first stages. The earth is changed and Adam and Eve are expelled from Paradise; but to soften this "sad sentence rigorously urged" (11: 109), Michael is to instruct them in the implications of the Son's judgment—the mixture of toil and pain with the covenant. Although the Son's and human being's resonant relation to the Father has modified the "law," Adam and Eve's act still has certain irreversible consequences. On the one hand, Adam says with some truth:

> . . . that from us aught should ascend to heav'n
> So prevalent as to concern the mind
> Of God high-blest, or to incline his will,
> Hard to belief may seem; yet . . .
> . . . .
> Methought I saw him placable and mild,
> Bending his ear; persuasion in me grew
> . . . .
> . . . that the bitterness of death
> Is past, and we shall live.
>
> (11: 143–58)

Adam and Eve take comfort from this persuasion and believe that they will remain in Paradise. Eve says gladly, "While here we dwell, / What can be toilsome in these pleasant walks?" (11: 178–79). However, this perception is too simple and unmixed. For as she speaks, Paradise itself is beginning to alter as a result of their psychic fall:

So spake, so wished much-humbled Eve, but fate
Subscribed not; Nature first gave signs, impressed
On bird, beast, air, air suddenly eclipsed
After short blush of morn, Nigh in her sight
The bird of Jove, stooped from his airy tow'r,
Two birds of gayest plume before him drove;
Down from a hill the beast that reigns in woods,
First hunter then, pursued a gentle brace,
Goodliest of all the forest, hart and hind.

(11: 181–89)

As God has said to the Son in answer to his effort to bend the judgment:

All thy request for man, accepted Son,
Obtain . . .
But longer in that Paradise to dwell
The law I gave to Nature him forbids.

(11: 46–49)

Adam and Eve must be expelled from Paradise not primarily as a "place" but from the third dramatic space of their resonant relation with God in Book 8, which is now literal. The meditative third space of consciousness must replace the space of resonant action. The primary locus of resonance, reciprocity, and evolution must be somewhere else, in some other "place" more appropriate to their new state of mind, which has as a result of their fall become sympathic and more fragmented. In a sense, Adam and Eve are not expelled from their familiar Paradise, but rather from the memory of it and the associations it has with their former state. For the character of Paradise is altered as their minds are altered; therefore it is no longer the same "place."

Paradise and earth are changing even before Michael arrives to expel them. As in the confusion of the collapse of the third space the "calm region" of Adam's mind becomes "tossed and turbulent," filled with the rising "high winds . . . high passions" (9: 1122–26), so at Adam and Eve's falls

Earth felt the wound, and Nature from her seat
Sighing through all her works gave signs of woe.

(9: 782–83)

Earth trembled from her entrails, as again
In pain, and Nature gave a second groan;
Sky loured and, muttering thunder, some sad drops
Wept at completing of the mortal sin.

(9: 1000–1003)

As Adam and Eve fall, Sin and Death build their bridge from hell to earth, and God, "calling forth by name / His mighty angels gave them several charge, / As sorted best with present things" (10: 649–51). The courses of the planets are distorted and the weather changed to the extremes of hot and cold as described in 10: 651–706.

> . . . Thus began
> Outrage from lifeless things; but Discord first,
> Daughter of Sin, among th'irrational
> Death introduced through fierce antipathy.
> Beast now with beast gan war, and fowl with fowl,
> And fish with fish; to graze the herb all leaving,
> Devour'd each other; nor stood much in awe
> Of man, but fled him, or with count'nance grim
> Glared on him passing. These were from without
> The growing miseries.
>
> (10: 706–15)

This new fallen world is the world first glimpsed in *Paradise Lost* in the similes in Books 1 and 2. What was simile in hell is now, in the epic dimension of the poem, "real." As after his conquest Satan sends Sin and Death on their mission to earth,

> . . . the blasted stars looked wan,
> And planets, planet-strook, *real* eclipse
> Then suffered.
>
> (10: 412–14; italics added)

Both God's angels and Satan's "substitutes" (10: 403) are agents of change, but they are secondary agents. In the resonant structure of the universe the altering of mind brings about the altering of the mind's setting. The "high passions" within and the "high winds" without correspond to each other. The instances of discord

> . . . were from without
> The growing miseries, which Adam saw
> Already in part, though hid in gloomiest shade,
> To sorrow abandoned, but worse felt within,
> . . . in a troubled sea of passion tossed.
>
> (10: 714–18)

This painful and sympathic world into which Paradise metamorphoses is the world into which Adam and Eve are expelled by Michael at the end of Book 12. In the final simile of the poem Adam is likened to a laborer homeward returning (12: 613–32), to the fallen laborer sentenced to till the ground "in the sweat of . . . [his] face" (10: 200–208), in the world the reader knows well. And a few lines later he and Eve descend from Paradise into this "real" world, the "subjected plain," the fallen world of history:

> In either hand the hast'ning Angel caught
> Our ling'ring parents, and to th'eastern gate

Led them direct, and down the cliff as fast
To the subjected plain; then disappeared.
They, looking back all th'eastern side beheld
Of Paradise, so late their happy seat,
Waved over by that flaming brand, the gate
With dreadful faces thronged and fiery arms.
Some natural tears they dropped, but wiped them soon;
The world was all before them, where to choose
Their place of rest, and Providence their guide:
They hand in hand, with wand'ring steps and slow,
Through Eden took their solitary way.

(12: 637–49)

This fallen world is not only the "real" world, but the sympathic world of hell and chaos, the world of pain and conflict where good and evil seem inextricably mixed, and where moral and perceptual distinctions are difficult to make. The eclipsed planet of the fallen world is the ruined angel of hell whose glory is dimmed by pain (1: 589–600). The "blustering" and "confounding" winds and thunder of 10: 664–67, are the winds and thunder of 1: 171–77. And the "pinching cold and scorching heat" of 10: 691 is the "frozen continent" of 2: 572–628. Adam's response to the "sight / Of terror, foul and ugly to behold, / Horrid to think, how horrible to feel" (11: 463–65) that he sees in Michael's vision of Cain killing Abel in the future history of the fallen world is similar to Satan's pain as he sees his followers' plight in 1: 604–8. The deceptive "marriage rites . . . feast and music . . . happy interview and fair event / Of love and youth not lost, songs, garlands, flow'rs, / And charming symphonies" of 11: 591–95, as the Sons of God join the lustful daughters of men, is similar in tone to the "lustful orgies" of Peor (1: 415), the "amorous ditties all a summer's day" of Thammuz (1: 449), and the harmony that "suspends hell" in 2: 554. The "sea without shore" of the flood in 11: 750 is the same chaos through which Satan voyages in Book 2 to find a shore for his sea in the newly created world (2: 1011). Likewise the Cherubim of God are likened to the meteorous evening mists gathering fast at the laborer's heel in 12: 629–32, and the sword of God before them blazes "fierce as a comet," images recalling and seemingly indistinguishable from the deluding mists that lead the peasant in Book 9 to his death and to the Satan who "unterrified like a comet burn[s]" in 2: 708.

Yet while Adam and Eve's sentence banishes them to the painful world of fallen reality and the world of hell, it simultaneously introduces them to the world of a new art. For Michael's mission is twofold: to expel them but also to instruct them, to "reveal / . . . what shall come in future days" and "so send them forth, though sorrowing, yet in peace" (11: 113–17). This revelation, beginning in Book 11 and continuing through Book 12, precedes the expulsion, and in it Adam and Eve enter the world of history for the first time. Here the archangel reveals to them first the effects of sin and the "world destroyed" by flood, and then the "world restored" by the first and second comings of the Son. Although this instruction may seem to be directly historical, more so than any representation of the fallen world after the actual expulsion, it takes place in the third space of vision and verbal "relation"—on the "top / Of speculation" (12: 588–89) to which Michael leads Adam and in the space of Eve's dream as she "sleep[s] below" (11: 368). In this space Michael's primary purpose, more poetic and spiritual than historical and theological, is to bring a new kind of art to succeed both Raphael's social, theological, and epic art and Satan's love-song; to repair the collapse of modality in Adam and Eve's fall; and to prepare the psyche for the more subtle and complex art of Milton's meditative counterplot, a world into which Adam and Eve enter, as they enter into fallen "reality" and hell, at the end of Book 12. For Adam, the laborer "homeward returning" becomes in this final simile of *Paradise Lost* the peasant who pauses on his delayed way home at midnight to watch the faery elves in Book 1, the wanderer like the pilots, explorers, and astronomer wandering in their uncertain journeys through sea, land, and sky. Thus there are two directions of movement at the poem's end: on the one hand, the similes in Books 1 and 2 move forward in the epic historical dimension into the "real" world into which Adam and Eve enter at their expulsion and into which hell will disgorge its fallen angels. In this first "falling" movement, the similes function as terms of comparison, likening the fallen world to hell. On the other hand, in a second "rising" movement—the movement of the "fortunate fall"— Adam and Eve enter a realm of mind that is in its next higher stage of evolution. The "real" world into which they are "expelled" is a new construction of mind, consisting of both the infernal sympathic world and the world of the similes that simultaneously lifts the mind out of the sympathic world. At the same time as human being "falls" on the heated and painful "subjected plain," he/she is distanced and lifted into the cool, fluid, third space of meditation, just as when Adam and Eve slunk into the wood in shame they found the cool pillared walks of the fig-tree. What we sometimes think of as the "real" world of empirical history does not exist so simply; it is a matter of choice in the face of or in the midst of this perhaps puzzling construction—this "troubled sea of passion" that is somehow also the liquid medium that sustains the pilot's "night-foundered skiff," and the cool vibrating air that sustains the Indian herdsman's spirit.

Paradise Lost "ends" by returning to its beginning; but this "return" is the latest stage in the "plot," a plot that has turned out to be a modal plot of consciousness more than a traditional epic of action. Expelled from Paradise, Adam and Eve enter what is more completely a world of mind than was their edenic being—this new world is the "paradise within," whose reality is as great as the more historical vision in Books 6 and 12 and the world that Adam and Eve now, after their descent into the world of this vision, more literally inhabit. The fallen world is primarily a construction of consciousness neither "inside" the ego's mind nor "outside" in the world, but in the third space of meditation and imagination that is the next stage of the evolution of the universe.

Although Adam and Eve's fall changes their psychic structure in ways that "cause" the painful changes in their world described above—the eclipses and storms—these changes are not simply a punishment. Rather, they occur in order to help restore the resonance between mind and universe, to make it more conscious and thereby allow the evolution of the universe to continue. The "plot" of *Paradise Lost* might be characterized as a sequence of experiments in creation. The first is the heavenly state of being in which the stillness-in-motion/motion-in-stillness of angelic kinesthesia provides the most perfect bliss but in which there is a lack of a corresponding structure of mind. Satan's revolt is an experiment that fails. The creation of Adam and Eve is an experiment on the part of God that attempts to remedy the flaw that prompted Satan to revolt. The judgment passed on them after their fall is a third experiment in creation that is perhaps the most significant because their fall is not allowed to be a failure: it is recognized that the fall is more the result of flawed mind-structure, consciousness, and communion between beings than the result of defects in the beings themselves. Instead of expelling Adam and Eve in the absolute "unmixed" way that he did Satan and starting over, God changes the structure and shifts the locus of the reciprocity and evolution from Paradise to the fallen world that includes instead of excludes hell; and paradise as a separate structure of being disappears.

On the one hand, this new world is painful and confusing: it is a world where the meteorous angels seem to be both good and evil. On the other hand, precisely because they are mixed and not separated or purged off as in the heavenly state, the mind can, indeed must, comtemplate all the forms of the universe and being and reach a resolution in relation to them. This is the "action" of the last two modes in the declension of mind, the meditative relativizing modes. Instead of distinctly separating into entities good and evil, heaven and hell, or even Adam and Eve, in this new "creation" God mixes the elements or entities of being into motions and forms that are more modal than ontological and that therefore are sometimes distinct (in ontological terms) and sometimes not. In this new creation the imaginative space is more definitively separated from the structure of the universe than was the third dramatic space that was Eden. It is less magnetic in its relation to action. At the same time this space is more immersed in and less protected from the sometimes painful movements and vicissitudes of yearning than was Adam and Eve's innocent state: the new mind is not in Paradise, but in the "paradise within" whose boundaries and locus are less clear. In this sense, the new space is less separated from the structure of the universe. The "distance" is the distance of attitude and mind, not of geography.

Although descending into the pain of yearning is a fall, it is a "fortunate fall" because the new psychic structure allows for greater consciousness of and resonance with the forces of the universe and being than did either the angelic or edenic configurations. It is more inclusive, more mobile, and more flexible. The masculine and feminine principles—upright central neutrality and fluid space—come to be more principles of mind—of each human mind—than principles of physical incarnation; and thus knowing and inter-knowing can become more articulate, more exact, and more refined, less encumbered by the obstacles of flesh even while subjected to the more encumbering physical toil on the fallen earth. Moreover, in its meditative action, consciousness can be reflexive, acting and contemplating distinctly and simultaneously since action and imagination have become more dis-tinctly separated and articulated in the judgment. Therefore the action of *Paradise Lost* can at the end of Book 12 circle into the space of meditation; and complementarily the greater consciousness of the counterplot circles back into the epic dimension of the fall and creation stories and becomes their measure, as we the readers listen to Milton, our Raphael, telling us this story to help us on our journey—as Raphael was supposed to tell the story of the war in heaven to help Adam and Eve in Paradise. But Milton brings a more subtle art than Raphael, an art that lifts the mind into the space of the meditative modes and restores the fluid sustaining resonance between earth and heaven. But between Raphael and Milton comes Michael, the warrior angel whose art with broader strokes than Milton's first begins to form and forge this new mind.[1]

In one sense, the future world of history that Adam is shown in Books 11 and 12 is direct, raw in its violent extremes, and sympathic to a degree that invites strong identifications. When Adam views Cain's bloody murder of Abel, "rolling in dust and gore," Adam is "much . . . dismayed" and re-sponds:

> . . . O sight
> Of terror, foul and ugly to behold,
> Horrid to think, how horrible to feel.
>
> (11: 463–65)

And when he next sees the diseases, he weeps:

> Sight so deform what heart of rock could long
> Dry-eyed behold? Adam could not, but wept,
> Though not of woman born; compassion quelled
> His best of man, and gave him up tears.
>
> (11: 494–97)

Likewise Adam identifies with the delusive delights of the lustful Sons of God:

> Such happy interview and fair event
> . . . .
> . . . attached the heart

> Of Adam, soon inclined to admit delight,
> The bent of Nature.
>
> (11: 593–97)

But these visions, despite their apparently unmediated quality, are modified
by the character of the third space in which they occur. First, the boundaries
of this space of "speculation" on the mountaintop are almost artificially
definite and clear, clearer than they will be in the world after expulsion and
in the subtle world of the similes. Second, the mountain offers a breadth and
distance of vision that surpasses normal physical sight within the confines of
space and time and stretches it into spiritual vision. This opening out into a
great spaciousness, similar to the imaginative spaciousness of some of Milton's similes, neutralizes the intensity of the more particular sights Adam
witnesses within it.

> . . . It was a hill
> Of Paradise the highest, from whose top
> The hemisphere of earth in clearest ken
> Stretched out to amplest reach of prospect lay.
> . . . .
> His eye might there command wherever stood
> City of old or modern fame, the seat
> Of mightiest empire, from the destined walls
> Of Cambalu. . .
> . . . .
> . . . In spirit perhaps he also saw
> Rich Mexico.
>
> (11: 378–407)

Michael gives Adam still greater powers of sight by removing the film from
his eyes caused by the eating of the fruit, and then

> . . . purged with euphrasy and rue
> The visual nerve, for he had much to see;
> And from the well of life three drops instilled.
> So deep the power of these ingredients pierced,
> Ev'n to the inmost seat of mental sight,
> That Adam, now enforced to close his eyes,
> Sunk down and all his spirits became entranced;
> But him the gentle Angel by the hand
> Soon raised, and his attention thus recalled:
> "Adam, now ope thine eyes, and . . . behold."
>
> (11: 414–23)

The state induced in Adam by Michael is a dream-state; but the "dream" he
dreams does not allow evil to "harbor" or run to "wild work" (5: 99, 112).
His visions are a lucid dream in which he does not sleep but "wakes to
foresight." In a sense, Adam on the mountaintop is being led into the imagi-

native space that was more proper to feminine being when he and Eve were in the edenic state. In this new human meditative "creation," Eve sleeps below the mountain, "calmed" by "gentle dreams" (12: 595), while Adam in the space of her dream is "formed" into imaginative life as in their first creation Adam slept while Eve was formed from his rib into incarnate life. As Michael says:

> . . . Ascend
> This hill; let Eve (for I have drenched her eyes)
> Here sleep below while thou to foresight wak'st,
> As once thou slept'st while she to life was formed.
>
> (11: 366–69)

In Book 11 Michael's presentation of the future history of humanity to Adam is in visual form; in Book 12 he changes his technique of revelation, as Adam's "mortal sight" wearies, from this direct vision to "relation" (12: 11). In this change the revelation shifts more definitely from the space of action into the more detached imaginative space of poetry. Yet the impact of this poetry is not less than the impact of the direct visions, because the style of Michael's relation does not differ from the style of Milton's relation of Michael's visions. Moreover, in his relation Michael says, speaking of Abraham, for example, "I see him, but thou canst not" (12: 128), and then follows this statement with a lengthy description that brings him to sight. Similarly, when referring to the Nile, he says, "See where it flows, disgorging at seven mouths / Into the sea" (12: 158–59). This technique makes the verbal art attain the immediacy of direct vision and a scope greater than that of direct vision, thereby giving the reader the sense of literally seeing through words in a vast imaginative space.

The visions of future history may be immediate to the eye and the sufferings of the fallen world immediate to Adam's sympathetic heart and invite pity, but within this space this pity is not indulged. Nor does this space of dream provide a lyric relief, or as Ferry and MacCaffrey would say, momentary indulgence for "mortal beauty." The sweet "imagined way . . . to the rich Cathaian coast" is blocked in 10: 289–93, by Sin and Death. The clarity, coolness, and precision of Michael's visions serve as much to distance their content as to make it immediate.

Michael is no "sociable Spirit" like Raphael, nor is he invoked by the young Milton of *Lycidas* to "look homeward . . . and melt with ruth." He is the warrior angel and comes to Eden as such. When Adam first sees him and his band in a "blazing cloud" in the distance, he fears him:

> A glorious apparition, had not doubt
> And carnal fear that day dimmed Adam's eye.
>
> (11: 211–12)

His fear abates, but his awe and respect do not as he says to Eve:

> . . . such majesty
> Invests him coming; yet not terrible,
> That I should fear, nor sociably mild,
> As Raphael, that I should much confide,
> But solemn and sublime.
>
> (11: 232–36)

When Michael then appears to Adam as a man, not as an angel, he is still dressed in a "military vest of purple" (11: 241).

But Michael is no longer the warrior of the war in heaven. He holds in despite the days of human "sword-law" that he reveals to Adam:

> . . . in those days might only shall be admired,
> And valor and heroic virtue called
> . . . .
> [men] . . . to be styled great conquerors
> Patrons of mankind . . .
> Destroyers rightlier called and plagues of men.
>
> (11: 689–97)

True virtue and valor are not accomplished by literal "duels" (12: 387) with swords, but by the alert and wakeful mind. Instead of the epic "griding sword" (6: 329) he used to fight physical battle on the plains of heaven, he now brings a swordlike art that, while not "terrible" or cruel, is disciplined, cold, and hard. It is not the lyric and "drowsy" art of Orpheus: the faces on his chariot

> Had, like a double Janus, all their shape
> Spangled with eyes more numerous than those
> Of Argus, and more wakeful than to drowse,
> Charmed with Arcadian pipe, the pastoral reed
> Of Hermes, or his opiate rod.
>
> (11: 129–33)

This chariot has the power of the Son's chariot in 6: 749–62, but it brings an art to teach and not to destroy.

Michael's presentation of future history, unlike Raphael's account of the war in heaven, is focused as much on Adam's responses as on the events themselves or their "meaning." His purpose in terms of the effect he wants to produce in Adam's mind is twofold. First, it serves to reinfuse into Adam's psyche the dimension of yearning that has been lost in the fall. To this end, the historical events are not presented in an objective or indifferent way detached from feeling, but are presented in an extreme form that specifically arouses strong feelings, as in the visions of Abel's death and of death by disease. This yearning aroused by Michael is proper to the lyric and ironic modes, but in such an extreme form as to become sympathic. This sympathic dimension, however, is gathered into a modality beyond even lyric and ironic modality by Michael's accompanying technique of specifically countering every sympathic response and thus detaching Adam's yearning from every identification with object, feeling, or judgment. This countering is Michael's second purpose, and it takes three forms.

First, he counters one sympathic response with another one that does not balance or work against the first one by opposition, but rather intensifies it such that the mental structure on which it is based collapses; and then the feeling, though more extreme, dissipates. This technique has the effect of making the bottom fall out of the mind, as it were, in its sympathic attitude. For example, when Adam feels pain and pity at the sight of Cain killing Abel, and asks Michael, "Is piety thus and pure devotion paid?" (11: 452), Michael counters not even with a vision of harsh justice, but with a comment that destroys the expectation of justice upon which Adam's question, and his pity too, are based:

> . . . th'unjust the just hath slain
> For envy.
>
> (11: 455–56)

The angel then proceeds to show Adam another equally painful vision of "injustice"—deformity and death by disease. Adam again weeps and questions the justice of this vision:

> . . . Why is life giv'n
> To be thus wrested from us?. . .
> . . . .
> . . .Why should not man,
> Retaining still divine similitude
> In part, from such deformities be free,
> And for his Maker's image sake be exempt?
>
> (11: 502–14)

Michael's answer shows that justice is not at issue, that the suffering is not a "punishment" but the consequence of dynamics caused and controlled in part by the sufferers themselves:

> Their Maker's image . . . then
> Forsook them, when themselves they vilified
> To serve ungoverned appetite, and took
> His image whom they served . . .
> . . . .
> Therefore so abject is their punishment,
> Disfiguring not God's likeness, but their own.
>
> (11: 516–21)

Adam answers, "I yield it just," speaking from a new conception of "justice." As God expresses the same concept in Book 3, they will be absolved "who renounce / Their own both righteous and unrighteous deeds" (3: 291–92). The true structure of the universe is dynamic and not moralistic.

In the second form of countering, one sympathic response is tempered by an opposite nonsympathic, but not necessarily detached response. At the sight of death by disease, Adam weeps in pain in the passage quoted above, but soon restrains pity with "firmer thoughts."

> . . .[he] gave him up to tears,
> A space, till firmer thoughts restrained excess.
>
> (11: 498–99)

This assertion of his nonsympathic, upright, masculine neutrality is made easier by Michael's preceding comment about the injustice of Cain's murder of Abel. Michael similarly counters Adam's sympathic delight at the sight of the low coition of the Sons of God and the daughters of men with stern judgment and sharp irony:

> . . . Judge not what is best
> By pleasure.
>
> (11: 603–4)

> . . . These fair atheists . . . now swim in joy
> (Erelong to swim at large).
>
> (11: 625–26)

The third type of countering occurs in the pacing of Michael's presentation, which is controlled by the alternation of vision/story and commentary. This pacing function of the commentary is as important as its "content." The visions are full and detailed, and the commentary measured and brief. Thus Michael corrects Adam's view of "patience" precisely and tersely:

> Nor love thy life, nor hate; but what thou liv'st
> Live well, how long or short permit to Heav'n:
> And now prepare thee for another sight.
>
> (11: 553–55)

Similarly, he makes his comment on the scene of the fair atheists brief and to the point:

> From man's effeminate slackness it begins,
> . . . who should better hold his place
> By wisdom, and superior gifts received.
> But now prepare thee for another scene.
>
> (11: 634–37)

With this "but," Michael refuses to allow his art to wander into indulgent discourse, and in this way repeatedly forces it back into the living but controlled space of the imagination.

Michael's art and the yearning it arouses have neither the fluidity of lyric nor the fixity of idea or ironic distance, because he distances the mind from these as well. Thus justice is distanced by the vision of "injustice," pity by firmness. It is not a unidirectional distancing but a multidirectional distancing or countering that allows no permanent "harborings," whether of evil, joy, fear, or sorrow. Michael's "intermixed" art trains Adam's mind into "temperance" and "true patience": one purpose of Michael's instruction is

> . . . to temper joy with fear
> And pious sorrow, equally inured
> By moderation either state to bear.
>
> (11: 361–63)

Temperance, or better, tempering, is an activity of mind, not a laxity, apathy, or quietism. It detaches Adam's vitality from identifications that distort it or entrap it. At first Adam interprets patience as nonactivity, saying proudly to the angel:

> Henceforth I fly not death, nor would prolong
> Life much, bent rather how I may be quit
> Fairest and easiest of this cumbrous charge,
> Which I must keep till my appointed day
> Of rend'ring up, and patiently attend
> My dissolution.
>
> (11: 547–52)

To this Michael abruptly answers in the passage quoted above, "Nor love thy life, nor hate; but what whou liv'st, / Live well" (11: 553–54).

While Michael's art may be incisive, it is never cruel or excessive, as Raphael's inadvertent art at times was. Michael's firmness is measured so that Adam experiences it as just and even gentle. As Adam says to him:

> . . . gently hast thou told
> Thy message, which might else in telling wound,
> And in performing end us.
>
> (11: 298–300)

Michael shares Adam's dismay at the murder of Abel; as he answers Adam's question about its justice, he is "also moved" (11: 453), but he does not allow his compassion to take sway. The poet himself empathizes with the necessary pain of Adam's education: as Michael presents the vision of the flood, he intrudes with:

> How didst thou grieve then, Adam, to behold
> The end of all thy offspring, end so sad.
>
> (11: 754–55)

The end to which this art of yearning and counterings leads Adam is a state in which, distanced from all sympathic and even lyric or ironic identifications, his mind is completely arrested in all its motions, but not in resignation or quietism. His mind is "fixed," but not *to* anything. Rather, in its stillness, it is in a suspended state, stripped of pity and judgment, of lyric and ironic pulls. This stripping does not cancel but allows vitality and a pure yearning that is both a fullness and a peace. The "sum of wisdom" to which Adam attains is this state, which he describes to Michael after the verbal vision of the second coming:

> How soon hath thy prediction, seer blest,
> Measured this transient world, the race of time,
> Till time stand fixed: beyond is all abyss,
> Eternity, whose end no eye can reach.
> Greatly instructed I shall hence depart,
> Greatly in peace of thought, and have my fill
> Of knowledge, what this vessel can contain;
> Beyond which was my folly to aspire.
> Henceforth I learn that to obey is best,
> And love with fear the only God, to walk
> As in his presence, ever to observe
> His providence, and on him sole depend,
> Merciful over all his works, with good
> Still overcoming evil, and by small
> Accomplishing great things, by things deemed weak
> Subverting worldly strong, and worldly wise
> By simply meek; that suffering for truth's sake
> Is fortitude to highest victory,
> And to the faithful the gate of life.
>
> (12: 553–71)

The sympathic motions of history—of time—stopped, Adam's mind returns to the vessel of the imagination, leaving both eternity and the abyss outside. This space is peaceful and filled, a tempered love and fear no longer conflicting or even countering one another. But this space is not isolated from the universe: for in its smaller motions the imagination accomplishes great things. The suffering involved in his instruction has been for the sake of truth and it gives him strength for a victory higher than epic victory.

Michael's art is both a gateway to the art of the meditative modes that will follow in human being's life on earth and a preparation for these modes. It has purified yearning, and it has cleared and defined the space of imagination, which may now be a container within which lyric and ironic may be used or engaged in more as tools than as ways in themselves. And in this art the meditative process of relativizing has begun. It is as if Michael has taken the violent motions into which the resonant structure has modulated as a result of the fall and used them to cancel out their counterparts in the mind and to imprint on it instead the idea of reciprocity and resonance. This education resembles Satan's punishment, except that it takes place in a defined space and in a controlled manner.

Michael's instruction follows a sequence that begins with the personal and mimetic, moves into the apocalyptic, and ends with the fixing of time and mind. The apocalyptic "predictions" function primarily to shake the mind *out of* theological attachments, almost as a spiritual exercise, rather than the reverse. As Adam words it, the prediction of the second coming quickly ("how soon") "measures" the race of time and almost catapults the mind into the suspended space.

Michael starts with the more personal visions, such as Cain's murder of Abel, the deforming diseases, the lax Sons of God, the sword-law, and the partly personal story of the flood. These scenes, though some of them are more historical and personal, are evoked in a lengthy, detailed, and almost directly mimetic style that serves to restore modality to Adam's fallen mind. The passages relating these visions are full of description and raw action. As Adam opens his eyes to see Cain kill Abel,

> . . . he . . . beheld a field,
> Part arable and tilth, whereon were sheaves
> New-reaped, the other part sheep-walks and folds;
> I'th'midst an altar as the landmark stood
> Rustic, of grassy sord; thither anon
> A sweaty reaper from his tillage brought
> First-fruits, the green ear and the yellow sheaf,
> Unculled, as came to hand.
>
> (11: 429–36)

The lines that describe the murder are direct and blunt and not in the least latinate:

> [he] smote him in the midriff with a stone
> That beat out life.
>
> (11: 445–46)

The style in this mimetic presentation is mostly unmediated by tone. The few instances of irony serve to counter rather than mediate, becoming a modality beyond the ironic. Lines such as the "now swim in joy / (Erelong to swim at large)," "Inductive mainly to the sin of Eve" (11: 519), and "great laughter was in heav'n / . . . to see the hubbub strange / And hear the din [of the tower of Babel]" (12: 59–61) are sharp and abrupt, serving to jolt the mind entirely out of sympathic or ironic indulgence rather than to gain the distance that gives shelter from yearning in order to buy indulgence.

The mimetic immediacy of the personal and historical presentation changes into the immediacy of more violent extremes in the less "realistic" and more apocalyptic visions and accounts of the destruction of the earth by flood, the plagues in Egypt, the first coming and the crucifixion, and the destruction of the earth by fire in the second coming. These visions serve to intensify the countering process to an extreme degree that makes the stripping of sympathic identifications absolute. It is important to be aware that the apocalyptic events do not necessarily fit into any "logical" pattern and are not primarily part of a scheme of "justice." They are extremes that like some kind of shock technique cancel each other out to produce a tempered state of mind. Thus the flood is both the wrath of God countering the laxity of fallen humanity by almost total "depopulation" (11: 756) and the overwhelming grief of Adam. This anger and this grief are so great that they are purgative: Adam experiences this vision personally and sympathically, but the extremity of his grief functions to cancel out the possibility of such a mode of response:

> . . . thee another flood
> Of tears and sorrow a flood thee also drowned
> And sunk thee as thy sons.
>
> (11: 756–58)

The flood is a transitional form between the personal and the apocalyptic visions.

The plagues of Egypt and the "crazing" of the chariot wheels (12: 209–14) are less a theological punishment for wickedness than "signs and judgments dire" (12: 175) to "compel" Pharaoh, the "lawless tyrant," into action, to break his "stubborn heart," his obdurate fixity. This functional aspect of the plagues corresponds to the functional nature of law, and also clarifies the apparently contradictory role of Satan as both a Pharaoh and a Moses figure.

Michael defines law not primarily as a reflection of some theological or even natural pattern of justice, but as a kind of goad that, by countering human mind in a stone-wall technique, arouses its sinfulness and foregrounds it so that it can be more clearly perceived.

> . . . therefore law was given them to evince
> Their natural pravity, by stirring up
> Sin against law to fight; that when they see
> Law can discover sin, but not remove,
> Save by those shadowy expiations weak,
> The blood of bulls and goats, they may conclude
> Some blood more precious must be paid for man,
> Just for unjust.
>
> (12: 287–94)

Similarly, Satan as scourge serves a useful "positive" function in the progressive declension of mind in the fallen world by attracting like a magnet the "draff and filth" (10: 630), not so much so that evil can be "unmixed" and purged off as so that it can be more clearly perceived.

The licking up of this draff and filth is a "natural" expression of Satan's mirroring and identifying psychic dynamic in which overly like is sucked toward overly like as in a vacuum. This phenomenon is half of the overall dynamic set in motion by the breaking of resonance. In such breaking, the material becomes more material, more "palpable" like the "palpable darkness" over Egypt (12: 188); and the resonance of energy then breaks or stretches into two complementary motions or states that may be described as vacuum and explosiveness. Though these motions are violent and may appear to be random, their nature has modulated in this way for a purpose: they are the expression of the universe striving to right itself, to restore the resonance. In one motion, the overly material attracts matter and thereby "creates" a yet more palpable mass of evil. Satan's agents Sin and Death lick up the filth and draff, and Satan as Moses calls up the evil locusts, his followers. In a second motion, because this structure of the gross and the vacuum is unnatural, a reaction, the explosiveness of energy hurls the gross masses against each other. To use a slightly different conception, if one vacuum center acts to draw matter into it and create a larger mass, it simultaneously creates a vacuum "outside" its own circle of influence, which then acts to suck the mass away from its center toward the new vacuum center. In this action two masses may collide. The plagues and Pharaoh are two such masses of "evil." The collision serves to counter and break false "obdurateness" or palpability into fragments that are then better able to move in the less violent reciprocity of resonance.

Satan as a Moses is "good" not by virtue of his intentions but by virtue of his dynamics and its effects. A skillful Moses who is more Moses than Satan or who has a perspective on the Satan in himself may not abolish such dynamics, but he may by "small" and "weak" motions of his own slightly alter the direction or speed, so to speak, of the motions around and within him, and in this way "accomplish great things."

The Son's crucifixion cuts in a different direction, and uses a different countering technique. Whereas Eve's assertion of love in Book 10 and her offer to ask God to let the whole sentence "light on her head" is sufficient in itself to "disarm" Adam and make him relent, the Son's offer is accepted. To "pay / The rigid satisfaction, death for death" (3: 211–12), to satisfy "justice" (12: 401), the Son offers his love and peace as a kind of wall against which the wrath of God may fall and spend itself, or as an enormous receptacle, larger than the wrath, in which this wrath may therefore dissipate itself and evaporate. The Son says to God, "On me let thine anger fall; / Account me man" (3: 237–38). The "justice" of this "Godlike act"—Michael in his account of it stresses that it is an act—is not the justice of "fairness," but the justice of dealing with and resolving certain "laws" that have been set in motion by the energies and vicissitudes of evolution. It is an efficient as well as a moral act; it is also an art, a dramatic art in which the Son, because he is able to, takes on the role of human. Because the Son makes his love and peace so great and so strong, they outlive the wrath not by opposing it but by absorbing it in a process similar to *t'ai chi,* the ancient Chinese martial art and meditation in which one finds enhanced strength in moving harmoniously with the forces around one. This technique is different from that in Book 6, where the Son used power to counteract Satan.

In the second coming, the countering is similar to the Son's action in Book 6: here in the apocalypse the violence of glory and power reaches its greatest extreme. The Son comes to destroy the world by fire, and

> . . . then raise
> From the conflagrant mass, purged and refined,
> New heav'ns, new earth, ages of endless date
> Founded in righteousness and peace and love,
> To bring forth fruits, joy and eternal bliss.
>
> (12: 547–51)

These multidirectional apocalyptic counterings, the motions of love and power complementing each other, serve to purge and refine the mind more than the literal world. The motions of Satan—vacuum and explosion— resemble the motions of the Son—love and power—but are different because Satan has less consciousness and control.

The effects of this technique are the suspension of mind that Adam achieves in 12: 553–71 and later the *fruits* of the suspension, joy and bliss, which are almost secondary consequences of the primary exercise of peace and love. The apocalpytic countering cancels out and clears away the chaotic residues of the war in heaven and the fall of Adam and Eve and refocuses the evolution of consciousness in the "smaller" subtler space of the meditative imagination, in which "love" and "fear" are not in conflict but together help define the space and insure flexibility of mind. It is a peaceful space, a "patient" space in which a more complex and subtle meditation can take place after the broader and blunter strokes of apocalyptic countering— in which at times "wrath / Impendent . . . distinguish[es] not" (5: 890–92)— have spent themselves. It is a space cleared of sympathic distortions and freed from that direct relation with God in which modality may too easily collapse. Adam has learned that it is better to "walk / *As in* his presence" (12: 562–63; emphasis added), in the "as if" of meditation and art. Michael's art has prepared Adam for the art of Milton's similes, in which "shapes immense" are reduced to "smallest forms" (1: 789–90) and by these "small things"—the peasant and the elves in the moonlight—to accomplish the great things. For when the mind has been cleared of gross distortions, it becomes more precise in its perceptions. When Adam skillfully interprets the meaning of the rainbow following the flood, Michael says, "Dextrously thou aim'st" (11: 884).

Another equally important effect is that Adam reaches a degree of empathy with God. In his own grief he comes to feel and know the pain of God: as he sees his offspring "all in a view destroyed at once," Adam painfully exclaims:

> O visions ill foreseen! better had I
> Lived ignorant of future, so had borne
> My part of evil only, each day's lot
> Enough to bear; those now, that were dispensed
> The burd'n of many ages, on me light
> At once, by my foreknowledge gaining birth
> Abortive, to torment me ere their being
> With thought that they must be. Let no man seek
> Henceforth to be foretold what shall befall
> Him or his children, evil he may be sure,
> Which neither his foreknowing can prevent,
> And he the future evil shall no less
> In apprehension than in substance feel
> Grievous to bear.
>
> (11: 763–76)

One purpose of Michael's instruction, to awaken Adam to "foresight," has been fulfilled. The empathy this foresight gives him impresses on him the reality of the reciprocity of feeling in the universe and of the dependency of God on his creations to lessen pain and turn it into creative evolution.

Beyond the attainment of the contentless suspension of mind and the complementary empathy with God is the positive vision of the cold paradise, "positive" because it has qualities of its own rather than being wholly stripped of quality. At the end of Book 11 Michael describes how in the flood of water and tears

> . . . this mount
> Of Paradise by might of waves [shall] be moved
> Out of his place, pushed by the hornèd flood,
> With all his verdure spoiled and trees adrift
> Down the great river to the op'ning gulf,
> And there take root an island salt and bare,
> The haunt of seals and orcs, and sea-mews' clang.
>
> (11: 829–35)

This paradise is clear and cold in its lack of confusion; and more, it has a positive precision of mood as well as of perception. The warm, luxurious Paradise of Book 4 is replaced by the cold paradise, which is an emblem for the more complex relativizing mode of the final stage of Milton's art to follow Book 12. The Son at the first coming came in the warmth of love, and at the second coming in the fiery violence of wrath and glory; but when he comes to judge after the fall, to adjust the nature of Paradise and human consciousness for further evolution toward the one heaven and earth in a newer recreation,

> . . . he from wrath more cool
> Came . . .
> To sentence man. The voice of God they heard
> Now walking in the garden, by soft winds
> Brought to their ears, while day declined.
>
> (10: 95–99)

God has become the spirit within, the living voice of poetry in the cool space. After the heats of joy and fear have been tempered, and after one has experienced the cold paradise of the next meditative mode, in this cool space of the imagination one's heart may like the peasant's in the soft moonlight "with joy and fear . . . rebound" (1: 788).

Paradise Lost ends with the same quick pacing that has characterized Michael's art. As soon as the last identification has been stripped from Adam's mind by the second coming, Michael responds briefly, saying that the suspension of mind that Adam has attained is the "sum / Of wisdom" and that now he will "not be loth / To leave this Paradise," but will possess the "happier" "paradise within" (12: 575–87). This said, Michael allows no lingering:

> Let us descend now therefore from this top
> Of speculation; for the hour precise
> Exacts our parting hence; and see the guards,
> By me encamped on yonder hill, expect
> Their motion, at whose front a flaming sword,
> In signal of remove, waves fiercely round;
> We may no longer stay; go, waken Eve.
>
> (12: 588–94)

Adam runs ahead of Michael to awaken her but finds her already awake. She tells him that she has understood their future in her dream and is ready to leave, but time is too pressed for him to answer:

> Whence thou return'st, and whither went'st, I know;
> For God is also in sleep, and dreams advise
> . . . .
> . . . But now lead on;
> In me is no delay.
>
> (12: 610–15)

> Adam heard
> Well pleased, but answered not; for now too nigh
> Th'Archangel stood, and from the other hill

> To their fixed station, all in bright array
> The Cherubim descended.
>
> (12: 624–28)

The "hast'ning Angel" catches them in either hand in the passage quoted earlier (12: 637–49) and leads them "direct" and "fast" to the gate and down the cliff, "then disappeared." In the last few lines of the poem the pace relents, as Adam and Eve slowly wander through Eden and into the world before them to seek their place of rest.

NOTES

1. From a slightly different perspective, John T. Shawcross in his article "*Paradise Lost* and the Theme of Exodus" discusses *Paradise Lost* in terms of the myth of exodus, a myth "distinguished from the myth of return by repetitive stages of ritual, moving linearly through time, rather than by cyclic recurrence." The poem presents the original exodus of Adam and Eve that leads to the successive exoduses of their descendents shown in Books 11 and 12. The aim of this sequence is to soften "the hardened heart into 'th' upright heart and pure,' to achieve the Paradise within," and so to reach heaven. The exoduses provide the means for this softening: "successive stages of trial and purgation" (p. 3). Each exodus is a fall, occasioned by human being's attachment to false gods; yet each exodus is simultaneously a "deliverance from [the] bondage" of these false gods. At each stage, guided by will and by the new knowledge attained in the fall, human being relinquishes a false concept of God and attempts to "reformulate a concept of true Godhead." On the one hand, the deliverance "is . . . no guarantee for the future"; on the other, "each fall becomes a successive stage upward to the final judgment, for each fall discriminates for humankind another factor of the dialectic" (pp. 9–13). These successive exoduses are the "degrees" by which human beings under long obedience tried," will "open themselves at length the way" (*PL* 7: 154–61; Shawcross, p. 20).

Yet humanity's successive exoduses are not simply repeated occasions for the manifestation of faith and obedience; in the terms of my study they are the struggle for consciousness and resonance, in which the softening heart opens itself to resonance and in which the mind discerns and forms an image and an understanding of God and the universe that is not too "hard" to allow resonance yet has sufficient form to prevent resonance from being annihilated by the raw power of God. As Shawcross says, "The highest good, God, is not the goal attained by exodus: it is the means to renewal" (p. 9). The end sought is not the direct "blinding splendor" of God that destroys, but the resonance between human and God, human and God's universe, in which the splendor is known in living, not in itself. Resonance in consciousness is the central "dialectic" of creation.

In the perspective of Shawcross's concept of exodus, the "return" in Book 12 of *Paradise Lost* to its beginning in Books 1 and 2 forces Adam and Eve, and the reader, into a new stage in the declension of mind by "expelling" them simultaneously into the sympathic world of hell and into the cool meditative world of the similes. The images of these worlds and the active meditation required and encouraged by the disjunctions between them provide the specific means and a specific illustration of the human mission. The "return" also emphasizes that the purpose and nature of this mission is meditative, that it is consciousness toward which the succession of exoduses tends, consciousness that will unite human and God in a union different from and surpassing the original oneness of God. "*Paradise Lost* and the Theme of Exodus," *Milton Studies* (1970), 2: 3–26.

12   The Meditative Modes: The Art of Milton

The art of Michael in Books 11 and 12 has strongly detached the mind from all possessions, identifications, and intermediation—the solutions to the sympathic and modal conflict found to be false at the end of chapter 3. The first meditative mode, simple relativizing, carries this process further, but because it now occurs within the third space it is less painful and is more of an exercise to awaken and strengthen consciousness. Its motions are less blunt and more precise.

The art of the second meditative mode, complex relativizing, is the most advanced stage of the declension of mind in *Paradise Lost*. Like simple relativizing, complex relativizing is detached from both sympathic and lyric-ironic identifications, but the particular nature of its detachment—which is more a central coldness of mood than a detachment—allows it, unlike simple relativizing, a deep resonance with the objects of former identification, a resonance of consciousness and psychic action that is not vague or transcendental but infinitely various and specific, precisely appropriate to each object, situation, or event.

These two modes, but most particularly the second mode, are the consummate form of Milton's art by which he helps carry forward the evolution of human mind, beyond even the apocalyptic art of the archangel Michael.

When the reader returns to the beginning of *Paradise Lost* after exiting from Book 12, the poem seems quite different from when he/she began reading it for the first time. Because of the final stillness attained by Adam at the end of his education, the aesthetic distancing and the counterings in the early books are now experienced with less pain. Whereas on a first reading they seemed either unidirectional or conflicting, now they are seen as a multidirectional process, an exercise rather than a theological or emotional debate, that springs the mind into a meditation more valuable than the singular directions of thought, belief, or opinion.

But this transition to the paradise within and the progress through the meditative modes does not occur simply and smoothly. Unlike *Paradise Lost* in its epic dimension, which proceeds from Book 1 to Book 12, the meditative "plot" must be constructed by the reader. For at the end of Book 12 the human mind is set on an uncharted sea of wandering, not a predestined way. This second plot consists of meditating upon certain passages in an order that bears no particular relation to the sequence of the poem.

Sometimes one passage is used more than once at different stages of the declension. This meditative sequence cannot exist on a first reading of the poem because in the first reading the passages are still attached to their epic-theological contexts. Therefore the process of really reading *Paradise Lost* requires several readings in which the mind moves back and forth between passages, between modes, between the various stages of the declension—sometimes gaining ground, sometimes losing ground—until finally the whole poem reads smoothly and resonance is attained.

On a first reading, the aesthetic distancing might be experienced as disturbing and frustrating. On a second or third reading, perhaps the various shiftings are experienced more gratuitously, simply as themselves. Detached from the effort to find their meaning, they function to break up the sympathic vision and imprint the principle of kinesthesia on the mind. In a next reading, the mind, its kinesthetic faculty awakened, might allow itself to be caught too deeply into the motions of a modality that offers itself as a new, more fluid connective to replace the more rigid theological ones. But as one reads on, this pleasant "imagin'd way" is blocked—like the northwest passage in Book 10—as modality collapses and loses the virtue of its own nature in the falls. Modality is then perceived as insufficient: it is seen that joy is insufficient to drive away despair (4: 155–56) and knowledge insufficient to detect hypocrisy (3: 682–83).

Nevertheless, a beginning has been made. The ironic mode in its characteristically abrupt haltings has started to imprint neutrality on the mind. The lyric mode has started to imprint the mood and motions of meditation. The "blocking" of the lyric Orphic way prepares the reader for the art of Michael, but the lyric and ironic modality has also prepared him/her for the meditative modes to take place during the final readings of the poem in the third space opened up and sharply defined by this blocking.

In this sequence of readings the character of any one instance of aesthetic distancing may change from one reading to another. Thus the Proserpine and fawn similes may at first seem ironic, or lyric, or confusing; whereas later they may be experienced both lyrically and ironically at the same time, their motions detaching the mind from modality and suspending it. Similarly, the line "hope never comes / That comes to all" (1: 66–67) might at first seem to be an instance of harsh divine injustice; but after seeing Satan in Book 9 turn away from hope and beauty, one might read it differently. Instead of being a simple inflexible opposition, it is a statement that gives itself away: because hope can come to all, it could come here, but it does not. Rigid fate does not exist; rather, free will helps determine its own reality.

The whale simile in Book 1 might at first be read as lyrical relief, as Ferry and MacCaffrey read it; and the editorial comment following it might be read either as vicious moralism or as a sane return to "reality" from delusion. Later, however, this countered pair can be read in two mutually supporting directions: the cold lyricism takes the mind away from a theological hell, while the editorial intrusion counters a possibly indulgent and dangerous lyricism to move the mind toward the meditative state defined by the tone of anger rather than its content and the cold mood of the moonlit scene joined together. Moreover, in this later reading, the content of the editorial comment gives itself away in the same manner as the earlier lines about hope: if Satan is left to his own designs, he need not choose to commit "reiterated crimes."

In the sequence of many readings, there are forks in the road. The first time the reader comes to a fork, he/she may see only one way, and following that way—like the lyrical way to the sweet orient—will find it a gate closed in front of him/her. But on a later journey, in the puzzlement of contemplating the fork itself, a gate slams shut behind, the fork disappears, and the reader is in a new space. Thus the dovetailed, lyric-and-ironic Proserpine simile finally acts to spring the mind out of the lyric-ironic ways into a new space. The closing of the gate behind one images the effect of the simple relativizing mode; and the entry into a new space images the complex relativizing mode, where discordance is replaced by resonance.

The Simple Relativizing Mode

There are three stages in the simple relativizing mode: a first preparatory stage, a second stage that might be called "pure" intellectual relativizing or simple relativizing proper, and a third stage in which the relativizing technique of the second stage is applied to less "pure" matters.

In the mental exercise that constitutes the first preparatory stage, the reader focuses on instances of countering without trying to resolve them and observes their motions until his/her mind is arrested. It is best to choose for this purpose instances of aesthetic distancing that are not fluid but whose elements rather are focused into a sharply dualistic relationship—into a pair of opposite concepts, images, or tones. In this stage aesthetic distancing like that in Books 11 and 12 is more useful than aesthetic distancing like the gradual shift from the earth seen as a globe to the earth seen as cedar trees. There are many such instances of dualistic distancing in *Paradise Lost*, some harshly so and others that are more perplexing and even amusing than painful. It is perhaps best to begin by considering the gentler instances of shifting and then gradually move into increasingly harsh instances.

The simile describing the "cany wagons light" sailing on the "windy sea of land" in Sericana, followed by the description of the relics, beads, and the like of the "eremites and friars," which are the "sport of winds" (3: 437–96), is a gentle pair in which the images are similar but the tones are different: one is lyrical and poignant, the other light and humorous. However, because these tones are very pure, almost entirely detached from judgmental concerns—the sailing wagons evoke neither strong pain nor delight but a more neutral beauty, and the fools are more sympathetically teased than viciously condemned—the disjunction in the implications of the wind image is experienced less as conflict and more as a neutral observation of motion.

The Proserpine and fawn similes in Book 4 offer a less neutral experience at first: it is harder to focus on both the ironic and lyric motions at once. But the tension in contemplating both the poignant evocation of Ceres' pain and the irony of inserting this image in the context of unfallen Paradise in the end arrests the mind more emphatically than the already neutral Sericana-fools juxtaposition. The fawns simile involves a similar motion, in which figure becomes ground and ground becomes figure, but it is less wrenching than the Proserpine simile and more humorous, closer to the tone of the sport of winds.

The two serpent images in 10: 168–69 and 218 ("justly then accurst, / As vitiated in nature" and "the snake with youthful coat repaid") engage in a conflict more of idea than of tone. The presentation of these two images with no attempt to relate or explain their implications stops the mind in puzzlement rather than sending it into pained outrage, for human minds and hearts are less involved in the fate of serpents than of humans.

The image of the "ambrosial fragrance" that fills heaven following God's stern pronouncements in 3: 135, and the image of the "fresh flow'rets" smiling beside the path of the Son's wrathful chariot of power in 6: 784, are slightly more jolting in their context than the serpent images because God's wrath more nearly affects the human reader. However, if the wrath and flowers are perceived simultaneously, the jolting of their implications modulates into a more neutral, uncomprehending suspension.

The opposition of "authors to themselves in all" and "my motions in him" (3: 122; 11: 91) are initially still more jolting, for the ideas expressed affect us strongly but cannot be visualized with a more detached pleasure and thereby be neutralized, as can the images of the chariot and the flowers. The discordant conceptual pair may be too difficult to experience with the detachment necessary to neutralize them because at this stage so much meaning is attached to these ideas of free will and determination.

God's outright derision at future scientists' attempts to understand the stars that follows Adam's question to Raphael about the intention and reasonableness of the stars (8: 70–84) may be felt as yet more wrenching because it sounds like such a "human" response. Yet after Books 11 and 12 this derision can be detached from sympathic meanings and intentions and seen as an objective response aroused by the sympathic nature of Adam's questions, and therefore experienced from a more neutral perspective.

The pairing of the whale simile and the harsh editorial comment following it may be experienced at this stage, if one focuses on the angry tone of the comment rather than on its content, as a kind of shock that arrests any movement into lyrical fluidity, a shock that again abruptly halts the mind in its motions and springs it into neutral suspension.

This sequence of passages falls into a continuum ranging from gentle to harsh relativizing. They need not necessarily be selected in this order; what is important is that the preparatory exercise be experienced in a variety of ways for a more articulated and thorough imprinting of the arresting of the mind and the resulting neutrality. This neutrality, as Michael stressed to Adam in his education, should not fall into apathy or quietism. The reader should choose the material for this meditation so that the discordant issues concern him/her, but not so much that they destroy the observing stance and throw the mind back into a sympathic chaos. At the end of the contemplation of each instance, the mind should be in a state of puzzlement or wondering somewhere between experience and consciousness. This preparatory exercise like the countering of Books 11 and 12 helps define the edges of the meditative space and clears the space itself.

In the second stage of simple relativizing one assumes or internalizes the central neutrality even though he/she may not understand it, and, maintained by it, enters into more extreme discordant motions. One may focus on the image of Adam suspended in fixed time (12: 555) as an emblem to aid in this next meditation.

In this exercise one contemplates the countering not of one frame of reference moving in relation to a fixed frame of reference, as in the initial experience of aesthetic distancing on a first reading of *Paradise Lost,* but of two unfixed frames of reference moving in relation to each other and in relation to the self. In this stage one yields more to motion than in the first stage. This yielding may seem passive, but the maintaining of the neutral center is active.

The purest example of this exercise occurs in Raphael's account of astronomical motion in the beginning of Book 8. The shifting in this pure relativizing is similar to the purely physical shifting discussed earlier, but transferred to the mind. Here the body "sits still" (8: 89) on the seemingly "steadfast" earth while the mind considers the relative motions of planets. This stage of simple relativizing is the most purely intellectual process in the declension of mind. Its purpose is to strip away, in a process that is more detached and more conscious than in Books 11 and 12, all identifications from both the planets and the object of perception and from all mental positions associated with them. In this process the pain and doubts arising from disjunctive perceptions and disjunctive notions are also stripped away.

The exercise begins when Adam expresses his "doubt" to Raphael in the opening of Book 8: his doubt is a fear of the "restless revolution" of the planets, of the "spaces incomprehensible," and of the "incorporeal speed" of the planets' motion. Specifically, it is the apparently unstructured character of the motions, the vastness of the space (similar to Pascal's fear), and the degree of a speed that can dissolve substance that are disjunctive to Adam on "the sedentary earth," as he characterizes it (8: 15–38).

Raphael answers Adam by saying that the heavens are a "Book of God" in which Adam must learn to "reckon right." The nature and "purpose" of the

heavens are epistemological as well as ontological (8: 66–71). The central
point Raphael makes in his following discourse is that if one "admits the
motion" of the heavens—a motion even greater than that imagined in
Adam's fearful speculation—rather than, like the future astronomers of fallen earth (8: 74–84), trying to "frame" it and kill the motion with their
rhombs, spheres, and centric and eccentric additions, then Adam's doubts
will be proved "invalid":

> . . . But this I urge,
> Admitting motion in the heav'ns, to show
> Invalid that which thee to doubt it moved.
>
> (8: 114–16)

The subordinating conjunction for "admitting" is to be read as "by means
of" instead of "although." To demonstrate this point, Raphael asks Adam to
detach his mind from the false frames and from his false laxity of mind that
attaches itself to them—a laxity indicated by his word *sedentary*—and instead allow it to be involved in all the motions at once. He asks Adam to
consider that "whether heav'n move or earth / Imports not" (7: 70–71); that
the "rhomb . . . needs not . . . [his] belief" if he imagines that the earth is in
motion (8: 134–40); and that it "imports not"

> Whether the sun predominant in heav'n
> Rise on the earth, or earth rise on the sun,
> He from the east his flaming road begin,
> Or she from west her silent course advance.
>
> (8: 160–63)

Adam is further urged to consider "what if . . . / The planet earth, so
steadfast though she seem / Insensibly three different motions move?" (8:
128–30). Although the body is steadfast on earth, the mind may consider
such motions without disorienting itself if it maintains its meditative neutrality.

Although Adam, to whom this exercise is specifically directed ironically
does not have this meditative neutrality, the reader may from his/her different perspective safely focus more on his/her own watching than on the
objects watched or their meaning. But for Adam heaven and earth are
realities that do have "import" for his state. This divergence between
Adam's and the reader's attitude is one instance of the forking of the poem's
path on a second reading. Adam and Eve and Satan focus either on the self
or on the object (star, moon) in their considerations of the nature of the
universe. They vacillate in their identifying mental motions between assigning priority and causality now to the stars and now to the self. For example,
in the dream he brings to Eve in Book 5 Satan says, "heav'n wakes with all
his eyes, / Whom to behold but thee . . .?" (5: 44–45). In this dream and

ultimately in Satan's temptation, the fluidity of mind cannot keep from attaching itself to object or observer. But for the reader, whose fluidity of mind is suspended by the neutral center, the question of such ontological priorities is irrelevant—the "reality" is the watching itself, the motions between or behind the mind and the stars. As Raphael says, God placed the stars far from earth, far from earthly "sight" and "human sense," so that the mind could "no advantage gain" from their limited use (8: 119–22). For it is not to the earth that the stars are "officious" but to "earth's habitant," the human mind.

The first effect of this relativizing exercise is that the neutrality, until now only assumed or experienced indefinitely, becomes positive, almost substantial in its impact. It is now conscious and imprinted into the core of the being. The second effect is a rushing of energy into the cleared space in the mind and into the being: the energy of the relativizing itself, the acceleration of its disjunctive unframing, is replaced by a contentless and raw energy that is energy itself apart from its manifestations. At this point the energy is no longer felt as "movement" in the usual sense, and is not disjunctive because it is totally stripped from any attachment that could cause friction. It is "still" in relation to motion that is defined and experienced in terms of its friction or disproportion with something else, but "moving" in relation to any sedentary quietism. It is a vibrant resonance or pulsation, a still kinesthesia. This stillness is yet more positive and "substantial" than the neutrality, and is less an attitude of mind than an experience throughout the being. The neutrality has become something positive, alive and "real."

Raphael next engages Adam in the consideration of the speed of his journey from heaven to earth and the speed of the planets—a yet more extreme exercise that yields a meditative experience of the greatest possible pure energy.

> The swiftness of those circles áttribute,
> Though numberless, to his omnipotence,
> That to corporeal substances could add
> Speed almost spiritual; me thou think'st not slow,
> Who since the morning hour set out from heav'n
> Where God resides, and ere mid-day arrived
> In Eden, distance inexpressible
> By numbers that have name.
>
> (8: 107–14)

These experiences of energy could be upsetting; but if the mind maintains its neutrality and thereby avoids destructive friction, it reaches a point where the stripping is complete, a point where "negative" relativizing in its extreme form turns into a "positive" and freely pulsating energy with which one can move and which one can use in consciousness. From a position of inertia, perception and consciousness are not possible. But through the controlled movement of the relativizing process one gradually reaches this turning point, after which Raphael's claim—that admitting motion in the heavens will show Adam's doubt to be invalid—bears fruit. For the acceptance of the motion ultimately yields a greater stability than the framing strategy of the astronomers.

Raphel's rhetorical question to Adam about the several motions of the earth may be read in two directions:

> . . . what if . . .
> The planet earth, so steadfast though she seem,
> Insensibly three different motions move?
> Which else to several spheres thou must ascribe,
> Moved contrary with thwart obliquities.
>
> (8: 128–32)

Superficially it appears that Raphael is saying "the earth might seem steadfast, but your senses deceive you: she is moving 'restlessly' in three different motions." But read more carefully, with reversal of figure and ground as it were, Raphael is also saying that although the earth moves in three different motions, she is steadfast, a truth supported by the evidence of the senses. In meditation the mind leaves the still body and involves itself in the extremes of disjunctive motion; but when the mind returns, it finds itself in the same still place: the being has not "moved" as a result of the meditation. The earth is experienced as steadfast as before.

This experience is not a deception. The word *seem* ("steadfast though she *seem*") is assigning no ontological priority but is serving to mediate on the level of experience and appearance between two truths. The more precise relation between these two truths is not a paradoxical but a causative and frameless one (paradox depends on frames): though the earth moves, the motions are insensible and the earth steadfast because the motions are related in such a way that they yield stability. It is the *right relation* of motions that produces steadfastness, not sedentariness or frames. Motions and bodies like the earth are related by the type, direction, and strength of motion, by flows of force. The principles by which these flows of force express themselves—such as gravity, mass, and the laws of inertia—may be lawful, but the structures or forms in which they become more manifest are secondary and therefore less predictable or definite. The structures are more consequential than causal.

In these relations of bodies and motions, there are different kinds of "motion" and different kinds of "stillness." A body may be in constant or disproportionate motion (as in acceleration), but the "constancy" or "disproportion" may be affected by the "constancy" or "disproportion" of another body in relation to it. The motions of two bodies may correspond in type, direction, or speed, or they may balance one another in "counterpoise." An unchanging speed may produce "stillness" according to the second law of inertia, and a correspondence or balance between two bodies in motion may also produce stillness. The "attractive virtue" (8: 124) between two bodies may produce motion toward each other, or, if balanced by motion of certain speed and directional impulse, it may produce the "dance" in "rounds" of constant orbital motion. Then the spinning of a body on its own axis may balance against its other motions and thus similarly produce stillness.

Moreover, the relation between two bodies may be affected by yet other bodies and their motions. Two bodies accelerating at the same rate in the same direction may be "still" in relation to each other but in disproportionate motion in relation to other bodies.

But even the "restlessness" of disproportionate motion is modified when it is seen as falling along a continuum, ranging from a dizzy disproportion to a more plastic relation; and one's place on this continuum—the degree of plasticity—can be modulated in meditation if not in action by shifting the focus of perception or by adjusting the degree of the central meditative neutrality. Even the dizziness of extreme acceleration can be put in counterpoise with this neutrality and thereby produce steadfastness.

The planetary bodies Adam beholds in doubt are not necessarily "restless" but are held "up" or "together" by forces in adjustment to each other. For it is not the particular identity alone of each body that defines its virtue, but its relation to other "like" (7: 240) and "unlike" bodies and to the "attractive virtue" itself—the "balanced air" (4: 1000) or the "spun out air" as Raphael characterizes it. For as he says,

> . . . great
> Or bright infers not excellence: the earth,
> Though in comparison of heav'n so small,
> Nor glistering, may of solid good contain
> More plenty than the sun that barren shines,
> Whose virtue on itself works no effect,
> But in the fruitful earth; there first received,
> His beams, unactive else, their vigor find.
>
> (8: 90–97)

Were he prepared by Raphael to "accept" these motions in this way, Adam could see that the relation of motions sustains and that space is plastic; and then his fears of the motion and the vastness of space would be allayed. His mind would concur with his senses in a fuller consciousness that the earth advancing from the west

> With inoffensive pace . . . spinning sleeps
> On her soft axle, while she paces ev'n,
> And bears . . . [him] soft with the smooth air along.
>
> (8: 164–66)

It is ascribing the motion to frames—to the "several spheres" and the "rhomb supposed"—that produces "contrary" and "oblique" disjunctions. An understanding of the principles of the right relation of motions obviates the need for such strategies. As Raphael says, "the rhomb . . . needs not thy belief" (8: 135–37) if Adam can imagine the earth and sun "rising" on each other (8: 161).

From the perspective of the living neutrality so strongly imprinted by the "pure" relativizing of the second stage, one can in the third stage return to matters that more nearly concern human being (8: 174–203). Using the same pure relativizing technique, one can now contemplate to a different end the pains of the sympathic, conceptual, and emotonal disjunctions that were considered in the preparatory stage only in order to arrest the mind.

This third meditation is different from the preparatory meditation because one can allow oneself more involvement in the disjunctions, and is different from the meditation of the second stage because the disjunctions are less "pure" and more sympathic. In this exercise, as one contemplates instances of aesthetic distancing in the gentle-to-harsh continuum, one can adjust the focus, using the principle of the right relation of motions, so as simultaneously to maintain the central neutrality and to avoid becoming too detached and sedentary. If the reader begins to feel a detachment in which modality begins to dissipate, he/she should focus on a harsher and more involving instance of aesthetic distancing, one that arouses yearning. Conversely, if his/her neutrality begins to be shaken by sympathic pains, the reader should focus on a less harsh or less involving instance of aesthetic distancing to restore the central neutrality.

The purpose of this third meditative exercise is to further strengthen the neutrality by stripping less neutral objects than planets of identifications, and to make the mind conscious of the articulations of the modal fabric—to bring into awareness the finer distinctions between objects, between faculties, and between modes, and also disjunctions in the perceptual act between object and mode, between object and faculty, and between faculty and mode.

As in the second meditative exercise, here an energy flows into the central neutral space as a result of this relativizing. This energy is less raw and more modal and emotional—though still contentless—than in the preceding stage.

This final stage of simple relativizing does not yet provide a resolution or resting place; but the neutrality, the consciousness of articulation, and the experience of energy allow involvement in motions that are comparable to the three motions of earth but are more particularly human and spiritual, whose right relation will in the next mode similarly hold "up" the soul and mind in "steadfastness."

A complementary meditative exercise, one that has the effect of stripping the *faculties* more than the object of perception, is to select instances of aesthetic distancing in which the mental or emotional correlates are purest and most extreme, and to contemplate these correlates, still from the neutral perspective, as the mind is abruptly shifted into them by the poetic technique. For example, one may focus on the sudden pure delight aroused by the flowrets in Book 6, or on the sudden kinesthetic interchange of hill and vale that Satan perceives in the midst of his evil intent, or on the pure wrath of God in Book 3 ("Ingrate! he had of me all he could have") and of the Son in Book 6. Or one can focus on the pure lyric fluidity experienced in Mulciber's fall, the pure vitality of Book 7, the pure desolation of the "seamews' clang," the pure glory of the Archangel Michael as he appears in Book 11, or even the pure "carnal fear" experienced when beholding power and glory.

Because in this mode there is no resolution of disjunctions that can be felt as final or fulfilling, it may be thought of as a primarily "negative" mode, whose purpose is stripping. However, these simple relativizing exercises help develop a meditative consciousness and control that facilitates perception and opens up the mind to free energy. What began as an exercise is now a skill. Knowing the principle of the right relation of motions, one can choose a slight acceleration, deceleration, or change in angle in order to gain a different perception. Or one can modulate from the consciousness of "still" position to the consciousness of contentless raw energy. Such choices are appropriate because they correspond to the evolving nature of the universe.

In this correspondence, however, there is an important difference between the relation of the meditative consciousness to the raw energy experienced in the second meditative exercise and its relation to the motions of the universe. This energy is the primal energy of the universe, the power of God in its uncreated or unmediated form at the point at which it is coming into expression. As such, it is the reverse of the process of the dissolution of substance that Adam fears, and the reverse of the meditative stripping process. Therefore, while there can be a more direct correspondence or relation between human motion and the motions of the universe, the relation between meditating mind and primal energy is an inverse relation. At the moment one comes closest to experiencing the pure power of God—at the moment of greatest empathy—one is furthest removed from it. At the moment of the consciousness of greatest energy, one is in the most still and neutral state. The neutrality and stripping are indeed necessary for the experience to occur. In a sense this experience is the structure of least empathy, for the mind cannot really "know" the change of energy into matter and form. It can only know this energy by receiving it in meditation from an entity that, as the source of energy, is an opposite.

But as a receiver, although the mind cannot create matter, it can direct and use this energy flowing into the third space in action, in communication, and in art. Raphael has described this process on a physical level in his account of the relation between the sun and the earth in 8: 91–97 (passage quoted above). In his description of the reciprocal light sent between sun, earth, and moon, Raphael shifts from physical creation into mental and spiritual creation:

> . . . What if that light
> Sent from her [earth] through the wide transpicuous air,
> To the terrestrial moon be as a star
> Enlight'ning her by day, as she by night
> This earth, reciprocal, if land be there,
> Fields and inhabitants?
>
> (8: 140–45)

These fields and inhabitants have their life in the same space as Galileo's "rivers and mountains" (1: 291) and Milton's "Day . . . the sweet approach of ev'n or morn" (3: 42)—the space of the imagination.

In its creative reflection and imagining, the mind turns away from its pure perception and lessens the purity of energy as this energy is changed into expression and form. But in its imagining the mind simultaneously reaches its greatest empathy with God, in the motions of energy into intermediates that are not false or rigid but in resonant and precise movement. Although the purpose of simple relativizing is to achieve the state in which all intermediates have been stripped away, it was not the principle of intermediation itself that was false, but intermediation falsely formed and falsely perceived. And although the raw energy perceived in simple relativizing may be "primary" or "purest," it is not necessarily the most significant or valuable reality. For primacy in terms of time and space is not the only primacy. Although the energy of the universe radiates from a "first" and "highest" or "central" source, the universe is developing in an evolution that has as its goal a reciprocity in both action and mind that is necessarily dependent on "secondary" beings. The "pure" has yearned to express itself in the creation of "intermediate" beings and forms, and in reciprocity has yearned for something "better" than purity; and its experiments in creation have produced a reciprocal universe between unlike beings, the primary "center" of which lies in the resonant and plastic movement itself, a movement that requires consciousness to evolve. It is at this point in the manifestation of energy that there is the greatest empathy between human and God. In the creative use of received energy the human mind reciprocally evolves the universe.

This reciprocal imaginative action is the work of the next meditative mode, complex relativizing, which is more positive and active than simple relativizing. In a way, simple relativizing is only a preparation for the complex mode, for in itself it is incomplete. However, each mode has functions specifically appropriate to it, which work best when the other mode is held in the background of consciousness. Each yields different kinds of knowledge that are equally "true," but the complex mode is more complete and can lead to resonant action and fulfillment in a way that simple relativizing cannot.

The Complex Relativizing Mode

The consummate meditative art of Milton's final mode is not the art of the warm sun, like the "sociable" art of Raphael, who as he appears to Adam and Eve "seems another morn" (5: 310). Nor is it the "excessive bright" of an apocalyptic fire too great to behold, like Michael's art. Rather, it is like the pale light sent and reflected between sun, stars, earth and other planets, and moons.

It is not the "premeditated" art (9: 24) of theology, nor the "unmeditated" art of "prompt eloquence" (5: 149)—the perfect patterns and "concord" of the heavenly hymns and mystical dances or of Adam and Eve's edenic hymns. It is not the art of the epic wars of heaven and earth that build and disrupt civilizations, as in the *Iliad;* nor is it the art of the domestic earth pictured on Achilles' shield that provides lyric relief from war. It is not the "opiate" lyrical art of the fallen angels that "suspends hell" and leads the poet Orpheus to his death.

Rather, it is the mixed but wakeful, disciplined, and clear art of the moon, emblem of reflection and reflected light, the orbed shield of Satan in hell seen by Galileo the astronomer-artist in 1: 284–91, and the "new lands" into which it "opens" the meditative "eye" and shifts the "darkened mind" of fallen humanity (9: 1053–54).

This shift is introduced to the mind returning to the poem's beginning, in a "horizontal" movement in a sequence of three similes in Book 1: first, the pilot anchored to the whale; then Galileo looking at the moon, "less assured" than Raphael and anchored to nothing but his telescope; and last, the peasant looking at the small elves of earth in the light of the moon—three voyagers in the worlds of water, sky, and earth. The first image is the last instance of anchoring in *Paradise Lost* after the unanchoring of the last two books. The pilot's anchoring on the whale is tentative and temporary; in the counterplot he does not go down with the diving whale as in the medieval bestiary, for we later see him and his counterparts sailing throughout the poem. Rather, he shifts his focus to the truer "anchorage" of the cold, still mood of the scene.

Galileo voyaging in the heavens beholds the moon and focuses his attention there—on the reflection of the sun's light, the light the moon sends to earth by night as the earth "as a star" sends her by day, the moon's "night." He further beholds the moon's imaging of "fields and inhabitants" who are perhaps similar beholders of light and lands that, though far distant, are clearly their own.

In the elves simile, Aeneas's sun gives way to the peasant's moon, now no longer an object of reflection and meditation, but an "arbitress" for the peasant's beholding the mysteries not of a distant land but of his own earth, the arbitress "justifying" and adjusting his seeing and his dreaming, his joy and his fear. Arbitrating has replaced anchoring.

The shift from sympathic to modal to meditative art is introduced in a more "vertical" movement in the three Galileo similes (1: 283–91; 3: 588–90; 5: 261–63), taken not in their order of appearance but in a sequence from simple to complex. The similes in Books 3 and 5 shift the mind from epic into simple relativizing and then tentatively into the third space, while the simile in Book 1 fully introduces the mind to the complex mode.

When Satan lands on the sun in Book 3, Milton says:

> There lands the Fiend, a spot like which perhaps
> Astronomer in the sun's lucent orb
> Through his glazed optic tube yet never saw.
>
> (3: 588–90)

The glazed optic tube recalls the clouded vision of Milton in the invocation to Book 3 and of Adam in Book 11. The irony in this passage correspondingly cuts against the limitations of human knowledge. But the word *perhaps,* the poetic representation of the sunspot-Satan regardless of the official negation, and the word *yet* all cut in the opposite direction. Satan has been seen; perhaps Galileo saw him; and if not, he may see him in the future. Also, the simile counters the deluded search for wisdom by looking only at the sun, but says nothing about using a telescope to look at the moon.

The image of Galileo in Book 5 similarly cuts in two directions.

> . . . he [Raphael] sees
> . . . .
> . . . as when by night the glass
> Of Galileo, less assured, observes
> Imagined lands and regions in the moon.
>
> (5: 258–63)

The irony of "less assured" in one direction diminishes Galileo in comparison to Raphael, but the picture of what he sees has more presence than what he sees in Book 3—is more of a third space—now that he is more wisely gazing at the moon. Moreover, his wavering vision and imagination will lead to greater knowledge than Raphael's "assuredness," for the irony also cuts back against the smug and limited self-righteous tone of the statement. Further, the pilot who "kens a cloudy spot" is introduced in the immediately following lines as a parallel figure to Galileo. Delos and Samos will soon appear more clearly to the pilot, whose vision is partly the result of a movement less precipitous than that of Raphael and more resonant with both the object of perception and the faculty of the observer.

The more extensive and complex simile in Book 1 is a triple pivot from the epic dimension into the meditative dimension. First, Galileo is the astronomer, who like Adam and Eve beholds and questions the nature of the stars above, and who like Milton calls on Urania, the muse of astronomy—of the precision of numbers. In this capacity Galileo shifts the declension of mind into the "reckoning" of simple relativizing. Second, he is an artist— Milton calls him the "Tuscan artist"—and through his eyes and imagination the reader enters more fully than in Book 5 into the "new lands, rivers, and mountains," into the vision of the complex relativizing mode. And third, Galileo himself is already in the third space, in the cool "new land" of Fesole that has been distanced from hell. Thus the imaginative gazing not only takes one into a third space; it is itself occurring in the third space. Like the pilot kenning the cloudy spot or the peasant watching the elves, or like God who "ponders all events" (4: 1001), Galileo ponders the moon-shield ("ponderous shield") hanging on Satan's shoulders in a meditation that, unlike Raphael's speedy flight and quick vision, has kinesthetic weight and resistance.

The importance of the moon as an emblem for meditation and the imagination is indicated in many ways throughout *Paradise Lost*. The sun is a source of energy whose direct reception by the earth yields life in the physical world (8: 91–97). But the less direct light of the moon—the "reflection" of the light of the sun—yields consciousness and a resonance that, aligned with universal forces, yields life of a slightly different sort.

The moon is an integral part of the reality of the created heavens and earth. The world hangs "in a golden chain" not only "fast by" the battlements of heaven but also "close by the moon" (2: 1051–53). Her role is to "enlighten" earthly consciousness and help protect the creation from an ignorance that could threaten its existence. "Night would invade, but the . . . moon . . . fills and empties to enlighten th'earth, / And in her pale dominion checks the night" (3: 726–32). She enlightens by being the "apparent queen" who makes things visible in reflection (4: 606–9). And in the time of the moon sings the "solemn bird" (4: 648), the "wakeful bird" (3: 38), the voice of lucid poetry. The consciousness yielded by reflection and meditation leads to a resonance with the energies and structure of the universe. For the "soft fires" of the moon and stars

> Not only enlighten, but with kindly heat
> Of various influence foment and warm,
> Temper or nourish, or in part shed down
> Their stellar virtue on all kinds that grow
> On earth, made hereby apter to receive
> Perfection from the sun's more potent ray.
>
> (4: 668–73)

This art of the moon replaces epic art. On the fourth day of creation, "the moon . . . opposite [the sun] in leveled west was set / His mirror" (7: 375–77). This new shield-mirror, like the shield of Perseus, is used not as a shield but as a mirror, a shield and light of mind that gives birth to the winged horse of poetry. The orb of the moon is not the "clouded," "glazed," or "dim" orb of poor vision (4: 607; 3: 590, 26; see also 11: 411–15) but becomes the eye of meditative and intuitive vision that Raphael calls angelic. As Milton says, the moon's "argent fields . . . / Translated saints, or middle Spirits hold / Betwixt th' angelical and human kind" (3: 460–62). The moon is a stage on the "way at length" to the one kingdom of heaven and earth.

This reflective and meditative process clarifies the nature of the puzzling, triangular, referential structure mentioned at the end of chapter 2 in which angels, stars, and grain or dewdrops are likened to one another (as in 3: 60–61; 7: 358). The answer to the question "what are angels?" is not "they are stars, or grain"; nor is it "they are like stars, or grain"; but is that if one contemplates and experiences the forces and principles informing stars, or enters into the lifted third space defined by the terms of the similes, one will enter into the spiritual state of mind in which the natures of stars, angels, and grain are known, and in which one is not an astronomer or an artist but both simultaneously. To Adam's attainment of the space of suspension in Book 12, Michael says:

> This having learnt, thou hast attained the sum
> Of wisdom; hope no higher, though all the stars
> Thou knewst by name, and all th'ethereal powers,
> All secrets of the deep, all Nature's works,
> Or works of God in heav'n, air, earth, or sea,
> And all the riches of this world enjoy'dst,
> And all the rule.
>
> (12: 575–81)

Although the primary purpose of simple relativizing was to strip all mental positions from both the object of perception and the faculties of mind, an understanding of the right relations of motions results in a resonant perception by the sensible being of the phenomenal world that is one of the "firstfruits" of the meditative modes and also a first experience of the richer and more complex resonance characteristic of the final meditative mode.

If the reader sets him/herself into gradual motion in relation to the object of perception—a plastic motion somewhere between inertia and the disproportionate motion that Raphael represents to Adam in the beginning of Book 8—and then watches this object, the perception itself and the appearance of the object will gradually change as he/she moves. This movement would be similar to Satan's "easy" movement after his initial "flight precipitant" in 3: 564–66:

> . . . [he] winds with ease
> Through the pure marble air his oblique way
> Amongst innumerable stars, that shone
> Stars distant, but nigh hand seemed other worlds,

or to Raphael's more gradual flight as he enters the created universe:

. . . through the vast ethereal sky
[he] sails between worlds and worlds, with steady wing
Now on the polar winds, then with quick fan
Winnows the buxom air.

(5: 267–70)

Because the observer's movement is modulated and neutral instead of fixed
or harshly disjunctive, neither the identity of the object nor the perception is
broken or stripped as in simple relativizing. In such perception in motion,
the mind can be aware of the two "appearances" or states on either "side" of
the change, of the change itself, of the identity of the object, and of its own
identity, all of which are experienced neither as fixed nor as chaotic.

In a similar perceptual experience the observer remains still as he/she
observes objects in plastic motion in relation to each other. Thus the fish in
7: 401–6 move in relation to the water and sun, and as they move the sun
glints off different parts of their bodies: the motion changes their appearance
but not their identities. Of course, since the object of perception is in motion
in relation to the observer as well, the observer's motion would achieve the
same effect.

Such perceptions may be considered as effects of simple relativizing and
at the same time as transitional exercises from simple to complex relativizing. In them one can begin to see and feel kinesthetically—in one's bones
and muscles—the principle and reality of resonant kinesthesia now that
simple relativizing has stripped away impediments to flowing perception.
Further, because such perceptions are similar in a physical sense to the
modal motions that take place in Milton's similes, they occur "as if" they
were in the simile space. If the reader, in a third exercise, recalls to mind and
replays the perceptions of the first two exercises after they have been experienced, or imagines that he/she will perceive something in this way, his/her
mind will have shifted into this third space.

Some of the disjunctive pairs used above in simple relativizing, such as the
two serpents or the "wondrous" change of the giant devils into small forms,
lend themselves to the same perceptual process, and in this process they
lose their disjunctiveness. Thus, in a fourth exercise, the reader reverses the
above exercises to entertain and indulge without identifying both of the
disjunctive motions: cursed serpent-new skin and giant-small. In this exercise one should not consider the two parts of the pair simultaneously as in
simple relativizing, but should in the mind move slowly back and forth
between them, without however losing awareness of either. The effect will
be that the process and nature of the linking change between them will
appear in the "space" between them as a positive reality in itself. Whereas in
the first two exercises the object of perception was less plastic than the
motion and it was the physical movement that was the medium of change,

here the change itself takes on a greater "substantiality" in relation to the object and the object takes on an evolutionary rather than a fixed identity. The change in the serpents would then appear as either a passage of time—from winter to spring when serpents shed one skin and grow another—or an evolution.

The change in the devils' size is slightly more complex. Here the change takes on a positive character because, although the change can be seen principally as a change in physical position—the observer moves farther away so that the devils then seem smaller—the reader is forced to generate this change in his/her imagination. The reader has changed the relation between him/herself and the devils in a "space" in the mind; therefore the change is both a physical and an imaginative act. The object of change—the relation—corresponds more closely to the medium of change—the mind—and this correspondence is the source of the substance and power of the change. For it follows that if the reader can imagine the change in position, he/she can also simply imagine that the devils are smaller regardless of space or time. If the object of perception is more material and the medium less substantial, as in perceiving a ship, the imaginative act would not change the ship itself but would yield a change in perception or attitude in relation to it that then might affect his/her action in relation to it. But if the object of change is more psychic than material, then an act of the imagination could change it more "substantially."

In these exercises, the issue of "truth" and "reality" becomes secondary, for both parts of the disjunctive pair are equally true and the change is true as well. Whereas harshly disjunctive perception based on rigid notions of identity and reality served to destroy both perception and object, the reality of the change serves to preserve them because it sets them into the motion of a free will and evolution whose magnetic and plastic "structure" holds them together.

These exercises show that the stripping process is necessary for the "right observation" of sensible phenomena—sometimes considered a basis for scientific knowledge—as well as for the "right intellection" of their principles, and that plastic motion is the medium of perception and knowledge. They also show that one can move without moving, that one can experience the liquid plastic medium as a positive reality in itself, and that there is a resonant continuum between the different kinds of motion. Such resonant perception forms part of the declension of mind that will in the end yield the "right reason" and the "right imagination" that is the sum of human wisdom.

While the strippings of simple relativizing allow a purified and right perception of sensible phenomena both in the world and in the mind, they are not sufficient to yield the resonant consciousness of the fully developed mind. Simple relativizing has led the reader to an experience of the primal raw energy of God; what remains is to experience and understand the energy that is the yearning for consciousness and reciprocity that prompted the expression of pure power in creation, a yearning that is by its very nature plastic and resonant, more so than the movements discussion in the transitional exercises. Complex relativizing is the process that purifies yearning of sympathic positions and telic modal pulls. This purifying is different from stripping because yearning is not "raw" in the same sense as primal energy. In its inverse empathic structure it exists of necessity reciprocally and two-directionally rather than unidirectionally. The correspondence of divine and human yearning *is* the primary resonance. Therefore, unlike the simple relativizing exercises, the central neutrality cannot remain still or "fixed" as does Adam's mind in its suspended state in Book 12, but must itself move in the motions of yearning in order for the mind to experience them. Whereas simple relativizing is a two-part process in which the stripping—mostly of ideological, emotional, and perceptual frames—must precede the experience of the energy and the return to the perception of phenomena, complex relativizing is a process in which modality and yearning are purified of their own tendencies to directionality, and are experienced positively at the same time.

To allow the flowing yet highly disciplined movements proper to this process, the central neutrality must be more of a cold neutral mood than a detachment as in simple relativizing. In this second mode as in the first, this centrality must be imprinted before the motions of the meditative exercise can begin. Reexperiencing the purely aesthetic shift from the mimetic into the seemingly unidentifiable space in 10: 342–43, and focusing on and absorbing the quality, tone, and various images of the "cold paradise" will serve as exercises to establish the necessary mood.

In the first exercise we recall that Satan returns "by night" after the judgment to the scene of his seduction of Eve and

> . . . list'ning where the hapless pair
> Sat in their sad discourse and various plaint,
> Thence gathered his own doom.
>
> (10: 342–44)

In this return Satan has entered into a time and a space that are not directly represented in the mimetic dimension of the poem until much later in Book 10, when in their discussion of their plight Adam and Eve first mention Satan's judgment. In this shift the mind seems to be lifted into a new space beyond the imagination. It is not the vacuum of Raphael's and Satan's heaven, nor the center of raw energy, but the stillness and energy—the life—of a pure and "empty" space that corresponds to the suspended space measured by apocalypse, yet is different. For it is not stripped only of sympathic and ideological quantity and quality; it is also stripped of the properties of art and poetry. For this passage owes its effect to its breaking through the whole

mimetic and narrative frame of *Paradise Lost* itself. Art itself is a structure
or barrier that must be relativized in order to free the imagination into its
truer space of meditation. It is as if the mind suddenly turns a corner into
another world, a pure imaginative space defined not in terms of idea or image
but in terms of its edges and tone. For within these edges the mind experiences the pure tone of yearning—not specifically Adam and Eve's or Satan's
or God's yearning, but the yearning common to them all.

This yearning corresponds to the raw energy of creation. As purely abstract idea is raw primal energy, so this experience of yearning is the experience of purely abstract feeling or desire and modality. The definiteness and
emptiness of this third space serve as counterpoise to the yearning that
allows a pure experience of both. In a sense this exercise is a culminating
experience of, rather than a preparatory exercise for, complex relativizing,
but it is difficult to make this distinction in this eminently reciprocal mode.

In a second preparatory exercise, the reader focuses—as he/she focused
on the image of Adam suspended in fixed time as a emblem for simple
relativizing—on the quality of pause or suspension that characterizes Milton's simile world, filled though it is with journeyings, wondering, and
doubting. In these similes space, time, direction, motivation, judging, and
feeling are all suspended. Identifications and identities are not made, having
been gently stripped away or having not yet come into being; and the pause
itself is so definitely felt that it has a positive quality of its own rather than a
negative quality as in simple relativizing.

In a third exercise, one focuses on the still, clear, and cold mood of the
simile world and allows it to infuse the mind. In this exercise it is as if one
allows the yearning to become "incarnate" in more definable tone. This
mood is most purely represented in the image of the cold paradise in 11: 829–
35, discussed above, the autumn-leaves simile, the windy sea of land in
Sericana, and the whale simile. In the whale simile, the mood of the pale
moonlight; the still night world at sea; its coolness, clarity, and silence; the
simple and restful rhythm of the poetry describing it; the pause in time and
space; and the absence of any sense of evil or malice all permeate the
imagery, action, and meaning of the scene. In the other three similes the
mind experiences a calm intensity and purity, and a sense of loss and yearning that is beyond lyric, that is yearning itself in a space "empty" of the
object of yearning, of the self who yearns, and of both pain and joy. For in
these similes the mind is distanced from what is personal or specific to its
situation. The evocation of such images as the leaves, the sea-mews, the
whale, and the winds of Sericana—drawn from the world familiar to the
fallen reader and even associated with the theologies of hell, heaven, and
Eden and yet belonging to the inhuman, neutral world of nature where
leaves are not pitied or whales judged—makes this space a space of shared
mind. What is shared is yearning. It is the same space as in 10: 342–43,
distanced from both desirer and desired and the particulars of their minds

and worlds, that has yet been chosen by yearning to image and define itself apart from the structures and forms of raw energy in order to give a clearer perception of its being and nature. In his/her experience in the space of pure yearning, the reader's mind is not arrested and stripped, but filled in a neutral flowing that prepares it for the complex relativizing meditative exercises in which it will move in relation to the object of meditation in the various currents of the modality connecting and upholding them.

In the meditative exercises proper after these transitional and preparatory exercises, the mind moves, maintaining its neutral center, in relation to the object of meditation. This exercise is the truest empathy, for the imaginative projection of one's consciousness into the being of another being or object that constitutes empathy remains "imaginative"—does not fall into sympathic identification—because of the central coldness. Yet it can "project" because, instead of staying still as in simple relativizing, here the central focus can travel.

In this meditation, the mind, no longer confined to pairs of disjunctions, "wanders" from pole to pole in the modal structure, with or through or into its motions and vicissitudes, considering all without identifying with any and shifting the attention or degree of engagement as is appropriate. It moves with the joy of the desired good and the pain of its absence, the uncertainty of knowledge and attainment, the certainty of yearning, the peasant's joy and fear, and the ploughman's perplexity. Here the yearning becomes further "incarnate" in modes and images. This movement is somewhat similar to Satan's and Raphael's journeys, but it occurs in the mind and it has no destination. The purpose is the experience of perception and consciousness while in motion.

The effect of this meditation, which corresponds to its purpose, is to purify yearning in all its articulations, to train the mind and being to move with modal motions, and finally to attain the *right relation of modal motions*. Though the motions, and hence the exact nature or configuration of the relation, are always changing, the character of this resonant state is constant: it is a state of peace; it is a state of consciousness, of the yearning, of the goal—empathy with God—and of the articulations of this process; and it is a state of action both psychic and physical in which one moves without obstacle in consonance and love.

To reach this state the mode goes through three stages. First the meditation takes place *within* the space of the simile world, a separate and protected place where the motions are not too discordant. This space is only temporary, however: once the mind has achieved a measure of strength it moves in its meditation from the poetic space into the "fallen" world, the psychic structure that is the latest "creation." In the second stage one moves into the epic plot dimension of *Paradise Lost;* and in the third stage one moves as if exiting from Book 12 for a second time into the subjected world in which the reader lives. In this final ending of the poem, the reader carries the inner paradise within the psyche instead of in the poem. There is a progression from Paradise, to Paradise in the poem, to paradise in the spiritual third space.

At first, then, one moves within the world of the simile sequence delineated above in chapter 1. Some similes are more complex or complete than others, including all the modal aspects; others are relatively simple. In the bees-elves-peasant simile at the end of Book 1, for example, one may experience all the poles and motions of the modal structure—the warmth and fulfillment of the thriving and sunny city, the ironic reminder of Aeneas's distance from his own future city, his uncertainty, and his yearning; and then the beauty and coolness of the faery elves, the delight they afford the peasant and the fear, and his distance from home.

Such a group of similes as the spicy shores of the East (4: 159–67; 2: 636–43), the rural delights enjoyed by the city-dweller walking in the country "on a summer's morn" (9: 445–54), the reviving fields (2: 488–95), and the "glistering spires" (3: 543–51) all offer a less complex experience of momentary delight, balanced as it were on a point of vision. The clarity of the images in the last two similes, the object of perception no longer dimly seen as from a distance, makes the beauty undiluted, yet the unexpectedness of the shifts places this beauty within sharp limits, a sharpness that intensifies the beauty even as it narrows its point of balance. This technique prevents the simile from falling out of the third space into lyricism.

The charmed rhythm of Mulciber's fall is a more fluid and neutral experience of delight. The picture of leviathan in Book 7 (quoted earlier) offers a yet more neutral experience of living motion in relation to its setting that is enhanced rather than threatened by the whale's enormous size:

> . . . There leviathan,
> Hugest of living creatures, on the deep
> Stretched like a promontory sleeps or swims,
> And seems a moving land, and at his gills
> Draws in, and at his trunk spouts out a sea.
>
> (7: 412–16)

In the "confused" and "forlorn" wanderings of the devil-explorers on the "frozen continents" of hell in Book 2 the reader experiences the pain of utter loss. In the whale, autumn-leaves, and craggy-bay similes in Books 1 and 2 his/her mind is detached from this extremity and moves in a sad or uncertain but fluid yearning.

In the fig-tree image in Book 9 the reader may experience several of these motions. First, almost as in 10: 342–43, he/she seems to turn a corner into the space of another world, which has the same suspended, almost empty, quality and the coolness of the whale simile, but a coolness less intense and crystalline. This coolness would then modulate to delight in the sunnier images of the glistering spires in the cool light of the morning and the fields reviving in the rich yet cool light of evening in Book 2.

In the image of the whale as serpent grown into the monstrous dragon in 10: 530–32 the reader experiences the fear of the grotesque, a grotesqueness similar to that of the hissing and ravening locusts in 12: 185–86.

In the image of the peasant following the will-o'-the-wisp through the swamp in Book 9, the reader experiences a different fear of disorientation, delusion, and loss of the very neutrality that in this meditation allows him/her to safely experience it.

One may experience these different lyric poles in a constantly modulating sequence in the series of mist images. The Satan gliding obscure and "wrapped in mist / Of midnight vapor" (9: 158–59) and moving through the underbrush "like a black mist low creeping" (9: 180) is sinister. However, in the picture of Satan rising up in the fountain by the tree of life "involved in rising mist" (9: 75), the freshness of the image almost detaches itself from Satan, or Satan from his evil. The "dewy mist" that rises up to water "all the ground" in 7: 333 and the rising and falling mists in Adam and Eve's hymns in Book 5 are beautiful, their fluid metamorphosing nature not delusive like the will-o'-the-wisp because their motion is allowed in the detached meditative space and not followed in the realm of identifying action:

> Ye mists and exhalations that now rise
> From hill or steaming lake, dusky or gray,
> Till the sun paint your fleecy skirts with gold,
> In honor to the world's great Author rise;
> Whether to deck with clouds the uncolored sky,
> Or wet the thirsty earth with falling showers,
> Rising or falling, still advance his praise.
>
> (5: 185–91)

The reader beholds these mists in a new space of "innocence" more conscious than the edenic state of mind.

During these exercises the reader should be careful not to lose his/her center and attach him/herself to any one point or slip into any one direction of motion. As in simple relativizing, he/she should adjust and readjust his/her focus so as to maintain the central coldness and yet engage in the empathic movement of this meditation. For once one is more conscious of the various modal motions and has experienced them empathically, one realizes that it is possible to direct one's own movement by shifting focus. By shifting his/her attention from Mulciber to the winds of Sericana— shifting focus in relation to the object of meditation—the reader can change his/her own modal response and motion from a pleasant languor to a more crystallized coldness. Or he/she can shift from one modal response to another—from pain to joy or from joy to pain—and thereby evoke a different image. This power of self-direction allows the mind to move more freely

with the modal flows, always strengthening the central experience of yearning, the degree of empathic engagement, the consciousness of articulations,
and the meditative control.

After the strengthening influence of these meditative exercises within the
third world of the similes, one can in the second stage turn one's attention to
meditate in the less-sheltered imaginative environment of the world of *Paradise Lost* at large, the "hell" of the fallen world where sympathic motions
clash with the edges of the modal space, and where similes clash with the
referential structure. The purpose is still to purify yearning in all its articulations, to move with the motions of the mind and universe without identifying, and to attain the right relation of motions, but here these articulations
and movements include the sympathic. In certain respects this exercise
resembles the third stage of simple relativizing; but whereas there the center
remained still and the sympathic motions were stripped, here the center
moves into and with them. Because of its strong center and powers of self-
direction, the mind does not fall into the identifying cycle but comes to know
it and to use it. For in this stage of the declension, meditation begins to move
into action.

Thus one may return to contemplate Satan as pilot in the modal world, the
Satan who "like a weather-beaten vessel holds / Gladly the port, though
shrouds and tackle torn" (2: 1043–44), in the referential context of his
viciousness and revenge. First the reader is conscious of the modal yearning
for shore, of the pain and difficulty of the voyage, and of the hope and delight
at the sight of the opal towers of heaven and the pendent earth. But then the
mind shifts to the consideration of Satan the enraged destroyer. Because the
reader has seen sympathic anguish and rage modulate into modality—into
stillness, suspension, and a pure yearning—in the autumn-leaves simile; and
because he/she has seen the sympathic-modal "interchange" in Satan's
psyche in Eden, he/she knows that the modal state of mind can be chosen
and knows therefore that there are not two Satans, but only one Satan.
There is a single object of perception modulated by modality. This knowledge helps keep the reader's center from splitting apart. Earlier, he/she
might have fallen into an identification with one Satan or the other, but now
he/she can understand and experience Satan's different manifestations and
his/her own different responses as different parts and stages of the modal
declension.

In this self-directed movement, the reader may choose one of two paths.
Seeing that Satan has refused to enter the modal space and has thereby
withdrawn himself from the space of shared yearing and shared mind, the
reader may choose to see Satan in modal terms in order to prevent a corresponding mirrorlike change in his/her own mind that could cause him/her to
fall into a nonmodal space where, like Eve, he/she is more susceptible to
rape. This inclusion or absorption of the sympathic dimension is similar to
the Son's absorption of God's wrath. On the second path, understanding the

reciprocal principle and the process of change between the two appearances in Satan's disjunction, the reader may choose to enter into the realm of action with Satan and use the various countering techniques on him to reverse the direction of his fall. But this choice requires much greater strength and would be difficult at this stage of the declension.

The similes of Satan as scout in 3: 543–51 and as city-dweller in 9: 445–54 are similar instances in which the meditative choice leads in the direction of lyric and away from sympathic rage. The "partial" lyric song that suspends hell in 2: 546–55 provides a slightly different meditation. While the image leads the mind out of sympathic hell into lyric modality, the referential context rightly warns that the simile is "partial" and must be countered by the discerning mind in the fuller perspective of the whole modal declension. Here again is another fork in the path: the fallen angels give themselves over to lyric while the reader moves on into the discipline of meditative relativizing.

Similarly, Mulciber's fall may be experienced as occurring in three different stages of the declension: judgmental, lyric, and meditative. Such a simile presents again the different articulations of the modal structure and the different forkings in the path of thought in *Paradise Lost*.

As a further step in this exercise, one may consider the same Satan as did the angels in heaven just before their fall: "his countenance, as the morning star that guides / The starry flock, allured them" (5: 708–9). The angels followed and fell, but Satan does not allure the reader in the third space of meditation where he/she admires the beautiful star with a cold mind, nor does the will-o'-the-wisp in Book 9 amaze and mislead him/her.

In these meditations the mind uses and strengthens the perception of modes and their effects and its agility in relation to them. What began as the control of maintaining the neutral center is becoming the ability to move with or detach oneself from modes, or to use one mode or stance to counter another in order to move in the desired direction, depending on the particular situation. It is in this way that the reader constructs the second plot in *Paradise Lost,* exercising his/her "free will" in relation to the motions of the universe of energy and yearning in order to achieve the goal of the right relation of motions in consciousness and action.

A consideration of the last mist image in the poem (12: 629–32) is a good instance of this multifaceted meditative process. The mind experiences the tension between the simile world and the sympathic referential world, yet goes through the meditative motions just described and resolves it. The mist risen from the river and gliding over the marsh is the band of punishing Cherubim who come "gliding metéorous" not to provide lyric relief but a "blazing fierceness." Yet the laborer's meditative mind, no longer clouded by "doubt and carnal fear," may counter this fierceness by perceiving, for example, the mist as a morning star, a "glorious apparition," and then counter any overly mild "notes angelical" this perception may have by reengaging his mind slightly in the fierceness. In this way he maintains the clear edges of his third space and keeps the mist "at his heel" as does the Son who in future days will "bruise Satan's head" (10: 181).

Although the contemplations of this stage are perhaps more disjunctive and more painful than the contemplation of flowers and serpents because objects of contemplation like Satan are more nearly "human," the resolution they achieve is far more thorough and more profound than has hitherto been possible, because in complex relativizing the reader experiences in the discipline of empathy all the motions of yearning—its pains, its power, and its purity. The mind of the reader-laborer, as in the passage just discussed, is clear, deep, and strong, unlike the mind of Satan, who, refusing modality, falls into the uncontrollable metamorphic process that deforms both mind and body, as described above.

Yet these deformative motions are inescapable vicissitudes of the structure of fallen consciousness, to be confronted and drawn back into the modal dimension. Whereas Satan's method of resolving pain is to "smooth" "each perturbation . . . with outward calm" (4: 120), the reader in the motions of meditation moves with and counters the harsh motions of the sympathic mind in a labor that perhaps molds the strongest consciousness and effects the greatest evolution in the world, whose "lifting" is partly the human mission.

In this more fully developed complex relativizing, giant devils become small, not primarily because they have changed their own size and shape or because the reader has changed position, but because he/she has imaged to him/herself in a meditative process involving several steps and movements first the "bees in springtime" in their rich scene and then the "faery elves" in the moonlight. This process has moved the reader's mind into the third space in which devils seem or become small.

In the third stage, having attained through Milton's counterplot a consciousness and control of his/her own psychic processes, the reader may leave the poem and create his/her own aesthetic distancing, modal perspective, countering, and meditations. After seeing the effects of the bees-elves simile, the reader no longer needs Milton's help. The transition here is not simply from "inner" to "outer" or from "imagination" to "reality," but from the counterplot inside the similes as a temporary heuristic frame to the counterplot in the post-edenic world. The definition of location may change, but the meditative process does not. For the complex relativizing mode has developed into a complex form that is no longer simply a certain kind of meditative exercise, but a state and way of mind. In its own mobile process it has grown to include the simple relativizing process as well as all the sensible, intellectual, and modal workings of mind. This new form of mind is better able to correspond to the complex plastic form of the world, which the reader began to perceive on the level of the senses as one of the first effects of simple relativizing.

The world is plastic, yet the degree of substantiality of the plastic medium in relation to manifest objects varies. The new form of mind must and is able to gauge this variation and adjust its modality in relation to it. For example, a variation in substantiality may require a modulation from meditation to action, a turning of the third space into the world. But the plastic stretching resonance always maintains, and action in the world is always "as if" in the third space. In the larger as in the smaller space of the counterplot, one's imaginative choices can stretch and change one's perceptions, and one's perceptions can change the influence of the object of perception on him/her and his/her influence on the object.

In the similes of Aeneas in Book 1, the ploughman at the end of Book 4, and in his picture of himself in the invocation to Book 3, Milton images this meditative process: the reader sees the mind in balance, weighing, observing, swaying in the motions of doubt and yearning in relation to building a city, reaping wheat, and the mind of the poet in a more sheltered space "Feed[ing] on thoughts that voluntary move / [the] harmonious numbers" of poetry.

The reader-poet whom Milton teaches to construct his/her own counterplot in the fallen world is no Orpheus, but a warrior. For there are in *Paradise Lost* disjunctions harsher than the clashes between simile and reference contemplated in the second stage of complex relativizing; and these serve to ensure the reader's eventual independence of mind, to break any lingering attachment to the separate third space, to the poem, and force him/her out of its sheltered world. These disjunctions may be seen as a parting meditative exercise to gird the warrior-reader for the descent to the subjected plain in the last stage of complex relativizing.

First, to prepare his/her mind, the reader should focus on something slightly too painful for meditative centrality. Then, as he/she begins to slip, he/she should call to mind a milder or colder object of meditation as a counter until his/her centrality is sufficiently restored to return to the first meditation and maintain its resonance. He/she may use the editorial intrusion in 1: 210–20, and the preceding whale simile (1: 196–210) for this purpose.

Then the reader may meditate upon the instances of extreme but pure manifestations of the sympathic mode, the pure anger of God and the Son in Books 3, 6, 11, and 12 and the pure "excess of joy" in heaven and the "wild" and "enormous bliss" of creation (1: 123; 5: 297). In simple relativizing this contemplation serves to strip the faculties; here the reader enters into them, his/her empathic strength allowing him/her to experience them fully without identifying with them or being wrenched by them. In this consciousness he/she may use anger and joy, precisely timed, measured, and aimed like the strokes of Michael's countering sword, to help evolve his/her own mind, the minds of others, and the universe.

This pure anger and joy are not sympathic. They are beyond the sympathic stage of mind, and beyond the modal stage of mind with its masks of tragedy and comedy. They are the pure emotions of the meditative being.

One can see the workings of the fully developed mind in the third stage of complex relativizing after it has left the poem represented "mimetically" in Milton's sequence of meteor images. These meteors are sometimes "real" objects and sometimes meditative images, combined in a space where simple relativizing and complex relativizing are dovetailed in mutually reinforcing movements.

In Books 1 and 2 there are several images comparing Satan to meteors and eclipses. As he rouses his abject followers into an epic march, his ensign "full high advanced / Shone like a meteor streaming to the wind" (1: 536–37). Satan himself:

> . . . above the rest
> In shape and gesture proudly eminent
> Stood like a tow'r; his form had yet not lost
> All her original brightness, nor appeared
> Less than Archangel ruined, and th'excess
> Of glory obscured: as when the sun new ris'n
> Looks through the horizontal misty air
> Shorn of his beams, or from behind the moon
> In dim eclipse disastrous twilight sheds
> On half the nations, and with fear of change
> Perplexes monarchs.
>
> (1: 589–99)

Later, in Book 2, as he confronts Death at the gates of hell:

> Incensed with indignation Satan stood
> Unterrified, and like a comet burned,
> That fires the length of Ophiuchus huge
> In th'arctic sky, and from his horrid hair
> Shakes pestilence and war.
>
> (2: 707–11)

These star images appear to be ordinary sympathic similes in which the star is a vehicle to represent a fiery, violent, and fearsome Satan as tenor.

However, in 3: 377–80, the same shorn-sun image is used to describe God; and in 4: 555–60 the fiery meteor is used to describe Uriel, a "good" angel. As the Son says to the Father:

> . . . when thou shad'st
> The full blaze of thy beams, and through a cloud
> Drawn round thee like a radiant shrine,
> Dark with excessive bright thy skirts appear.
>
> (3: 377–80)

When Uriel comes down to the gates of Paradise to warn Gabriel of Satan's arrival, he is pictured as

. . . gliding through the even
On a sunbeam, swift as a shooting star
In autumn thwarts the night, when vapors fired
Impress the air, and shows the mariner
From what point his compass to beware
Impetuous winds.

(4: 555–60)

These similes mark a turn of metaphorical events that introduces a disjunction in the referential structure. While the identity and quality of the vehicle
have remained the same, the tenor has changed from "evil" to "good."

In a further and perhaps more disturbing development, Lucifer-Satan and
Mulciber are described in terms of star-vehicles that are accompanied by a
lyrical mood that is peaceful, beautiful, and spiritually relieving.

Men called him Mulciber; and how he fell
From heav'n, they fabled, thrown by angry Jove
Sheer o'er the crystal battlements: from morn
To noon he fell, from noon to dewy eve,
A summer's day; and with the setting sun
Dropped from the zenith like a falling star,
On Lemnos th'Aégean isle.

(1: 740–46)

His [Satan's] count'nance, as the morning star that guides
The starry flock, allured them, and with lies
Drew after him the third part of heav'n's host.

(5: 708–10)

There has been a perplexing crossing-over of connotation in which the
"good" is perceived as threatening and the "bad" as beautiful. The disjunctions in *reference* mark the transition from the sympathic-theological dimension into the modal dimension; and the *connotative* exchange of associations
marks the transition from lyric modality into meditative relativizing, which
then incorporates all stages of the declension of mind in its workings. At this
point there is a fork in the path: the purely modal path leads to the simile in
Book 9 in which the peasant falls into the bog, and the relativizing path leads
to the laborer homeward bound in 12: 629–32.

The "paradox" in which evil often appears as beautiful may now be clearly
explained. If one takes the sympathic or modal path and identifies with or
follows the object without first experiencing the relativizing process, the
object may be "evil" and the follower may fall. The pilot who anchors
innocently on the whale-island and the angels who follow the beautiful star
run a risk in the modal dimension as real as that of the angels who "consciously" follow Satan's announced intent of revenge in the sympathic dimension of hell.

But in the relativizing stage of the meteor sequence, the pilot unanchors
his ship from the whale and sets sail in the motions of meditation, attached to

neither anchor nor guide. The resolution he then achieves of the disjunctions above is not primarily related to whether the heavenly bodies are "good" or "bad," for they are "wand'ring fires" (5: 177) just as the pilots are wanderers.[1] Their "true" natures, like the "true" nature of the whale in 7: 412–16, is described in a passage praising Lucifer in Book 5 as neutral:

> Fairest of stars, last in the train of night,
> If better thou belong not to the dawn,
> Sure pledge of day, that crown'st the smiling morn
> With thy bright circlet, praise him in thy sphere
> While day arises, that sweet hour of prime.
>
> (5: 166–70)

The star's true nature is uncertain—does it belong to night or day? Lucifer "is" not Lucifer-Satan; it is simply "fair." Its uncertainty is its truest nature, its transitional "position" between night and day that can lead from night *to* day.

The "determining" issue is not what these objects of perception are but how they are perceived and used. Angels and peasant fall because they attach themselves to phenomena. The mariner in 5: 555–60 is safe not because Uriel is good but because he contemplates the meteor-Uriel from a distance and uses it as a perceptual measuring device.

The mariner's contemplation, like the laborer's in 12: 629–32, is not direct and simple. His mind has already progressed through several stages and movements in relation to the star in order to achieve the state of mind represented in the simile. The simile represents only the final right relation of motions—modal as well as universal. But the workings of the mind that maintain this state—the lines of force—are represented only by the entire complex of meteor similes. Each simile is a fragment of a whole image or process; each simile implies or requires the others.

The Uriel-mariner simile implies, for example, that the mariner's first response to the comet might have been fear. But he has used the lyrical Lucifer images detached from their tenors to strip this fear from the object of perception, the comet, so that he could experience the comet sensibly in its aspect as a manifestation of universal energy. Such a meditative strategy incorporates the simple relativizing technique and prevents the mind from following a delusive image of fear. For just like undistanced beauty, undistanced fear can lead to a fall.

A complementary meditative strategy would be to use the fearsome comet to counter the lyrical pull of the Lucifer image in 5: 708–10, and then use the resulting stripped and colder beauty to enter the meditative third space distanced from Satan. The angels, by contrast, use the beautiful image of the star not to distance their minds from Satan but to "smooth over" the evil and the danger. They identify it with him and follow both into action, and fall. This Lucifer is then different from the Lucifer in 5: 166, hovering between night and day.

The state of mind imaged in the Uriel simile implies that such complex meditation has preceded it, while the Lucifer-Satan simile rather implies the need for such meditation because of the fall it portrays. The lyrical star images used to describe Mulciber and Lucifer are not so connotatively direct and simple as they appear, and their disjunction with their referents serves to signal their "partiality." They become complete only if their context is expanded to include fiercer images.

Conversely, to the meditative mind the star images used to represent Satan in 1: 537 and 1: 589–99 and the shorn-sun image of God in 3: 377–80 are not so univocally "evil"; they are beautiful too. Yet these images are not double or ambivalent; they are terrifying and beautiful at the same time. The terror and the beauty, if considered separately, counter each other to drive the mind into a perception not of the misleading lyrical beauty but of the beauty of the "glorious apparition" in Book 11. The shorn-sun image of God and Satan seems double because the beauty it offers can be either terrifying or inspiring depending on how it is perceived modally. Its doubleness can be either upsetting or useful. Satan may be the eclipse that "with fear of change perplexes monarchs," but it is partly the beholders' resistance that makes it disastrous and fearful. Rightly understood, such an image can be used either as a direct emblem of the cold paradise and the warrior art, or it can be used as a countering device. If it becomes too frightening, one can call to mind the lyrical star images as partial meditative tools in order to distance the mind from fear and the danger of fear and thereby maintain resonance.

In the final simile in the meteor sequence, the meteor is combined with the fearsome mist of Book 9—"vapors fired" with the "wand'ring fire . . . kindled through agitation to a flame"—as the Cherubim "on the ground . . . [glide] metéorous, as ev'ning mist / Ris'n from a river o'er the marish glides, / And gathers ground fast at the laborer's heel" (12: 629–32). But the laborer-warrior, having gone through the movements of meditation, is in a state where he no longer fears such apparitions, and is "homeward return-ing" with the mist at his heel.

After the reader in these various motions has fully experienced both simple and complex relativizing, his/her mind is able to work in an intricate complex of articulations and movements whose purpose and function is to achieve consciousness of both the principles of reciprocity on which the universe was founded and the vicissitudes and warpings in universe and mind that result from their original nature and from their history. The fully developed mind becomes the fully developed being, exercising control in both its psychic and physical action in relation to this universe.

Although in the final "one kingdom" the structure of yearning and the structure of created forms and matter are in perfect resonance with each other, until this end is reached the resonance is stretching, not imitative—now opposing, now yielding—in the reciprocal movements that produce evolution. The shape of the world into which Adam and Eve go to work for this evolution has been affected by several kinds of "warping." First, the structure of the universe even at its origin was potential: an answer to a desire that itself demands an answer from its created beings. Second, in its varying in the degree of substantiality, much of the creation is material. Hence often one's relation to the creation can be changed more than the creation itself can be changed. The resistance of matter often leads more to consciousness than to reciprocal action: the material world cannot be evolved in the same way as the spiritual world. Yet the structure of "raw" energy and matter is a medium in which yearning can express, form, and evolve the structure of love and consciousness, a medium that may sometimes cause painful resistance but that simultaneously slows down heavenly kinesthesia to a plasticity that makes consciousness and action possible. In a third warping, the universe has been marked by the two falls. In the first fall, the resonance has partly modulated into the more violent sympathic motions discussed above; in the second fall, the third space of action has been more separated from the third space of meditation in order to enhance the possibility for consciousness. This separation is less a duality than a division of evolution into stages: as Raphael says in Book 7, human being was created to be "self-knowing, and from thence / Magnanimous to correspond with heav'n" (7: 510–11). After the fall this division between self-knowledge and correspondence has been more clearly articulated.

But the fully conscious psyche can move in these vicissitudes and warpings and turn them into forces of evolution. For example, after the training of the two final meditative modes one is able to distinguish between the motions of "raw" energy, the motions of yearning, and mixtures of these. And one is able to call to mind techniques of adjusting to them, such as the countering of absorption used by the Son in Book 12.

During history these warpings unavoidably exist, necessitating such multidirectional and complex movements of mind that often the resonance is felt less than its articulations. It is this way of mind and state of being that is imaged by the mariner-Uriel and the laborer-mist similes. But in some moments the being experiences the full truth that the uses of energy always occur in the reality and power of yearning and in the context of the final resonance. The best image of the experience of this resonance is to be found not in the series of similes expressing the relation of wanderer to guides that sometimes turn into obstacles, but in a series of similes expressing the relation of wanderer to the obstacle itself that turns not into a guide but into a propelling and inspiring force.

Winds are pictured throughout *Paradise Lost* as obstacles to the wandering ships and the wanderers' hopes, as in the craggy-bay simile in 2: 285–90, the steersman simile in 9: 513–15, and the iceberg simile in 10: 289–93. In the intermediate stage of meditative suspension, the winds in the ploughman simile become less determinate: the wheat bends "which way the wind blows" it, but the wind does not always blow in the same direction or with the same force. In this image the wind and wheat are moving together, the wheat yielding to the motions of the wind as the ploughman's mind moves with the motions of his hopes and doubts in meditation. Yet in this doubting he "stands," unlike the Adam and Eve of 9: 1120–26, whose "inward state and calm region" is "shook sore" by the "high winds . . . within."

In 11: 5–32 Milton brings together the pilot, wind, and bird—the voice of yearning—sequences. The painful and unutterable sighs of the winds within become winged prayers of meditation and of the mute voice of meditative poetry expressed in the silent images and tones of the third imaginative space—prayer, ships, birds, poetry—that no longer "miss the way" to heaven "by envious winds / Blown vagabond or frustrate." These prayers are, as the Son says, "first-fruits" in the world of consciousness and are more valuable than the "fruits . . . which . . . all the trees / Of Paradise could have produced, ere fallen / From innocence." Here human prayer has made "dimensionless" contact with "grace . . . the wingèd messenger" (3: 227–29), who comes "unprevented, unimplored, unsought" as the evening sun comes to reextend her beam, as the morning star comes, and the "sweet interchange of hill and valley, rivers, woods, and plains. . . . "

But perhaps the central image of resonance in *Paradise Lost,* more resonant than the mariner-Uriel and laborer-mist images yet less "dimensionless" than the passage just discussed, is the image of the "cany wagons light" sailing over the "windy sea of land" in Sericana. These ships do not image the complex of articulations in the adjustment of motions of mind to the vicissitudes of the universe, but rather image a pure and final resonance so great that it is expressed as a resonance between pilot and obstacle itself. Here the ships have left the water for the less substantial windy sea of land, have become almost as light as the air that propels them. The ships sail in a medium that is at once water, earth, and air; they "wind" in a "wind" whose resistance and opposing force is not an obstacle but a source of energy. Here the only "warping" is the curving of the sail that is the visible manifestation of their resonance. Wind and sail cannot be separated; the sail properly adjusted shapes the wind as the wind shapes the sail in a graceful but powerful image of motion that does not go straight but "winds" in a yielding and assertive receptivity that literally and metaphorically—scientifically and poetically—lifts the boat through the waves and over the land, and lifts the mind into meditation.

Similarly, Milton brings together the images of the sword, shield, moon, and grain (fruit) in the ploughman simile, resolving a yet harsher disjunction. The Satan who stands "on th'other side"—opposite the ploughman and Gabriel's angelic squadron—is "alarmed" instead of "careful" and meditative. His spear and shield are indistinguishable from one another (he holds "in his grasp / What seem[s] . . . both spear and shield") because he does not understand that the "dreadful deeds" of unmeditated epic battle are arts of the shield and the cane posing as a spear in the cycle of identification. True action is not defensive and reactionary, but is the art of the shield become moon, the object of meditation and the agent of distanced and enlightening reflection. Here in Book 4 the full moon "sharpens" into the crescent-shaped scythe, an image that signals a fork in the path of *Paradise Lost*, epic as well as meditative—whether the creation will renew the war in heaven, collapsing the modality of the moon into the war of the sword, or whether it will take the new path into the new modal structure of human mind. On the first path the weapon will kill the lyrical field of Ceres introduced earlier in this book. On the other path of meditation, it is the "ported" spears themselves, held aslant, that pause as though in a momentary harbor (port), that bend as the "bearded grove of ears," that listen to the art of Milton's left hand instead of bowing before or waging the military art of God's "red right hand"—that bend and yield to the wind of the "careful" and "doubting" ploughman who doubly "stands / Lest on the threshing-floor his hopeful sheaves / Prove chaff." In such meditation Satan the dragon can help guide and pull the ship.

The state of mind attained at the end of Milton's counterplot is a state of resonance, and it is also a coition of the principles that were in the edenic creation expressed in the configuration of male and female. This coition occurs between principles within the psyche—self-knowledge—and between psyche and universe—"magnanimous . . . correspond[ing] with heav'n."

That this state can be both a resonance, which is characterized by distance, and a coition, which is an intercourse or intermingling, is not a contradiction or a paradox: for distance and joining are not spatial concepts but principles. Distance is the meditative neutrality that allows a more entire empathic intermingling. What is at first perceived as male and female modulates into the consciousness of the principles of the masculine upright neutrality and the feminine fluid third space. These then modulate in the evolution of mind into the simple relativizing mode and the complex relativizing mode, or into right reason and right imagination. Simple relativizing may perhaps be considered more "masculine" because the neutral center is more upright, still, as though "standing." Complex relativizing may be considered more "feminine" because it is more fluid, spatial, shaped, and yielding; but the cold neutral mood at the center is its masculine component. Likewise, the process of mind involved in confronting the more substantial manifestations of the structure of universal energy as perceptible objects may be thought of as more "masculine" and "rational"; and the process of mind involved in moving with the structure of yearning, in which the medium between objects is more substantial and the objects more evolutionary, may possibly be thought of as more "feminine" and "imaginative." But since all manifestations and all meditation occur in the context of yearning, these distinctions are not dualities but modulations. In the resonance of evolved mind in its correspondences it is difficult to identify what is mas-

culine and what feminine in substantial terms. Its true nature is perhaps best
expressed by Raphael's description of angelic love:

> [we] . . . obstacle find none
> . . . .
> Easier than air with air, if Spirits embrace,
> Total . . . [we] mix, union of pure with pure
> Desiring.
>
> (8: 624–28)

The shape created by sail and wind is perhaps the best visualization of
resonant coition occurring in the world of "dimension," or perhaps the image
of an embrace between two beings or forces that are simultaneously wres-
tlers and lovers.

The final resonance is also a coition of human yearning with God's yearning in the structure of greatest empathy of complex relativizing that is the
inverse of the structure of least empathy in simple relativizing. As the energy
of God is slowed down in creation so as not to overwhelm human consciousness, the energy and consciousness of human being are evolved to receive it.
This two-sided adjustment is the drama of the wrestler-lovers. As Adam
expresses part of this action:

> [By] . . . Nature's law
> . . . all causes . . . according still
> To the reception of their matter act,
> Not to th'extent of their own sphere.
>
> (10: 805–8)

In the evolution of creation, the "cause" limits the extent and power of its
sphere while the strength of receptivity is increased.

In another image, the transformation and interchanging of energy described by Raphael in 5: 404–26 express heavenly kinesthesia along the
"chain" of "procession" and "return," but in the processes of yearning,
reciprocity, history, and evolution, the linear shape of the chain is warped
and curved such that linearity loses its visual and conceptual aptness.

This final coition may be thought of as "high" because it is the way or state
of heavenly love toward which human love tends. As Raphael has defined it
to Adam in Book 8, love is "the scale / By which to heav'nly love thou
may'st ascend." But it is more appropriate to think of high coition in evolutionary rather than in hierarchical terms, for although the universe was
created in yearning, or love, this temporally "primary" love and the love that
answers it are not enough: true love is love moving in consciousness.

In this final state of mind, the disjunctive pair of theological concepts,
"authors to themselves in all" and "my motions in [them]," are no longer so
disjunctive. In Milton's description of the interchange between God, human
being, and the Son in 11: 5–30, the human prayers formed in the openness to

grace compel God to listen: in response to the prayers and the Son's mild urging, God "therefore bend[s] . . . his ear / To supplication, and hear[s]." He yields and bends as the fields of grain bend, and as God bends again after the flood in the covenant of the rainbow (11: 864–901). The violent reciprocal motions of the pain and ire of both human and God have been bent by their own motions and by the relenting of the "one just man" and the "binding" of the sea and of God's wrath by the rainbow covenant. This rainbow gives "bounds" to the raw energy of universal forces like the waters and also serves as a sign for God to "call to mind his cov'nant" in his own meditation. It is a sign of his self-consciousness in response to and in his evolving relation with human being. For in the images of the cloud-shorn sun, it is not necessarily the shading misty air that arouses fear in the beholder, but the "glorious brightness" and "excess of glory" that God partly veils by "drawing round" him the skirts of cloud in order to allow the meditative shelter of the "shady covert" and the "pillared shade / High overarched."

In this final stage of the declension of mind "long-wandered" humanity (12: 313) finds a port and rest, not in an apocalyptic resolution, nor in a place, but in a state and process of mind. The sweet port sought in the spicy shores of Cathay, the Hesperian gardens of old (3: 567–70), or the new lands of 1: 290–91, 5: 263, and 9: 1115–18 may at first be a separate space in the world or mind, but in the end it is the colder but clearer paradise within, where the yearning of human and God can come to move in resonance. For God "áttributes to place / No sanctity, if none be thither brought / By men" (11: 836–38). But in this bringing we are guided by Providence (12: 647), the guide that is seen to be prior to meteors, signs, and angels. This guide is the "Comforter," the "Spirit within," and the "spiritual armor" of a new warrior art (12: 486–91) and the strength of mind in which we are awakened to vision ("to foresight wak'st") in closest empathy and resonance with God.

As Adam and Eve descend from Paradise, "The world was all before them, where to choose / Their place of rest." Their literal place of rest is a matter of choice. But the solitary meditative journey, the wandering now beginning, will lead to the mind in a counterpoise corresponding to the astronomical counterpoise of earth, to the mind "self-balanc't on her center hung" in the space of meditation. In this space the mind creates, as Milton the poet—the "wakeful bird"—creates, in a slightly different way from that of the brooding bird in 1: 21 and 7: 235, by moving into the flight of the bird of paradise, the poet-teacher-bird whose plume is the pen of poetry, who as Andrew Marvell expresses it in his commendatory poem to the second edition of *Paradise Lost*

> . . . soar[s] aloft
> With plume so strong, so equal, and so soft.
>
> (ll. 37–38)

This bird of meditation never finally alights, but finds its resting-place, its port, the shore for its sea, in flight—the flight toward reality that becomes the flight as in reality that is reality.

NOTE

1. The word *planet* etymologically connotes "wandering" or "erring."

PART III

Milton's Kinesthetic Vision: The Nature of the Universe

The vision into which Milton's art resolves through the workings of the declension of mind is closely related to the intellectual revolution that was reaching a peak of simultaneous exhilaration and doubt in the seventeenth century. The scientific revolution in which the discovery of the telescope verified the speculations of Copernicus challenged not only the astronomical conception of the universe but the intellectual and spiritual conception to which it was inseparably allied.

The medieval worldview was a conceptual incarnation of both mind and sensibility. In the Renaissance sensibility was finding a new vigor and delight in action and the world of phenomena, without, however, relinquishing the intellectual structure of the medieval worldview, which in its all-inclusiveness and flexibility actually served as a sanction for the new stirrings. Now, in the seventeenth century, these movements of body, mind, and spirit became focused into a structural conflict between the ladder or chainlike hierarchical picture of the universe and the circular picture introduced in a new way by the discovery that the known universe was probably heliocentric and by the implications of this discovery.

Both these pictures are present in *Paradise Lost*. The chain of being is represented by Raphael several times in Books 5 and 7, as discussed above in such statements as "One almighty is, from whom / All things proceed, and up to him return . . . various degrees . . . more refined, more spiritous, and pure, / As nearer to him placed . . ." (5: 469–76). The human spiritual mission in this structure is to "return" up the chain to God. In his discussion of food, Raphael illustrates the step-by-step ascent of matter into spirit—"corporeal to incorporeal"—in passages such as 5: 414–26 and 478–505. Adam expresses this ascent in more explicit conceptual terms in his response to Raphael's representation:

> O favorable Spirit, propitious guest,
> Well hast thou taught the way that might direct
> Our knowledge, and the scale of Nature set

> From center to circumference, whereon
> In contemplation of created things
> By steps we may ascend to God.
>
> (5: 507–12)

Here Adam combines both a chain and a circle picture. The conception of a circular structure per se was not first introduced by the heliocentric discovery: as can be seen in the preceding quotation, the chain and the circle could exist comfortably in the same picture. The chain is the steps by which one goes from the center to the circumference.

Another circular picture expresses a similar order and peace, not disjunctive in spirit from the order expressed in Adam's picture:

> . . . th'empyreal host
> . . . .
>   . . . in orbs
> Of circuit inexpressible . . . stood,
> [And] orb within orb, the Father Infinite,
> By whom in bliss embosomed sat the Son,
> Amidst as from a flaming mount.
>
> (5: 583–98)

and

> That day, as other solemn days, the [angels] spent
> In song and dance about the sacred hill;
> Mystical dance, which yonder starry sphere
> Of planets and of fixed in all her wheels
> Resembles nearest, mazes intricate,
> Eccentric, invervolved, yet regular
> Then most, when most irregular they seem;
> And in their motions harmony divine
> So smooths her charming tones that God's own ear
> Listens delighted.
>
> (5: 618–27)

Although in tone these two passages express no conflict with Adam's picture, they differ from it in ways that have far-reaching though here buried implications. In Adam's picture the ladder proceeds from earth at the center "up" to the circumference, which is God. In the last two passages, however, God is at the center and the angels and stars—God's creations—are at the circumference. Of course neither picture is necessarily truer than the other: from the point of view of the "procession" of spirit into matter, the ladder is best represented visually by having God at the center, while from the point of view of human being's "return" by means of contemplation, the "scale of Nature" is best represented by having earth—where the contemplation takes place—at the center.

As separate pictures, these two circular conceptions are not disturbing. In an age such as the Renaissance when the spiritual sense of the medieval structure of things still intuitively held despite the new discoveries, the pictures served less as rigorous formulations than as "poetic" representations whose discrepancies did not invite questionings. Each picture provided certain spiritual comforts. The picture of human being proceeding from the center up to God was perhaps spiritually satisfying because the circumference of the circle was pictured as an enclosing, containing shell or sphere within which all other planets and their spheres had their place. The other picture with God at the center was also comfortable because it was articulated and shaped into the structure of "orders and degrees": the orbs of angels "for distinction serve / . . . [in] hierarchies, . . . orders, and degrees" (5: 590–91). The motions in these two pictures were conceived of as ordered by the pleasurable and delicate patterns of music and dance. The power or energy responsible for the creation was thought of as almighty and infinite, but such concepts were grasped only in a vague way and represented in terms of military glory, a human power that was itself subject to strict order or, again, in terms of dancing and music.

In the seventeenth century this intuitive sense gave way to intense doubts that demanded more absolute answers. For once one becomes aware, as does Adam, of motions that imply an energy and power in the universe infinitely greater than musical impulse, the comfortable conceptions become disjunctive and disturbing. The pains caused by this new awareness are reinforced rather than alleviated by considering these two circular structures as traditionally conceived, because the comforts they once offered metamorphose into pictures of terror before the pressures of the new awareness. When the mind is beset by radical doubt, it yearns for one answer, not two whose conflict serves to cancel both or that individually function to enhance the terms of the doubt.

Thus the honor paid human being by the conception of a geocentric universe contained in the shell of encircling musical spheres explodes and flies apart if the motions are suddenly accelerated to speeds capable of dissolving not only structure but substance as well. Of what use is the centrality of the earth—become a "spot, a grain, / An atom" (8: 17–18) in a vast space—in the face of such new truths? How can "restless" motion and "incorporeal speed" produce the civilized musical harmony of medieval and Renaissance music and frame a universal order? On the other hand, a heliocentric picture in which an infinitesimal earth is at the circumference of the "spaces incomprehensible" is hardly a more comforting arrangement.

These fears are reflected in Adam's speech to Raphael in the beginning of Book 8. Though relinquishing the geocentric view is perhaps unsettling to the Renaissance mind, the idea of a tiny frail earth at the center being served by so much power in such "restless" motions seems more terrifying than the reverse; therefore Adam seeks comfort in the wishful formulation that if the earth were moving to serve a stationary sun—which by virtue of its greater nobility and brightness might be better able to stay put—then the earth "better might with far less compass move" (8: 33), and the universe as a whole could slow down and become smaller.

Raphael, of course, does not allow Adam this comforting possibility. His answer instead carries the process of conceptual dissolution still further. By saying, "Great or bright infers not excellence," he destroys the centers of both circles; and by saying "whether heav'n move or earth / Imports not," he destroys the two structures. When the new astronomical considerations of size, distance, and motions allured scientists to "behold this goodly frame, this world / Of heav'n and earth consisting, and compute / Their magnitudes," such "computing" begins to take precedence over the "goodly" aspects of the object of computation. The "goodly frame" that consisted of the now destroyed earthly and heavenly conceptions loses its poetic aptness for representing spiritual realities. This loss is the familiar Cartesian split in which astronomy and cosmology begin to part ways. In sum, the introduction into awareness of distance, motion, and energy destroys the possibility of traditional structural formulations, of frames, altogether, and requires a new un-Cartesian concept of *forces* to restore stability to the view of the universe and a measure of peace to the mind. Paradoxical solutions such as Nicholas de Cusa's "God is a circle whose center is everywhere and whose circumference is nowhere" are sophisticated but hardly helpful. Without the conception of forces the mind falls into a state that might be described in cosmological terms as an acceleration of the "proceed"-and-"return" motions into an alternating or indistinguishable centrifugal explosion of vast energy out of the center and a centripetal sucking into a vacuum, a central abyss, a double process that is invisible and incorporeal.

Adam falls into this state, but for the reader Raphael's strategy is the simple relativizing that takes the mind on a different path. In simple relativizing, the Cartesian split is avoided because *both the planets and the mind* are detached from the frame and thus neither is lost. By contemplating the motion of objects in relation to one another rather than building thought-structures on quantitative computations or building spiritual structures on "poetic" patterns, Milton springs the psyche into a consciousness of the invisible energy, the forces, and principles of motion behind visible or corporeal manifestations such as planets, and into a consciousness of the reciprocal nature of these forces in right relation to one another and to mind.

In this strategy Milton actually saves the appearances of all the pictures described above—the two circle structures, the chain structure, and the musical conception. All have their place and function in the new picture that emerges from the two relativizing modes. The chain represents the steps or pulsations of resonant energy between two poles that are the two centers of two circles. One center is the center of the original creative energy (the raw energy experienced at the end of simple relativizing)—or God. The second center is the center of meditative consciousness, of the mind structure created to achieve wisdom in resonance with God—the human mind that is placed on earth but not to be identified with it.

This picture is ironically articulated most clearly by Satan as he beholds the created universe, still young in the evolution of created structures, just prior to his "descent" into the serpent:

> O earth, how like to heav'n, if not preferred
> More justly, seat worthier of gods, as built
> With second thoughts, reforming what was old!
> For what God after better worse would build?
> Terrestrial heav'n, danced about by other heav'ns
> That shine, yet bear their bright officious lamps,
> Light above light, for thee alone, as seems,
> In thee concentring all their precious beams
> Of sacred influence! As God in heav'n
> Is center, yet extends to all, so thou
> Centring receiv'st from all those orbs; in thee,
> Not in themselves, all their known virtue appears
> Productive in herb, plant, and nobler birth
> Of creatures animate with gradual life
> Of growth, sense, reason, all summed up in man.
>
> (9: 99–113)

God extends from a center, and human mind "centers" in its meditative reception, to make created "virtue" known virtue, a reciprocity that makes virtue productive both physically and spiritually.

In this picture and, more important, in the account of the creation in Book 7, Milton articulates the nature of his new universal "structure" based on principles of the relations of motions and speeds, and on the principle of reciprocity of both matter and mind. This new picture alters the seventeenth-century pictures in several significant ways. First, in the steps of the "extending" or "proceeding" of all things from God, there is a flow of energy and vitality so great that it takes conceptual precedence over the structured steps of the chain or ladder. In Raphael's description of universal alimentation in 5: 413–26, the focus now falls on the process of substances turning into one another up and down the ladder more than on the degrees of change.

Second, there is a variation in the speed of the motion of energy that accounts for both the "incorporeal speed" that Adam fears and the delicate patterns of music and dance and stars, and for structures perceived as still. It is this principle of variation that indeed makes creation possible. For as God creates and energy is incarnated, he slows down the motion of the original explosion of energy that is of "speed almost spiritual."

As described in Book 7, the first act of God-Son's creation is to proceed into the abyss,

> . . . the vast immeasurable abyss
> Outrageous as a sea, dark, wasteful, wild,
> Up from the bottom turned by furious winds
> And surging waves, as mountains to assault
> Heav'n's highth, and with the center mix the pole.
>
> (7: 211–15)

This setting is similar to the world into which the human meditative mind proceeds—or wanders—in the structure of consciousness after the expulsion from Eden.

The second step is to establish a mood of "peace" and "silence" to end the discord of the abyss:

> "Silence, ye troubled waves, and thou deep, peace,"
> Said then th'omnific Word, "your discord end."
>
> (7: 216–17)

The third step is to circumscribe the raw explosive power of God:

> Then stayed the fervid wheels, and in his hand
> He took the golden compasses, prepared
> In God's eternal store, to circumscribe
> This universe, and all created things.
> One foot he centered, and the other turned
> Round through the vast profundity obscure,
> And said, "Thus far extend, thus far thy bounds,
> This be thy just circumference, O world!"
>
> (7: 224–31)

This act is one key to the process of creation, the implications of which God has spoken as he announced his intentions to the assembled hosts of heaven (7: 139–61) and commanded the Son. In order to create a structure in which humans may "open to themselves at length the way / Up hither . . . and earth be changed to heav'n, and heav'n to earth" (7: 158–60), God, using the agency of the Son, circumscribes his power:

> . . . bid the deep
> Within appointed bounds be heav'n and earth;
> Boundless the deep, because I am who fill
> Infinitude, nor vacuous the space.
> Though I uncircumscribed myself retire,
> And put not forth my goodness, which is free
> To act or not, necessity and chance
> Approach not me, and what I will is fate.
>
> (7: 166–73)

These lines can be read in two ways. First, God can be understood as saying: "Though I am infinite and uncircumscribed, I can if I wish retire and not put forth my goodness; or I can extend myself—put forth my goodness and thereby express my infinite and uncircumscribed essence." The point of this reading would be that God is infinite goodness and acts to exercise this goodness not out of any necessity but as an act of free will. But in a second reading, God would be understood as saying: "I am infinite, but *unless* I myself am circumscribed, I will not put forth my energy because it will not be good, and I will retire instead. But I choose the Son to circumscribe me so that I can create, to bid the deep—the boundless deep that is myself—within appointed bounds be heav'n and earth." Thus in the use of the compasses the Son is circumscribing God (the deep) as well as the universe.

The two circles described above are not "separate" in the sense that they occupy different parts of space. Rather, they are two principles: it does not say "where" the Son centers the one foot of the compasses, or where the circumference is. The center is in the pause, peace, and silence; the circumference is the principle of limitation, of slowing of energy, of counterpoise. This principle is "sapience" or wisdom, the sister of Urania (7: 9–10), and this sapience is a new weapon that the Son girds himself with, one that he did not have in the war in heaven.

> . . . the Son
> On his great expedition now appeared,
> Girt with omnipotence, with radiance crowned
> Of majesty divine, sapience and love
> Immense.
>
> (7: 192–96)

In the bounded, creative, meditative space that God has created for himself with the compasses, he now "infuses" the "vital virtue"—his measured energy—into the deep:

> . . . Darkness profound
> Covered th'abyss, but on the wat'ry calm
> His brooding wings the Spirit of God outspread,
> And vital virtue infused, and vital warmth
> Throughout the fluid mass, but downward purged
> The black tartareous cold infernal dregs
> Adverse to life; then founded, then conglobed
> Like things to like, the rest to several place
> Disparted, and between spun out the air,
> And earth self-balanced on her center hung.
>
> (7: 233–42)

The planets are created with gravitational and orbital forces that keep them "disparted" yet connected through the "spun out air," a principle similar to the "magnetic beam" of light (3: 583) soon to be created, principles made possible by the combination of energy and circumscription.

The variation of the speed of motion and the adjustable circumscription partly account for the apparent paradox that the creation is patterned and numbered on the one hand and spontaneous and bountiful—even wild and wanton—on the other. It is patterned because the energy moves and materializes according to principles and hence appears as the "starry dance in numbers" of 3: 580, and as the song and mystical dance of the angels in 5: 618–27, and the other heavenly and edenic hymns. The creation is bountiful because it is in motion, because it is an expression of energy. Eden is described as

> A wilderness of sweets; for Nature here
> Wantoned as in her prime, and played at will
> Her virgin fancies, pouring forth more sweet
> Wild above rule or art, enormous bliss.
>
> (5: 294–97)

This passage focuses on the part of the creative process in which energy is turning into matter. This kinesthetic perception of energy is the reverse process of the astronomical exercise of simple relativizing in which stripping leads to the perception of the energy "behind" the stars.

The second key principle of creation is reciprocity. The universe is bountiful, spontaneous, unpredictable, and in motion because the energy has been circumscribed and its speed slowed, and also because it is reciprocal and evolving. In his yearning for reciprocity God chooses to create; he is no "unmoved mover" in either a physical or a spiritual sense.

Satan expresses this principle in his speech admiring the earth: the beings created by God do not simply proceed from the "one Almighty" as Raphael represents it in 5: 469–76, or "descend" "unmeasured out" as Adam puts it in 5: 399. Rather, the energy of God, circumscribed, is infused into the deep, an infusion that sets into motion a generative process in which often a substance or energy that is initially receptive and impregnated becomes invigorating and impregnating in relation to another substance or energy. This reciprocal generative process then yields the living articulation of forces, elements, and substances.

On the first day of creation, God's voice—his word—speaks into the deep and in answer light springs forth from it. Light, now a force itself, journeys through the "airy gloom" and then pauses to "sojourn" in a "cloudy tabernacle" while the purely physical creation proceeds. Light is then divided from darkness in the articulation of night and day. Similarly, on the second day, God's speaking into the waters yields the division of firmament from waters.

On the third day, the earth is in the "womb of waters" that then infuse and ferment the earth as "great mother" with their "prolific humor," and the earth then gives birth to the dry land. Again, inspired by the voice of God and the "dewy mist," the land puts forth grass, herb, and trees; and on the fifth and sixth days the waters and land give birth to fish, birds, and animals.

These infusions, conceptions, and births are not to be identified primarily with either place, object, or being. They are principles by which the bursting vitality of the birth of creatures, for example, "proceeds" from the reciprocal energy of God and his creation. The chain of being does not descend from God but rather ascends from the productive deep, waters, and earth in response to his infusing virtue and voice.

On the fourth day God creates the sun and moon as both receivers and senders of the light that has been sojourning. The light, "sphered in a radiant cloud," is both the first answer to God's voice and the first image of God; and the sun and moon are agents of both energy and illumination, infusing the energy and articulation of consciousness into the articulation proceeding from raw energy. The sun is a form created to receive and "drink the liquid light, firm to retain / Her gathered beams" (7: 361–63) and to "keep distance due," to "dispense light from afar," and to "shoot invisible virtue to the deep" of the different parts of the universe (3: 571–87). The moon is set opposite the sun to "mirror" its light in reflection. The light of the sun and moon are "communicating male and female light, / Which two great sexes animate the world" (8: 150–51). Again, these two sexes are principles, not beings or even the lights that are themselves receivers as well as senders.[1]

On the sixth day, infusing breath into a form made from dust, God creates human being, who through self-knowledge will come to know him. This entire reciprocal process is summed up by Satan in the passage already quoted.

The animating reciprocal relation of all these creative principles sets in motion a continuing generation: the creation does not "stop" when it is "finished" but is now itself alive in relation to God. Satan in 1: 650 says "space may produce new worlds," a statement that, while it is an oversimplification, expresses the fertility of a universe that is space filled with energy, for the warmth of suns may animate and urge other "terrestrial" planets to give birth. As the angels sing in their hymns celebrating God's work, "every star [is] perhaps a world / Of destined habitation" (7: 621–22). And as Raphael says to Adam,

> . . . What if that light [the light reflected from the sun off earth]
> Sent from her [earth] through the wide transpicuous air,
> To the terrestrial moon be as a star
> Enlight'ning her by day, as she by night
> This earth, reciprocal, if land be there,
> Fields and inhabitants? Her spots thou seest
> As clouds, and clouds may rain, and rain produce
> Fruits in her softened soil, for some to eat
> Allotted there; and other suns perhaps
> With their attendant moons thou wilt descry,
> Communicating male and female light,
> Which two great sexes animate the world.

> (8: 140–51)

This reciprocity is not only a physical principle; it is also a psychic principle. As Raphael says to Adam, the earth in receiving the vital virtue from the sun gives this virtue its vigor, "Yet not to earth are these bright luminaries / Officious, but to thee, earth's habitant" (8: 98–99). The structure of energy and matter expresses and serves the structure of love and consciousness set into motion by God's yearning.

The motion and life of the creation give God and his angels great delight, as is expressed in their many hymns. The "grateful vicissitude" of day and night (6: 8) in heaven has been created not only from necessity or function but for pleasure, as was the variety of hill and dale: "For earth hath this variety from heav'n / Of pleasure situate in hill and dale" (6: 640–41). The glory of the Son and the flow'rets in his path bring the angels "unexpected joy" (6: 774). The last day of creation is set aside simply to "behold" and enjoy and praise this "new-created world":

> . . . Up he rode
> Followed with acclamation and the sound
> Symphonious of ten thousand harps that tuned
> Angelic harmonies. The earth, the air
> Resounded . . .
> The hev'ns and all the constellations rung,
> The planets in their stations list'ning stood,
> While the bright pomp ascended jubilant.
> "Open, ye everlasting gates," they sung,
> "Open, ye heav'ns, your living doors; let in
> The great Creator from his work returned
> Magnificent, his six days' work, a world;
> Open, and henceforth oft; for God will deign
> To visit oft the dwellings of just men
> Delighted.
>
> (7: 557–71)

The kinesthetic energy moving through the creation is powerful, but principled. The image of the air moving through an instrument discussed earlier expresses more precisely than before the nature of this creation. It is an instrument in which the infinite power of God is "attuned" as human mind "attunes" itself to resonate with this power, and just as the "airs, vernal airs" of Eden "breathing the smell of field and grove, attune / The trembling leaves" (4: 263–65), and as God in the wrath of more violent motions "bellow[s] through the [apparently] vast and boundless deep" of hell (1: 177).

The creation "answers" God's "great idea" (7: 557). It is the answer as much as the idea that is creation. The human being God has created out of his yearning for communication, consciousness, and mutual praise is not simply an inferior in a hierarchy of identical beings. Though made in God's image, this being is different rather than unequal—with a different structure of consciousness and different capabilities. The evolution of creation to the one kingdom of heaven and earth depends on the "answer" of evolving human consciousness; and God, though "infinite ascents" above the creatures he has made, is "alone from all eternity" and desires the happiness of human converse (8: 399–411). When Adam and Eve hide after the fall in the "thickest trees," God asks:

> Where art thou, Adam, wont with joy to meet
> My coming seen far off? I miss thee here,
> Not pleased, thus entertained with solitude.
>
> (10: 103–5)

It is the loss of reciprocal converse with human being and the resulting solitude that pains God most, and he hastens to a judgment that will heal the breach and ensure the continuing reciprocity.

But this attainment of consciousness and reciprocity does not occur as a direct "ascent" or "return," just as God's creation was not a direct "descent" or "proceeding." Wisdom is not simply the inverse ladder of the "contemplation of created things / By steps . . . [in ascent] to God," as it is ambiguously expressed in 5: 511–12, but is a two-part process of self-knowing and correspondence with heaven. In this self-knowing the mind must "retire" into its meditative space, as Milton the poet retires into the shady covert where he can feel but not see the light that nevertheless "irradiates" "the mind through all her powers" in a different kind of "sight." This circle of meditation and the meditative space of God described by the circumscribing compasses of the Son strive in evolution to correspond to one another in consciousness, empathy, and wisdom. In this way the disjunctive heliocentric and geocentric conceptions are resolved. In this meditative "centering" (9: 109), the mind ultimately reaches and is subsumed by the center that is God, thereby "returning" the creation ex deo to one substance in a new interknowing consciousness and bliss. As God says to the Son in Book 3, he has placed "Conscience"—right knowing—in human being as a guide,

> . . . whom if they will hear,
> Light after light well used they shall attain,
> And to the end persisting, safe arrive.
>
> (3: 195–97)

Then there will be no need for scepter or the mind's strivings; there will be no more pain, no more shiftings. The yearning for reciprocal consciousness that impelled God's creation of the universe—of stars, angels, creatures, humans—and the evolution of this creation toward reciprocal union will have become one motion, one substance: "God shall be all in all" (3: 341; cf. 1 Cor. 15:28).

However, this evolution is not predetermined. The abyss out of which creation springs is "the womb of Nature and perhaps her grave" (2: 911). And in the counterplot the mind journeys into the same "outrageous" seas of the abyss that the Son had to silence with his word (7: 211–17). The course of evolution depends upon the reciprocity of the forceful and fallible beings and energies that constitute it.

In the beginning God is a power, infinite raw energy, yearning but not "just," "human," or even "good." His road is "flaming" like the sun's (8: 162) and his sword is "flaming" (12: 643). His only "humanness" lies in his desire for reciprocity. And during the course of the creation's history, the lag between yearning and a "fit answer" and the vicissitudes and warpings of universe and mind described above result in outbursts of violence as erring perceptions and actions produce reactions. There is the rage of the thunder (1 and 2) and the flood (11), the openly expressed "incensèd" wrath of the Deity demanding to be "appeased" (3: 186), and "in time," "lest the wrath / Impendent rag[e] . . . into sudden flame [and] distinguish not" (5: 890–92). At times this rage gains a force that leads to talk of destroying the creation entirely, a possibility mentioned by Satan, the Son, Raphael, and Adam (2: 370; 3: 162–66; 4: 995; 8: 235–36; 9: 943–50). In such destruction the womb would become grave.

But the "unjust" vicissitudes of the creation move equally in the direction of spontaneous and unexpected delight (as in 6: 784), of song and dance, and in the direction of pain and pity as in the visions that " by . . . foreknowledge gaining birth / Abortive . . . torment . . . ere their being" (11: 768–69). The strife of both mercy and justice plays continually over the face of God (3: 407) in the uncertain evolution of his creation and his own reactions to it.

Sometimes an act sets forces in motion that then become irreversible—determining—as when the golden scepter rejected by Satan (5: 886) like the "bounty scorned" by Adam and Eve (10: 54) turns into the "bruising" and "breaking" iron rod that now "determines" Satan's fall (5: 887; also 2: 327).

But although such movements and reactions cause pain and breaking at one time nothing is ever absolutely "remédiless" even though it cannot be "recalled" or "undone" (9: 926–27), even by "God omnipotent." For in the forward-moving progress of evolution each moment is a new moment, not entirely "free" and disconnected from preceding moments or from the principles informing the movement of moments, but not entirely connected either. As the hymning angels say after the creation of the world:

> . . . Who seeks
> To lessen thee, against his purpose serves
> To manifest the more thy might: his evil
> Thou usest, and from thence creat'st more good.
> Witness this new-made world.
>
> (7: 613–17)

If creation is rightly understood as primarily a structure of consciousness rather than a structure of matter, the iron scepter called into being by Satan's breaking of resonance, like the law that "stirs up" and "evinces" sin and as Michael's use of the apocalypse, serves a positive purpose in the declension of mind. For the inner state of mind must share responsibility for iron scepters in the reciprocity of psyche and world. As Michael says to Adam:

> . . . since he permits
> Within himself unworthy powers to reign
> . . . God in judgment just
> Subjects him from without to violent lords. . .
>
> (12: 90–93)

This justice is not the justice of intention or justice proceeding from a static moral frame, but the enactment of secondary principles called into being by created being in its response to the universe.

Because of the warps in the universal structure, the responses to it on the part of its creatures often demand that they take risks and act from an intuition of underlying principles rather than from obedience to obvious and superficial dictates or literal-minded concepts of justice. Abdiel acts to leave Satan's council in Book 5 to escape the possible destruction; he does not complain that such an undistinguishing extinction would be "unjust." Similarly, the angels in 8: 229–326 put extra guard at the gates of hell when God is creating the world, "Lest he incensed at . . . [an] eruption bold, / Destruction with Creation might have mixed." This is an act of judgment based on dynamic rather than moral principles. Similarly, the Son accepts the Father's need for "appeasement," and Raphael tells Adam the story of the war in heaven even though it is "perhaps / Not lawful to reveal" (5: 569–70). Eve asserts her love in the face of rage in Book 10, and Michael and the Son use firm and flexible but not violent opposition to counter the sometimes divine manifestations of the universe.

In this struggle to forge an "answerable style" (9: 20) in action and mind, one uses a combination of yearning, love, wits, patience, and temperance, knowing always that a reciprocal response is usually forthcoming, that while fire and flood may be aroused, the rainbow appears and the ear bends. Although the universe is not predetermined for good, neither is it random or chaotic. In time the dramatic struggle of evolution in which mind strives to know self and world and then to "add / Deeds to . . . [this] knowledge answerable," as Michael instructs Adam, will become a harmonious and energetic resonance between God and his created beings occurring in the one third space of action and mind that were divided in the second fall.

As human being—man and woman—struggles to help evolve and shape the initial power in its yearning toward the one kingdom, the state of love, as we wander in the space of meditation sometimes with the guidance of angels like Raphael and Michael and sometimes "solitary," in our lucid waking dream we are also moving, small figures—pilot, peasant, astronomer, poet— in the vast dream of God. The third space is a world in which we move

together. As he describes Michael leading Adam to the "top / Of speculation," into the same space in which Eve dreams below, Milton states in the
briefest and most direct sentence in *Paradise Lost,*

> . . . So both ascend
> In the visions of God.
>
> (11: 376–77)

As the statement stands forth from the winding complexity of the poem's
verse paragraphs, so the vision and yearning stand forth from the intricate
and at times painful way at length. This moment of greatest contact simultaneously opens into the greatest distance, into the vastness of God's vision of
love that in its promise takes away the possibility for any contact that human
could know as human, whose real home thus seems to be the strangeness of
a sadness wedded to an uplifting joy.

NOTE

1. Cf. Joseph H. Summers, *The Muse's Method: An Introduction to "Paradise Lost"* (Cambridge, Mass.: Harvard University Press, 1962), chap. 4, "The Two Great Sexes," pp. 87–111.

Selected Bibliography

Abrams, M. H. *The Mirror and the Lamp: Romantic Theory and the Critical Tradition*. New York: W. W. Norton and Co., Inc., 1958.

Aristotle. *Poetics*. Translated by Gerard F. Else. Ann Arbor: University of Michigan Press, 1967.

Barker, Arthur, ed. *Milton: Modern Essays in Criticism*. New York: Oxford University Press, 1965.

Coleridge, Samuel Taylor. *The Portable Coleridge*. Edited by I. A. Richards. New York: The Viking Press, 1950.

Cope, Jackson I. *The Metaphoric Structure of "Paradise Lost."* Baltimore, Md.: Johns Hopkins Press, 1962.

Dante. *Dante's Inferno, Italian Text with English Translations*. Translated by John O. Sinclair. New York: Oxford University Press, 1961.

de Man, Paul. *Blindness and Insight: Essays in the Rhetoric of Contemporary Criticism*. New York: Oxford University Press, 1971.

Eliot, T. S. *On Poetry and Poets*. New York: Noonday Press, 1961.

———. *The Complete Poems and Plays, 1909–1950*. New York: Harcourt, Brace, & World, Inc., 1952.

Empson, William. *Milton's God*. London: Chatto & Windus, 1965.

Fergusson, Francis. *The Idea of a Theater: The Art of Drama in Changing Perspective*. Princeton University Press, 1949. Reprinted. Garden City, N.Y.: Doubleday Anchor Books, 1953.

Ferry, Anne Davidson. *Milton's Epic Voice: The Narrator in "Paradise Lost."* Cambridge, Mass.: Harvard University Press, 1967.

Fish, Stanley Eugene. *Surprised by Sin: The Reader in "Paradise Lost."* New York: St. Martin's Press, 1967.

Freeman, Kathleen. *Ancilla to the Pre-Socratic Philosophers: A Complete Translation of the Fragments in Diels, "Fragmente der Vorsokratiker."* Cambridge, Mass.: Harvard University Press, 1948.

Frye, Northrop. *Anatomy of Criticism*. New York: Atheneum, 1966.

———. "The Argument of Comedy," in *Shakespeare: Modern Essays in Criticism*. Edited by Leonard F. Dean. New York: Oxford University Press, 1967.

Gardner, Helen. *A Reading of "Paradise Lost."* Oxford: Clarendon Press, 1965.

Hartman, Geoffrey. *Beyond Formalism: Literary Essays*. New Haven and London: Yale University Press, 1970.

Hyman, Lawrence W. *The Quarrel Within: Art and Morality in Milton's Poetry*. Port Washington, N.Y.: Kennikat Press, 1972.

Kermode, Frank, ed. *The Living Milton: Essays by Various Hands.* New York: Barnes & Noble, 1960.

Knott, John Ray. *Milton's Pastoral Vision: An Approach to "Paradise Lost."* Chicago: University of Chicago Press, 1971.

Kranidas, Thomas, ed. *New Essays on "Paradise Lost."* Berkeley and Los Angeles: University of California Press, 1969.

Lewis C. S. *A Preface to "Paradise Lost."* New York: Oxford University Press, 1961.

Lieb, Michael. *The Dialectics of Creation: Patterns of Birth and Regeneration in "Paradise Lost."* Amherst: University of Massachusetts Press, 1970.

MacCaffrey, Isabel G. *"Paradise Lost" as "Myth."* Cambridge, Mass.: Harvard University Press, 1967.

Martz, Louis, ed. *Milton: A Collection of Critical Essays.* Englewood Cliffs, N.J.: Prentice-Hall, 1966.

———. *The Paradise Within: Studies in Vaughan, Traherne, and Milton.* New Haven, Conn.: Yale University Press, 1964.

Milton, John. *The Complete Poetical Works of John Milton.* Edited by Douglas Bush. Boston: Houghton Mifflin Company, 1965.

Nashe, Thomas. *The Unfortunate Traveler,* in *Elizabethan Prose Fiction.* Edited by Merrit Lawlis. New York: Odyssey Press, 1967.

Rajan, B. *"Paradise Lost" and the Seventeenth Century Reader.* Ann Arbor: University of Michigan Press, 1947.

Reich, Wilhelm. *The Murder of Christ.* New York: Noonday Press, 1972.

Ricks, Christopher. *Milton's Grand Style.* Oxford: Clarendon Press, 1963.

Sewell, Arthur. *A Study in Milton's Christian Doctrine.* Hamden, Conn.: Archon Books, 1967.

Shawcross, John T. *"Paradise Lost* and the Theme of Exodus." *Milton Studies* 2 (1970): 3–26.

Sophocles. *The Theban Plays.* Translated by E. F. Watling. Baltimore, Md.: Penguin Books, 1960.

Stein, Arnold. *Answerable Style: Essays on "Paradise Lost."* Seattle and London: University of Washington Press, 1967.

Stevens, Wallace. *The Collected Poems of Wallace Stevens.* New York: Alfred A. Knopf, 1967.

Summers, Joseph. *The Muse's Method: An Introduction to "Paradise Lost."* Cambridge, Mass.: Harvard University Press, 1962.

Tillyard, E. M. W. *Milton.* Rev. ed. New York: Barnes & Noble, 1967.

Tuve, Rosemond. *Images and Themes in Five Poems by Milton.* Cambridge, Mass.: Harvard University Press, 1957.

Waldock, A. J. A. *"Paradise Lost" and its Critics.* Cambridge: University Press, 1961.

Whaler, James. "Animal Simile in *Paradise Lost.*" *PMLA* 47 (1932): 534–53.

———. "Compounding and Distribution of Simile in *Paradise Lost.*" *Modern Philology* (February 1931): 313–27.

————. "Grammatical Nexus of Miltonic Simile." *Journal of English and Germanic Philology* 30 (1931): 327–34.

————. "Miltonic Simile." *PMLA* 46 (1931): 1034–74.

Yeats, William Butler. *The Autobiography of William Butler Yeats*. New York: Collier Books, 1965.

Index

For references to individual similes see the Index of Similes.

Abdiel, 45, 54, 56, 138–46 passim, 149, 162, 179, 194, 196, 293; compared to figures in similes, 146; fixity of, compared to Satan's, 144

Abel, 231, 234. *See also* Cain and Abel

Absence: of object of desire as determining poles of lyric-ironic structure, 71–72, 73–90 passim, 79. *See also* Presence

Absolute, absoluteness, 71–72, 73–90 passim, 79–80, 84, 87, 105, 127, 181–82

Abyss: role of in creation, 285–86. *See also* Chaos

Acceleration, 29, 250–51, 283

Accommodation, strategies of, 77. *See* Intermediates

Achilles: shield, 225. *See also* Perseus: shield; Satan: shield

Action, 85, 197, 198, 209, 267, 269, 272, 274, 276; in complex relativizing, 263; human, in a dynamic universe, 293; meditation moving into, 266; in relation to consciousness, 274; in relation to imagination, 228; in relation to setting of *PL*, 25; in relation to time shifts in *PL*, 63. *See also* Plot

Active: state of desirer in lyric and ironic modes, 72, 80, 81

Active yielding, 81

Adam, 14, 21, 48; colloquy with God, 131–32; compared to Abdiel, 157; countering of Eve's sympathic despair, 219; deference to Raphael, 152, 153, 159, 163; diction, 47; disarmed by Eve, 217–18; dynamic relation to God, 155–56; educated by Michael, 37, 222, 228–42; education of by Michael compared to creation of Eve, 230; empathy with God, 240; on Eve's dream, 19, 66, 119–20, 133; fall, 211–13; false perception of Eve's fall, 212–13; fear, 247, 251, 283–84; formed into imaginative life in the space of Eve's dream by Michael, 229–30; imaged as reaper, 116; lack of wisdom, 173; mind contrasted to reader's, 152–53; misconception of Eve, 159–60; nature of as corresponding to principle of centrality, 156–57; perception of

tree of life, 37; on possible destruction of creation, 56; as principle of pure structure, 157; and Raphael discussing astronomy, 29, 93–96, 246–52; and Raphael discussing Eve, 159–63; and Raphael discussing war in heaven, 45–46; role of responses in education by Michael, 231–32; Satan's perception of, 196; self-devaluation, 174; state of mind after Michael's education, 90, 235, 239; story of his and Eve's creation, 153, 155–66; on structure of universe, 281–82; style, 165–66; thirst for knowledge, 147–48. *See also* Adam and Eve; Eve; Human being; Raphael

Adam and Eve, 13, 30, 47, 104, 106, 120, 128; breach between, 172–73; colloquy preceding fall, 168–75; colloquy preceding fall as potential evolution, 168–70; creation of, 155–58; defined and summarized, 168–69; descent from Paradise, 278; disjunction in representation of, 14; effects of Raphael's visit on, 147–54; evolving beyond hierarchical structure, 218–19; expulsion from Paradise, 222–25; fall of, 151, 167–221, 239; "inner storms," 116–17; morning hymn, 41; nature of as knowledge, 161; nature of as revealed through irony, 130–31; nature of as two instead of one, 155–56; nature of contrasted to Abdiel and Satan, 144; nature of contrasted to angels, 145–46; and nature of Paradise, 125–34; purpose of creation of, 131–32, 145; relation between, 159; relation to Satan, 163–64; as representing human mind, 58; response to fall and judgment, 215, 217–20; responsibility of, 61, 103; Satan's response toward, 183–86, 191, 193, 194; shifted into pure aesthetic space, 62–65. *See also* Adam; Eve; Human being

Adoration: confused with love, 190. *See also* Worship

Aeneas, 102, 115, 255. *See also* Similes

Aeneid (Virgil), 115

Aesthetic: ideology as aesthetic frame, 19; pure aesthetic shift, 261–62; pure aesthetic

ing, 240–41; happier of future, 14; in relation to Paradise (place), 22n.3, 264. *See also* Paradise

Paradise Lost: mimetic and narrative frame of broken through, 261–62; overall plot of as combination of relations between story, plot, counterplot, and declension of mind, 110; as a poetics, 21; purpose of, 68; reader distanced from as last stage of complex relativizing, 269; as revolutionary poem, 89–90; subject of as modal reality and modal consciousness, 135; Urania as muse of, 256–57

Paradise of Fools, 99–100, 104, 120–21, 124, 245–46

Paradise within, 226–27, 264, 278

Paradox, 14, 138, 210, 250, 271, 276, 284, 288

Pascal, Blaise, 247

Passion, 161–62. *See also* Love; Sex

Passive, passivity, 127; of Paradise, 126; state of desirer in lyric mode, 80–81. *See also* Yielding

Pastoral: Milton's Paradise as anti-pastoral, 126

Patience, 122, 156, 233–34, 239, 293

Paul, Saint, 154

Peace: as first step of counterplot and of creation, 218; of meditation, 239, 263; role of in creation, 286; Son's 238–39

Peor, 225

Perception: clarified in simple relativizing, 252–53; and complex relativizing, 103; "determining" nature of, 272–73; difficulty of in fallen world, 225; disjunction in, 29–32; free will in, 269; kinesthetic perception, 25–39, 259; perceptual exercises in complex relativizing, 258–60; perceptual kinesthesia, 62, 93; relation of viewer to object of, 34, 269

Permanence: of conceived object of desire, 71–72

Perseus: shield, 257

Personal: in Michael's art, 236

Pharaoh, 237, 238

Philosophy, 33; Adam's, 197

Pity, 198, 292; countered in Michael's education of Adam, 230–31; countered in simple relativizing, 97; and fear in tragedy, 84–85; and judgment in conflict with ideology, 58, 61; in Nashe's *Unfortunate Traveler*, 88; reader's for Satan, 54–55, 58; sympathic, 187–89, 191. *See also* Redefinition; Sympathic; Sympathy

Place: hell as, 49; relation of mind to, 223–24

Plagues of Egypt, 237–38

Planetary forces, 287

Plasticity: creation as structure in which heavenly kinesthesia is slowed to, 274; of evolution, 260; in perception, 251, 259; plastic nature of world, 269; of third space, 193; of yearning, 261

Platonic energies: modal structure in relation to, 75

Plot: disjunction in, of *PL*, 19; double-plot structure of tragedy, 84–87; indeterminacy of, of *PL*, 14; meditative, as constructed by reader, 243–79; of *PL* as more modal than epic, 226; of *PL* as sequence of "experiments of creation," 227; redefinition of in *PL*, 54; of war in heaven as defective work of art, 138. *See also* Action; Counterplot; Epic

Poem: fallacy of concept of "poem itself," 67; in relation to author and reader in *PL*, 67; in relation to mind and reality, 68

Poet: imaged as bird, 105. *See also* Milton, poet in poem

Poetics (Aristotle), 83

Poetics: *PL* as a, 21

Poetic space: as empty space, 62–64

Poetic structure: disjunctiveness of in *PL*, 15, 19; new in *PL*, 35. *See also* Frames

Poetry: insufficiency of poetic patterns, 284; lucid, 257; and science, 275; self-awareness of, 67; as vision, 230; voice of as spirit within, 241

Point of view, 156; disjunctiveness of, 13; in ironic mode, 125; loss of in sympathic mode, 39, 51; in lyric-ironic modal structure, 81; relation to poet, reader, and character, 35; shifting in, 19, 28, 36, 43, 62, 78, 89, 102, 118; in similes, 31, 32

Possession, 105; in lyric-ironic modal structure, 79–80

Potentiality: of structure of universe, 274

Power, 168; Adam and Eve detached from, 157, 164; contest of between God and Satan, 57–59; of God in creation, 253, 285–87; of God in relation to human being, 253; in heaven, 180; in second coming, 239; of Son ending war in heaven, 144; in sympathic mode, 179, 187–89, 191. *See also* Energy; Force, forces

Practical judgment, 72

Prayer, prayers, 275, 277–78

Predetermination: absence of in evolution, 156, 291. *See also* Choice; Determination, determinacy; Fate; Free will

Presence: de Man on, 221n.5; of desired good as pole of lyric-ironic modal structure, 71–72, 73–90 passim; nature of, 79

Primacy, 254

Principles: of creation, 285–90; of motion, 250; of sensible phenomena, 260. *See also* Female, feminine principle; Male, masculine principle; Universe

Providence, 278; as meditative state of mind,

104–6; in Nashe's *Unfortunate Traveler*, 88
Psyche; Adam and Eve's psychic work, 174; articulation of, 221; complementarity and difference of principles in the, 201; human, in Milton's poetics, 67; increasing consciousness of psychic motions in complex relativizing, 99; as locus of union, 105; psychic energy, 49; psychic modality, 156; psychic motions, 36–38, 48, 53, 61, 64–65; psychic relation of viewer to object, 38; psychic space, 34, 38, 48, 54, 188; reader's control of psychic processes in complex relativizing, 268; reciprocally aligned with universe in meditative state, 106; reciprocity with world, 293; redefinition of conceptual structures into psychic motions in sympathic mode, 53–54; split into fancy and reason in Eve's fall, 209
Puns: Satan's in war in heaven, 124

Quality: in relation to substance, 50
Quantity: insufficiency of quantitative formulations, 284

Rage: in war in heaven, 136–37, 140. *See also* Anger; Wrath
Rainbow, 293. See also Covenant; Flood
Rape, 187; Eve's and Satan's mutual psychic rape, 177, 179
Raphael, 50, 57, 72–73, 125, 274; Adam's deference to, 152, 153, 159, 163; Adam's discussion with about astronomy, 29–30, 93–96, 247–54, 258; Adam's discussion with about Eve, 159–63; compared to Galileo, 255–57; compared to Milton, 228; compared to Satan, 151, 167, 256; deficiencies in art of, 147–54; description of, 133; devaluation of Eve, 148; diction, 47–48; discourse with Adam as groundwork for fall, 169; discussion of eating and sex, 203–6; distortion of human being, 153, 163; effect of mission of on Adam and Eve, 147; imagery, 45–46; inconsistency in use of imagery, 203; Michael contrasted to, 230–31, 234; mission of, 133–34; motion of, 115; motion of in relation to appearance of setting, 26–27; representation of structure of universe, 281, 283–84; style of, 148–49, 165–66
Reader: compared to Michael, 269; contrasted to Satan, 268; preconceptions about nature of Paradise, 166; relation to author and poem in *PL*, 67; sense perception, 28–30, 32–35. *See also* Desirer; Reader's mind; Reader response
Reader's mind: as chorus in *PL*, 89; in complex relativizing, 255–79 passim; contrasted to Adam's, 152–53; contrasted to Satan's, 122–23; in declension of mind, 38–39; dis-

tanced from poem as last stage of complex relativizing, 269; effect of Michael's art on, 230 (*see also* Adam, subentries relating to Michael's education of); effect of similes on, 31; final independence of in complex relativizing, 269; free choice of in complex relativizing, 244, 265; in ironic mode, 37, 124–46 passim; in lyric-ironic modal structure, 77–78 (*see also* Desirer); in lyric mode, 111–23 passim; meditative plot as constructed by, 243–79; in meditative state, 83; movement through lyric-ironic modal structure summarized, 69–71; purified in meditative modes, 92–107 passim; response to disjunctiveness of *PL*, 13–21; in relation to structure of declension of mind and counterplot, 69, 109–10; return to Book 1, 243; in simple relativizing illustrated, 245–55; in sympathic mode, 40–41, 51, 53–54, 58, 61–65. *See also* Consciousness; Faculties; Mind; Reader; Reader response
Reader response: Stanley Eugene Fish on, 22n.13; insufficiency of concept of, 67
Reading *PL:* frustrations of, 13, 17; necessity of several readings for, 244
Realism, 87, 211, 237; and garden of Eden, 126
Reality, 44, 199, 209, 224–26, 260; as flight toward reality, 279; and imagination, 43; inner and outer, 268; kinesthetic nature of, 249; real and fabulous, 52; relation to poem and mind, 68
Reason, 122, 152; contest between force and, in war in heaven, 139–40, 142; distortion of by Adam, 174; in heavenly structure of mind, 138–39, 142; in human mind, 134, 158, 171; and imagination, 156–57; intuitive and discursive, 206; and love, 162; psyche split into fancy and, in fall, 209, 221
Reciprocity, 20, 87, 162, 191, 223, 238, 254, 273; consciousness of in complex relativizing, 273; as essential nature of reality, 185, 194; of God and creations, 240, 292–93; of God and human being, 156, 158, 291; of heaven and earth, 176; of human being and universe, 106; lack of in heavenly structure of mind, 143–44, 180; of love and sex, 204–5; in Michael's education of Adam, 236; psychic and physical as principle of creation in Milton's vision, 285, 288, 290; reciprocal evolution of psyche and universe, 68; regained in meditative state, 106; true union as, 105
Recognition: absence of in plot of war in heaven, 138; mutual in Dante's meeting with Ugolino, 87; in tragedy, 83–85
Redefinition: of contest between anger and pain into contest between pity and judg-

Index of Similes

Similes are listed chronologically by Book and line numbers, followed by identification of the vehicle and, in parentheses, the tenor. Three of the "similes" are more properly images, but are included here because they are discussed in the text as having similar effects as similes.

1: 192–209, pilot of night-foundered skiff, whale (Satan), 16–18, 20, 31, 37, 41, 53, 66, 71, 99–102, 112–13, 117, 244, 246, 255, 262, 264, 269, 271–72; quoted 16

1: 227–33, torn earth (hell), 44–45; quoted 45

1: 283–91, Galileo, moon (Satan's shield), 32, 116, 254, 255; quoted 32

1: 299–304, autumn leaves (fallen angels in hell), 16–17, 20, 37, 100, 111–12, 193, 262, 264; quoted 111–12

1: 304–13, scattered sedge on Red Sea, Pharaoh, Moses and Israelites (fallen angels in hell), 42, 118; quoted 118

1: 338–43, Moses and locusts (Satan and fallen angels in hell), 42

1: 536–37, meteor (Satan's ensign), 270–71, 273; quoted 270

1: 594–99, shorn sun, eclipse (Satan), 43, 103, 270, 273; quoted 43, 270

1: 612–15, scathed trees (fallen angels in hell), 45, 55; quoted 45

1: 675–78, pioneers (fallen angels in hell), 115

1: 740–46, Mulciber (image), 19, 36–37, 71, 100, 102, 112, 124, 253, 264–65, 267, 271, 273; quoted 36, 271

1: 762–88, bees, pygmies, elves, peasant (fallen angels reducing their size to enter Pandemonium), 15, 17, 19, 31, 37, 43, 50, 60, 66–67, 98–102, 112–13, 115–17, 226, 241, 257–59, 264, 268–69; quoted 15

2: 285–90, hollow rocks, craggy bay (murmur of fallen angels), 100–101, 112–13, 264, 274; quoted 100

2: 488–95, sun returning, fields reviving (fallen angels rejoicing), 16–17, 20, 31, 37, 71, 100, 112, 194, 264–65, 275; quoted 16

2: 570–618, explorers (fallen angels in hell), 115; quoted 115

2: 636–43, fleet hanging in clouds (Satan), 114; quoted 114

2: 707–11, comet (Satan), 42, 225, 270; quoted 270

2: 1011, sea without a shore (Satan), 55

2: 1043–44, weather-beaten vessel (Satan), 41, 266; quoted 41, 266

3: 60–61, stars (angels), 46, 258; quoted 46

3: 377–80, shorn sun (God), 43, 273, 278; quoted 43

3: 437–41, cany wagons on plains of Sericana (windy sea of land on the outer shell of the universe), 104, 112–13, 120–21, 245–46, 262, 265, 275, 277; quoted 104

3: 543–51, scout and glistering spires (Satan and newly created world), 115, 264–65, 267

3: 588–90, Galileo and sunspot (Satan on sun), 116, 256–57; quoted 256

4: 114–19, Pandora (Eve), 127–28, 149; quoted 127

4: 159–64, sailors and spicy shores of Araby the Blest (Satan, Eden), 42, 100–101, 264, 278; quoted 42

4: 183–87, wolf (Satan), 52

4: 196, cormorant (Satan), 52

4: 268–72, Proserpine, Enna (Eve, garden of Eden), 77–78, 82, 98, 121, 125, 127, 244–46; quoted 78

4: 395–408, fawns, beasts of prey (Adam and Eve, Satan) (image), 52, 244, 256

4: 555–60, mariner, shooting star (Uriel), 42, 103, 112, 270–75; quoted 103, 271

4: 977–85, ploughman and wheat (angelic squadron), 46, 102, 269, 274–76; quoted 46, 102

5: 261–63, Galileo (Raphael), 116, 256–57; quoted 256

5: 266–77, phoenix (Raphael), 43–44, 50;